Cutting the Red Tape

Cutting the Red Tape

How Western Companies Can Profit in the New Russia

MARK TOUREVSKI

EILEEN MORGAN

THE FREE PRESS
A Division of Macmillan, Inc.
NEW YORK

Maxwell Macmillan Canada
TORONTO

Maxwell Macmillan International
NEW YORK   OXFORD   SINGAPORE   SYDNEY

Copyright © 1993 by The Free Press
A Division of Macmillan, Inc.

The Free Press
A Division of Macmillan, Inc.
866 Third Avenue, New York, N.Y. 10022

Maxwell Macmillan Canada, Inc.
1200 Eglinton Avenue East
Suite 200
Don Mills, Ontario M3C 3N1

Macmillan, Inc. is part of the Maxwell Communication
Group of Companies.

Printed in the United States of America

printing number
1 2 3 4 5 6 7 8 9 10

Library of Congress Cataloging-in-Publication Data

Tourevski, Mark.
  Cutting the red tape: how western companies can profit in the new
Russia / Mark Tourevski, Eileen Morgan.
      p.   cm.
  Includes bibliographical references and index.
  ISBN 0-02-932715-6
  1. Soviet Union—Commerce. 2. Soviet Union—Economic
conditions—1985–1991. I. Morgan, Eileen. II. Title.
  HF3624.T68 1993
  332.6′732′0947—dc20   92–10751
                                                          CIP

*This book is dedicated to
Eleanora Golbert,
translator and friend*

Contents

Preface

This book is based on the results of a research study of American companies doing business in the Soviet Union and of their Soviet partners during the period of perestroika. It is intended to help American businesses understand how the deeply embedded cultural dynamics of over seventy years of Soviet communism impact attempts to do business there. Tens of thousands of enterprises have been granted the right at this time to establish direct contacts with the West, and new types of ownership have emerged, such as cooperatives, leaseholding companies, and private enterprises.

Positive developments which have emerged under the new structures include companies which have become partners of American companies, a new form of business alliance, the joint venture, and the right of foreign companies to have 100 percent ownership. Examining the experiences of these companies, both successful and unsuccessful, has provided insights into how viable and efficient decisions are made which can lead to tangible results in the unusual and complicated business environment which the former Soviet Union presents for Western businesses.

Due to the openness allowed by Gorbachev, the co-author, Dr. Mark Tourevski, had a unique opportunity to conduct a study of the activities of both American and Soviet companies who had just "been through the battle." The objective of this book is to derive from these experiences the information necessary to make efficient business decisions when dealing with the Soviets, ranging from whether or not to enter into the business at all to determining how to repatriate the profits. (The authors chose to retain the use of the term "Soviet" when referring to the people and country, because it captures the culture and mentality that are still present.)

Over the course of the last twelve to eighteen months, when the authors were compiling the information and writing the book, many friends, colleagues, and business associates expressed concern about its relevance now, under conditions of disarray and confusion, while trade barriers are falling, travel restrictions are being lifted. The republics are attempting to enter the financial markets as major recipients of capital from the West; meanwhile, the economic crisis is becoming worse and political instability and the unpredictability of the future are evident. Some business executives with whom we spoke were adopting a "wait and see" attitude, waiting to see how market-oriented reformers were faring and waiting to see how the unrest in the former republics would resolve itself. The attempted coup in August 1991 was, on the one hand, an indicator of political instability and, on the other, a demonstration of the increasing strength of democratic market-oriented forces. This generated new business opportunities, though expectations for fast development of business with the former Soviet Union turned out to be unrealistic.

So, is it timely to tackle the problems of doing business with the Soviets and raising the efficiency of decision making in one of the most unpredictable moments in Russian history, when every day messages about dramatic events are received and the future is unknown? As we will consider later, some companies may even use the present situation in all its flux and instability to their advantage. There are companies currently doing business with the former Soviet Union who have been quite successful. Many businesses still perceive both positive long-range and immediate possibilities. Waiting until the situation becomes clearer means that the cost of getting in will be much higher.[1] However, for other companies, the situation is not the best time for trying to gain access to the Soviet market and does not call for prompt action.

In the survey, one of the representatives of an American company trading with the Soviet Union drew an interesting analogy regarding the timing issue when he said, "The weather is not favorable for starting a trip." However, if one remembers the Russian proverb, "Prepare sledges in summer and the cart in winter," maybe it is *just* the time to explore the route with all its obstacles and pitfalls encountered by other travelers. In this way, when the weather is favorable enough, new would-be travelers can be well prepared for the hurdles which earlier travelers couldn't overcome. They may then be able to solve such difficulties, and identify quickly emerging opportunities. In this case, being on time means being too late. There is not time for reading books, for research, or for analysis when the rush begins.

Another reason why the content of this book only becomes more timely and important with each new wave of openness is that it is more critical than ever, now that opportunities are becoming more accessible, for potential business partners to understand the complex cultural and historical context in which they are about to engage, and the myriad partners from whom to choose.

With decentralization, the loss of power of the Communist party, and establishment of independent states instead of the former Soviet republics, more and more potential partners will be emerging. It will be more critical than ever to be able to evaluate who's who, and where the best business relationships can be built. Even the hard-liners who staged the coup understood that economic reform and increasing trade with the West were imperative for the country's survival.

Infusing $100 billion into the new states of the former Soviet Union, as was proposed recently, might begin to bring about some prospects for more enlightened political and trade interactions, but there is still the unfathomable scale of the infrastructure with which to deal. And while a law approving private ownership was approved, there are still millions of individuals to deal with who were born and raised knowing only the Communist system and how to survive within it. And even though democratic forces have won, it will be many years before there is a real possibility of dealing with the former Soviet Union as a true business partner or consumer market. It is only now that businesses have the kind of "time out" to analyze and consider the experience which has been accumulated. As one of the American interviewees stated, "It might not be the right time for big monetary investments, but it is the time for 'information investments,' " i.e., for accumulating information, for developing an infrastructure of personal contacts, and for preparing personnel to work under the unusual conditions of a fledgling market economy in the former Soviet Union. The keen entrepreneur will gather information in advance and then be in the best position to decide whether to enter the market and, if so, how and where.

This book is also intended to help readers identify those opportunities which are there now for the business or individual who understands the risks, who is willing to engage in them, and hopefully find some ways to circumvent them.

For as John Lamb, Citibank attorney said, "If it's part of your business mission in life, you have to be prepared to hit the air pockets. Fasten your seat belts!" The authors hope that this book will help you weather the air pockets and find the best altitude for your journey should you decide to take it.

Acknowledgments

Writing this book was a joint venture between a Soviet management consultant and an American management consultant. However, the authors could never have accomplished it without the interest, assistance, and support of many, many people in both countries.

We wish to thank our families, Natasha and Konstantine Tourevski and Francis Warman, for learning to live with endless months of strewn papers, computer printouts, trips to the post office, and fax machines going off during all hours of the night and day. Their patience and encouragement were islands of stability during a chaotic and stressful time. We are particularly indebted to Dr. Alexei Morozov, a leading Soviet in organizational development, whose participation in our discussions helped us to interpret our research findings better and to James P. Baughman, director of the General Electric Management Development Institute, whose interest and support in the project were instrumental in its birth. We thank Michael Morgan of Conoco-Du Pont for his assistance with interviews and Patti Jones Morgan for her encouragement and sharing of resources and information. Nils Svensen, also of Conoco-Du Pont, was helpful in steering us through some corporate bureaucracy, as was James McNerny of General Electric Capital Corporation. Many people were interviewed and we wish to thank them for their invaluable information and time, including Richard Worthy of General Electric Transportation Systems, Jim Stuckey of Gronich and Company, Jeff Furman of Ben and Jerry's Homemade, Inc., John Lamb of Citibank, Norman Gershman of Mebinvest, and many others, particularly Soviet politicians and leaders who could not be quoted by name.

The unflagging love and support of friends during this long and sometimes difficult process helped us get through with our good spirits intact. We thank Deborah Shah, president of Management Partners, for lending us her office in New York so we could work together, Mary Speed for her many referrals to excellent interviewees, Keith Melville and Nancy Lesser for their endless encouragement and support, and Louise Zak for her uncanny ability to call and lend support and critical analysis when it was most needed, whether day or night. We also wish to thank Louise for her sharp editorial eye, which provided a much-needed additional perspective. We also owe a special debt of gratitude to Joanne VanDeusen, the transcriptionist and word processor who graciously processed garbled tapes, unreadable manuscript pages, and endless revisions and corrections with goodwill, spirit, and loving support, and who didn't flinch when asked to pull "all-nighters" on occasion in order to meet very tight deadlines. We are especially grateful to Eleonora Golbert, who assisted in collecting, processing, and translating various sources which were used in the process of writing this book, as well as in translating and preparing the findings of the interviews.

Finally, we benefited enormously from the overarching support of Bob Wallace and Lisa Cuff, editors with whom we worked at The Free Press. Their confidence in the project and our ability to deliver it occasionally exceeded our own. Their insights, comments, sharp editorial eyes, and total professionalism made this book a far better product than it would have been without them.

Introduction

The key focus of the data for this book is the human or interpersonal dimension of business activity, which is so important in doing business with the Soviets. (As mentioned earlier, the authors chose to retain the use of the term "Soviet" when referring to the people and country because it captures the culture and mentality which are still present.) Since, historically, Americans have not been strong in this orientation, most analyses have come from the political-financial perspective. In addition, what we have learned about Soviet-American business relationships has come largely from Americans, through the filter of American culture, and is based on anecdotal superficial information.

Very few Americans have actually seen a Soviet factory up close or talked with a Soviet plant manager. Americans do not understand the sources of deeply rooted traditions, values, and principles from which Soviet management evolved. The American view of trade with the Soviets is loaded with negatives, real and imaginary, mental and emotional, about cutting through bureaucracy and negotiating with them. It is characteristic for Americans to talk with U.S. ethnocentrism about the Soviets as "unreliable," "unprofessional," and "unpredictable," instead of placing these characteristics within the context of the Soviet environment.[1]

Former officer of the United States Embassy in Moscow, Raymond F. Smith, observed:

Despite its surface opaqueness, the Soviet Union is not Churchill's "riddle wrapped in mystery inside an enigma". . . . At best they [American negotiators] have been exposed to a few articles on how the Soviets negotiate, manuals on avoiding negotiating pitfalls. They are unlikely to be asked or to have been told why the Soviets negotiate the way they do. And this is the crucial question. If we do not ask it and attempt to answer it, we will continue to substitute our own psychological or ideological projections for Soviet reality. . . . We can negotiate more effectively with the Soviets if we understand them better. To understand is not to accept. . . . It is a tool, like any other form of human knowledge, which hopefully we can use for the good of mankind. The beginning of understanding is willingness—willingness to stand outside our own framework, to try to see the world through other eyes. . . . The Soviets were not inscrutable. They were merely different.[2]

The information presented in this book was compiled by analyzing several years' worth of videotapes made by co-author Dr. Mark Tourevski, as well as one-on-one interviews with directors of large enterprises, professionals, and high-ranking Soviet party leaders. The videotapes, never before permitted, were made during actual negotiation sessions and training seminars. During the seminars, participants looked at their own behavior and that of Americans and other Westerners. This original perspective is due to the fact that for the first time professional psychologists participated in negotiations in two capacities: as trade consultants facilitating Soviet-American trade and as experts who help to identify sociocultural barriers that are obstacles to achieving positive results. It is also the first time that officials of the highest level have been videotaped. Particularly important were the sessions in which Americans and Soviets worked together to determine joint decisions on given assignments. The findings on these tapes of interactions between Americans and Soviets were particularly illustrative of the dramatic differences in business communication and technique between the two. We gained valuable insight into the specifics of dealing with the Soviets due to direct participation in the work of joint ventures. Our analysis focused on concrete Soviet-American business projects, the striking and implementation of contracts and agreements, the processes of joint operations and production management, accomplishing programs in the fields of education, science, and culture requiring joint cooperation, and joint research and development activities. While conducting case studies, we attempted to determine what specific characteristics and behaviors of Soviets facilitated or impeded achieving an agreement. On the other hand, Americans were studied for how they achieve success in their interactions, neutralize negative interactions and processes, and take advantage of the positive aspects of their partners' business conduct.

In order to verify the conclusions, a study of Soviet-American business contacts in the field of converting the military-industrial complex was conducted, including a deeper analysis of cooperation strategies in the sphere of space technology. Those interviewed included officials of Glavkosmos (the State Space Administration), representatives from related centralized ministries, chief designers from the industrial conglomerate engaged in designing and launching space technology, as well as Soviet cosmonauts. Among the cosmonauts were a participant in the joint Soviet-American flight "Soyuz-Apollo," General Leonov, Georgi Grechko who made three space flights, as well as Alexander Balandin and Anatoli Solovyov who together made a long flight. More than 1,000 Soviet and American business people, representatives of practically all major sectors of business, participated in the study either on tape or through interviews. Representatives of major political forces of the former Soviet Union—radical reformers, centralists, and hardliners—were also interviewed, along with representatives of the former Soviet military elite who voice the interests of the military-industrial complex.

The decision-making experiences of companies doing business in the former Soviet Union were studied along the following lines:

- Making choices about what can be sold
- Locating the right customer which, as a rule, is an organization, not an individual
- Figuring out who is worth dealing with and whether they will be able to pay in hard currency
- Figuring out whether it is reasonable to open an office in Moscow, set up a joint venture, or an enterprise with 100 percent ownership
- Figuring out how to receive hard-currency profits from investments
- Figuring out which commodities might be sold on the world market.

But is all of the above realistically applicable? Is the situation changing so dramatically, and will it continue to change to the degree that this is all a moot issue? Do increasing political instability, turmoil, and financial crisis set back the prospects for business development so far they may never realistically recover? The attempted coup proved once more the political instability of the Soviet Union. Is the environment for business changing as rapidly? Won't the lessons drawn from other companies' experiences be out of date and the tactics and strategies which previously proved valuable turn out to be inappropriate in a totally new business environment? Life itself has recently carried out an experiment that proved the persistence of sociocultural factors of doing business which are the focus of our book. It has demonstrated that however rapid the ongoing changes in the former Soviet Union might be (victory of democratic forces, formation of new independent states, disruption of economic ties, sharp slowdown of production), only those business strategies that are in keeping with the persisting sociocultural factors are successful. It is because any changes are distorted by these factors that experience gained today will be adequate for the business environment which emerges and will emerge as a result of ongoing and upcoming changes.

It is not the objective of this book to prompt American companies to decide to begin doing business with the former Soviet Union. The findings do not serve as guidelines for one-way decisions. The information in this book may rightfully convince some companies that now is *not* the time to develop business with the Soviets. For others, it may be the basis for deciding to start or expand a business.

The study of doing business in the former Soviet Union extends beyond the considerations of its current probability. The analyses of business experiences under uncertain, absurd, and paradoxical conditions within a cross-cultural context has independent significance. It expands and deepens the understanding of the difficulties which might arise in the course of any business. The exceptional peculiarities and complexities of the business environment in the former Soviet Union force a person to seek creative, flexible business arrangements, be more open to new business experience, overcome stereotypical models, and develop divergent business thinking. In virtually every example of successful business development, creativity and flexibility were evident all along the way. Mastering the challenge of the former Soviet Union will help make the reader prepared for any eventuality under extreme conditions anywhere. Soviet managers struggle to acquire the expertise and skill needed to operate effectively under the constraints of a bureaucratic system. Their daily management activities resemble an model of equilibrium when conducted against the backdrop of risk, bypassing of laws, responsibility for things beyond their control, and necessity to comply with conflicting obligations that are unavoidable and a part of their daily routine.

How did the opportunities develop which led to the collection of this unique and informative data?

Beginning in 1980, Dr. Tourevski gained support among some high-level economic leaders who were less influenced than others by ideological dogmas and motivated by economic achievements. These leaders, realizing the need for skills in human relations, saw that directors and managers cannot function effectively without them. Dr.

Tourevski designed the original training program aimed at providing a broader vision of the world, sensitivity to new experiences, professional creativity, and change management. In his training program, Tourevski showed that years of the communist experiment subjected Soviet officials and industrial leaders to all kinds of manipulations as pawns in the administrative command system. Accordingly, some participants perceived the training as bourgeois provocation designed to discredit the high-level Soviet leaders. The grounds for accusations were the use of foreign training techniques by the instructor. While accusations came from the diehards motivated by ideological considerations, Dr. Tourevski found support among those leaders who were oriented toward economic reforms and motivated by professional values and by the desire to increase productivity.

The situation changed in 1985 when Gorbachev came to power and Tourevski's work received official recognition. With his participation, a training program for new leaders from industry and regional bodies has been designed and implemented, along with a textbook.

Beginning in 1986, Dr. Tourevski started using his training program for the leaders of trade union organizations. Over one hundred trade union leaders from all over the country have been participants. In 1987 Dr. Tourevski began training groups of managers in Western business practices, negotiation techniques, and the operation of joint ventures. He also arranged their direct on-site exposure to business operations in the United States during two- to three-week visits to America and provided assistance in establishing contacts with American companies. His co-author, Eileen Morgan, principal consultant of the Morgan Group, an international consulting and organizational development firm, has taught in these sessions, providing the American management perspective first-hand. In 1989, based on his training and consulting experience with the Soviets, Tourevski began to conduct seminars for American companies on strategies for doing business with the Soviet Union. He also became involved in cross-cultural support while American companies were hosting Soviet delegations and conducting negotiations. A relatively new undertaking became joint video-training sessions for American and Soviet businessmen.

What do many hours of unique videotapes recorded during training the Soviet managers tell us about the difficulties that might arise between Americans and Soviets while trying to conduct business?

Americans and other Westerners frequently talk about the difficulties associated with the lack of basic fundamental business concepts on the part of Soviets in general. Americans sit down to negotiate and discuss "strategies," "marketing," "compensation," "pricing," "payback," etc., and do not realize their conversations are often analogous to a joke in the Soviet Union: An instructor was showing a student a modern IBM computer, explaining all the various functions that the computer could perform. The student was listening attentively and his face expressed full understanding. He then said he had understood everything but had one question, "Where does the gasoline go?" He understood the words, but he did not understand the fundamental principles of electronics that were behind them and ascribed inadequate familiar concepts (working on gasoline) to the new notions he was trying to perceive.

The following example illustrates this lack of fundamental business orientation typical of the Soviets: A member of a Soviet group had been participating in a management training program at a U.S. university where the Soviet students were familiarized with a number of basic business, finance, and economic concepts. The day before their departure for the Soviet Union this particular student bought a watch for ten dollars from a street vendor. The watch had a fake logo with a brand name. On the day of departure, this student saw an expensive watch in one of the airport stores that seemed to him just like the one he had bought on the street. He immediately went up to the shop assistant and offered to sell his watch for one hundred dollars. He was convinced this was a bargain both for him and for the store because the item in the store window, with which he was comparing his watch, cost over two hundred dollars.

On the other hand, Americans frequently do not understand Soviet reality. It is interesting to cite the opinion expressed in the American Management Association management briefing by an experienced American businessman: "Oztemel is discouraged to note that many American companies have not learned the lessons of the détente experience. He watched with amazement and amusement when the developer, Donald Trump, flew to Moscow with the aim of selling the Russians on his plan for a luxury hotel complex. 'He was proposing to buy a part of Red Square,' says Oztemel. 'Not even to lease!' "[3]

Another analogy of the different fundamental levels of understanding comes from Gwen Kennedy, an independent business development consultant who has lived and worked in the Baltics while developing aviation-related business. The following is an excerpt from her journal:

> I played tennis Saturday morning. The tennis court was a community gym floor, eerily set up for a soccer game and later to be used for basketball. We took over the court made of wooden planks and painted with lines for at least three different sports. The soccer goals remained at the

far ends and the basketball nets hung over the courts. We strung the net the width of the room making do with a chain and turnscrew intended for heavy construction work. The net hung lower than regulation and certainly there was not enough room on the sides or back to recover hard hit or angled balls.

I began play with a young man whom my friend had introduced as the strongest member of their threesome. His racket would have been a K-Mart leftover and the balls had long since lost their bounce.

I soon learned that this game we call tennis was an entirely different game than the one I was used to playing in the States. With limited space in which to move, substandard equipment and facilities, and an interest in only volleying the ball back and forth between two players, I quickly tried to adjust my play and to think of the exercise as an entirely new game. I worked on control, not strength. The wooden floors and the bounce of the ball had to be taken into consideration with every volley. What would have been a "nice shot" in the U.S. was an inconsiderate shot on this court. I worked on my concentration, on controlling the power of the stroke and direction of the ball. Though I did not chase down balls or race to pick up well placed shots, I found myself more tired than usual after an hour's play . . . (after some time) I was beginning to find my rhythm to this new game.

In my interactions with the Soviets I am having to learn a new way of perceiving reality. I must accept and at times expect, limited and substandard resources. I must learn how to control what I can and appropriately respond to limitations. I feel fluidity is more an asset than directness, control more important than strength, that skill and knowledge are only as useful as their relevance to the environment . . . and that sharing experiences and one's love of life is how real learning takes place. . . . I hope to play tennis again soon.[4]

The videotapes and interviews also highlight the superficiality with which Americans tend to respond to these very deep cultural differences. A standard response by Americans in a discussion about Soviet bureaucracy is to laughingly acknowledge our own experiences with bureaucracy (such as our own governmental bureaucracy), failing to grasp the all-encompassing pervasiveness which dictates a Soviet's every waking minute at work or at home. Americans do not understand how this total pervasiveness has generated a nationwide schizophrenia, an absurdity in everyday dealings. Americans will laugh and say, "Oh, yes. We have crazy people, too!" The issue, however, is not that every nation has some individuals who are unreasonable, but that this is the fundamental element in getting by in everyday life and work in the Soviet Union. It is not to be seen as aberrant, but rather as useful survival skills. When Americans say, "Oh, yes, we have people who will not give you an opportunity to make money," they are missing the point of the primary cultural peculiarities and basic differences. This book is about those basic ethnic, cultural, and national differences, differences which are usually minimized because Soviets look more Western than other business cultures which we are trying to understand. It is because of that very assumption, however (that Soviets look more Western, more European, so will think and act that way), that Americans run into so many obstacles and are brought up so short by them.

Finally, the video and interview data repeatedly confirmed that the keys to business success in the former Soviet Union are flexibility and creativity. If a business person wants to build a hotel in France, he evaluates the resources in terms of money available, location, labor, and other such business considerations. On the surface it would seem to be the same in the former Soviet Union. However, he would also need to ask if there were enough resources of the "soul." Is there enough creativity, flexibility, and perseverance to deal with this totally new situation? Is the business person willing to stretch himself in ways he has not tried before?

People are different, of course, and business resources, values, and missions are different, as well. For some individuals, entering the Soviet market is a challenge to be relished for its own sake. Others will decide it is not for them. All in all, preparing to do business in the former Soviet Union, and conducting the business itself, is an investment for an American company of any size. There is an investment of time up front in making general contacts, making personal contacts, and personal ties, getting people interested, following up in person, and in writing and calling over and over again, following through—and then starting over.

Over the course of the study it became apparent that doing business in the former Soviet Union develops some important qualities in American companies because they are an immediate requirement in Soviet life. These qualities are being shaped because they are in constant demand. Stephen J. Simurda sums up what many experienced business people cite as the indispensable qualities required: "The need for creativity and flexibility is surpassed only by the need for patience when dealing with the Soviets."[4]

Now that the number of players has increased a hundredfold due to changing laws and regulations, the situation is both simpler and more complex. Simpler because a lot of business can be generated and conducted outside of the behemoth of centralized government; more complex because choosing the right partner in this new environment is much more difficult.

Difficulties arise in business situations when Westerners continue to operate out of the framework of their own business systems and fail to acknowledge and understand the fundamental gaps and differences between the systems. It is necessary to gain an insight into these fundamental differences and set aside preconceptions based on individual experience in one's own system. This book attempts to help the reader do that.

For underneath it all, as we will see in the chapters to follow, the politics have changed, but the mind-set of the people, to a great extent, remains the same.

The Human Dimension of Doing Business: A Key to Success in the Former Soviet Union

The Impact of Political Developments on Business Opportunities

For many years the perception existed that trading with the Soviet Union meant strengthening the "Evil Empire," but this has changed dramatically. Equilibrium with the West does not rest on worsening the Soviet situation in order to strengthen the American one. In fact, the position has reversed: The worse things are for the former Soviet Union, the worse they are for the Americans, for their children, and their grandchildren. The consequences of the Chernobyl disaster showed how closely we are all tied together, that we are not isolated and secluded from each other. We are more aware than ever that the threat of social and economic Chernobyl is quite realistic. Now that the situation has changed dramatically, with the central government removed and the republics spun off into independent states, the former Soviet Union is not likely to become a strong rival whether America trades with it or not.

There is currently a pervasive attitude among American business people that when things stabilize and change for the better in the former Soviet Union they will do business with them, but that attitude simply won't work. Today, bloodshed, disruption, and civil war in the former Soviet Union potentially have more than local consequences. In a country with a huge nuclear potential, chaos and loss of control might lead to a nightmare for the rest of the world.

The change in the Soviet political position has been precipitated by the necessity to survive. No matter who holds the power, no matter which political mottoes are used for gaining power, the development of a market economy and the forging and maintaining of business partnerships with the countries of the free world are necessary for survival. Even those Soviet political figures who are in favor of an iron fist policy realize that only a market economy will work. They see the goal of a military dictatorship which bans democratic freedoms as enforcing market mechanisms which might stabilize their economy. The new market economy places people into the private enterprise system, making them shareholders of commercial banks and participants of joint ventures.

We asked one of the representatives of an American computer company whether or not it would be ethical to trade with the Soviets if the balance of forces swings to the right and democracy is limited, strengthening hard-liners with the trade. He responded:

> If I see that the balance of forces is in favor of conservative forces, I'll shift the focus of trade and will pursue business contacts with representatives of the alternative economy: with private enterprises, cooperatives, and foreign trade organizations of national republics. To put it another way, I'll deal with those who are the stronghold of the democratization processes. Maintaining business contacts with them will facilitate strengthening of the democratic forces. In this light, the crucial issue becomes not whether to deal or not deal with the former Soviet Union, but who you are dealing with. In other words, the temporary shift of power towards conservative forces, a possibility which cannot be excluded in the future, does not mean that I reject my business contacts with the Soviets. It means I'd better learn to deal with the private sector or with those new states, which have replaced the former Soviet Union, where the situation is more favorable.

While some feel a sense of "help the people help themselves," still others feel a regular transition to open markets can and should occur.

Another point of view about initiating the new era in Soviet-American trade was expressed in a survey interview by an experienced American businessman who believed the new era in doing business with the former Soviet Union was already beginning to resemble normal international trade. Admitting that there are peculiarities and specifics of trade with the former Soviet Union, and difficulties related to them, he felt the difficulties compare with any trade in its ups and downs.

No one concludes that because a particular industry, such as the automotive and steel industries, has declined in the United States, that there won't be any business at all. During the Iraqi invasion, doing business with Kuwait was impossible, but now that the war is over, trade has resumed and even bigger opportunities appear. Omitting the relatively short periods of disarray, chaos, and political aggravation in the former Soviet republics, the business curve will show steady increase. There can be temporary decline, and probably, at some points, no trade at all. But generally, it will be subject to all the inherent laws of international business. Even now that the old Soviet Union has collapsed, business is continuing with the new countries that emerged in its territory. Too much is at risk. The United States and the Soviets have to learn to understand each other on a deeper level than the "balalaika" and "cowboy hat" clichés. They have to overcome transnational barriers and to move closer to each other through the positive elements of both cultures.

The Human Dimension of Doing Business in the Former Soviet Union

The survey findings demonstrate repeatedly that one of the most frequently overlooked problems in doing business with the Soviets is a failure to acknowledge and understand the complexity of the individuals' interactions. Even though there are nations seemingly more different in culture and traditions from the Americans than the Soviets, Americans seem to have many of the great difficulties in dealing with the Soviets.

Over seventy years of social experimentation totally distorted the normal processes of business life and business interactions. They were systematically and deliberately destroyed by the communist powers over all those years, and in the former Soviet Union, more than anywhere else in the world, business is specifically determined by factors outside the realm of the business world itself. More than anywhere else it is determined by sociocultural forces.

Soviet interpersonal relationships and business relationships are inextricably intertwined throughout all business activities. The "human dimension" of personal interactions might not be the only pertinent factor in doing business in the former Soviet Union, but its significance is enhanced by the fact that it is consistently neglected by American companies. It is the least known of all its aspects. It is less of a problem to obtain information about things such as taxes or credits than information about doing business from the angle of human interaction. The analysis of our discussions showed that to a lesser or greater extent problems were caused by ignoring the human factor. The difficulty lies not only in obtaining the information about American-Soviet business interactions at all, but also in correctly interpreting the information that does exist. As was revealed in the interviews, many of those who were unsuccessful in the former Soviet Union could not overcome these interpersonal obstacles and stumbled over the human dimension of doing business. Interestingly enough, many of them had read Dostoyevsky's novels, heard about the enigmatic Russian soul, and recognized the specifics of Russian character, but these concepts somehow did not penetrate the business sphere and cultural specifics as reflected in their decision-making strategies.

On a personal, social level, Soviets and Americans have few difficulties in relating to each other. Fundamental differences will probably not be observed. In fact, they may share common visions and beliefs. They reveal similar traits when discussing their daily routines or showing family photos. Those who were unsuccessful in doing business with the Soviets made a crucial mistake when, having observed little social difference between themselves and Soviets, they extrapolated these feelings into the business sphere. In negotiations and business contacts with the Soviets, they expected the same kind of civilized business conduct in conformity with familiar business laws and customs.

Assumptions are made around business basics that Americans take for granted and are understood and agreed to by their counterparts:

- The concept of business, what it means in terms of principles of operating, transactions, agreements, commitments, ethics, mutuality
- Principles of capitalism, including risk, profit, motivation, investment
- The concept of a consumer market, and subsequent advertising, dealing with and satisfying customers
- The elements of decision making, how decisions get made, and who can (and does) make them
- The concept of timeliness in business transactions, doing things within supposedly agreed-upon time frames
- The separation of "business" from the "social"
- The concept of accountability—"the buck stops here."

It is true that there will be varying degrees of intelligence among Soviets, just as there are among Americans. But intelligence is not the issue. When the Soviets enter the business world, they are not businessmen at all. They reflect a distorted and absurd system in which they have always lived and which is an economic system but not a business one. In their "business" behavior they naturally act as parts of the system which they represent. They strike us as no longer being the "nice people" with whom you might have felt comfortable at lunch, but rather, carriers and tools of the system which exists and reproduces itself through them, a system which is dramatically different from the American free-market economy system. And while the effect of culture on the political negotiation process has been examined by a number of scholars, fewer studies have been devoted to the impact of cultural variables on the commercial negotiations process. Moreover, in studying political and commercial negotiations, scholars considered only diplomats and officials of the former state foreign trade organizations. But today this specific category of negotiators cannot serve as a typical example of the many people who are currently engaged in business, cultural, scientific, and public relations contacts with the West.

Many Americans have admitted the importance of considering sociocultural specifics in making business decisions in the former Soviet Union:

> US executives who have negotiated with the Soviets have identified differences between the negotiating style of the Soviets and that of negotiators from other capitalist countries. A questionnaire by A. C. Gorlin found that a large majority of respondents, 85.2%, agreed that "the Soviet negotiating style was different from that of Western countries. . . . There is often very little of practical value to guide executives from different cultural backgrounds in their interactions with their counterparts. This is especially true if we consider the literature dealing with the Soviet Union. . . . By contrasting cultural biases that are considered typical of US executives with the biases of Soviet negotiators, conclusions can be drawn that would address the problem and would thus improve understanding between the parties."[1]

In preparation for delivering seminars for representatives of American companies who were planning to start doing business with the Soviets, we asked the participants what kind of information they were looking for. Most, and sometimes all, the questions were of a standard nature and were the same questions they would likely ask if they were going to start up business in any Western country. It was obvious that they were not seeking the information that could help them the most, and were underestimating the very specific nature of the Soviet business setting, especially the human dimension of the business activity. They did not realize that understanding this dimension is the very essence of a successful enterprise. It also helps Americans to comprehend many of the paradoxes of the Soviet business environment, such as:

- Why $7 billion worth of equipment purchased overseas was not installed and is rusting?
- Why Soviets might buy equipment that is more expensive and is not compatible with the existing units, when it is possible to purchase less costly equipment of the same quality and compatible with the existing production facilities?
- Why, after a warranty expires and it is necessary to buy spare parts to replace damaged ones, the Soviets buy the entire expensive piece of equipment which might cost hundreds of thousands dollars just to break down into pieces and take the component parts?

Understanding these business decisions, which will be discussed further through the prism of the human dimension, can provide answers to other questions as well, such as:

- Why, under identical conditions, some companies find customers who are able to pay in hard currency or have something to offer for barter trade?
- Why, given the shortage of office space, some companies manage to find it?
- Why, for some companies, transportation and deliveries in the former Soviet Union might not be a problem?
- Why some companies experience no delays in payment or can obtain hard-currency credits from Soviet banks for their joint ventures in the Soviet Union?

As we will show in following chapters, the efficient decision-making performance of some American companies is, as a rule, permeated with sociocultural considerations and special concern given to the problems of dealing with Soviet business people. Those companies that performed effectively in the Soviet Union showed sensitivity to these sociocultural dynamics, learned to identify the new trends and processes, and monitored them so well that they were able to anticipate changes in the climate.

An experienced director of a joint venture stated that judging by many features in the performance of the ministry officials, such as their intonation, gestures, the time they make you wait in the reception room, etc., he can determine whether changes are under consideration for the work of the joint ventures, whether the favorable new laws and regulations might be passed, or conversely, whether tough measures and restrictions are under way. He stated, for example, that three weeks ahead of adopting restrictions for the joint venture activities, the Ministry officials showed a sharp turnaround in their behavior. Everything about their bureaucratic style, their arrogant manner, and casual attitude revealed themselves vividly. They all indicated that a tighter twisting of the screws was approaching. The power of observation towards sociocultural specifics enabled the joint venture director to take protective measures so that the joint venture which he headed was less affected than others by the approaching changes.

A representative of Ben and Jerry's Homemade, Inc., the Vermont ice cream company, told us in our interview that they sent an employee to a small northern Soviet town in the province of Karelia, in order to maintain a personal presence while trying to pull together the deal for the joint venture Iceverk, an ice cream store in the town of Petrozavodsk, and to learn first-hand the idiosyncrasies of establishing a business there before they actually began to try and do so. Before going to the Soviet Union, the employee learned enough Russian to manage to "get around." He also had the benefit of many hours of instruction, storytelling, and preparation by Ben Cohen, one of Ben and Jerry's founders, who had been to the Soviet Union several times, as well as assistance from several friends of the owners, one of whom had lived in the Soviet Union for many years.

Norm Gershman, director of the joint venture Mebinvest, which operates in fourteen republics, spent a year studying the language and culture before going on his first trip to the Soviet Union. "Such an investment pays off because the personnel sent to the site have a much better understanding of the environment, and thus perform better, while the buyer's personnel welcome the extra effort by the seller."[2] A willingness to be flexible when difficulties arise is also critical. "Personal rapport, individual credibility and a receptiveness to mutual trust form a basis for closing a deal involving millions . . ."[3] How long will findings such as these be up-to-date and retain their value for determining decision-making priorities?

It is indicative of the persistence of the old mentality that even when the market adherents came to power and made an attempt to introduce a capitalistic system in the former Soviet Union, resulting in crucial transformations of business life, this old mind-set is continually regenerated even under the new conditions. However crucial the impact of those dramatic changes might be, the sociocultural determination of the people's behavior will retain the links with those deeply rooted traits of Russian mentality originating and shaping themselves over all Russian and Soviet history. All the new trends will still be lived out through the screen of peculiarities in the Russian and Soviet mind-set. The crucial impact on the business sphere will still be the impact of the importance of the business connections with its system. That is still the legacy. The former system of business connections, with the same sociocultural characteristics, will be replicated. During our training session a student, the director of an enterprise, asked what would happen if suddenly all the buildings and plants and factories of some developed Western country were destroyed? He gave a hypothetical answer himself. "After some years it will be rebuilt and better than ever." When asked what would happen if the same thing happened in the Soviet Union, he replied, "It will be worse because the bottom line is not in the destroyed equipment and buildings, but in the ugly business system which reproduces inefficiency. And that would not be destroyed along with the buildings. It will come back again and again."

Many misperceptions and illusions exist now about what is really going on inside the former Soviet Union and about the prospects for success which are complicated by the swiftness of political changes in Eastern Europe and the former Soviet republics.

New Soviet Business Partners of American Companies: A New Focus of Study

The business that has been done with the Soviets in modern history has been won through the arduous and long-term process of developing contacts with the various ministries or enterprises. Finding the appropriate parties to deal with, gaining access to them, and then carefully nurturing those relationships through repeated trips abroad and careful attention to individual needs, has culminated in working relationships that *can* produce results, even though they are still difficult and time consuming.

A good example of this is the case of General Electric Transportation Systems, which designs, builds, and delivers locomotives. Richard Worthy, USSR program manager for GE Transportation Systems, told us in an interview:

GE has been sending people to the Soviet Union for about fifteen years to develop business. And why not? Just look at the numbers: (1) it is the largest locomotive system in the world, bigger than the rest of the world combined; (2) four million people work in the system; (3) the head of the system reports to Gorbachev's cabinet; (4) it is a key national security and strategic asset. For years the Soviets engaged in reverse engineering, that is, they would copy our locomotive, and that worked for them until electronics became so prevalent. Reverse engineering can't conquer the technology of a microprocessor controlled engine. After fifteen years, our strategy was to give up if nothing happened by Summer of 1990. With the increase in electronic value-added technology, all the players, including the Railway Ministry, Venesheconom Bank, and the Ministry of Heavy Machinery began to get coordinated. We went to a factory in Breiansk where they had a great deal of unused capacity for building locomotives. We had to build in a lot of support in the top layers and that takes time. We had to do lots of homework. We'd go for long periods of time and sit around offices and waiting rooms. You need a lot of patience to do this kind of business. Things also take a long time because part of developing a deal over there is bringing the top guys here, so a one year/five trip venture can easily be turned into a two year/ten trip venture.

The Ministry of Heavy Machinery needed to get on board because they had the connections to get the hard currency. And we wanted the big deal. Getting to Velecko, the ex-Ministry of Heavy Machinery and new Deputy Prime Minister in charge of hard currency, was our biggest challenge and accomplishment. In seven months I made four trips, in addition to a lot of work done by the GE office in Moscow.

Perestroika, and decentralization, and the creation of new independent states resulted in a dramatic influx of potential business partners. Where once an American business had only the single option of working through the centralized Moscow office in a ministry, it can now deal directly with many decentralized offices in the republics. It can also negotiate directly with any number of cooperatives, private enterprises, or joint ventures.

American business people with long-standing contacts in the former Soviet Union are confused about this new influx of potential partners. Their previous ability to conduct business was due to their ability to cut through bureaucracy and go to decision makers. Today, some of their old contacts among the trade apparatchiks no longer exist. Little is known about who their replacements are or how they operate.

This chaos is the result of the impact of three factors:

1. Emerging new forms of property ownership such as the cooperative, and private enterprise
2. More and more new laws being passed permitting various ways of investing foreign capital in the economy of the former Soviet Union.

3. Decentralization of Soviet trade, granting the right to Soviet enterprises, organizations, and cooperatives to engage directly in business and deal directly with foreign companies.

Before perestroika, the circle of the foreign trade elite was very limited. As one Soviet manager told us, "It was a peculiar breed of people raised in an incubator under artificial breeding grounds." This was a specific cast, a specific homogeneous group of people endowed with the right to go abroad. It is easier to understand the breeding grounds shaped for this specific cast in light of the analysis in the books *Negotiating with the Soviets* by Raymond F. Smith and *The Russian Mind* by Ronald Hingley:

Access to housing, material goods, but most of all travel abroad, gave them a very high status. However, it was an important component of the highly structured and artificial world designed by the Soviets to create a false impression of the Soviet business world. In some sense, it was meant to foster the same erroneous impression about the Soviet Union as its "licensed liberals" who "are sanctioned to tour foreign countries demonstrating that the Russians, too, are human beings . . ." and that the country "does tolerate political opposition."[4] Naturally, this group does not now represent the whole spectrum of new foreign trade participants, and with the liberalization of travel in general, will cease to be such a privileged minority.

One retired foreign trade official who was very experienced in this secluded sphere of Soviet life said in our interview:

It was a very specific phenomenon of Soviet business life when, in the country where there was no business, it was necessary to raise an artificially secluded privileged group of people provided with the business training which was essential in order to navigate in the international trade system. Otherwise, the country would not have been able to trade oil, furs, and gold, or buy technology, consumer goods and food products. Due to the Western companies' exclusive dealings with this secluded group, they acquired expertise and knowledge of their behavior patterns. Foreign companies' perceptions of the Soviet businessmen are based mainly on this experience. The American ear is not trained to distinguish between two similar names of organizations from the point of view of principle differences of the people who represent them. But, as a matter of fact, people representing these organizations seem to come from two totally different worlds. In no way could the skills acquired in dealing with former foreign trade monopolists be transferred and be applicable to those who have never before had access to foreign trade and whose entire activity was subordinated to the fulfillment of the plan and was directed by the Ministry, Gossnab, Gosplan, and Communist party organizations.

(Nor is this experience applicable to those who came into cooperatives from a shadow economy or underground businesses.)

For American companies that gained an insight into the peculiarities of behavior of the former foreign trade monopolists, these people were quite predictable. But their knowledge and attitude have turned out to be unapplicable to the representatives of state enterprise, all of whom only recently acquired access to direct business contacts with foreign companies, as well as to the directors of commercial banks, cooperatives, and stock exchanges.

The complexity of this picture is compounded by the very contradictory nature of the transition period which has no equivalent in history because it is transition from socialism to capitalism. Up to this point, neither the goals nor the direction of change have been identified with any degree of certainty.

We researched the following six categories of Soviet business people who comprise most of the business contacts with American companies. These potential business partners for Americans were categorized and grouped together after the interviews, and it was discovered that the various categories differed greatly in the degree of their actual versus declared independence, motivation for developing business contacts with foreign companies, their powers to enter into business relationships with foreign partners, as well as their reliability, business ethics, professional competence, and professional business performance.

In analyzing the experiences of successful American companies, it was evident they instinctively make distinctions among these various categories and have a sense of their specific characteristics. While establishing and maintaining business contacts with various categories of these new businessmen, the effective companies weigh and consider the advantages and disadvantages of dealing with each group and choose their business partners consistent with these considerations. The six categories are:

1. Representatives of the foreign trade elite, often the head of former All-Union foreign trade organizations who are losing their monopoly and try to retain at least some of their positions including such an alternative as transforming some of these organizations into stockholding companies
2. Ministry officials who used to exercise control over the country's economy and attempt to secure for themselves new positions in the market economy structures
3. Heads of the enterprises who have recently been granted the right to engage directly in foreign trade and who try to engage in those

activities in the midst of the dramatic struggles with bureaucratic hurdles
4. Representatives of new, independent economic entities originated under perestroika, e.g., heads of the cooperatives, leaseholding companies, commercial banks, stock exchanges, etc.
5. Representatives of the economic structures of the new states. Their specific position is characterized by the fact that their independence has only recently been achieved and their political status and the relationships with other parts of the former Soviet Union are still unclear
6. The Soviet partners of joint ventures.

Books other than this one on related subjects which can be classified in American literature under three main categories are:

1. Negotiating with the Soviets
2. Soviet bureaucracy and Soviet managers
3. The Russian mind-set and Homo sovietikus.

The first category is represented primarily by the literature which considers the negotiation styles, techniques, and behaviors of former foreign trade monopolists and participants in political negotiations. The second category is represented by books which treat the organizational issues of Soviet management at state industrial enterprises as well as the structure and system of management operations, styles, and practices. Some have addressed the problems and conditions under which managers at state enterprises operate. There are also some similar findings in books devoted to the phenomenon of the Russian mind-set (Homo sovietikus), the Russian sociocultural legacy and tradition, and the historical roots of the Russian and Soviet mentality.

Consistent with our principal goal of providing a comprehensive analysis of the new and complicated phenomenon of "millions of Soviets acting in the capacity of business people" and entering into business relationships with American companies, our book differs from other publications in some major areas. First of all, the authors focus attention on a far broader context of current Soviet reality, an unprecedented influx of new entrepreneurs from the various segments of the alternative economy, such as those from the former Union Republics, managers from semi-private and private enterprises, and negotiators other than those previously selected, few of whom have appeared on the business scene over the last few years. They brought with them all the confusion of the new breakthroughs in the country which has always been inscrutable in many ways for the West. Specially designed experiments, a lot of interviews with partners from both sides, personal involvement in Soviet-American business contacts, and the flow of publications in the years of glasnost enabled the authors to see from a new angle who and what American companies are actually dealing with.

The illustrative information is taken from the American and Soviet press. A lot of examples come from the weekly newspaper *Commersant*, the daily newspaper journals *Deloviye Lyudi/Delovoi Mir*, and the *Business in the USSR*, *Moskovski Biznes*, and *Moskva* which have won popularity in Soviet business circles over the last few years. We cited also the well-known Soviet newspapers *Izvestiya, Moskovskie Novosti, Literaturnaya Gazeta*, and others.

CHAPTER 2

Ten Advantages of Doing Business in the Russian Federation and Other Former Soviet Republics

Is it worthwhile for our company to start doing business in the former Soviet Union? Do we have the necessary resources for this? Should we postpone it or give up the whole idea entirely?

Many businesses have been asking themselves these questions over the last several years. Americans evaluate opportunities for doing business in the former Soviet Union in black and white. Some say that it is an impossible environment in which to do business. Picking up on this American attitude, the president of the Chamber of Commerce and Industry of the former Soviet Union quoted the words of Mark Twain: "Sirs, the rumors about my death have been exaggerated."

The other extreme is idealizing business opportunities in the former Soviet Union. When an American businessman is communicating with his Japanese partner, the physical appearance of the Japanese is a constant reminder to the American about cultural and psychological differences. Therefore, there is the illusion that the Soviet businessman understands business strategies and uses business techniques in the same way. Actually, in terms of business performance, he differs much more from his American counterpart than the Japanese businessman. As individuals, there are many similarities with the Soviets, but as participants of foreign trade contacts and as representatives of a business culture, Soviet businessmen differ dramatically from Americans. Ignoring these differences, and developing unrealistic idealized expectations, generates disappointment and causes other failures.

The analysis of the experience of American companies indicated ten advantages of the Soviet market which successful companies used, and ten drawbacks that they tried to neutralize, or avoid. Obviously, the advantages which have been formulated by the surveys are not the only avenues to follow. There are limitations and difficulties in exploiting them. As is said in Russia, "not everything which shines is gold," and "even the sun has its dark spots."

At the same time, the drawbacks of being in the Soviet market are not insurmountable, and as the experience of American companies shows, can be successfully neutralized or eliminated. Here, there is also a Russian proverb: "There are no bad things that can't be turned to your benefit."

Advantage No. 1. The Former Soviet Union's Growing Dependence on Western Supplies: The West's Political and Economic Motivation to Develop Business There

More than any other imports, the former Soviet Union depends on Western supplies for food products, consumer goods, medical equipment and supplies, material for the automotive and tractor building industries, oil exploration and development technology, etc. A number of industries cannot function without the regular import of technology and components. For instance, at the time when the amount of oil developed in the Soviet Union was high and the price of oil was high too, large amounts of hard currency were generated for the country. It was a normal process to buy technology and components overseas to maintain production, resulting in dependency on the regular importing of technology and components, even when the oil situation changed and went into sharp decline, generating less hard currency. One hundred percent of the instant coffee, baby formula with meat and milk products, pasteurized milk, and franks are produced with imported technology. From 85 to 95 percent of dry non-fat milk, margarine, candies, and juices from the total volume of the USSR production are produced with the use of imported technology.

It is interesting to consider the tobacco crisis in the former Soviet Union, which started in the middle of 1990. Cigarette shortages aggravated the social unrest due to poor economic conditions in the country and resulted in increased riots. The director of the tobacco factory Yava, Leonid Sinelnikov, said that the crisis had not occurred by accident: "This crisis was bound to happen when, in 1988, the amount of tobacco products available for sale was reduced. Tobacco shortages are the worst kind of deficit. Seventy million consumers became outraged all at once. When the industrial segment, including the tobacco segment, operates on imported technology and not a kopek is allocated to [developing technology] over six years, the crisis is inevitable. The money is allocated when it is obvious that there is no other way. The crises occurred in 1969, 1976, and in 1980. There were some small increases in supplies, and then it was reduced again. A fast way to get out of the crisis was to allocate currency to renovate the equipment with the participation of manufacturing firms. We conducted negotiations with them. They have already studied the state of affairs. Today, the government has agreed to allocate the money. And if we buy new equipment, it will be supplied in a year and a half. While there is the necessity, it also costs a lot. But to import cigarettes will be even more expensive."[1]

We will show how the Soviet dependence on imports generates specific opportunities for American companies in various business segments. In the current situation, the United States has an objective, strategic interest in the economic revitalization of the former Soviet Union and its viable economy and in the development of business there.

Advantage No. 2. Market Economy Transformation in the Former Soviet Union: Formation of Independent Economic Structures

In spite of all the contradictions, paradoxes, and absurdities, and in spite of inconsistency in accomplishing political and economic reforms and establishing market structures, the proportion of new independent structures in the economy is increasing. On April 1, 1989, cooperatives, leaseholding and private enterprises, as well as commercial banks and stock exchanges, were granted the right to engage directly in foreign economic activities, and many of them have become partners of American companies.

Soviet and American stock exchanges have started to create joint auditing firms which envision putting Soviet shareholding companies in quoting lists of American stock exchanges. One of the new avenues for cooperation is selling Soviet securities in American stock exchanges. The first steps are being made in buying brokers' places in U.S. stock exchanges. For example, Moscow Central Stock Exchange is negotiating buying brokers' places in the New York Stock Exchange. Opportunities for buying oil, oil products, and non-ferrous metals generate interest among American companies in becoming members of Commodities and Commodities-Raw Materials Exchanges. For example, the American financial group Revco has become a member of the Moscow Commodities Exchange. American companies operating at the stock exchange in Moscow and in the Baltic states are making their first steps in selling the shares of American companies, such as General Motors and Boeing. Among the founders of a number of these Exchanges are American citizens.

Both cooperatives and state enterprises have created alternative foreign economic structures, such as associations of business cooperation, consortiums, leaseholding organizations, and trade houses. One such example presenting an alternative in the fields of construction and construction materials to the State's foreign economic structures is Vneshstroikomplex, the Association of Business Cooperation with Foreign Countries. This organization united about one hundred enterprises over a one-year period, representing their interest in the external markets. In an interview with the journal *Business People*, the general manager of the association, Yakov Minasov, discussed the role of the middleman in a new environment of direct engagement of foreign trade. He claimed that due to the complexity of the foreign trade field, professionals are required to help an organization navigate through the customs, laws, assumptions, and proprieties. In promoting his new association, the general manager emphasized the advantages of its broader-based business representation for his clients over traditionally narrower specializations of the former monopolists—state foreign trade organizations.

The second advantage in using the services of this new middleman consortium is its ability to work within the government structure, eliminating the possibility of customers outside the plan being excluded for a longer time frame for order filling. During the year the association has operated, many clients have begun to understand the advantages it offers. For instance, one customer applied to a former state foreign trade organization to buy component equipment. The fulfillment term he was given was six months. The Association of Business Cooperation's term was two months. Cost of services is lower as well, since they charge low commissions and seek volume.[2]

The creation of an independent economy is hampered by obstacles to the market economy: vague contradictory laws and regulations, limited access of the new business entities to natural and financial resources, the lack of entrepreneurial skills, the business culture, and the long-term orientation of new businessmen.

The independent economic organizations operate differently from other economic sectors. An analogous situation would be a country where under the same traffic regulations public vehicles drove on the left-hand side of the road (as in Great Britain) and private cars on the right-hand side (as in the United States). But despite these difficulties, independent structures are a dynamic impetus for the reforms, and, although they are experiencing periodic crisis they are beginning to predominate in the economy.

Alongside the disastrous reduction of production in the state sector of the economy, the volume of production and services in independent economic structures was 15 percent of the gross national product. At the beginning of 1991, 245,000 cooperatives were registered. The total number of personnel working in cooperatives was 6 million. In the middle of 1991 there were 197,000 cooperatives and 5 million people working in them. This reduction is explained by transforming some of the cooperatives into stockholding companies and private enterprises.

Independent economies have become a serious political factor. The interest of more than 25 million people hinge on them. Public, political organizations such as the Regional Cooperators' Unions and the Association of Joint Ventures have appeared, that stand up for this sector of the economy.

Advantage No. 3. Significant Changes in Soviet Laws

Since January 13, 1988, according to the decree of the Supreme Soviet of the USSR "about the issues related to the formation on the territory of the USSR and operations of joint ventures, international associations and organizations with the participation of Soviet and foreign organizations, firms and administrative bodies," foreign companies have been given the right to create joint ventures in the USSR. Beginning in 1989, restrictions were lifted that had previously barred foreign partners from owning more than 49 percent of initial joint venture capital. Now the split is according to the partners' agreement. The chairman of the board or general manager of the joint venture can now include foreign citizens as well as Soviets, unlike before.

According to the decree of the Council of Ministers of the USSR of December 2, 1988, "about further development of foreign economic activity of the state, cooperative and other enterprises, associations and organizations," after April 1, 1989, all state enterprises and cooperatives were given the right to enter external markets independently after their registration as participants in foreign economic activity. Under this new approach, foreign economic regulations reflected more openness in this decree in the Soviet economy. This approach was a prerequisite for involvement in a broad realm of business connections, such as coordination of tariff and non-tariff regulations with the international standards and, correspondingly, the Soviet Union entering into GATT and other international organizations.

According to the decree of the Council of Ministers of the USSR, "about the development of economic activity of Soviet organizations overseas" of May 18, 1989, the rights of enterprises are being expanded in another area which had been closed to them before: Development of economic activities overseas through setting up enterprises with a Soviet share of the capital and participation in the management as well as investment in the securities of other enterprises, and operations of fund and commodities exchanges. According to the decrees, Soviet state enterprises, and organizations in which they participate, could set up foreign enterprises and engage in securities operations if they were registered as participants of foreign economic relations.

The Soviets buy brokers' seats on American exchanges, for example Moscow Central Funds Exchange is considering the possibility of buying a broker's seat on the New York Stock Exchange. The company Lickon (in the State of Delaware), is a joint venture created in the United States by the Foreign Trade Association, Licenzintorg, and is engaged in selling Soviet licenses in the United States. A Russian restaurant venture Tyodorov, on Long Island, New York, was set up by one of the first and most famous Soviet cooperative restaurants on Kropotkinskaya Street. There are successful Soviet ventures in some European countries. For example, the enterprise Sillprint FRG trades Soviet postage stamps and Soviet anniversary coins overseas and also purchases printing equipment.

Beginning in the fall of 1990, foreign companies were given the right to open their subsidiaries in the former Soviet Union, and to be founders and 100 percent owners of these businesses in the territory of the former Soviet Union. 3M was the first foreign company to take advantage of this new rule, and did so as an exception even before the adoption of the law upon agreement with the Soviet leadership. Due to the size and high visibility of the company, 3M was able to generate interest with the Soviet leadership to arrange the agreement.

The second example of registration in the USSR of a foreign firm with 100 percent ownership is the creation in November 1990 of Cuperwood,

Inc. Its founder and full owner is the American trading and broker company, Cuperwood Enterprises. Foreign firms have been given the right to open ruble accounts in the former Soviet Union and invest ruble profits there. Joint ventures have gained access to hard currency auctions. By converting rubles to hard currency at the auctions, they overcome many difficulties related to ruble inconvertibility.

In 1988, "Free Economic Zones (FEZ)" projects were started. Free Economic Zones play some role in the development of business in the former USSR. These capitalist economic islands ("Soviet Hong Kongs") function separately and independently and can survive in periods of economic and political crisis, social unrest, and disarray, making them a preferred place to do business. The attitude of the various political forces and the population to these Free Economic Zones is not unanimous. Independent experts at the Academy of National Economy conducted surveys which reveal various attitudes towards the project. For example, in Novgorod, more than half of the respondents have a positive attitude to these Free Economic Zones, 20 percent are against, while the rest are uncertain as yet.[3] Another example of the disagreement of opinion is the extreme point of view of one of the opponents of Free Economic Zones, The People's Deputy of the former Soviet Union, N. Strukov. He believes that such zones are necessary, however they should not be given to foreigners, but populated by criminals, wrongdoers, and other enemies. "An iron rod and discipline will provide an opportunity to build cities of the future quicker than with the help of the Japanese," he believes.[4]

Advantage No. 4. New Opportunities for Western Companies Due to Independence of the Former Union Republics

In our interview, the director of a Ukrainian foreign economic consortium commented on the increasingly favorable opportunities for Western companies aiming to enter the markets of the former republics due to their newly achieved independence.

According to the director, republics have been interested in cooperation with Western companies even if they did not benefit very much from it economically. Just having these contacts was recognition of their independence and a step toward strengthening their sovereignty.

They have been creating a more favorable environment for foreign businesses than the former central government, because they have been ready to compromise, give concessions, discounts, and exclusive rights. Republics also resort to help from American experts for the development of market reform strategies. For example, the Kazakhstan leadership invited a Korean-American economist, Chan Yan Bang, one of the authors of the South Korean economic miracle, and he currently occupies the position of the vice chairman of the Committee of Economic Experts of Kazakhstan. He is the closest adviser to the president of the republic. Another example would be two ministers of Armenian government who are American citizens.

The former republics differ in their laws passed by the Supreme Soviets which, for the first time, were elected on a democratic basis. These differences appear in the varying legal frameworks for foreign companies doing business in the territory of the former USSR. This enables American companies to identify the new states with the most favorable conditions for their business.

It is also important that republican government bodies follow the principle of establishing more favorable conditions for independent economic structures. The opportunities for economic alliances with republics are illustrated by the example of the Russian Federation's potential and the results of its foreign economic activity in 1990, the first year of Russia's relative economic independence from the center.

According to *Commersant*, by the end of January 1990, 14,500 enterprises were registered as participating in foreign economic activity in Russia. Russia's imports totaled almost 23 billion rubles. Exports totaled 25 billion rubles, leaving a foreign trade deficit of 2 billion rubles. In general, the structure of Russian exports was identical to that of the former central government, with major exports falling into three categories: (1) oil, gas, coal and ores; (2) concentrates; and (3) lumber. Import structures between Russia and the central government didn't differ significantly either. The only difference in the Russian Federation's imports from those of the centralized economic structures was that in Russia the proportion of imported equipment and technology was higher. In the territory of the Russian Federation, the major industrial enterprises were in constant need of supplies of goods that may be invested in production. By the end of January 1991, 2,516 cooperatives which participated in foreign economic activities were registered. The proportion of total Russian exports coming from free enterprise organizations in 1990 was 0.06 percent, or approximately $14 million. The proportion of total Russian imports coming from free enterprise organizations was 0.07 percent, or about $18 million. However, other estimates show that the foreign trade operations of non-centralized structures were far more efficient than those of the centralized ones. According to statistics on commodities which commercial, non-state structures were selling overseas, the following were priorities:

- technology and equipment
- lumber
- industrial goods for mass consumption.

These differences in the foreign trade of commercial entities compared with centralized ones testify to the potential development of Russian exports through independent structures. It is obvious that commercial companies free from the obligation of supplying the state operate more effectively in their import trade and sell goods which can yield profits. The import structure of commercial entities also has a progressive character: Goods which are intended for investment in production prevail, such as machinery and equipment, which constitute more than 50 percent of the total worth of cooperative imports in 1990.

It should be noted that commercial entities run more efficient import operations than the state enterprises. Commercial firms import almost 100 percent of their operating equipment. The same index for state enterprises in various kinds of technology and equipment ranges from 40 to 90 percent.[5]

Advantage No. 5. Unexplored Opportunities for Establishing Business Contacts

To a great extent, previous connections with American companies which had been doing business in the Soviet Union have now been destroyed, because beginning April 1, 1989, Soviet enterprises, organizations, and cooperatives were granted the right to enter the foreign market independently. They account for tens of thousands of new participants in foreign economic activities.

Previously, state foreign trade organizations had been monopolists in the specific fields of foreign trade, as in the case of V/O Medexport, for example. If anyone wanted to sell medical supplies to the Soviet Union there was only one door. Some companies established close ties with these foreign trade monopolists, but today the situation has changed drastically. Before, only a very small group of people could make foreign trade decisions. Today, new participants in foreign trade are becoming more and more active. Now, not only Medexport, as it was before, but also state enterprises, commercial entities, and local city officials have the authority to buy medical supplies for the employees of enterprises, for local medical offices, and hospitals. With hard currency, an enterprise can buy, for example, disposable syringes for the hospital, or clothes, or food products for its employees. An enterprise can also buy technology and equipment on the outside market.

Some of the hard-currency earnings of the enterprises are allocated to city needs. The policy of allocating some of the hard-currency earnings to city needs, many directors of enterprises indicated, is for two reasons. First of all, laws were adopted which obligate them to transfer part of their currency profits to the city budget. Second, the reality of the situation in which their enterprises operate makes them do this. They depend on city authority for such critical functional issues as facilities, energy and materials supplies, means of communication, housing construction, etc. Currency proceeds from enterprises are used by the city for overseas purchases. City authorities sometimes also try to establish cooperation with foreign countries on a regional basis, i.e., to create some permanent arrangement of the region with another region or the city with another city.

Many of these new foreign trade participants have not yet established stable business contacts and have just started seeking business partners. Therefore, Americans can now enter Soviet markets in which there was previously a business vacuum.

The Soviet market is extremely responsive to all investors, not just Western business giants such as IBM. As shown by the polls, new Soviet participants in foreign economic activities often do not make distinctions between Western firms according to the usual criteria of business reputation. In most cases, the single fact that this is a Western firm might generate interest from a Soviet enterprise or cooperative. In a sense, the situation of the Soviet market provides a chance for a Western company of any size, reputation, popularity, or experience to be successful.

Advantage No. 6. Vast Amounts of Natural Resources and Possibilities for Business Partnerships in Exploration and Processing

In the territory of the former Soviet Union, large reserves of natural resources have been explored and developed:

- Oil reserves are being developed in Western Siberia, the Volga-Urals Region, Kazakhstan, North Caucasus, Transcaucasus, and the Komi Autonomous Republic. Oil is also being developed in the sea in the Caspian, Okhotsk, Baltic and Karsk seas.
- Gas reserves are being developed in Western Siberia, the Komi Autonomous Area, the Near Caspian Depression, North Caucasus, and in the Central Asia and Orenburg Regions.
- Coal is mined in the Kuznetsk and the Donetsk Regions (in

Ukraine), the Karagandinski Region (in Kazakhstan), in Siberia, and the Far East.
- Non-ferrous metals, lead, zinc, copper, tungsten, nickel, and iron ore are mined in the Urals, Siberia, and Kazakhstan.
- Major diamond deposits are found in Jakutia. Gold is mined mostly in the Russian Federation (Jakutia, Buryatia, Tuva, Khakassia), Uzbekistan.
- Chemical resources (potassium, salt, sodium chloride, sulphur, apatites, and phosphorites) are abundant in the Ukraine, Belarus, the Urals, and Volga Regions, Siberia, the Central Regions of Russia, and in the European North.
- Timber resources are available in the North of the European part of the country, the Far East, and Siberia.

In addition, oil exports from 1975 to 1990 brought profits of $100 billion to the USSR. There is also major potential for business partnerships to cooperate in the fields of processing by-products, in particular scrap metal, paper recycling, timber by-products, and oil by-products. According to a key figure in the Soviet foreign economic complex, large amounts of scrap metal are being dumped in the country. Environment cleanups are necessary in places where it is being dumped, such as on the banks of rivers and seashores. At the same time, the scrap metal which has been dumped, totaling 8–12 million tons over the last five to seven years, is not being used for industrial purposes. Existing capacity for processing ship scrap metal allows for processing only 80,000 tons. There are no facilities and no technology for its preparation for foundry, so the government has decided to create joint ventures with foreign firms for processing the scrap metal. For example, Minrybkhoz, the former Ministry of Fishing of the USSR, was assigned the task of creating four joint ventures with American firms that will engage in disassembling and processing sunken and old ships. These ships are currently sailed to closed bays where they remain for many years, rusting and sinking. Of the approximately 500 ships that have sunk to date, 232 of them are from the merchant marine fleets which had sunk before World War II.

They should be removed just because they contaminate the environment, if not for other purposes. In this endeavor the state appears to be lagging behind independent entrepreneurs.[6]

Advantage No. 7. Cheap Labor

Analysis of Soviet-American joint ventures revealed two avenues for using cheap Soviet labor:

- in construction and industrial joint ventures, primarily computer assembly
- in the development of new technologies equipment, software, research, and development.

In those scientific and technological fields where the former Soviet Union met world standards, Soviet specialists had received good professional training and were well qualified. These were in the following fields:

- synthesis of small grain solid substances
- rare substances
- space, energy technology
- nuclear technology
- welding through explosions
- high-frequency radio technology
- impulse energy sources
- production of modern ceramic materials
- research of monocell albumen
- lasers
- materials for the electronics industry
- medical, ultrasonic equipment
- catalysts for chemical processes
- modern materials
- nuclear reactor technology
- modern software[7]

Engineers, scientists, and inventors have been solving sophisticated scientific and engineering problems under the poor conditions of nonexistent facilities, poor materials, and scarce financial resources. The personnel engaged in research and development are highly motivated and creative workers and their experience, knowledge, and skills can be useful in American firms and joint ventures. For Soviet specialists, work in American firms might be the best practical school for studying modern technology.

But with many other categories of the Soviet workforce, the reverse side of cheap labor is lack of motivation, poor performance, and low-quality products. A popular saying in the Soviet Union went, "You pretend to pay us, and we pretend to work." A good illustration of this is found in the comments of a Japanese businessman who had been doing business in the Soviet Union for a long time:

The first Russian book which I could read myself is the novel *Oblomov*. It often seems to me that I have met, if not with Oblomov, himself, then with his grandchildren and great-grandchildren until now. You are indifferent to what you are doing. In Japan, you will not hear anecdotes about poor quality of products, though the defective products do occur. Workers and engineers are ashamed of this. Most of your anecdotes are about bad-quality products that you manufacture. You are especially willing to laugh at these anecdotes. For example, why not create a joint venture for the production of TVs, PCs and robots?

   . . . I see before my eyes the Volga Automobile Plant. Zhigulis seem to be very much like Fiats, but this is only on the outside. As for quality, they have as much in common as a real tiger and a paper one, and the tiger from the picture may create an erroneous impression about the tiger from the jungle. This was the case with the Zhiguli and the Fiat. If I engage in joint TV production with you, I am running a risk that the same production of mine from Japan will be rejected in the same way as Fiat is being rejected somewhere in the world now.[8]

If seen in terms of Western culture and the concepts of market economy, the approach of many of the Soviets to hiring and entering into relationships with employers appears at times to be ridiculous and absurd. An example comes from the following story about the attempts of the Soviets to obtain employment overseas. Many sociopsychological traits are strikingly illustrated here, specifically, (1) the psychology of deficit and therefore the lack of skills to sell oneself, (2) the dependence on the authoritarian state which is supposed to find the solution to someone's problems, and (3) the projection of this parasitic attitude onto other societies. This story relates how the Soviets responded to an ad by American lawyer Emily Silliman for the employment of foreigners overseas. Emily Silliman agreed to answer the readers' questions about the legal side of such arrangements, but there were actually very few questions about legal issues. The Soviets demonstrated a complete lack of awareness of how to generate business correspondence. Typically, the Soviets seeking this opportunity assumed that, as in their home country, they could apply by writing a letter to some institutions of authority where one could ask any question and from where a letter would be forwarded to other places these institutions might consider appropriate. The usual practice in the Soviet Union is to write letters to the editorial boards of the central newspapers, to the Supreme Soviet or the ministries or somewhere else at the "top" from where their letters would be readdressed to the local authorities, to the courts, local head offices, and so on. The American way of sending the letter to the actual organization from where they can receive specific answers was unknown to Soviets. The following excerpt is from one reader, Ilyin, from the Moscow region (the letter has been chosen from many just like it):

> I have some "know-how" to offer a Western firm engaged in production of computer technology and software. The production of an entirely new product is possible.

Some people did not even type their letters but wrote them illegibly. It is hard to imagine how such letters would be deciphered in Western firms and how they would translate them into English. The assumption that their letters would be answered at all stems from the Soviet policy of obligating any organization to answer a letter from the people. The Soviets didn't realize that when they offer their labor in the international market nobody is obliged to them.

Another letter to the lawyer Emily Silliman stated:

> Dear Emily,
>
> I read your article in the newspaper and decided to seek an employment overseas too. But how can I find an employer? Could you possibly help me? For example, to advise me on the addresses of the employment agencies (Finland, Sweden, Norway . . .). Or maybe you can provide some more information about this? My best wishes to you. I hope to hear from you soon.
>
> Ivan

It is amazing that the letter writer hopes to figure out the addresses of the employment agencies in other countries from the U.S. lawyer. And it is even more amazing what kind of information he hopes to obtain if he does not inform anyone about his profession, experience, age, proficiency in English, etc.[9]

Another example is about the lack of a work ethic. It reveals itself in the Soviets' underestimation of quality issues. According to the opinion of one Western businessman, expressed in the press, one of the factors that hampered long-term business contacts with Soviet partners was that one and the same traded product might have different grades over the entire contract period. Because the necessary adjustments were required with every shipment, it caused a lot of trouble and generated a lot of expenses.

In our interview, Jeff Furman, vice president of Ben & Jerry's Homemade, Inc., described his experience in trying to get a Soviet commodity for a new flavor of ice cream. The idea was to mix walnuts from Karelia with Vermont maple syrup in their ice cream to make the international flavor of "Karelia Maple Crunch." "It was impossible to get the quality standards met for the walnuts," he stated. "We can't put rotten walnuts in our maple walnut ice cream, no matter how cute the name is and how wonderful the concept. The quality just wasn't there. And they didn't seem to know or seem particularly interested in how to ensure it. We even offered to pay in hard currency just to get what we needed, but it never worked out," stated Furman.

Many Western businesses also complain about the performance of secretaries and other office employees. Soviet clerks are sloppy in their contacts with clients. A representative of an American company said: "The telephone might ring and our Soviet managers don't answer. They might pick up the receiver and put it down again. They are not used to asking who's calling. I may come back to the office and they will tell me 'Somebody called you.' In the long run, I taught them to write down the number."[10] Secretaries and clerks also often lose faxes, don't answer them, forget to coordinate meetings or notify participants about their dates and times, and generally cause overall confusion through inattention to detail.

The experience of American companies in the Soviet Union indicates that to some extent these problems might be solved through the following:

- A serious approach to the choice of employees. One can choose from thousands of applicants who would be eager to work in a joint venture in a foreign firm. The Moscow McDonald's restaurant had 25,000 applicants for 630 jobs.
- Creating an effective incentive system which might include imported goods, trips abroad, etc.
- Training of both managers and office employees and workers. The experience of the Soviet-American joint venture Perestroika might serve as an example. Training programs for Soviet managers abroad, such as, for example, those arranged by American universities, might also contribute to solving these problems. According to the Soviet press, the chairman of the board of directors of Fuqua Industries, Jack Fuqua, personally invested $4 million in the training of Soviet specialists at Duke University Business School. He believed it was a timely move to render financial assistance in the form of training executive personnel of Soviet enterprises. He also hoped that as a result of the changes in the economy, the former Soviet Union would become a stronger partner and would benefit the Americans in the international market.[11]

Advantage No. 8. Two-Hundred-Eighty-Five Million Eager Consumers

Before the ruble becomes convertible, the opportunities for entering one of the largest untapped markets are limited. Analysis of the surveys and available sources highlighted five sales strategies currently used by American companies for gaining access to this huge market. (Chapter 4 will provide specific examples of companies using these strategies in various business fields.)

1. The biggest potential for the development of enterprises in the former Soviet Union seems to be extensive ruble sales, with further investments of ruble proceeds into the enterprise. This strategy enables companies to enter the market without large, hard-currency investments, positions them in the Soviet market for the time the ruble becomes convertible, and provides growth opportunities for companies and publicity back home. In the head office of the Levi Strauss Company, there is a huge world map on the wall with yellow continents showing green areas where their jeans are distributed. "We still have more yellow space," complains a representative of the company, pointing to the former USSR. One strategy is creating joint ventures oriented to the internal demand of the country. They do not promise big profits, but enable the company to get a toehold in the new marketplace.[12]

   McDonald's logos in Moscow and long lines in the street for the crowded restaurant caught the attention of mass media worldwide. This contributed to even higher visibility for the company and helped offset its hard-currency expenses.

2. Sales for rubles with further purchase of hard currency at the auctions through joint ventures.

3. Sales for rubles with hard-currency compensations from the government, as in the cases of priority items.

4. Sales for rubles with further purchases in the former Soviet Union of commodities, which can be sold for hard currency in the world market.

5. Sales to Soviet hard-currency owners. The Soviet press has cited findings about the estimated disposable hard-currency income of Soviet citizens. According to the estimates, the consumer population of the Soviet Union currently has $2 billion at its disposal and other estimates figure it is closer to $5 billion. According to calculations made on the basis of the findings of the Public Opinion Poll Center, the total hard-currency income of Soviet citizens

might be worth about $10 billion a year in the near future. Given the cultural norm for Soviet citizens of a 12 percent savings rate from personal income, $8.8 billion a year could make its way into the retail system.[13]

One of the positive factors for trying to gain access to the Soviet market is the low requirements of the Soviet consumer for product quality. Low quality requirements also mean less production expenses when the opportunities for joint production are considered.

Advantage No. 9. Opportunities for Commercial Application of Scientific Developments, Inventions, and Technologies

According to expert estimates, only 1 percent of all inventions (i.e., 800) in the former Soviet Union from the total 80,000 that are registered yearly are introduced into production.

A Japanese businessman told about his search for ideas in the appendices of small Soviet journals and publications under the heading of "Do It Yourself." He sold these ideas to American, Soviet, and Japanese firms and made an estimated $35 million. He is continuing this search now. He admits that he has been trading Soviet ideas for twenty years and the profitability has been fantastic. He also believes that Russians are extremely talented and thinks they are in the forefront in many areas of scientific-technical progress, but they often import their own ideas, paying in gold for their own inertia. The financial prosperity of this Japanese gentleman's firm hinges on the Soviet lack of initiative and inability to make use of what is under their nose.[14]

There is a narrow market for scientific developments and inventions in the country, since enterprises often try by all means to avoid them, although the representative of the Academy of Sciences of the Russian Federation said in our interview that the possible scientific fields where American companies can buy licenses for Soviet scientific development are software, albumen research, lasers, semiconductors for explosive welding, and materials for the electronics industry.

An Estonian engineer, L. Sulbe, developed a device for processing oils with high water content, in the 1970s. This device was very economically efficient and could be used in environmental protection activities. However, not a single Soviet enterprise started producing it, in spite of the requests from abroad and in spite of the direction from the former chairman of the Council of Ministers of the USSR, who knew about this device and assigned GKNT (the State Committee for Science and Technology) the task of introducing it. The inventor could not license the invention and sell it that way, either, since former officers of the GKNT neither endorsed introduction of the development nor selling of a license. Their reasoning was that, "They will start its production abroad and will sell it to us." Their caution, while having some merit, did not solve the problem.

Another example is that regarding the proverbial shortage of electrical batteries, which are produced in only a few varieties for domestic appliances. There are numerous varieties of batteries being used in Western Europe, many of which are based on Soviet licenses sold in the 1970s.[15] Additionally, research on the new DNA structures conducted by M. Frank-Kamenetski generated interest and received recognition all over the world, but has no support in his home country. This research study received support all over the United States which is financing the project.

Soviet designers invented a deep drilling device a quarter of a century ago, at approximately the same time Americans were developing such designs. It received recognition by the State Committee for Inventions and Discoveries, and got American and West European patents. A sample was made and tests proved that it could be fully operational. The device only required an adjustment to increase its reliability before it could be put into production. Instead of making the adjustment, there was a hiatus of several years as a new sample was made and new testing began. The new sample proved to be fully operational, but again, certain components were unreliable. Every year, research and development plans were written into the reports, but it is still a long way from being put into production. The inventor of this device, Mr. Kotlyarov, protested the situation and was forced to retire. The Designing Bureau he created never earned a single dollar from his design because the patent expired before it was operational. And now, Kotlyarov's idea can be used by anyone. The millions of rubles spent on developing the device did not result in savings which could have totaled billions. According to the people's deputy of the former Soviet Union, engaged in the oil development industry in Siberia, V. Gustov, this story is typical of the general situation. He pointed out that the program of technical reconstruction for Western Siberia's oil industry had practically come to a standstill. Out of sixty-four kinds of new technology critical for oil and gas development and production, only one novelty device had arrived, a control and measuring instrument.[16]

Addressing American businessmen, Gorbachev said: "I . . . visited the big Moscow association Kvant. I was shown two medical inventions which seem very promising for medicine. The FRG [West Germany] is working to set up a joint venture for producing this kind of technology. I am saying this because the FRG is offering to cooperate in introducing Soviet engineering developments. While you are establishing contacts, I would ask you, when you establish contacts, to try first and foremost to use those R&D achievements which our countries have already attained."[17]

According to a *Commersant* analyst, Oleg Utitsin, Soviet achievements in the field of biotechnology will be developed in the United States, with the help of American money and American scientists, by a joint Soviet-American firm that has been created by Sierra-Ventures and the Clintodale Group, and the Soviet partner, the Albumen Institute of the Academy of Sciences. The middleman services in this deal were rendered by GKNT. The project is based on new technology for albumen production developed by the Soviet institute, which does not require the use of living cells. The firm also sells joint developments and licenses to other companies. It is one of the first examples of a Soviet company acquiring ownership of a large part of the shares of a foreign firm. The Albumen Institute involved in the project took advantage of the fact that at the time this transaction was concluded, the terms for such kinds of deals were not spelled out in Soviet legal documents. According to the agreement, the American company is supposed to initially invest about $2 million, but over the next few years the investment will be significantly increased.[18] Another example of the joint development of Soviet products involves the Eastern European division of Du Pont which has established contacts with some Soviet pharmaceutical research centers.

Soviet-American cooperation is developing along other lines, too. FloraGenetics developed a data base under an agreement between the Research Bureau of the U.S. Agricultural Department and the Plant Studies Institute, named after N. Vavilov. In the future, Soviet scientists will be able to help farmers protect fields from insects, which are eating up crops. According to scientists, an important part of the agreement is combining the plant collections accumulated by the researchers of two countries over two centuries. The international data base will provide information for scientists all over the world.[19]

One of the joint ventures concerning intellectual property is Mebinvest, a product of Norm Gershman's consulting company, the Moscow-based Center of Patent Services, and Syntez, a private company headed by Dr. Mark Garber, whom Gershman met during his years of international exchange work. Gershman told us in our interview that in his opinion, intellectual property is the most underutilized resource in the former Soviet Union, with no more than 1,500 patent applications out of approximately 150,000 per year being developed in international markets. Today, Mebinvest has an office in every republic and can deal with each republic independently.

Advantage No. 10. Former Soviet Military Complex Conversions Open New Avenues for Cooperation

Conversion of the military industry of Russia and other new states is opening up potentially extensive new avenues for cooperation. The reduction of military production frees up vast amounts of industrial facilities. Enterprises embarking on paths of conversion avail themselves of highly qualified, disciplined personnel and significant scientific-industrial potential. For example, the field of space technology is confronted with the task of peacefully re-orienting production. Starting first with the production of medical equipment, food equipment, and consumer goods, 1 million square meters of industrial space have been released. The conversion can be accomplished through cooperation with Western companies, compensation deals, and the creation of joint ventures. These trends towards conversion have met resistance from opponents to the reform, from the military-industrial complex, and from the conservative military, which has resulted in few conversions; however, with the changing direction and leadership of the military as a result of the events of 1991, the prerequisites for the lessening of resistance have emerged.

Examples of inefficiency regarding developments in military complex conversion are cited in the Soviet press, such as the Volgograd washing machine plant, where of the thirty-seven different features designed for the machine, the Soviets are manufacturing only six. Export of this machine is impossible because it does not stand up to competition in the international market. In one of the interviews, we were told that ski poles are being made from titanium because there is an excess supply of this metal at some enterprises, although ski poles could be made from cheaper metals, and titanium used for mountain-climbing supplies. The enterprises, however, have no idea of how to locate the firms to generate the mountain-climbing supplies.

A special study was commissioned to discover strategies for American-Soviet cooperation in the field of the military-industrial complex, such as the use of high technology developed in this complex for civilian purposes. The survey polled more than fifty key Soviet experts, including chief designers and directors of enterprises, and also officials from the ministry in charge of military industry. Particular attention was given to a detailed examination of how these enterprises could be potential partners for American companies, and how different they were from other Soviet enterprises. These organizations are powerful because for many years they have had a special position in society and special support from the government. They should be considered as dependable partners.

Six distinguishing characteristics were most evident in these military complex enterprises:

1. A high level of responsibility, discipline, and reliability with partners (by Soviet standards).
2. A high professional level, with good knowledge of the production and operations processes.
3. An interest in working together with American companies and a willingness to tackle important projects in line with their qualifications. They also want to do this through the creation of joint ventures and selling their products for hard currency.
4. A lack of preparation and ability to take responsibility and risk and, as a rule, lack of initiative and independence caused by the specific management style in this field (only chief designers have authority, power, and responsibility).
5. A lack of openness in relationships with foreign firms due to many years of secretiveness in this sphere.
6. An absence of information about international markets resulting in poor preparation for working in international markets, in particular, lack of awareness about actual demand and overestimation of the commercial significance of some of their projects and an underestimation of others. Their estimation of a project's value is based on the recognition of those achievements in the domestic market. They also underestimate the role of marketing and middleman services.

A project developed by the Texas-based Space Commerce Corporation and a Soviet machine building organization is one of the first successful projects to convert the Soviet aerospace industry into the commercial production of useful civilian services, by selling commercial satellite photos. The project is the third commercial source of satellite images in the world. It follows the American Landsat and the French Spot, and while they rely on visual images, the Soviet Almaz remote-sensing satellite uses radar. "The whole project has been oriented toward being an extremely rapid delivery product. We see that as very important to the market," said Arthur M. Dula, president of the Space Commerce Corporation.[20]

Problems in conversion projects with American companies have important sociopolitical impacts affecting many people, which create difficulties in implementing the projects. In order to discover the attitude of the workers involved in the conversion process, the Moscow-based Institute of the International Labor Movement conducted a poll at the Yoshkar-Olinsk Mechanical Plant (it is no secret that many defense industry enterprises are machine building works). Of the respondents, 44.9 percent stated that they believed that their salary would be reduced through the conversion process, 4.8 percent believed that it would increase, while 7.4 percent thought that it would not change. Some 44.9 percent of the workers couldn't answer the question, while 54 percent believed that if a conversion were made, they would have to change their professions, while in fact the overwhelming majority would have retraining programs at the plants, according to the administration. It did not appear that the workers had been notified about this. Of the workers who were polled, 91.4 percent didn't know where they would have training in case they have to change their professions, and only 5.8 percent of them answered that it would be through training programs arranged by enterprises, while 2.6 percent believed that it would take place somewhere else. The lack of information compounds the tension at the enterprises and generates uncertainty and anxiety. Some 43.8 percent of the respondents answered that they would seek fairness by organizing and creating an alternative workers association. As we see, the idea of paternalism through the government's patronage which has been fostered in the minds of the workers and other social strata of the society over decades has been snuffed out, and though the willingness to fight for their rights now, without the government's help, seems to be just an emotional outburst, it is very probable that it will require some structure and rational strategy in the future.

Among the conversion problems as they are perceived by the employees from the military industry there is also a sociopsychological issue related to the prestige of being in this industry. To the question "Will your prestige be affected if the production at your enterprise is converted?" 36.3 percent answered that it is not high anyway so there will be no changes; 43.3 percent believed that their prestige would not be affected because it does not depend on the place of their employment; 17.6 percent thought that they would lose the prestige; while 1 percent answered that prestige does not depend on the place of work but on the salary. These evaluations may have a negative impact in terms of employees quitting their jobs at their enterprise and seeking employment at other enterprises.[21]

As our interviews have shown, a major reason for resistance by the military elite to the reforms in the army and military-industrial complex, is the fear of dismissal from the army as a result of reductions in the armed forces. Managers of military enterprises are extremely sensitive to the importance of their military activity, and they fear a loss of prestige if they go from "producing rockets to producing pots."

Soviet-American cooperation in this area is a chance to involve them in their professional activities, generate hard-currency earnings, and provide an opportunity to go abroad where they can see for themselves Western life and give up many dogmatic assumptions about the free enterprise world. This is designed to reduce their resistance to reforms. An important element of such cooperation is arranging trips to the former Soviet Union for American businessmen and politicians interested in conversion processes. During one such trip, in autumn 1990, a delegation of high-profile American businessmen and politicians visited Soviet military enterprises in the fields of space technology, manufacturing electronic equipment for naval shipbuilding, and communication technology for military purposes. Participation in these projects helped us put together video-training programs for the Soviet military and managers of the military-industrial complex. The program is aimed at preparing them for commercial activities and helping these unique specialists use their strong qualities—discipline, responsibility, and high qualifications—in commercial entities, including joint ventures. Alongside other moves being undertaken by the world community to employ these people in peaceful pursuits, the program is designed to make use of their skills in the market economy and prevent them from selling their knowledge to terrorist regimes.

CHAPTER 3

Ten Obstacles to Developing Business in the Former Soviet Union

In a country where bureaucracy interferes with every-thing, where foreign trade provisions are passed of which participants are unaware, where structural and infrastructural resources are scarce or non-existent, the process of developing business can seem like the game of Chinese baseball proposed by consultant Ralph Siu. In the game of Chinese baseball, a mythical game which captures the idea of constantly changing context, whenever the ball is in the air anyone is allowed to pick up any base and move it—anywhere.[1] Such has been the experience of many companies attempting to locate and realize business opportunities in the Soviet Union. Players, boundaries, and rules are constantly shifting, and the obstacles are usually wider and deeper than even the most savvy company anticipates.

In an interview, the general director of the former state foreign trade organization observed that Americans are very well trained as experts in such fields as marketing and finance. These skills, however, often turn out to be needless in the Soviet business environment. In order to overcome those specific obstacles that a foreign businessman encoun-ters in the former Soviet Union, a businessman needs a lot of other skills. The following are key obstacles which Americans encounter and their experiences in overcoming and bypassing them:

Obstacle No. 1. Social and Political Instability

The impact of social and political instability is less surmountable than other obstacles that might be overcome by a company's strategies. The chairman of the Chamber of Commerce and Industry of the former Soviet Union suggested the following analogy to describe the situation in the Soviet Union: "Imagine an aircraft is flying. It takes off for the journey and travels over half way, but doesn't have enough fuel to fly back. There are no intermediary stops. Passengers are nervous, but the crew is experienced with strong nerves." We would like to hope that those political leaders who are at the head of the reforms in the former Soviet Union are just this kind of a crew. But setting aside the experience and strong nerves of the specific crew, the key analogy recognizes the fact that there is no alternative to developing free markets and attracting foreign investments for the former Soviet republics. All this does not, however, exclude the possibility of a slowdown in this direction, and even counterattacks of anti-market conservative forces. Now that we can look back at perestroika years, one can say that this analogy was too optimistic and that Gorbachev's crew was not able to prevent the coup. But the dynamics of all the unfolding events shows that the key issue remains the same: there is no alternative to the market economy. The newspaper *Izvestiya* cited the following comments from a Hong Kong newspaper: "There is no other place with such a bundle of contradictions as the Soviet Union. There is ethnic unrest, class struggle and ideological disputes, regional liberation movements, unscrupulous battles for power and uncivilized practices of dividing the economic pie . . ."[2]

Before the coup, the main obstacles for doing business in terms of the instability of the situation in the Soviet Union were the resistance of hard-liners and anti-market, anti-perestroika tendencies. After the victory of democratic forces and the failure of the coup, there was an obvious shift. The major problems may now become ethnic unrest, instability of relationships between former republics, and, because of the economic aggravation, disruption of economic ties, inflation, sharp increase of prices, and an increase in riots and strikes.

A sociological survey has been conducted on some of the new social phenomena in the life of the former Soviet Union such as strikes. Publications and other materials reported the well-known miner's strike in Kuzbass and the demands of the strikers. The listed demands, in order of priority, are as follows:

· Giving full economic independence to enterprises and lifting the ministry's control

- Increasing prices on coal in compliance with mining expenses
- Firing local city officials, and enterprise executives who do not deserve the people's trust
- Further democratization of society with the adoption of laws aimed at social protection of the people
- Improvement of the wage system and retirement plans
- Improvement of environmental protection
- Increasing funds for the neighborhood councils
- Development of the construction industry in the cities of the region.

The sociologist, A. K. Nazimova, found that the strikes were due to low wages, a poor labor organization, poor working conditions, undemocratic personnel management methods, and the slow restructuring of enterprises.[3]

We attempted to figure out the strategies of successful American companies operating under growing instability in the former Soviet Union at a time of highly probable economic collapse, social unrest, and worsening political tension. If implementation of market reforms prevents disaster, these reforms will lead the former Soviet Union to a civilized route of development. If crisis is unavoidable, collapse will occur and the country will live through a tragic disaster. But either of these options will end with the beginning of a renaissance. The following might be the elements of long-term strategies by companies attempting to position themselves in the Soviet market by that time:

1. Small investments are being made in establishing a position in the Soviet market, e.g., opening up offices in the former Soviet Union, training personnel for working in the former Soviet Union, establishing stable contacts, creating a distribution network, and acquiring information.
2. They are establishing cooperation with authorities of the former republics and with local powers in various regions of the country, especially where democratic forces have established their positions.
3. They are participating in the creation of Free Economic Zones.
4. Small trial deals and setting up joint ventures with small investments aimed at gaining experience in operations within the Soviet market under the conditions of decentralization of foreign trade, introducing free market elements, and developing new categories of business partners and new forms of cooperation.
5. They are generating ruble earnings with a minimum of hard-

currency expenses and investing the ruble profits in strengthening their positions in the Soviet market.

Short-term strategies of companies aimed at making quick profits under the conditions of rapid political changes and instability include:

1. Taking into consideration expert evaluations of the state of the political and social tension in various regions of the country while contemplating the deal and considering the short-term forecast (for two to three months).
2. Being able to forecast and quickly respond to business opportunities temporarily emerging in the Soviet market. This was the case with the exchange of scrap metal for computers, raw materials, and mineral fertilizer exports, middleman services of joint ventures, and publishing opportunities when censorship was lifted.
3. Sale of goods on the terms of a Letter of Credit opened in a Western bank, or according to the principle "Money in Advance."
4. Barter deals.
5. Selling goods for rubles, with further purchasing of hard currency at auction through joint ventures.

Getting positioned in the Soviet market entails risk because of the instability of the situation, but, on the other hand, also has many advantages, such as opportunities to locate competitors and enter the market for the least expense. Alongside this advantage, however, carrying out the above strategies can help minimize risks. Leon Anderson, director of marketing at Atwood Richards in New York, said:

> [S]imply waiting on the sidelines is rarely a recommended business strategy. . . . The challenge to business today is the same as it has always been. If you aren't willing to take a risk, somebody else will. A number of those "somebody elses" will fail, but others will succeed. The winners will be your competitors well into the next decade.[4]

John Lamb, a Citibank attorney who served as counsel to McDonald's from 1976 to 1980, stated, "It's not an environment where quick-buck artists are appreciated—nor is it possible."

An example of a company which has no immediate plans to place its products on Soviet shelves, but is already winning good publicity, is Duracell, which co-sponsored the First International Play Exchange in the fall of 1988. Duracell backed the project because many of the popular toys are battery operated.[5] The leader of the British Labour party, Neil Kinnock, called for all Western countries to participate as quickly as possible in financial support for the former USSR. Otherwise, according to him, every car on the former USSR's highways will be German,[6] because of Germany's financial support for the country.

The chairman of the Chamber of Commerce and Industry of the former Soviet Union, V. Malkevich, in his presentation at a seminar in New York in 1989 said:

> The domestic market in the USSR and the foreign economic mechanisms corresponding to it are in the process of taking shape. Thousands of Soviet enterprises are entering the international market and seeking business contacts, and are trying to locate partners for industrial cooperation and joint entrepreneurship. There are many difficulties and unsolved problems in this process. The moment is critical. Future priorities hinge on the formulas worked out today. It is possible to take a "we'll wait and see" stand. We'll wait till Russians create a healthy market economy and make the ruble convertible. We'll see what opportunities this will open for Americans. However, in this case, the old law of international business will work—"first come–first served." Traditional trade partners of the Soviet Union—Germany, France, Italy, Finland, and others—have realized this and are acting accordingly. I believe that it is in our common interest to include Soviet-American business cooperation in the sphere of mutual priorities. For a long time our business was a hostage in the political fight of two superpowers, and we both paid a high price for this.

Obstacle No. 2. Strong Resistance by Bureaucratic Power Structures to Streamlining Businesses

Among Soviet power structures, the strongest resistance is from those groups for whom introduction of a free market economy, decentralization of foreign trade, and streamlining of business connections mean losing their monopoly positions and the power and privileges that go along with them. This component of the bureaucratic apparatus is afraid of the reforms because it is not able to adjust to the changes and find a niche for itself in new commercial structures. It tries to prove by every means possible that without total control on its part over foreign trade activity of the enterprises, organizations, and cooperatives, disarray and chaos are inevitable. It manipulates public opinion, for example, by blaming the new commercial structures which sell scrap metal and old paper overseas by saying that this accounts for the raw material shortages the paper and metal-producing enterprises are experiencing. By saying this, they ignore the fact that vast amounts of by-products are just dumped or abandoned in the country and that the business venture only uses an insignificant amount of them, anyway.

The following overview by a well-known Soviet businessman, Artyom Tarasov, illustrates the Soviet business setting dominated by bureaucratic interference.[7]

The situation is aggravated constantly. For example, the Ministry of Foreign Economic Relations is creating an auditing board which will be given the right to control the activities of not only any independent entity engaged in foreign economic relations, but also to close it. Many will probably not survive after their examination. The point is that the reasonableness of any contract could be in doubt. They might say "the goods were sold for such and such a price. And in Singapore it might have been sold for a higher price." You have to prove whether it is or isn't so. That an outsider decides whether a cooperation is profitable and whether it is worthwhile to continue, and not the parties of the contract, is part of the preposterous mind-set under which businessmen work.

Obtaining licenses depends on a lot of things in our country. Such as whether Gossnab, Gosplan, and other organizations are contemplating anything to do with these commodities. In general, it is amazing how internationally accepted foreign trade norms and practices have been distorted in our country, and have not only been integrated into the administrative system, but have strengthened it as it has applied this distorted form. Let's consider, for example, foreign supplies quotas. Other countries enact them in order to protect their markets from the influx of cheap, imported goods that might destroy fixed economic mechanisms. In the Soviet Union, quotas were used to restrict exports. By doing so, the administrative command system had powerful leverage. There are also other ways to restrict exports. Now, for instance, the miners from Vorkuta have been granted the right to export their products after fulfilling their contract obligations. But with the help of quotas and license regulations, all this independence means nothing. This is what we are having now.[8]

One example of bureaucratic interference is a joint venture that could not ship its merchandise by air because of bad weather and wanted to do it by rail. To use rail required so many permissions that by the time all the necessary endorsements were obtained, the weather had changed.

Creating a food processing plant in the former USSR was negotiated, requiring the installation of long furnaces. The Soviet administrative body suggested that the equipment should be placed in four-storied buildings, which were not big enough. The American firm advised them to build a new facility on another site, but the administration responded that there was no other place (in this huge country).[9]

*   *   *

Bureaucracy interferes with everything. In addition, many provisions are being passed of which foreign trade participants are unaware. The director of one of the joint ventures said he spends a lot of time just obtaining new instructions so he can stay informed. And obtaining is what is meant here, because officials who have them do not provide much information about them in order to maintain control over the situation. If business people knew about the instructions and were able to comply with them at least in part, the bureaucrats' power of interference and denial would be diluted. In other words, they would lose power which they treasure. And not knowing these provisions, foreign trade participants involuntarily violate them, and allow bureaucrats to retain their power by either allowing or forbidding deals. As the Soviets say, "A real man is one who has the proper forms in his hands."

Thus, one director of a joint venture who spends a lot of time studying and obtaining those instructions studies them thoroughly. Bureaucrats are astonished when they see that he knows *and* understands the instructions. Once he had to ship a certain kind of mineral fertilizer, and under the directions these fertilizers had to be shipped in sacks of five layers. Since few people know about this, fertilizers are frequently brought for shipment in thinner sacks. He was forbidden to send his shipment without their checking to see how many layers his sacks had. The bureaucrats believed that if nobody knew the directions he wouldn't know them either. When they saw that he had sacks of five layers the officers were shocked. "How did you know this?" He has become somewhat of a folk hero in Moscow through the retelling of this story. One definitely needs strong character and strong nerves to be able to deal with the Soviet bureaucracy.

Is the attitude of resistance on the part of bureaucracies to the progressive transformation of the economy changing today? The answer is yes. A certain shift in the bureaucratic attitude to the market economy is obvious today. A significant part of the bureaucracy is trying to use its high-ranking position in the hierarchy of State economic structures to attain some position in the privatized economy and in new commercial structures instead of generating resistance. An example of this is the way they are buying out state property at prices lower than market value. In our interviews with officials from the ministries this strategy became clearer. Local city authorities and officials from the ministries are acquiring lead positions in stockholding companies, joint ventures, and associations. It appeared in our interviews with the representatives of alternative economies that the opposition to this process is growing. The opposition disagrees with the policy of allowing state officials to engage in commerce and having their stake in businesses through state property. Probably exaggerating a little bit, one of the members of the Russian Parliament said in our interview: "The reason why the coup failed is that thousands of state officials who were supposed to support putschists already had their stakes in market economy structures, were welcoming the opportunity of big earnings, and were afraid that anti-market punitive measures might follow."

However, while one still has to deal with the excruciating level of bureaucratic detail and can deal with it alone, the job can also be given to people in Moscow who solve these kinds of bureaucratic problems. Small companies, incidentally, due to the flexibility are more successful in overcoming these bureaucratic hurdles. A small company that offered to export seeds to the former Soviet Union was delayed waiting for permission from Soviet officials to send the samples to the country. The president of the company put these seeds in his briefcase, got on a plane, and brought them himself. Only big fish get stuck in bureaucratic nets, small ones can come through the nets. Some companies delegate the responsibility of doing business in the former Soviet Union to their subsidiaries or affiliates. As we have seen, part of the bureaucracy that continues to oppose reforms is definitely an obstacle to doing business, but there are ways to neutralize it.

Obstacle No. 3. Absence of a Full-Fledged Legal Framework for Doing Business and Protecting Foreign Investments

The laws do not embrace all business spheres, and in the spheres where they do exist, they are far from being perfect. The wording of clauses is vague and contradictory, and the regulations and provisions which spell out the rules for doing business are constantly changing. The deeply rooted tradition of vague formulations is well-reflected in the Russian proverb, "One law can work many ways."

We shall consider in detail the peculiarities of the legal framework for doing business in the former Soviet Union in Chapter 6. Here we shall consider an example of a rather extreme situation that was the result of an absence of a full-fledged legal system regulating business.

The absence of a full-fledged legal framework for doing business can lead to rather extreme situations, such as the story told by *Commersant* analyst Igor Svinarenko: The Soviet-American joint venture Spark was created in December 1989 for the production and distribution of batteries in the USSR and overseas. The founder on the Soviet side, the enterprise Magadannerud (Magadan), was transformed from a state enterprise into a cooperative in December 1988. The American partner is the Fairbanks, Alaska, firm, Alaskan Battery. Three-thousand automobile batteries, some destined for the United States and manufactured by the joint venture, were declared smuggled merchandise. The customs administration refused to let them through, arguing that the merchandise was not the production of Spark only (the batteries were produced jointly with the cooperative Avangard). Paragraph 8 of the Council of Ministers Decree No. 203 of March 7, 1989, allowed exports only from sole exporter products. The joint venture turned its products back to the warehouse and started correspondence with customs, in an attempt to prove their innocence. Meanwhile, through regular bureaucratic channels, the case was reported to higher authorities and the regional KGB office arrested an entire shipment on the same grounds. Tsvetkov argued that the extent of participation in production of products was not spelled out in the decree. The argument did not work. Alaskan Battery sent letters to Presidents Bush and Gorbachev, asking for protection from prosecution for their Magadan boss. Tsvetkov advised his deputy to also appeal to Yeltsin, the governor of Magadan, Vyacheslav Kobets, and to the Rotary Club.

In his fax to Alaska, Tsvetkov was optimistic: "Good day, my remote friend! There is the Russian proverb that there are no bad things that can't be turned to one's benefit. We should take advantage of this situation for winning good publicity for our venture . . ."[10]

Obstacle No. 4. The Destruction of Economic Ties and Production in the Former Soviet Union

One of the major reasons for the economic crisis in the Soviet economy, and hence the necessity for market-oriented reforms as was realized by Gorbachev who came to power in 1985, was that the resources consumed by the country under the Soviet system had been exhausted.

Under Stalin, these were the people resources, the labor of slaves. It was in the Stalin era that the proverb "If you saw timber, the chips will fly everywhere," became very popular and was used to express the idea that no human price is too high for achieving certain goals. But, if a canal can be built just by having tens of thousands of people work at it, the computer cannot. The kind of performance required for a job such as making computers cannot be achieved by simply using a large quantity of people.

The system remained alive for an additional time at the expense of consuming another resource—natural resources—primarily because of oil dollars. Over fifteen years before the beginning of the nineties, the

Soviet Union received about $100 billion from oil exports. The absence of work incentives and centralized management resulted in the inability to feed the people in the country. Every second or third kilogram of sugar, every third kilogram of vegetable oil, and every seventh kilogram of butter were imported. World oil prices slumped. A reduction in oil extracted from the former Soviet Union because of an absence of technology sped up the crisis. The Soviet government became aware of the need for reforms and creating incentives for a motivated labor force. The only way out was to lift restrictions on private initiative, generate business, and attract foreign capital into the Soviet economy. The whole complex of political and sociocultural factors made the process of reforms extremely painful and generated conflict. There were indications that the economic crisis was becoming deeper over time. Production output was decreasing drastically, including production of consumer goods, as well as basic meat and dairy products. At the same time the Soviet population increased by approximately 20 million people. Because the republics established their independence, their allocations to the state budget were decreasing. There was a significant increase in the total budget deficit and the internal state debt. Ruble inflation was continuing. The disruption of economic ties in the country and the disruption of production escalated economic and social disruption. In 1991, the volume of production decreased by 14 percent compared to 1990.

A large percentage of the gross national product was continually allocated to the military with disastrous effects. Former national security adviser to the president of the United States, Professor Brzezinski, in his presentation to the scientists and students of the Moscow-based Diplomatic Academy, noted that the average Western European country, Japan, and the United States spend a far lower percentage of their gross national product on defense than the Soviet Union, and this is given the fact that the revenues of the Soviet Union are significantly less than the revenues of the United States. Nobody knows the numbers for sure, because of the absurd statistics and pricing systems, although one can get an idea by just looking at the shelves in the stores. In a country with enormous natural resources and very talented people who are ready for sacrifice, according to Professor Brzezinski, there is no reason for such disarray in the economy.[11]

At the same time, a significant reduction in defense expenditure, affecting the interests of the military, may cause serious political and economic aggravation. Such a development requires resources providing housing and peace jobs for the military. Given the fact that these resources are non-existent, this policy may adversely affect the military's choice in the balance of political forces, making them side with opponents of democracy and a market economy.

Chances for joint entrepreneurship in the Soviet Union are limited because of the state of its economy. Difficulties arise with the Soviets, when deciding issues about ruble investments, obtaining ruble credits, supplies to joint ventures, and transportation of raw materials and products. Here is an example of the difficulties that a joint venture with a lot of construction work involved can encounter. Western Siberia is one of the regions of the country where shortages of construction supplies and the small capacities of construction companies result in large uncompleted state projects. A local oil chemical plant, Tobolskhimstroi, has been under construction for fifteen years. There are 104 uncompleted projects, with the remaining cost of construction at 250 million rubles. Because of these existing uncompleted projects, Promstroibank of the former USSR, could not fulfill a contract to generate 124 million long-term credits to the joint venture Sovbutital, which was contemplated for construction under the Tobolskhimstroi plant.[12]

The dissolution of the Soviet Union and formation of independent states became a catalyst for the disruption of economic ties, the slowdown of production, and the further aggravation of the general economic situation. For example, Turkmenia stopped gas supplies to Ukraine, resulting in a breakdown of operations at many plants. In a reciprocal move, Ukraine threatens to block gas pipes on its territory from Turkmenia to Europe. The Russian Federation significantly reduced supplies of timber to Ukraine. A countermeasure on the part of Ukraine was the reduction of food supplies to Russia. A decrease of cotton supplies from the Central Asian republics to Russia resulted in a drastic fall in production at textile and sewing factories. A general indication of the breakdown of economic ties is the curtailing of work schedules at many plants in the former republics. These plants function either two or three days a week or have ceased functioning altogether.

In interviews, the directors of large Soviet enterprises and foreign trade organizations admitted that it is impossible for the former Soviet Union to survive without opening its market to Western companies, yet they were concerned that the faltering Soviet economy would become a lucky break for international businesses. Their concern was caused by the possibility of very lucrative deals the Western companies could make by participating in the process of privatization. Given the specifics of hard-currency transactions on the Soviet market, Western companies could buy out Soviet enterprises for virtually nothing. The fact that the restrictions on the activities of Western companies in the Soviet market remained was justified, according to the directors interviewed, by those reasons.

Obstacle No. 5. The Chaotic Character of the Markets Makes Evaluating the Reliability of Partners Difficult

The president of Phoenix International said: "It is getting more and more chaotic. . . . The old power structure has collapsed and the new one has not been created yet."[13]

The Soviet economy is giving up the command-administrative economy management style, but it is a long way from free-market structures. Today, both new and old economic structures operate simultaneously, and the clashes between representatives of various political and economic orientations are becoming dramatic. Given the orientations come from representatives of such strongly antagonistic groups as the advocates of actual market economy, the anti-market economy, and the *purported market economy*, the complexity of the scene becomes even more evident. Decentralization of foreign trade under these conditions leads to chaos and disarray, to disruption of stable economic ties and to difficulties in locating appropriate business partners. As a result, the previous ways of doing business by American companies, which were fruitful before, are inadequate today. At the same time, American companies often have not capitalized on new business opportunities which have emerged from the restructuring of Soviet foreign trade, and overcoming the monopoly of the central foreign economic bodies. Today, in order to be positioned in the Soviet market, it is essential to enter into relationships with the new foreign trade participants, to shift and focus company marketing strategies on the outlying areas, remote regions of Russia, and the former republics. In the new situation, even if an American company has something to sell or to purchase in the former Soviet Union, it is confronted with a major difficulty in locating the right, specific partner, figuring out whether its proposals are serious, and then determining whether the partner is reliable enough.

On April 1, 1989, all Soviet enterprises, organizations, and cooperatives were given the right to engage directly in foreign trade. Many of them have not had any experience in international business dealings and exaggerate their expertise and experience. Today, many ideas and proposals are coming from many foreign trade participants, and it is difficult for a foreign business person to figure out:

· which ones are realistic and which ones are not
· if they are able to get licenses for export of raw materials and by-products
· whether they have hard currency to buy products which they are interested in

· whether they will be able to provide regular supplies, resources, and materials which are necessary for stable production in joint ventures.

A directory of the financial and economic state of all Soviet foreign trade participants compiled by the Soviet Chamber of Commerce and Industry of the former Soviet Union can provide good leads to cut through this chaos. Until recently, there was no reliable source of information in the former Soviet Union about the financial and economic state of Soviet enterprises and organizations. The lack of reliable information was one of the reasons for caution by foreign firms. The directory gives some information regarding foreign trade participants (both state and non-state enterprises and organizations), their financial position and business reputation. The information in the directory is supposed to be regularly released in the international business information publication *Mercury*, as well as in other business publications. In order to be included in the directory, enterprises, organizations, and cooperatives must meet the following requirements:

1. An enterprise must act as a person legally, and have a hard-currency account in the bank
2. An enterprise must have been profitable over the last three years
3. An enterprise must have a foreign trade participant certificate
4. The ratio of profits to production expenses must be over 15 percent
5. The ratio of the total sum of the enterprises own, and owned equated assets to the total sum of its assets must exceed 50 percent
6. The ratio of the working capital to short-term debt must not be less than 2:1
7. An enterprise must have no arrears on bank credits.

The East-West Association—The Center for Business Development, Inc. in New York offers American companies business information which is essential for adequately assessing the reliability of Soviet partners.

Some companies have been successful in establishing contacts with local authorities. These assist in forging business relationships with the enterprises which are located in the territory of their region. While in the central regions of the country, in Moscow, there are many Western representatives resulting in competition, there is practically a vacuum in the remote regions. Present confusion can cause a lot of difficulties for

Western companies, but an understanding of the peculiarities of potential Soviet partners helps to surmount them. (In Chapter 7 we shall consider in detail categories of Soviet organizations and individuals as possible partners of American companies.)

Obstacle No. 6. Inconvertibility of the Ruble

There are different points of view about when the ruble should become convertible. Some people feel that it is necessary to convert the ruble immediately. There is also an opposite opinion that first it is necessary to make the economy more viable and then convert the ruble.

There are some grounds to believe that the ruble will soon become convertible. This measure is included as one of several principal reforms needed to solve the problems of the Soviet economy. But, even now, without convertibility, many American companies are successfully overcoming difficulties related to the inconvertibility of the ruble. These include barter deals, compensation deals, and the use of internal hard-currency markets and hard-currency auctions. The need for finding ways to overcome the inconvertibility is emphasized by many American businessmen.

Ken Petrilla, deputy general manager of Creditanstalt-AWT Trade Finance Company, an export-finance services firm in San Francisco, says, "If you are competing with someone for a sale, and he is willing to work with a country to eliminate the balance of payments problem, or enhance the economy in that country, he is willing to do counter-trade and you are not, he is going to get the sale." John Well, chief executive of Ernst & Young—Eastern Europe, comments, "I wouldn't like to underestimate the difficulty of currency inconvertibility. . . . It's difficult, but our experience is that if the deals are demonstrably valuable to both sides, the convertibility issue tends to fall in place."[14]

According to Laura B. Forker, "Making use of countertrade allows a Western firm to enter the Soviet market, thereby expanding its sales volume and utilizing more of its productive capacity at home to meet the increased demand. Without countertrade, items considered non-essential by the Soviets are typically untradeable, because the former USSR generally requires countertrade when trading for anything other than essential goods. Similarly, in a countertrade transaction, a Western firm may be able to sell products that are technologically out of date, and therefore, unmarketable in the advanced, industrial countries. . . ."[15]

Leon Anderson, director of marketing at Atwood Richards in New

York, says: "Trading for cash is a simplistic game and at the wholesale level, a relatively modern development. The history of world trade is wrapped up in barter, not in Letters of Credit. To a large extent, Americans have become spoiled and we have forgotten what a Yankee Trader used to be. The opportunities for trade are enormous for those firms which still have a little entrepreneurial spirit. . . . After all, barter's primary advantage is that the buyer's credit is seldom a problem."[16] An effective form of barter for a company is to purchase products from the Soviet enterprises, generating their hard-currency reserves as a result. Large amounts of a company's products are bought later for this hard currency.

Obstacle No. 7. Loan Defaults

Loan defaults by the former Soviet Union are estimated to run at over $70 billion. Over half of the hard-currency earnings which the former Soviet Union is supposed to generate in 1992 must be paid to clear interest on the loan. The insolvency of the former Soviet Union threatens operations, such as rail and sea transportation. The amount of debt that the former Soviet Union owes to foreign companies for railway passenger service totals $75 million. Here is one more example. Because of late payments by Soviets, their ships have been detained in the Suez Canal.

According to some estimates, the loan defaults by enterprises which have started to engage independently in foreign trade exceed $2 billion. Because the payments by their Soviet partners are overdue, over 20,000 foreign companies incurred losses. Representatives of one company, that might run into bankruptcy because of non-compliance with the payment terms by their Soviet partners, demonstrated near the "White House" in Moscow where the leaders of the Russian Federation Parliament work.

One of the problems of working in the Soviet market is the identification of the financial reliability of Soviet partners. Our analysis demonstrates that informal contacts with Soviet partners enable Americans to find ways to speed up the payments. Western businessmen in Moscow say that some companies are paid and others are not paid, and there is the impression that some companies are paid at the expense of others. With informal contacts, these problems are solved more easily. Difficulties like these are taken into consideration by American companies when drafting contracts and choosing the forms of payments and business cooperation.

The companies that were setting up their operations under these conditions work out secure business arrangements, such as: (1) agreements in which the payment terms envision using the natural resources reserves as collateral; (2) shipments on terms of 100 percent prepayment; and (3) barter deals. Other business forms include selling the products for rubles and converting the rubles into hard currency by various means (for example, through a joint venture) and investing the ruble proceeds in the country. Americans also may find partners who have hard-currency accounts in foreign banks and use them to pay for their purchases overseas. This practice of keeping money overseas has spread widely now. According to different estimates, the sums of money in foreign banks total from $5 to $25 billion.

Obstacle No. 8. Undeveloped Business Infrastructure

Based on the impressions of American businessmen who have been in the Soviet Union, it is possible to single out the six most significant indicators of an inadequate business infrastructure:

1. Underdeveloped business information systems, including the absence of a regular and timely supply of financial, legal, and commercial information
2. Poor telephone and fax systems
3. Transportation difficulties (lack of railcars, overloaded seaports, poor packaging, delays at customs, etc.)
4. Lack of office space and living accommodations for representatives of the companies
5. An underdeveloped service industry, a lack of proper protection of foreigners' property
6. Major differences between life and business styles in Moscow and other cities of the Soviet Union, particularly in remote regions.

A foreign businessman from China felt frustrated and humiliated by his encounters with the Soviet power structures and services delivery. The date of his arrival in Moscow was erroneously listed as one day later than was indicated in his documents. When the train from Beijing approached the Soviet border and his passport was examined by the Soviet border officers, the Chinese businessman was rudely treated like a criminal, resulting in his fear and anxiety.

A sales agent from South Korea was also shocked when, in the lobby of the Moscow Hotel Belgrad, two robust militiamen held him up by his suit and asked for proof of his hotel registration. The would-be Soviet customer tried to resist and the military men threatened him with rubber truncheons. The South Korean could not understand any of this. He complained: "I have visited over 40 countries and I have always been greeted by smiling service people in hotels. In this country I was welcomed with rubber truncheons."

One businessman from Hong Kong complained, "I cannot live for more than a month in Moscow. I get tired and have to go home or to Western Europe for a rest. I am exhausted from waiting and trying to obtain what I need. Everyone has to please salespeople, be able to lie to the traffic inspection officers, be able to repair his own car, carry heavy loads, stand in lines for hours, and squeeze through crowded busses. There are no people on earth more patient and more tolerant of hardships than yours!"[17]

Let us look at how these difficulties show up in specific situations and how things have changed, given the fact that providing services to Western firms has become a profitable business in the former Soviet Union.

Because the existing infrastructure differs in various regions of the country, it becomes important to locate areas where business might be better than in other regions. For example, Texaco decided to center its exploration on potential oilfields in the Soviet Union west of the Ural Mountains, where the infrastructure is better. As reported in the Soviet press, a number of companies are considering projects to provide various services to Western businesses in the former Soviet Union. The Moscow bureau of Reuters is considering the possibility of disseminating, including through the videotext systems of the Agency, information about the Soviet market and deals that have been concluded at trade exchanges. Reuters increased the number of Soviet consumers of videotext information by 50 percent from the beginning of 1988 through 1990. About 150 videotext monitors of the agency have been installed in Moscow. They are used by fifteen Soviet banks and foreign trade organizations.

AT&T, in conjunction with the Moscow telephone system, is developing an international telephone system. Both foreign and Soviet firms have gotten a chance to install telephone systems manufactured by AT&T in their offices. The Moscow city telephone network modifies these systems for Soviet telephones. The Association for Segol is planning to create the consumer telephone system in the Soviet system, radio-telephone connections, and mobile telephones. Sprint International created, in conjunction with the USSR Ministry of Communication and Latvian Institute of Electronics (LIE), the joint venture Telenet USSR.

Quick delivery of parcels and documents to 175 countries and territories around the world is provided by the joint venture UPS-Sovtransavto, using the network technology and experience of the United Parcel Service of America. Federal Express is considering a transportation distribution system in the former USSR, making its own satellite communication stations and data bases on the commodities inventory available for the country.[18]

Problems with supplies and transportation are serious obstacles to joint entrepreneurship in the former Soviet Union. Items may not be successfully delivered. Less than 30 percent of roads are paved. There are severe railcar shortages, and inefficiencies in freight handling can waylay shipments for weeks. Recently, joint ventures have appeared offering services for transportation and storing merchandise. One such joint venture, Molcom, has a customs office on its site and offers its clients leasing services for warehouse space and storage and delivery from joint venture terminals to receivers in Moscow and the Moscow region. They facilitate the customs clearance of their declared merchandise.[19]

Business people complain about the lack of buildings. Honeywell's joint venture, Sterch, has had difficulties in finding an appropriate facility in the city for housing its technical center. James Verrant, senior vice president for international operations, says, "Lots of people are looking for buildings. We just have to fall into the queue."[20] Representatives of 1,500 foreign firms are in line for living accommodations in Moscow. American company representatives who have come to the former Soviet Union for a long stay are deprived of many amenities, so many companies give them subsidies for shipping basic items for their everyday use, such as food products, fresh fruits and vegetables. Over the last several years, the number of crimes against foreigners has greatly increased, including robberies of apartments, offices, hotel rooms, and automobiles, as well as murders, attempted kidnapping, etc. Some American firms have applied to commercial entities that offer security services. There are indications that the projects that are being accomplished now contribute to the development of infrastructure.

Obstacle No. 9. Cold War Remnants as Obstacles to Soviet-American Business Relations

The Cold War has left a legacy which continues to affect Soviet-American trade, including COCOM's restrictions, high tariffs on Soviet products imported to the United States, and restrictions on obtaining credits for trade with the former Soviet Union.

COCOM was set up to prevent the transfer to communist countries of modern Western technology, which could be used for military purposes. At present, we are witnessing some loosening of this and other trade restrictions. One perspective on this problem is reflected in the statement by the vice president of the U.S. Chamber of Commerce and Industry, U. Archi: "Those people are naive who believe, that the times when the Soviet Union was regarded as the 'Evil Empire' as it was at the beginning of 1980, are gone. There are powerful people who are sure that by exporting plastic knives and forks to the Soviets we are assisting them strategically, because these knives and forks might be used by Soviet soldiers."[21] According to Brzezinski, some of COCOM's restrictions will have to be loosened, since some of them are out of date. It is time to give the former Soviet Union easier access to Western technology. Moreover, in many arenas, this technology doesn't necessarily enhance military potential, but could make efforts to modernize, decentralize, and streamline the economy easier. And he stated that is why he is not against lifting some of COCOM's restrictions.[22]

Prior to mid-1990, the number of Soviet representatives of various organizations allowed to be in the United States at the same time was limited. Many of them were involved not in commercial activities but in espionage. Now that the relations between the United States and the former Soviet Union have thawed, these restrictions have been lifted. The victory of democratic forces over the putschists in the 1991 coup became a catalyst for the process of overcoming the remnants of the cold war in Soviet-American relations.

Obstacle No. 10. Unreliable and Unmotivated Business Partners

Many Soviet partners exploring a potential deal are not reliable and are not interested in generating successful business. Americans often complain that problems which are quickly solved in the West require months of waiting in the former Soviet Union. Matters that are solved in the West by one person must pass through multiple agencies and approval systems in the former Soviet Union. Soviets lose letters and faxes. They receive correspondence and often do not answer it. Often, Soviets ignore the norms of business conventions, laws, and technicalities. One key Soviet economist, P. Bunich, president of the Union of Leaseholders and Entrepreneurs of the former Soviet Union, admits that many Western firms are just not able to adjust to the obstacles or comprehend the enigmatic soul of the Soviet economic bureaucracy and the nuts and bolts of the Soviet economic mechanisms. It is impossible to establish fast business ties, to obtain what is needed in time, if at all. As P. Bunich said bluntly, there is nobody worse than a Soviet partner for being unreliable. For the Soviets, decency and commerce are different things.[23] This trait of the Russian mentality is reflected in the proverb, "Keep an eye on the one you trust."

Some American companies have already acquired experience and take into account the peculiarities of their Soviet partners. In Moldavia, the experiment of growing Virginia tobacco was a failure because of the violation of technology requirements by Soviet specialists. A famous Soviet businessman and doctor comments that on the factory site, expensive equipment has been rusting for many years, and thousands of workers and engineers are passing by every day through these machines that "belong to them." In their dacha lot, the same worker will be in a hurry to take away the shabby armchair when it starts raining. Here, he is an owner, and he is concerned about his property. At work, a man often perceives national property in an abstract way, as belonging to nobody, and he treats it accordingly, because he sees that the owner of the property, the state or the people as a whole, is also an abstract notion. This state of affairs is one of the major reasons for the weakness of our economy.[24]

An illustration of the paradox of the lack of motivation by Soviet government agencies can be seen in the fate of West German credit to the former Soviet Union. The credit was obtained for financing West German supplies of machinery and equipment to update and renovate Soviet light industry. The credit was not fully used, and what was used was not used effectively. For the first time in the history of Soviet-West German business cooperation, a loan of this size was obtained from FRG banks for processing segments producing consumer goods, i.e., in segments where it could give quick reward and therefore, tangible results for the USSR population and not just raw materials and heavy machinery. The loan was structured for eight and a half years on favorable terms. The term for using the credit line expired one month before the end of 1989. By that time Vnesheconombank of the former USSR had used 1.5 billion West German marks. In order to use the credit fully, it was allowed to conclude deals on supplies after the expiration date, enabling the Soviets to use 8 million marks more. From the 3 billion in credits, the Soviet Union used 2.5 billion, with 80 percent of the credits being used for orders to West German firms. From these West German orders, forty-four sewing factories, forty-two shoe factories, thirty-one stocking and sock factories, tens of bakeries, cheese plants, etc. were supposed to receive machinery and equipment. In explaining why the loan has not been fully used, the Soviets stated that there were no acceptable offers from FRG firms, or they did not satisfy the Soviet customers and "did not meet competitive standards." The initiative in this case, however, had to come not from West Germans, but from the Soviets in the form of corresponding requests. The major reason for the puzzling Soviet performance was an absence of a clear plan for using the credit and the formal, disinterested approach of the officials. The primary objective of the credit appeared to be in obtaining the credit itself—a typical behavior of the command administrative management style. According to the credit agreement, the Soviet economic organizations could not conclude the deals independently, and so the effectiveness of the agreement was reduced. More modern forms of industrial cooperation were inaccessible to this deal. The regulations regarding minimum credit amounts of the deal (not less than 5 million marks), which Vnesheconombank insisted upon, practically excluded many small, efficient FRG firms from being participants, and deprived the Soviets of flexibility. Of course, to buy twenty complex cracker production lines with a yearly capacity of 120,000 tons of crackers isn't all bad, but they were not among the basic necessities of Soviet consumers.[26]

One of the most important lessons which the American companies have learned in the Soviet Union is that without enormous patience, without the willingness of the representative to spend a lot of time there, without a willingness to wait for one year or more for the first successful deal, business is impossible. Companies looking for fast results just don't work in the former Soviet Union; such orientations are inadequate there.

One of the survey questions asked business people was: "Why is it better to leave your watch at home when you go to the Soviet Union to do business?" The various answers were categorized and in turn formulated ten reasons why everything takes so much time in the former Soviet Union:

1. There are many decision-making entities where one has to get varieties of signatures to approve the deal.
2. There are peculiarities of the national psychology in terms of a different tempo of life and different tolerance of difficulties. Encountering difficulties does not necessarily call for activity to overcome them, but a move to put up with them. Tolerant waiting for something bad that is gong to happen is common.
3. Time is not money in the former Soviet Union.
4. There are no incentives for concluding a deal and bringing the project into operation.

5. There is diffusion of responsibility because many entities and officials tend to be decision makers.
6. Initiative is punished. "Don't show yourself."
7. There is a suspicion that an official is being bribed if he is too interested in concluding a deal and does everything without bureaucratic procrastination.
8. A Soviet delegation that represents ministries or state foreign trade organizations often has no power at negotiations to change a position which has been previously approved by their authorities. Even if they would like to make small changes, they often have to make all kinds of bureaucratic provisions and ask permission for making changes from their bosses.
9. Delaying meetings and putting off decision making are techniques used for conducting negotiations.
10. Dragging out the decision-making process by state foreign trade organization officials is a way to test potential new Western business partners. The Western partners will figure out for themselves if they are prepared to work in the former Soviet Union. If they cannot wait, and have no patience, they are poor partners for Soviet negotiators. One does not achieve results quickly in the former Soviet Union. A bureaucrat will lose nothing if such a businessman leaves and doesn't undertake business. But if a Western businessman successfully goes through the initial testing period, through the "initial control stage," he has a higher probability of successfully working in the former Soviet Union for many years. It can be expected that he will be patient in situations of uncertainty, bureaucratic procrastination, and the lack of commitment to schedules and deadlines on the part of his Soviet counterparts.

CHAPTER 4

Potential Opportunities in Trade and Investment Activities for American Companies in the Former Soviet Republics

Since the State's monopoly on foreign trade has been lifted and enterprises have been granted the right to engage in foreign trade, tens of thousands of enterprises and organizations have been registered as participating in foreign trade activities. According to the journal *Moskovski Biznes*, for the five-year period starting in 1986, foreign trade conducted through the Ministry of Foreign Economic Relations of the USSR decreased from 99 to 54 percent and the USSR central government lost over 50 billion rubles in revenues.

The USSR traded with over 140 countries, and in 1990 according to the Council for Mutual Economic Assistance (or SEV, an organization for economic cooperation of socialist countries which has now been dissolved), the trade was broken down as follows:

• Former SEV members	43.8%
• Capitalist countries (including)	38.1%
Germany	14.8%
Japan	2.7%
France	2.1%
USA	2.1%
• Developing countries	11.6%

The major exports of the USSR in 1990 were fuel and energy resources, timber and lumber and other raw materials and resources. The major Soviet imports included machinery, equipment, and transportation vehicles which were worth 31.7 billion rubles in 1990, and the imports for the agro-industrial complex and food products for the population (14.5 billion rubles).

In 1990, imports of industrial consumer goods increased sharply by two billion rubles compared with 1989. Also in 1990, 30 percent of drugs, almost 30 percent of detergents, and 35 percent of sewing goods from the total consumption of these products in the USSR were imported.[1]

According to Vitali Zvolinsky, a scientist from the Institute of the United States and Canada, the former USSR and the United States, with combined populations of more than half a billion people, may seem distant countries separated by an ocean. But actually, they are neighbors. The distance between two islands belonging to each of them in Diomida archipelago is only four kilometers—a one-hour walk. The variety of natural resources found in the two countries create favorable conditions for exchanging deficit energy resources, various kinds of raw materials, and food products.

The two countries produce over one-third of the world's industrial products but all trade between them is only 0.7 percent of total world trade. The former USSR's share in the total international trade exchange with the United States is only 0.6 percent and the former Soviet Union's total exports and imports fall within 1.2 percent and 0.1 percent of all American exports and imports. The U.S. share in the total international trade exchange of the former USSR is only 2.4 percent. The United States, the biggest trading country in the world, is in thirteenth place in the trade exchange of the former USSR. According to American analysts, the improvement of economic ties would enable the yearly trade exchange to increase by up to $10–15 billion in the next three to five years. Eighty percent of Soviet imports from the United States consist of food products, 12 percent of goods for current industrial use (chemicals, rolled pipes, pulp, etc.). High-level processed commodities constitute only about 8 percent.[2]

At the same time, American companies have been more active than other countries in the area of cooperation, such as creating joint ventures. For example, in the Russian Federation alone, American companies have set up 300 joint ventures. That constitutes 25 percent of the total number of joint ventures created by American companies in the former Soviet Union. After America, the countries which have founded joint ventures in the former Soviet republics are, in order of importance, Germany, Finland, Switzerland, Italy, Great Britain, Sweden, and Japan.

Analysis of interviews with American and Soviet respondents revealed significant differences in their expectations for doing business and the types of business arrangements. The most common expectation of the Americans is to sell their products or in some cases to buy raw materials. For the Soviets, it is to obtain equipment, by encouraging American investment in a joint production agreement with the former Soviet Union, and exports. This difference in expectations can be demonstrated by two pyramids representing the various levels of attractiveness of different forms of joint entrepreneurship for Americans and Soviets.

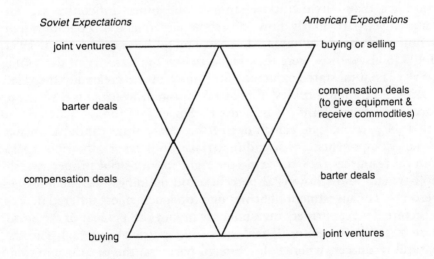

As is seen here, the most attractive opportunities for doing business for Americans turn out to be the most unattractive opportunities for Soviets. It is highly likely that the reason for the disagreements between American and Soviet partners in joint venture discussions is the desire of the Soviets to export their joint production and the unwillingness of Americans to have more competitors in the Western market. The Americans would rather win a new market than introduce new production into an already tapped one. It becomes obvious that the problems of compromise and taking into account a partner's expectations turn out to be critical. Subsequent chapters will show how these problems might be overcome and how a compromise might be worked out.

One of the goals of the interviews was to analyze the experiences of American companies in different business and economic sectors of the Soviet market to determine the ease or difficulty in starting up businesses.

Opportunities for Joint Entrepreneurship in the Former Soviet Union

Statistical information on the activities of joint ventures in the Soviet Union published by the newspapers *Delovoi Mir* and *Izvestiya*, and the magazine *Deloviye Lyudi/Business in the USSR* (based on State Statistics Committee and other sources) shows the dynamics of the development in 1990–1992. The chairman of the Board of Joint Ventures Association of the USSR, Lev Veinberg, believes that joint entrepreneurship is developing successfully in the former Soviet Union. He considers that bureaucratic resistance and other difficulties are surmountable, particularly now that some experience of operating joint ventures has been accumulated. According to the data of April 1, 1991, 3,400 joint ventures were then registered on the territory of the former USSR. The total stated capital of the joint ventures created in the USSR was over 3.3 billion rubles, almost 1.5 billion of which was invested by foreign partners. Joint investments by Soviet and foreign partners totaled 34 percent. The remainder of the total initial capital is in machines, components, units, and materials (36 percent), the right to use natural resources (8.8 percent), the right to industrial property, technology, and know-how (7.2 percent), and buildings and facilities (14 percent). The investment of Soviet and foreign partners differed in their structure. Soviet partners invest mainly money (38 percent of the Soviet part of the joint venture), real estate (22 percent) and rights to use natural resources, whereas for foreign partners, the proportions were equipment and technology (about 59 percent of their capital), money (a little over 20 percent), and technology (12 percent).

Under such arrangements, Soviet partners are able to import technology and equipment without spending hard currency and asking for credits. Their foreign counterparts avoid expenditure on constructing facilities and paying for resources. About 30 percent of the total number of registered joint ventures were actually operating. Most of them

(42 percent) were industrial enterprises and companies offering all kinds of services, such as hotels, tourism, transportation, advertising, and publishing, while others included trading companies, restaurants, scientific-research and designing companies, and construction companies. Most joint ventures are consumer products-oriented, but only a small number of them are engaged in production. Only a minority of joint ventures have been quite successful. The production of the first Soviet-American joint venture Pris, which produces technology for the petrochemical industry, can compete both in the Soviet and foreign markets. The same can be said of the joint ventures Khomatek, Stankovendt, Festo-Pnevmoavtomatik, Rotor-Reza-ABB, and Kranlod. The most successful joint ventures in the field of supplying production computer technology were Interquadro, Soyuzforinvest, Dinamika, Intermikro, and Atlant.

Considerations affecting the kind of products produced by joint ventures include market demand, the availability of raw materials, the supply of human resources, the attitude of local authorities, and so on. Priorities in joint venture production are not determined by existing shortages in the Soviet market. For example, despite the acute need for food products in the former Soviet Union, food products account for only 1.8 percent of joint venture sales. It can be expected that because of the worsening food shortage on the one hand, and a number of agrarian reforms on the other, the sales volume of food products might increase.

It is well known how much construction materials are in short supply. But they represent only 0.33 percent of joint venture sales. The major production of joint ventures are computers (46 percent) and consumer goods (25.9 percent). These commodities are also scarce, but if market demand had been the principal criterion taken into account, the proportions of investment and production would have changed. This state of affairs is related to poor hard-currency reserves in the domestic market, shortages of raw materials, multiple difficulties in setting up operations, orientations to short-term profits, and so on.

In 1992 most of the joint ventures in the Russian Federation (about 70 percent) were industrial enterprises. In 1989, the same index was 30 percent. At the beginning of 1992, the number of personnel working in joint ventures in the Russian Federation totaled 137,000, while their wages totaled 1,287,200 rubles. The foreign partners' share of the stated capital totaled 1.9 billion rubles.

In 1991, the proportion of total Russian exports coming from joint ventures was 1.4 percent. Major exports included machinery and components, oil, fertilizers, lumber, footwear, and fish products. Over 70 percent of exports went to Japan, West Germany, Italy, Austria, Finland, the Netherlands, Poland, and Hungary. In 1990, when many enterprises were in the process of being set up and produced practically nothing, the volume of imports was four times greater than the volume of exports. In 1991, the volume of exports increased by 2.2 times. Compared with 1990, the volume of imports decreased by 36.5 percent. Commodities that were bought by joint ventures overseas were mostly lacquers and paints, calculating equipment and components, copiers, cars, alcoholic and non-alcoholic drinks, and food products. Over 62 percent of commodities imported by joint ventures in the Russian Federation came from Germany, Japan, Denmark, Austria, the United States, Switzerland, and Finland. That joint ventures operate more efficiently follows from the fact that the volume of production by one worker is two times higher than that produced by a worker at state enterprises.[3]

Under the joint venture structure, there are several ways to produce and distribute products in the Soviet market. One way is to use rubles to purchase export commodities to cover hard-currency investments and raise currency earnings (given the existing system of export licensing). Second, hard currency can be purchased in hard-currency auctions. Third, ruble earnings can be invested in the former Soviet Union. Joint entrepreneurship in the area of business services is one effective way to generate hard currency in the internal market, including providing various services to foreign businessmen, diplomats, and tourists.

An effective strategy for avoiding risk due to changing legal frameworks is the use of diverse arrangements in the activities of joint ventures. First, a joint venture may include a larger scope of activity in its initial documents (in the event the situation changes, it may stop the operations that became unprofitable and switch over to a more profitable business), and second, it could operate in various regions or republics that are now independent states. Mebinvest operates in 14 republics, actually generating business that way.

Creation of joint ventures with small investments in hard currency enables many American companies to enter the Soviet market without substantial financial risk. This scenario can be implemented through two primary strategies. A business can create a small joint venture in which American investment is the larger part of the stated capital, or create a large joint venture in which American investment is a small part of the initial capital. In the joint venture Dialog, the American investment is 21.8 percent of the initial capital. The stated capital of the joint venture Perestroika includes American investments (20 percent), and investment into Perestroika by one of its founders, the joint venture

Dialog (7 percent). Among the joint ventures where American investment is a smaller part is Sovelanaromo. American companies with a larger part of the initial capital are Forbesprogress, Sinergia International, and DAB International (over 50 percent). Small joint ventures are usually created in the fields of advertising, import-export activities, consulting and service businesses, printing, video and audio productions, development of software and new technologies, health care, and pharmaceuticals.

Large joint ventures usually are generated in the construction industry, consumer goods production, food products, production for industrial use, electronics, wood processing, etc. Significant Soviet investments are typically found in construction, consumer goods production, and products for industrial purposes. The reverse is found in sectors such as agricultural production, food production, wood processing, and by-products processing, where large hard-currency investment is typically required. Some joint ventures, such as oil and gas exploration and development, coal mining, chemical production, and fertilizers, are generated by the modernization of Soviet enterprises, with the expenses paid off by products produced as a result of the modernization.

Difficulties of Joint Entrepreneurship in the Former Soviet Republics

Because of the serious difficulty in operating joint ventures in the former Soviet Union, 20–30 percent of those registered have been actually operating Enterprises that manufacture products for industrial use have the lowest percentage of operation. Out of the total number of those joint ventures which are actually operating, the highest percentage falls within service businesses such as consulting, middleman businesses and brokerages, and the general service industry.

According to a poll taken among Americans and Soviets, the most common difficulties perceived by both Americans and Soviets in operating joint ventures include:

- Negative attitudes of certain types of Soviets towards joint ventures
- Unclear political forecasts for the former Soviet Union
- Frequent changes within the legal framework for joint ventures
- Unreliable supply systems because of the chaotic business environment in which central management structures have been destroyed and the system of market relationships has not yet been established
- Bureaucratic hurdles, including the disinterested attitude of some Soviet officials

- Difficulties in obtaining hard-currency credit
- An undeveloped infrastructure and communication system for doing business, including lack of office space, living accommodations, and general business services.

Americans specifically cited the following:

- Lack of reliable economic information about the state of various sectors of the Soviet economy and specific enterprises
- Necessity to come to the country often because even the simple problems are not solved without involvement from company executives
- Lack of experience by Soviet business partners in conducting joint ventures, including knowledge about marketing, management, and the business culture in general
- Non-professional performance, including lack of ethics and motivation by Soviet employees of joint ventures.

Soviets cited the items below as specific concerns of theirs:

- Impatience of American businessmen, specifically their unwillingness to take into consideration the specific problems and peculiarities of doing business in the former Soviet republics
- Underestimation by Americans of the "unwritten rules" and use of informal contacts
- Stereotypical vision of business opportunities in the former Soviet Union on the part of Americans, i.e., cheap raw materials and labor, ignoring alternative opportunities
- Serious discrepancies between Soviet and American accounting systems.

Many of the failures in getting joint ventures off the ground and successfully operating can be traced to these issues. Next, we shall take a look at several of the major industries and services where the greatest business potential exists.

Exploration and Extraction of Natural Resources, Chemical and Petrochemical Processing, and By-products

According to Soviet estimates, the former Soviet Union is first in the world in oil extraction. In 1990, 571 million tons of oil were extracted in the Soviet Union. About 90 percent of all oil is extracted in the

Russian Federation, 4 percent in Kazakhstan, and 2 percent in Azerbaijan.

The facilities for oil development, storage, and transportation differ in various regions of the country. For example, the oil extracted in the Mangishlak peninsula has to be heated while piping, as it thickens at air temperature because of a low paraffin content. In the Komi Autonomous Republic the thick, heavy oil is not extracted from holes but from oil mines. The oil extracted in the Volga-Ural Region contains a lot of sulphur and has to be refined. In the 1960s, about 70 percent of all oil was extracted using less costly facilities such as oil gushers. Today, the same amount is extracted through pumping. Traditionally, oil processing enterprises were located close to the oil reserves, but currently there is a tendency to locate them close to the oil-based production, resulting in difficulties related to the lack of necessary facilities.

Oil extraction in the former Soviet Union is one-third less deep than in the United States. One example of the inefficiencies of the oil development industry is the speed of drilling and operationalizing the holes which is three times slower than in the United States. Financial losses from oil extraction totaled 3.4 million tons per year. Financial losses from transportation and storage problems equaled 12–15 million tons.

The former Soviet Union extracts 40 percent of the world's natural gas, or 815 billion square meters. About 60 percent comes from Western Siberia, 75 percent from the Russian Federation, and 10 percent from Turkmenia. A small amount of natural gas is also developed in Uzbekistan, Ukraine, and Kazakhstan. Eighty percent of the gas consumption in the former Soviet Union is used for industrial purposes such as fuel supplies and processing, and the rest is consumed for utilities. Oil gas is used by enterprises producing synthetic rubber and other products of organic synthesis, and production facilities are located primarily in the Volga-Ural Region, Western Siberia, the Ukraine, and Azerbaijan.

Chemical and petrochemical industries include:

- *organic synthesis of oil chemicals (methanol—over 3 million tons per year; ethylene—also over 3 million tons per year)*; cokechemical (*senol—over 500,000 tons per year*); synthetic polymers (polypropylene—about 1.5 million tons per year)
- production of polymeric materials (synthetic resins and plastics—over 5.5 million tons per year)
- processing of oil chemicals for the production of resin-technical items, tires, etc.
- production of mineral fertilizers: nitrogen fertilizers (40 percent),

potash and phosphate fertilizers. Production is located mainly in the Russian Federation (50 percent), Belarus (20 percent), Ukraine (10 percent), Kazakhstan and Central Asia. Yearly production of mineral fertilizers exceeds 37 million tons.

- production of sulfuric acid both on the basis of minerals and on the basis of gas by-products of the metallurgic and oil processing industries. The annual volume of sulfuric acid production in monohydrate is 30 million tons.
- production of soda based both on minerals (in the Russian Federation and Ukraine) and on the basis of processing by-products of potassium plants (in the Russian Federation and Belarus). Production of calcinated soda totals 5 million tons per year.
- microbiological industry, including production of albumen fodders (from hydrocarbon and plant resources), amino acids, ferments, and bacteria fertilizers (in the Russian Federation, Lithuania, and Uzbekistan).

According to Soviet estimates, it is the world's largest producer of mineral fertilizers and the third-largest of chemical fibers. Over 50 percent of the world's potassium salt reserves, and over 30 percent of phosphate resources are concentrated in the former Soviet Union. Annual production of nitrogen fertilizers is 13 million tons, of phosphate fertilizers 9.5 million tons, of potash fertilizers 9 million tons.

Coal reserves in the former Soviet Union total over 6.5 billion tons, 30 percent of the total world reserve. Ninety percent of the reserves are found in Siberia and the Far East. Over half of the reserves suitable for mining in the near future are over 300 meters deep, and are found mainly in the Urals and Kazakhstan.

The former Soviet Union leads the world in the amount of iron ore extracted (which totals 40 percent of world volume), smelted ferrous metal, and industrial coke, although the metal is of low quality. In comparison with developed industrial countries, the major type of steel produced in the former Soviet Union is open-hearth steel, followed by converter and electric steel. One of the difficulties in operating the ferrous metal industry is the distance of ore reserves (the west of the country) from fuel supplies (primarily in the east). There is 77.4 percent of iron ore reserves in the European part of the former Soviet Union (13.2 percent of this figure is in the Ural). The Asian part of the former USSR has 22.6 percent of the iron ore reserves. More than 40 percent of cast iron is produced in the Russian Federation, over 40 percent in Ukraine, and the rest in Kazakhstan and Georgia. Sixty percent of steel and rolled metal is produced in the Russian Federation and about

35 percent in Ukraine. Non-ferrous metal enterprises are engaged in extracting, enriching, and processing the by-products of non-ferrous ores, and rare and precious metals. These metals are mined and processed primarily in the Urals, Siberia, Central Asia, and Kazakhstan. The major metals processed in non-ferrous metallurgy are copper, aluminum, zinc, lead, nickel, and cobalt. Eighty-eight percent of the world's manganese ore reserves are concentrated in the former Soviet Union.

The amount of gold mined yearly in the former Soviet Union exceeds 300 tons. The export of non-ferrous, rare, and precious metals has increased lately, making them a more significant source of hard currency for the former Soviet Union. Export of gold in 1989 was 320 tons, in 1990—400 tons, in 1991—500 tons. Export of platinum has increased from 400,000 ounces to 1 million ounces in 1991. In 1990 and 1991 the former Soviet Union sold about 10,000 tons of uranium at half the world market price. In 1991 the former Soviet Union sold about 1 million tons of aluminum. One of the chemical products exported to the Soviet Union by American companies is ammonia. The biggest deal in this field was concluded by Occidental Petroleum whose contract envisions shipments of 60–90 million dollars worth of ammonia supplies to the United States each year. According to the compensation agreement, superphosphate acid is supplied to the former Soviet Union.

Oil exploration and extraction industries lead the investment activities of foreign companies. It is absolutely critical for the former Soviet Union to generate hard currency from oil exports, yet at the same time, the crisis in the oil industry in the former Soviet Union (dependency on imported technology) is directly related to that country's lack of hard currency to buy the necessary technology, as well as the fact that information about the latest developments in the oil industry don't reach specialists working at remote oil locations and therefore workers have no exposure to the specifics of Western technology. On the other hand, oil specialists in Moscow might be unaware of the realities of the current situation in the regions, and do not always have unofficial contacts there and access to unofficial sources of information. In the constant situation of flux typical of the Soviet paradox, the specialists in Moscow often do not know the specifics of certain reserves, and cannot realistically estimate the advantages and disadvantages of specific holes and transportation facilities. We participated in creating a working team which consisted of specialists from both Moscow and the regions. The advantages of cooperation in a team made it possible to use the experience of both categories of specialists and neutralize their shortcomings. The purpose of forming this group was to help Western companies set up operations to extract oil using sea platforms.

The advantage of such production is that it is far more efficient to construct the platforms in regions located close to the oil reserves, such as the Asian Republics and the Caucasus Regions, than to ship them from Europe. Because the platforms are of heavy metal construction, Soviet metals can be used for them.

It has become easier to export oil, however. The regions and the enterprises themselves have now been given the right to engage directly in export activities. In spite of many difficulties, a number of Western companies are successfully engaged in oil exploration. An example of the enterprises engaged in oil exports from the former USSR is the Soviet-Canadian joint venture Yugansk-Frakmaster.

Analysis of the interviews can help determine how large, middle-size, or small companies can effectively engage in the oil business. Most large companies are dealing with the highest authority and do not need assistance in establishing or maintaining contacts with potential partners. However, smaller companies may need help in locating the right partner for a joint venture.

One of the authors took part in an Oil and Gas Symposium sponsored by Arthur Andersen in 1990. During discussion of his report, an outdated stereotype of the Soviet Union held by American representatives of oil companies revealed itself. This stereotype goes back about five years. Many believed that they could deal only with the government in setting up a joint venture and that only ministry officials had the authority to make decisions. Many felt that only the largest American oil companies could be players in the joint venture market with the former Soviet Union. Many were truly surprised to learn that they could deal directly with oil companies and develop and export oil together. Small companies were also surprised to learn that their size may actually have advantages in this market. Being smaller, they can respond quickly and flexibly to changes in the business environment, such as the legal framework for joint ventures, taxation policies, and operational changes. They deal directly with the local regions, develop personal contacts and make timely, on-site decisions, bypassing a lot of bureaucratic hassle.

Given the general underdevelopment of the Soviet infrastructure and the enormous problems of transportation, delivery, and so on, it is important to identify the regions where a better infrastructure does exist. The Timan-Pechora Region, where rich oil fields straddle the Arctic Circle, has been identified as a potential site by several oil companies, and Texaco is conducting feasibility studies to determine the possibility of joint production with the former Soviet Union. Texaco decided to center its exploration west of the Ural Mountains where the chance of generating actual production will soon be possible. Texaco agreed to cooperate with the Ministry on geological research, and supply and install computer facilities at the Ministry of Moscow offices as part of the overall agreement for cooperation on geological research with the former Soviet Union. The Soviets visited the company's Harrison, New York, headquarters and engaged in a two-week business seminar where basically they were learning Western business practices. Texaco began its endeavors in the former Soviet Union by purchasing several geological data packages offered by a London broker licensed by the Soviet Union to sell such information on its oil regions.[4]

Now that the former Soviet republics have gained control over their national resources and are interested in attracting foreign investment, a number of other companies, including Amoco, Arco, Chevron, Exxon, British Petroleum, MacDermott, and Du Pont, are also seeking business opportunities in the republics and regions which have potential for sizable projects. For example, the government of the Russian Federation is discussing handing over in concession the abandoned oil reserves to Du Pont. These are the oil fields from which the upper reserves have been extracted and the lower layers are not developed because of the non-existent facilities.

New opportunities in the Soviet oil trade are opening up due to the founding of Commodities–Raw Materials Exchanges. A number of Soviet Commodities–Raw Materials Exchanges obtained permission to sell large amounts of Soviet oil overseas. Several Western exchanges became interested in developing oil reserves in the former Soviet Union due to the possibility of selling the extracted oil through the Commodities–Raw Materials Exchanges. The Tumen Commodities Exchange, and the Surgut Commodities–Raw Materials Exchange appeared to have the most potential for such arrangements. One American broker bought 100,000 tons of oil for $12 million at the Tumen Commodities Exchange.

One of the new opportunities for American companies in the former Soviet Union is the processing of uranium for direct sale in the United States. Nuexco, a uranium brokering company, arranged a deal in which a Soviet plant processes uranium for direct sale in the United States for four U.S. utilities. As much as 6,000 metric tons of natural, unprocessed uranium will be shipped from the U.S. utilities to the Soviet Union. The Ural Electrochemical Integrated Plant based in Yekaterinoburg (formerly Sverdlovsky), a town in the Southern Urals, then enriches the material into a form that can be used by light-water nuclear reactors. The contract with Yankee Atomic, Vermont Yankee Nuclear Power Corp., Main Yankee Atomic Power Company, a subsidiary of Central Maine Power Company, and New Hampshire Yankee, a unit of the Public Service Company of New Hampshire, will be completed between 1994 and 2002, according to the spokesman. If U.S. nuclear fuel processing plants were to fulfill the full requirements of the four utilities, the costs would be 25 percent higher, industry sources say.[5]

The example of the joint venture Pris tells how many years of experience of doing business with the Soviet Union and overcoming the multiple obstacles has resulted in setting up a large, successful joint venture. The example also describes difficulties even a prosperous joint enterprise might encounter, and illustrates the potential of joint production in such beneficial areas as oil and the petrochemical industries. Various aspects of Pris's experience have been described in American and Soviet sources, such as the American Management Association's *Management Briefing, Business Month*, and the Soviet weekly *Commersant*.

ABB/Combustion Engineering has had many years of experience in trading with the Soviet Union and a great deal of expertise in overcoming its roadblocks. In 1985, Charles Hugel, the chairman and chief executive of ABB/Combustion Engineering, signed a $12 million contract to upgrade process controls at an ethylene plant in Siberia. This undertaking involved a meeting with the senior Soviet foreign trade official with whom he started to talk about the possibility of a joint venture, even though Soviet law at the time did not permit such arrangements. As Hugel described the conversation to the *Journal of Commerce*: "I said to him I knew their system wouldn't permit it, but times are changing in the world, and I would like to talk about doing a joint venture with this Ministry." In two years, those talks bore fruit as Combustion Engineering signed a joint venture contract to modernize a Soviet oil refinery and manufacture process control equipment.

The joint venture Pris was created by the firm ABB/Combustion Engineering, Inc., and the former Soviet Union, and is the first of the most successful Soviet-American joint ventures.

Pris is involved in automation control systems for enterprises in oil, chemical, refining, pulp and paper, and other industries. In 1990, the joint venture started a project to outfit a number of pulp and paper plants with automated control systems. The project was designed to eliminate the paper deficit in the Soviet Union in two to three years, saving about $40 million a year in the state budget. The estimated profit of the joint venture to the American firm when the project is completed will be $15–17 million a year.

According to *Commersant*, this successful joint venture developed a serious disagreement between American and Soviet partners in the course of the management process, though judging by the successful outcome of the joint venture it would appear that the conflict was overcome. According to *Commersant* which quoted Pris representatives, the disagreement between the American and Soviet partners was caused mainly by a personal conflict among the joint venture executives. Some Soviet representatives of the joint venture believe that the Americans were displeased with its general director, Vatsli Krontov. *Commersant* quoted American representatives as saying that one of the reasons for the Americans' discontent with their Soviet partners was the performance of the Soviets in the domestic market. The Soviet partners had not complied with the terms of the initial agreement and the firm was not able to control joint venture activities on the implementation of joint projects. American partners refused to confirm the information from the Soviet side about joint venture profits in 1989 totaling $75 million, because according to them ABB authorities were not given all the necessary financial documents on the joint venture activities. This publication reveals that the Soviets and Americans have different perspectives on the reasons for the conflict. For the Americans, the main reason is that the Soviets did not comply with some of the terms of the agreement, and did not submit the necessary financial documents about the joint venture operations. For the Soviet authorities, however, the joint venture is seen in light of personal conflicts such as Americans' discontent with the general director.[6]

In our interviews, the respondents told us about analogous situations which clarify the nature of such conflicts. While personal and professional roles are inextricably woven for the Soviets, they might not want to hand over the documents about the performance of the joint venture. In the Soviet scheme of things, any business information can be used for personal purposes, such as if a general director is not on good terms with other executives from the staff, he may use such information to fire them. By hiding information they retain control over the situation.

Along with the promising potential that the exploration and processing of natural resources offer for sizable projects, progressive developments are hampered by vague legal framework regarding property laws for joint ventures in the event they cease to exist. The provisions which envision and ensure the return of investments and determine the firm market value of the enterprise in such cases have not been developed. This creates considerable risk for Western companies.

Soviet-American cooperation in natural resources is developing in the following areas:

- exploration and processing of natural resources
- exploration of oil reserves, extraction of oil from deep and "dry" holes
- processing of natural gas, oil and peat
- manufacture of chemicals, products of organic synthesis, fertilizers, chemical agents, lacquers and paints, and lubricators
- processing of timber, production of plywood and paper
- tanning of hides and furs
- processing of old paper, scrap metal and recycling of waste
- processing of by-products of ores of ferrous and non-ferrous metals, and by-products of oil extraction and gold mining
- processing of by-products of chemical industry
- processing of by-products of cable industry, of lumber production, food and fishing industries.

Products for Industrial Use and Construction Materials

This industrial segment includes:

- heavy machinery—the production of heavy metal and its technology
- production of railway cars, ships, locomotives
- production of tractors and various agricultural machinery
- production of buses, trucks and cars
- production of machine tools, metal items, etc.

The former Soviet Union leads the world in the production of many construction materials, such as glass and asbestos. About 140 million tons of cement (about 14 percent of world production) is produced in the former Soviet Union. Due to the acute shortage of construction materials in the country and the willingness of the Soviet enterprises for self-supplying one of the most common types of technology for Soviet enterprises, hard-currency owners buy small-sized plants overseas for producing bricks from clay (with glazing). This enables enterprises to be independent from the construction companies and the suppliers of the bricks and allows them to engage in industrial and non-industrial construction. The enterprises can also make barter deals, exchanging bricks, for example, for automobile parts.

The major investments in commercial structures are in the production of construction materials. One of the avenues for cooperation in this industrial segment is the production at Soviet enterprises of technology and equipment for the Third World countries, e.g., Africa, the Middle East, and India. Soviet exports of these items are quite unusual. One rare example is the annual export of 2,000–3,000 Soviet-made tractors.

Five specific difficulties in arranging joint production in the fields of products for industrial use and construction materials emerged from the interviews:

1. The necessity for large investments in hard currency under high risk in the current state of Soviet political and social instability, and the related difficulties in obtaining credits from Western banks.
2. Lead time is long for creating these joint ventures, including coordination of the many bureaucratic entities, installation and adjustment of the equipment, startup of production operations, and so on.
3. It is difficult to operate Soviet construction companies efficiently, especially if it is necessary to do a lot of construction or renovation of the building production facilities. Soviet construction companies cannot complete many projects in five to ten years.
4. Poor wholesale trade system leads to difficulties with raw materials, components, spare parts, and materials. It was assumed that wholesale trade would develop in the country and that it would become the source of materials and supplies for joint ventures, but under the worsening deficit, possibilities for wholesale trade continue to be very limited, and difficulties with supplies destabilize production.
5. Overloaded, unreliable, inefficient transportation creates additional difficulties for both delivery of supplies and delivery of the finished products.

We encountered situations when enterprises and organizations, especially state ones, are not interested in buying retrofitted technology or technology which is not quite modern. Americans are usually surprised at the rejection of the offer that seems to them reasonable and realistic. Being motivated by the prestige, some representatives of state organizations would like to buy expensive equipment which would not fit into the existing system and which requires raw materials of a certain grade and quality not always available. Besides, the personnel might not have the necessary training to operate this equipment. What drives them here is just the chance to report that they purchased the most up-to-date technology and to estimate profit based on unrealistic estimates of the equipment's efficiency.

The following examples demonstrate how success can be achieved when a company abandons the traditional stereotypes of trading for hard currency and seeks non-traditional business arrangements in structuring a deal. These are examples of firms which offer non-priority items breaking into the Soviet market through countertrade. San Francisco-based Transisco Industries, Inc., which manufactures and services railroad equipment, launched a three-way joint venture with Soviet and Finnish partners. The project was to install heat exchangers in railcars and lease the retrofitted cars back to Soviet petroleum refineries. Customers use the cars to keep petrochemicals from congealing in transport through frigid climates. "The joint venture generates mostly hard currency today, but recently we were granted a trading license" that will allow Soviet customers to pay Transisco in petrochemicals, says Mark C. Hungerford, the company's chairman and chief executive.[7]

Soviet-American cooperation in the manufacture of industrial products is developing in the following areas:

- industrial robots, metal-cutting tools, optics, production of equipment and apparatus for scientific research
- the manufacture of bearings, press-molds for the production of plastics, and the manufacture of haulage carts and packaging for chemicals
- the manufacture of insulating materials, hermetic materials, polymer films and equipment for manufacturing plastic items (bags and other products)
- manufacture of refrigerating equipment, ventilation equipment, and haulage equipment
- manufacture of machinery for the metallurgical and metal-processing industries, for oil processing, masonry, and bottling equipment, and the development of technology for non-ferrous metallurgy
- manufacture of gas turbines, typographic, and copying equipment
- manufacture of sewage equipment and equipment for environmental control; technology for the development and use of ecologically safe energy sources; production of equipment for rescue measures and for operating in natural disasters
- manufacture of passenger, sports, and cargo aircraft and the production of aircraft engines

- assembly, distribution, and maintenance of cars
- manufacture and repair of fishing vessels and production of ship engines
- transportation of cargo and airline passenger services.

Computers and Software, Tele- and Radiocommunications

East Asian computer companies from South Korea, Taiwan, and Singapore, who took the initiative in the Soviet market, have to some extent been losing the position they initially achieved as they are being forced out by well-known American and West European firms. According to an assessment by Soviet experts, while computers from East Asia are cheaper, they are far less reliable. Currently, the demand supported by hard-currency purchasing power in the Soviet PC market is rather low. According to GKNT of the USSR, this demand in the middle of 1990 was approximately $300 million.

The history of the computer boom in the Soviet Union has been discussed in some major Soviet economic sources. The computer boom has been a result of both "humanitarian" and economic issues. Humanitarian issues include accumulation and transfer of quantity into quality in terms of Soviet citizens' awareness of the possibilities of computer technology and the emerging prestige of computers in the sphere of personal and public consumption. Simultaneously, potential buyers appeared, such as enterprises operating on a cost accounting basis and cooperatives. The Soviet market could offer only indigenously made PEVM, (personal computing machines) which were not only a generation behind, but also in very short supply. There is no reliable source of information regarding the number of personal computers imported into the former Soviet Union, including those being assembled from imported components and units. There have been many attempts to make estimates, the lowest one being about 200,000 items per year during the period 1989–1990. With minimum prices being 20,000 rubles, the total value will be approximately 4 billion rubles a year. However, according to computer analysts, a more realistic estimate would be 1.5–2 times higher than the 4 billion ruble figure. The State Committee for Science and Technology has estimated the demand for PCs to be thirty million units (without taking individual consumers into account).

The computer industry has turned out to be a forerunner and a driving force of general economic transformations. Its development facilitated the formation of a private sector, leading to independent and sharp increases in prices. Contrary to the traditional situation, an unusual balance between supply and demand has been achieved in this sector of the economy with the buyer dictating specific preferences to the seller. Low prices for computer technology in the world market and high prices for it in the former Soviet Union make it profitable to buy foreign-made computers using money generated from the sale of raw materials, by-products, and other cheap Soviet commodities overseas.

At first, the private, non-state computer sector was comprised of enterprises with a small sales volume. Later companies came on the scene which could generate output similar to the state sector, such as the Soviet-German joint venture Aquarius Systems Integral (ASI), which was created in the Soviet Union in 1989 by the German firm Tebimpex GmbH, and the research and manufacturing conglomerate Informatika to produce several tens of thousands of computers, including the computer based on the 486 processor. According to the joint venture's estimates, ASI, with the assistance of its foreign partners (members of the ASI groups: ASI-Germany and ASI-Taiwan) will be able to produce 900,000 PCs annually for the domestic and export markets after new production capacities have been introduced. Having become one of the top Soviet computer manufacturers, ASI generated interest from a number of foreign companies, such as suppliers of peripherals and software. Among them are the Japanese companies OKI and Epson, the American companies Quantum, Hewlett-Packard, and Novell, and others.

In starting its operations, ASI was confronted early on with the typical problems facing Soviet computer manufacturers. While they have to solve many complicated problems, such as creating an infrastructure, developing new products, and developing effective personnel management practices, their competitors, whose products arrive fully assembled, operate under far more favorable conditions. One of ASI's principal goals is a gradual transfer from assembling PCs from imported components to domestic production at Soviet enterprises.

Production of computer technology became one of the biggest areas of joint venture activity. Every fifth joint venture stated in its initial documents the intention to engage in computer or software production. Two types of such ventures began to emerge. On the one hand where joint ventures producing computer systems, such as dumping imported computers manufactured by a foreign partner onto the market, supplied more or less with a program package (this was actually the Soviet side's input). The other type of joint venture that emerged was computer manufacturing enterprises. These enterprises were of particular interest because an analysis of their activities showed that most of them included "production of computer technology" in their founding documents, but, according to some people, only as a tribute to fashion, as a means to simplify and expedite the process of forming and registering a joint venture. Realistically, the status of these joint ventures is the same as all the others, even given the fact that they don't have traditional joint venture supply problems. Practically all they are doing now is a "screwdriving assembly" operation, as the components and units are received from the foreign partner. In the distant future on-site production of the components will begin. Such are the plans of one joint venture called Inkompex.[8]

Beginning in the period 1989–1991, top American computer companies started large-scale marketing campaigns to expand their presence in the Soviet market. Here is the story of IBM activities in the Soviet market, as provided by American and Soviet sources. IBM has had an office in Moscow since 1972, and until 1980, it traded computers, typewriters, and copiers. After the trade embargo was passed in 1980, and IBM computers fell under COCOM restrictions, the Moscow office engaged mainly in rendering services. In 1989, the corporation resumed its business activities. According to *Commersant*, IBM created a dealership network in the former USSR for more than twenty business partners.

Twenty percent of the total sales of IBM products in the country are sold through dealer networks. In Western Europe, by contrast, sales through dealers totaled 95 percent. The same proportion is targeted in the former USSR. By the beginning of 1991, the Moscow IBM office received 4,000 business offers from potential partners. An IBM spokesman said that the company has signed two types of agreements with Soviet dealers: remarketing and representative. A third type, integrated, is envisioned. According to the IBM representative, the remarketing contracts call for the dealer to give priority to IBM sales in his overall business, with the requirement to invest the proceeds in expanding distribution and service. Remarketing contracts with IBM have been concluded by the joint venture Computerland (USSR-USA), the joint venture Microage (USSR-Canada), the Rossia association, and other Soviet organizations and foreign firms which are allowed to sell foreign products for rubles.

Michael Armstrong, senior vice president, chairman, and president of IBM World Trade Corporation, helped IBM develop the "education project in the Soviet Union," which resulted in a $20 million sale, the firm's largest in the USSR. "Our approach was to show them the value of IBM by implementing a project at twenty pilot schools. We invited eighteen professors to IBM and we put together support software for assisting blind and deaf Afghan war veterans. This was all done before we sat down and talked about price." Eventually an agreement of intent was signed involving computers for 1,250 Moscow area schools. The Soviet government gave the sale priority status by issuing a Central Bank guarantee for hard-currency payment. "This sale is only the first phase," says Armstrong. "The key issue is hard currency. We will participate in countertrade, but what the Soviets need to do is prioritize. We are looking at over 100,000 schools, not just 1,250." IBM is going to open offices in republics of the former Soviet Union and also in St. Petersburg.[9]

According to Soviet sources, a number of American software manufacturers, including Borland, Microsoft, Oracle, and Seagate Technology, are trying to break into the Soviet market using a variety of strategies and business structures. Some of them began their endeavors in the Soviet market with ruble sales, with the aim of encouraging Soviet consumers to identify with American products. Such strategies as special discount prices, programmer contests, using the production of the firm, and creating computer clubs and associations are also designed to win popularity with software consumers.

One would expect the Soviet side to be ready to set up joint ventures oriented to ruble profits. This could result in gradually overcoming acute shortage problems and satisfying a huge untapped demand. On the surface, lack of interest by Soviet joint venture partners in ruble-oriented operations in the domestic market seems paradoxical, but actually it is quite understandable. As one head of a joint venture put it in an interview, "We'll earn rubles ourselves in big amounts and with less effort. We need joint ventures which are able to generate hard-currency earnings."

In order to break into the Soviet market, Microsoft embarked on extensive ruble sales so the consumer would identify with its products. The firm is supposed to sell all its products for rubles and invest the proceeds to create the firm's support team and the construction of their training center. According to *Commersant*, conflict arose between Microsoft and the joint venture Dialog when Dialog lost the exclusive rights for distribution of Microsoft's software. Dialog wanted to sell Microsoft programs primarily for hard currency, but because Soviet consumers lacked hard currency, sales volume was small. Microsoft was interested in ruble sales, with the aim of breaking into the market quickly, with maximum distribution, an important part of their strategy. Insufficient ruble sales volume of the joint venture Dialog's software significantly held up the expansion of these products into the Soviet market.[10]

*   *   *

The prospects for initiating joint ventures in computer technology and software development in specific Soviet industries (oil exploration and development, environmental protection, production control, and so on), establishing computer production in the former Soviet Union, and translation of software into Russian, seem to be promising now. According to Soviet and American sources, Control Data is expanding its presence in the Soviet market along the following lines:

• The Academy of Sciences of the former Soviet Union and Control Data signed a cooperative agreement regarding development of projects related to new ways of securing nuclear installation safety and environmental protection. They plan to supply six computers designed to improve the safety of Soviet nuclear power stations. When Control Data decided to embark on a sale of six CYBER mainframe computers for use in Soviet nuclear safety programs, the Cold War had not quite ended. The computer data processing rate was six times higher than the standard set by COCOM, and nothing above the guidelines could be approved. When President Bush changed the policy, negotiations over the $32 million sale began between Control Data and U.S. government agencies. Jim O'Connell, director of international trade policy at Control Data, argued his company's case: "It is in America's own interest to prevent another Chernobyl disaster." This culminated in the granting of the export license for Control Data and an extensive safeguard package was arranged.

• Under the agreement with the Academy of Sciences, joint projects to ensure safety at civilian nuclear plants, to control the production and energy transmission, and to work out computer programs and develop oil reserves are envisioned. American specialists are interested in gaining access to Soviet computer software in order to find a wide commercial application for it. Joint production in the USSR of work station supercomputers is anticipated, with the building of a plant with a capacity for generating 20,000 units a year. The Soviet partner was chosen by the vice president of the Academy of Sciences, Evgeni Velikhov, during Gorbachev's visit to the headquarters of the corporation in June 1990.[11]

We have analyzed a case in which the partners who intended to set up a computer manufacturing joint venture could not reach an agreement in spite of the obvious interest of both sides in the project. One of the reasons why they could not reach an understanding was that Soviet counterparts did not contemplate business deals in terms of cost-efficiency. They acted to their own detriment, giving unrealistic estimates of their portion of the stated capital, such as the cost of facilities, communications, leasing land, etc. They inflated these expenses for the sake of a bigger percent of the stated capital on their part. It is quite typical for them not to think how the proceeds will offset the expenses. They may be motivated by the mere fact of entering the foreign market, starting production, or trading services. Quite naturally, foreign partners considered the entire deal from the point of view of its profitability and when their estimates showed it was not beneficial they abandoned the project.

One of the fastest developing areas of cooperation of the former Soviet Union with foreign companies is tele- and radiocommunications. Secession of the former Union Republics and declaration of their sovereignty make it possible to obtain the exclusive rights to large-scale, long-term projects with the republics of the former Soviet Union, which seems to be a very promising opportunity under the changed conditions. In our interviews with representatives from their foreign trade organizations, it was concluded that in the present situation, such monopoly rights can be obtained for a very small price. This is because of three factors:

1. Republics have a high need to involve the West in the process of economic revival.
2. The republics are free from the central government and can establish their own international business contacts.
3. Republican foreign economic bodies do not yet have stable foreign contacts or experience in operating in international markets.

One of the first examples of a sizable telecommunications project in the republics is the development of cellular phone systems in Belarus. According to Soviet sources, the Belarus ministry in charge of communications and the company Commstruct International negotiated an agreement which envisions granting exclusive rights to the American partner.

A preliminary agreement to provide cellular phone systems in Moscow has been signed by US West, Inc., the Soviet firm headed by Svyatoslav-Fyodorov, a Moscow-based eye surgeon and entrepreneur, and the Soviet's Ministry of Communications. The sides were negotiating a definitive pact, including financial terms and a network equipment supply contract. The companies expect to begin service by the third quarter of 1991, and plan to jointly bid on cellular service projects in other Soviet cities. US West, of Englewood, Colorado, is one of the regional Bell Telephone Companies. Millicom, New York, is a cellular and paging service company. Moscow's cellular plan calls for the group, including US West International Holdings, Inc., a US West unit, and Millicom International Cellular, S.A.R.L., a Millicom affiliate, to run one of two networks in the Soviet capital. The group also includes the Moscow Territorial Operations Center for Long Distance and International Circuits, Voronez Research Production Association, and the Moscow Local Telephone Network.[12]

According to Soviet sources, some other companies in communications systems, including Walker Telecommunication Corporation, an association of the American-Canadian companies Segol and Easton, have shown their interest in joint projects for developing modern communications in the former Soviet republics.

Soviet-American cooperation in tele- and radiocommunications is developing in the following areas:

- development of satellite communication
- creation of mobile cellular phone systems
- manufacture of telephones
- manufacture of antennas for satellite TVs.

Consumer Goods and Medical Supplies

P. J. O'Rourke, writer and philosopher, recently commented in *Rolling Stone*: "The best thing about our victory [the demise of communism] is we did it with Levis 501s. Seventy years of communist propaganda got drowned out by a three-ounce Walkman. A totalitarian system has been brought down because nobody wants to wear Bulgarian shoes."

In 1989, scientists from the Moscow-based research institute specializing in the consumer goods market and in researching consumer demand conducted a research study among Moscovites buying consumer goods. Among the respondents there were residents from all districts of Moscow. The findings of the survey show the untapped demand and the new opportunities in this market. Certain characteristics of consumer behavior were determined to be typical under the conditions where severe shortages were commonplace. These behaviors included:

- Frequent visits to various stores which often do not result in buying commodities because they are not available.
- Buying commodities outside the official distribution chain.
- Making purchases which do not fully meet their demand and requirements.

- Buying commodities in short supply when they are available, not necessarily when they are needed.
- Borrowing money to buy commodities in short supply when they are available.

The proportion of people who are willing to borrow money to buy commodities when they are available constitutes 14–16 percent. The decision about buying certain goods is determined by the unwritten law of the current situation: "Buy today if it is available, because tomorrow you might be too late."[13]

There is a joke in the former Soviet Union that the only thing in abundance is shortages. And this is alongside the fact that the former Soviet Union accounts for about 18 percent of the world's production of cotton fibers, making it the third-largest world manufacturer. It also produces over 4,000 tons of raw silk.

The largest part of foreign investments go into production and trade in the consumer goods sector of the economy. It is well known that Soviet-made commodities are of low quality and cannot compete with foreign products.

An analysis of the consumer goods sector of the Soviet market, based on interviews with Soviet light-industry executives and managers, reveals three reasons why potential for the next few years is promising:

1. The Soviet people possess ample hard currency, and beginning in 1990, a legal opportunity to purchase goods in stores in hard currency.
2. Part of the hard-currency earnings of enterprises may be spent on purchasing consumer goods for their employees. In addition, enterprises have been granted the opportunity to obtain hard currency at auctions.
3. There are new opportunities to surmount one of the major obstacles of Soviet entrepreneurship in the area of buying consumer goods, i.e., the difficulties in obtaining the necessary raw materials of the required quality in a timely fashion. Raw materials can now be obtained at the Commodities–Raw Materials Exchanges.

An example of structuring a deal in the consumer goods sector is as follows: Foreign-made commodities are bought for hard currency, then are sold for rubles with further purchase of hard currency. The highest profits which can be made through this cycle can be made on knitted items, outer clothing, sneakers, computers, car radios, and videocassettes.

Hard-currency profits of joint ventures can also be obtained by selling consumer goods outside the former Soviet Union. For example, this is similar to clothing and footwear supplies to the American market generated in countries with cheaper labor.

One of the ways of getting around many difficulties related to a poor supply system is creating a chain of joint ventures sharing their operations and oriented to some specific kinds of products. For example, companies in the sequence of producing leather goods can work cooperatively by creating several joint ventures for shearlings. One joint venture might be engaged in processing hides, another will be for dyes, and the third will sew shearlings. Under such an arrangement, the only source of supplies on which these joint ventures will depend is the meat processing plant from which they would buy hides.

Given the dramatic shortages of consumer goods in the former Soviet Union, its internal hard-currency market appears to be a promising opportunity, drawing from foreign business people, diplomats, tourists, and Soviet hard-currency owners. At the same time, bureaucratic hurdles, unstable legal frameworks, tariffs, and duty regulations make operating such stores difficult. Such hard-currency stores offer men's and women's clothes, lingerie, footwear, sportswear, domestic appliances, electronic appliances, automobile parts and supplies, jewelry, drapes, bedspreads, office supplies, and audio- and videocassettes. Hard-currency stores also offer food products and pharmaceuticals.

One of the ways to overcome the problems of ruble inconvertibility is through manufacturing goods by a joint venture which replaces or substitutes for imports. For example, a joint venture for the production of razors may obtain hard currency from the resources allocated by the government for overseas purchases of this commodity.

The findings of our interviews with companies trading consumer products in the Soviet market showed that their success was determined in great measure by adequate answers to three questions:

1. What they choose to sell in the Soviet Union
2. To whom they sell their products
3. Determining the best way to sell.

One of the first moves that the president of the New York-based trading firm Le Monti Leon Gandelman made in the Soviet Union was opening a showroom at the Exhibition of Economic Achievements in Moscow and also arranging temporary showrooms in some regions of the country. Showing samples of their products to the enterprises which own hard currency enabled the firm to determine which consumer products are in greatest demand. It turned out that in spite of shortages and sometimes the total unavailability of practically all basic commodities, Soviet consumers still have their preferences, based on tastes, current fashion trends, and prices, which together determine a decision on what commodities an enterprise would be willing to spend hard currency.

The need to be flexible while breaking into the Soviet market may be illustrated by the fact that, though Soviet consumers are highly attracted by American commodities, for some kinds of clothes they prefer a European style.

While contemplating whom they might target in the Soviet Union Le Monti chose enterprises possessing hard currency with which it could deal directly. The strategy of trading their products in non-central regions of the country has also contributed to the company's success.

One of the company's activities in the Soviet market is running a hard-currency store, which was opened at the Exhibition of Economic Achievements at the beginning of 1992.

Besides trading for hard currency, Le Monti also developed business arrangements such as selling for rubles, or exchanging their production for by-products and raw materials. These flexible strategies helped bring about the company's successful breakthrough in the Soviet market.

The company's assistance to Soviet business people in finding contacts in the American business world and its seminars for American companies with the participation of Soviet representatives have also contributed to strengthening Le Monti's positions in the Soviet market. The company has also put together a directory of business proposals from Soviet organizations, such as their export and import potential, interest in creating joint ventures, and so on.

An intermediate strategy for achieving long-term access to the Soviet market might be in doing business with some Eastern European countries and having enough patience and persistence to wait for other opportunities.

Wolverine World Trade, Inc., a Michigan-based company, opened a successful Hushpuppies shoe store in Sophia, Bulgaria. Why Bulgaria? "We felt that it was the best way to gain access to the USSR," Wolverine chairman and CEO Thomas D. Gleason explains. "We wanted to get a showcase, an example for the rest of the Eastern Bloc." Although negotiations for licensing with both governments began around the same time, the Bulgarians were quicker to take action. But persistence paid off, because the deal with the Soviets has been concluded. Wolverine got a licensing agreement with Kirov shoe and tanning combine, for the production of Hushpuppies footwear and tanning of pigskin leather. Wolverine found out that patience is a must when doing business in the former Soviet Union. It took more than two years of negotiations before pen met paper. Wolverine relied heavily on its own international group in the United Kingdom which, through private contacts, finessed its way through its negotiations with the appropriate Soviet department. Wolverine set up a two-day technical seminar for the Soviet footwear industry, sponsored by the Soviet agency. Attendees at the seminar inspired department officials to start negotiations with Wolverine. The specifics of the licensing agreement include production of the footwear, the technology for skinning and tanning pigskin leather, the use of the Hushpuppies brand name, and the option to go into a joint venture. Under the terms of the licensing agreement, Wolverine should enjoy a royalty based on sales, part in hard currency, and part in barter trade for raw pigskins.[14]

Lack of basic market and trading mechanisms by the Soviets and their confusion with ideological concerns which have nothing to do with business hamper the Soviet ability to trade goods with the West. In one of our interviews, the president of an American company related how the company wanted to buy hardware from the Soviets. The Americans sent their product catalog, indicating the items they needed, and asked the Soviets to choose which ones they could produce and quote the prices. The Soviets examined the catalog with its retail prices and quoted their prices which were only slightly lower than those in the catalog. They did not take into consideration the cost of promotion, advertising, and other expenses that the retail system involves. There is no need for such basic business considerations in the former Soviet Union. Total shortage of goods makes people buy out quickly whatever is on the market.

The Americans tried to explain that the prices were unreasonable and did not correspond to the reality of the market and the Soviets decided that the American partners were trying to cheat them. To make their argument, the Americans told the Soviets they bought the same products in China for a price twice as low. The Soviets were insulted by the comparison with China and said they didn't consider themselves an undeveloped country. This illustrates how ideological considerations distort the Soviets' attitude to business and how non-business factors have a direct impact on how the Soviets approach issues of trade and business.

Most authorities conclude that working with an experienced consultant is the best way to start up business in the former Soviet Union. Consultants also help cut through red tape. For example, they can register a joint venture with the Soviet Ministry of Finance in Moscow, and in America verify from the Department of Commerce's Bureau of

Export Administration that the proposed venture is in compliance with export controls and regulations. Legal advice is also needed because the former Soviet Union has only a skeleton of corporate law and thus, it is vital that every conceivable step be taken to ensure the enforceability of any joint venture. Even with a consultant's help, Thurston confronted difficulties.

Thurston Sails, a maker of custom, high-performance sails, did not think about expanding their operations, but when consultant-attorney Eric Fisher proposed a Soviet venture, Thurston accepted the challenge. Thurston and his Soviet partners launched a sail-making firm in a loft, a former high school gym, in Odessa and called it Aquation. Fisher explains why the consultant services are worth the money:

> "A lot of companies approach the Soviet Union cold, and 80% come away frustrated. It is not only the problem of visas, cars, and communications. It is knowing the right people and being able to establish contacts and negotiate deals."
>
> "First, there is a lack of business culture. Profit is not the only concept alien to today's Soviet employees," Thurston says. Aquation's five employees seemed not to see any relation between having a goal and working towards it. "They just had no idea what we were talking about when we said that time equals money," he says. On the other hand, Thurston was impressed with the resourcefulness of Aquation's workers. "When they were confronted with a difficult challenge, they went off and met it, which was the most frustrating part."[15]

Many American businessmen become convinced that personal, private ties play a significant role in business with the Soviets. According to Moreton Binn, president and CEO of Atwood Richards, "A lot of companies want to do everything through committee, but the Soviets are getting jaded with all this field research. The key is to have our people on the ground and give them responsibility to make deals. Since the players are constantly changing, if you do things by committee, it will take forever to get anything done."

Atwood Richards, the oldest barter company in the United States, which has offices in Prague, Budapest, Warsaw, and Moscow, is taking excess inventory from companies like Elizabeth Arden and Adidas and remarketing these goods in the East. The companies receive "trade credits" from Atwood, which are good for anything in Atwood Richard's inventory, from raw materials to advertising time. According to Leon Anderson, director of marketing at Atwood Richards, "To reduce your exposure to risk and to use the experience to train your own employees in the art of barter, it might be a good idea to begin with your surplus, overstock or excess inventory. If you use this old inventory and are realistic about its true value, your barter experience is almost certain to be worthwhile." Atwood takes a principal position in the goods and contractually agrees to remarket the clothes only outside the firm's regular distribution network. The most ambitious of Moreton Binn's projects is the opening of a wholesale distribution center in the former USSR that should remarket Western clothing for Soviet citizens, while selling office equipment and supplies to Western companies.[16]

An interesting example of the niche for small business trade with the former Soviet Union is the partnership called Soviet-American Woolens formed by farmers Peter Francis Haggerty and his wife Marty Tracy, when they put together an idea for blending American and Soviet wool and selling it in both countries. There was fruitless correspondence with Soviet ministries for two years. Then they joined a farmers' tour going to Moscow and made the right connection through the office of Chilewich Corporation, a White Plains, New York-based firm, whose late founder began trading with the Soviets in the 1920s. Making the right connection helped Haggerty finalize a deal rather quickly. Haggerty manufactures yarn made from a blend of medium fine wools from Soviet and American sheep. The blend is jobbed out to be dyed and spun, and is marketed by direct mail throughout the United States in kits that include patterns for sweaters, mittens, scarves, and totebags. The idea caught on. Soviet-American Woolens was finally netting a small profit. A new project began which was investing about $10,000 in cash and goods in a pending joint venture with a Soviet cooperative. According to the project, the cooperative will provide Haggerty with a new product, knitting needles, and he will buy wooden dowels from a Maine lumber mill and ship them to the Soviet Union. There, they are to be made into hand-painted knitting needles of varying sizes, shipped to the United States by UPS, and marketed through the Peace Fleece Catalog. The retail price envisioned was $5 a pair. Even including duty and shipping costs, a profit is expected. The wood for a pair of needles costs $0.22 due to cheap labor. "It isn't just a matter of dollars and cents," says Marty Tracy. "The main value is that it reflects on the credibility of our Peace Fleece business in the United States." She adds that they are looking for other products to barter for the wool they buy in the Soviet Union.[17]

The New York Times reported how the worsening cigarette shortage which added to public outrage over basic foodstuffs resulted in substantial orders for America's two largest tobacco companies. The order for Philip Morris, the nation's largest tobacco company, called for selling more than 20 billion cigarettes to the Soviets. RJR Nabisco, the second-largest tobacco company, planned to sell 14 billion. The demand came from Soviet smokers after shortages led to street demonstrations and reportedly, in some cities, to riots. It is an indication of the government's strong need for cigarettes that it agreed to pay in scarce, hard currency. The Tobacco Merchants Association, a trade group, estimated that Soviet consumption totaled about 418.5 billion cigarettes in 1989, or about 80 percent of the 524 billion smoked in the United States.[18]

Italy was one of the first countries to open world markets to Soviet goods. It began with a mechanical watch called Raketa, produced by Petrodvorets. Forced out by newer electronics, they went out of business when demand had been exhausted. It was well known that the watch was out of date, and nothing seemed to predict a market increase for the "Raketa." But the gut feeling of some Italian businessmen saved the archaic watch. The Verona firm Visio decided to sell it in the West as the Russian "Retro." In over two years, 400,000 units were sold. Visio also decided to sell another watch from a Cristopol plant called "The Commander" in the USSR. They also were mechanical, waterproof, with bright spots on the clock face, with pictures of tanks, paratroopers, airplanes, and soldiers, and most of all, the red star. What Italians advertised was not the watch itself, but the images embodied in them: The idea of the army as an envoy of peace, which replaced the aggressors' stereotype and the link with the past which is so dear to peoples' hearts. For "The Commander" watch, the Italians developed a fancy package made of wood and leather. Preliminary marketing expenses cost Visio a half-million dollars but the gamble was worth it; the watches were sold out. Inspired by this good luck, the firm offered the watches on the American market as the Soviet "military watch" and sold it to both men and women for $149. By comparison, the Japanese quartz Seiko is sold in the United States for $100.

The cooperative called Symbol has extensive expertise selling T-shirts with sports logos popular among admirers. The business has the capability of responding quickly to opportunities, such as the "Save the Whales" T-shirt with pictures of whales in caps duplicating the flags of both countries, made three days after joint actions by American and Soviet fishermen. At the Soviet exposition of goods exported to the United States, Symbol exhibited the T-shirts with logos of Soviet universities and institutes, which were bought by American firms and sold out quickly. Their popularity suggested to U.S. manufacturers the idea of producing shirts with the words "USSR" and "Perestroika" and the logo of Moscow State University, named after Lomonosov. The commercial success of the T-shirts is obvious, but the cooperative failed in its attempts to enter the American market. The tariff is almost 90 percent of the cost of the T-shirt. Normal cost-effectiveness is necessary, and to sell T-shirts at prices exceeding competitors' is not realistic. Striking a deal is also hampered by the difficulties confronting cooperatives in the former Soviet Union. The cooperative could have competed with the Americans if it had had modern equipment and had bought raw materials at wholesale prices. Nevertheless, the trade fashion, "Soviet chic," seems to have struck some sensitive chords among American consumers.[19]

An important factor in the development of the medical supplies sector of the market is allowing Soviet enterprises to keep export earnings and use foreign currency to buy directly urgently needed medical supplies. Now not only Minzdrav (the Ministry of Health), but enterprises themselves, such as oil, coal mining plants, and metallurgical enterprises, which have hard-currency income, may become the customers of foreign medical companies.

The American magazine *American Medical News* cited examples of opportunities in the health-care sector. The 500-bed Magadan Hospital bought a used computer tomographic scanner which was sold and installed by a subsidiary of the Linc Group. "The reform improved the way the Soviets communicate with each other," said Orlando Holway, whose group, Linc Equipment Systems, refurbishes and remarkets CT scanners. "Hospital officials told the Mine, which is a local hard-currency earning enterprise, 'This is what a scanner costs. With your money, we can buy the equipment, diagnose and treat your people, and get them back on the job.' "

Chronic drug shortages in the former Soviet Union give foreign firms additional opportunities for trade and business cooperation. Some sales are obtained due to emergency drug funding or release of hard currency for emergency drug imports which people can't live without. When, in 1989, the Supreme Soviet released 500 million rubles in hard currency (a more than 400 percent increase over foreign currency allocated for this purpose in the government plan), Upjohn Company got a good-sized share: a $45 million sale of pharmaceuticals, including anti-inflammatory drugs.

To be able to produce quality medical items, the Soviets were banking on joint ventures to bring in the Western capital and know-how. But many problems existed for businesses operating "outside the plan." They could find that all supplies had already been allocated, and even theoretically available items might not be successfully delivered.

According to *American Medical News*, such problems helped stall talks with the Upjohn Company several years ago on a pharmaceutical plant venture. "It just didn't happen," says Godfrey Grant, a spokesman for the Kalamazoo, Michigan-based drug maker. "We asked, can you supply these raw materials of such and such quality by such and such time . . . and they didn't know if they really could or not." However, with the USSR's chronic drug shortage, pharmaceutical plant ventures are a government's priority. That is why, in spite of the problems with supplies and deliveries which stalled Upjohn's talks some years ago on pharmaceutical plant ventures, the company was optimistic about new plant talks. Upjohn recently opened a Moscow office. Projects like Upjohn's are being looked upon as the tool to gradually put the Soviet drug industry on its feet.

Often, much of a company's success will be due to its willingness to "take a long-term view" and build relationships. The best-known old Soviet hand in U.S. health care is North Chicago's Abbott Laboratories, a member of the American Medical Consortium, which was created to unite the efforts of American health care and facilitate its cooperation with Soviet colleagues. Abbott built an infant formula plant in Ukraine in 1976, and now supplies drugs, hospital products, and diagnostic equipment, including HIV test kits, to more than 300 Soviet facilities. Richard McMahon, Abbott's divisional vice president for Soviet affairs, feels that much of the company's success was due to a willingness to take a "long-term view and build relationships." Most Soviet trade veterans echo this approach.

However, companies selling products not needed urgently enough to be paid for in dollars face more complex entanglements. In order to solve currency problems, Phoenix International, for example, considered the possibility of exchanging drugs for minerals with Kazakhstan, the large cash-poor central Asian republic which is rich in natural resources.[20] One of the opportunities for cooperation in this area is buying licenses and operationalizing Soviet development in medical technology and equipment. The American firm U.S. Surgical Corporation bought the license for the production of stitching surgical instruments and successfully introduced them into the Soviet market.

Soviet-American cooperation in the field of consumer goods and medical supplies is developing in the following areas:

- manufacture of men's suits, shirts, women's lingerie, dresses, pantyhose, jeans; sewing state-of-the-art items from natural silk
- processing of wool and manufacture of knitted clothing, and leather and fur items; manufacture of footwear

- production of cosmetics and razors
- manufacture of domestic appliances, office equipment, and supplies
- manufacture of furniture, hardware, bulbs, lamps and electric fixtures, wallpaper, and linoleum
- manufacture of cards, albums, marble and granite items, and items made of china, ceramics, and crystal
- musical instruments, electronic toys, and sporting goods
- manufacture of yachts, motorcycles, and bicycles; assembly and distribution of automobiles
- manufacture of diagnostic equipment
- manufacture of dental equipment and supplies
- collecting and processing herbs.

Food Products

A consortium comprising more than fifty Soviet enterprises, including coal mines, chemical plants, metallurgical plants, and so on, asked one of the authors to represent their interests in the United States. They had been trying unsuccessfully for over six months to buy small meat-processing plants for hard currency before they asked for our assistance. These plants were designed to provide their employees with sausages, franks, ham, etc., and to motivate them to accomplish their jobs under difficult conditions. This is particularly significant since little is sold in the stores and workers have almost nothing on which to spend their salary. They tried to buy plants in the United States but failed. At the same time, some American companies manufacturing meat-processing equipment were unsuccessfully trying to sell their production in the Soviet Union. Why did they fail?

First of all, they offered their equipment to the ministries, enterprises involved in food processing which as a rule have no hard currency, while overlooking the opportunity to offer these products to such hard-currency owners as coal mines, and oil exploration and development enterprises, etc.

Second, Soviet customers have quite definite requirements for food-processing equipment which need to be known to American companies trying to enter the Soviet market. Analysis of requests from other Soviet organizations revealed five requirements for this equipment.

1. The capacity for such a plant which is designed to provide meat products for its employees must be one to one-and-a-half tons per day.
2. It must be a turnkey production line from slaughterhouse to

smokehouse because they are not specialists in this field and are not able to buy the parts and put together the entire production line themselves.

3. The equipment must not be so sophisticated that it requires highly qualified specialists for maintenance.
4. The equipment must be reliable and not subject to breakdown.
5. The equipment must not be very expensive, if possible.

These requirements were also difficult to meet because the representatives of these enterprises were new to foreign trade and unable to clearly articulate their requirements about the products they wanted to buy. An absence of realistic information about the market, inadequately formulated business proposals due to lack of knowledge, and establishing contacts with the wrong partners who do not possess hard currency, were obstacles which hindered American companies from taking advantage of a favorable situation.

Let us look at the example of a company which showed creativity and patience in its endeavors to enter the Soviet market. Pepsico is one of the companies which started to win market share in the former Soviet Union many years ago and now is expanding its presence in that market, capitalizing on high visibility and popularity won long before perestroika began. Now the company is using new strategies which are in keeping with the new opportunities presented by the Soviet market and the ongoing political and economic changes.

Donald M. Kendall, chairman of Pepsico's board, decided to attempt a trading relationship with the Soviets long before perestroika. The Pepsi invasion was made possible by a barter agreement signed in April, 1973, between the Purchase, New York food giant and Sojuzplodoimport, a Russian export and import company. The agreement traded soft-drink syrup, which the Russians used to produce and bottle Pepsi in their own plants, for Stolichnaya Vodka. When economic restructuring was introduced, Pepsi-Cola was already well known in the Soviet Union and the product's growth has been steady. There are plans for 28 more facilities by 1995. Such growth poses its own challenges for Pepsi, which started to generate foreign exchange with other things besides vodka. Part of the exchange is selling Soviet-made tanker ships. Kendall says the company sells the ships to commercial shipping firms worldwide for a profit after buying them outright from the Soviets.[21]

Another example of a company which uses flexible business arrangements while structuring a deal with the Soviets is Coca-Cola. It has taken apple juice concentrate for use in its Minute Maid line out of the Soviet Union to offset its sales of Coke and Fanta orange soda.

Coke's primary method of earning hard currency for soft drink sales has put it in the automobile business. The company helps the Soviets export the Lada automobile to the United Kingdom.[22]

Though the former Soviet Union is a difficult market, perhaps best suited to large companies that can afford to wait for profits, Sarah Carey, an attorney with the Washington, D.C., firm of Heron, Burchette, Ruckert, and Rothwell, argued that "in some ways it is easier for a small company to do business in the Soviet Union than it is for a large one. The small company is less bureaucratic and can start with a small capital investment . . ." Others risk going in without a barter deal because they think the economic opportunity is too good to miss. One of Carey's clients is literally banking on the future. The Tabard Corporation, a privately held company that runs the Tabard Inn in Washington, D.C., and the Tabard Farm in Middletown, Virginia, worked out a project to manufacture and distribute its Tabard Farm Potato Chips in Moscow, through a joint venture set up with a Soviet cooperative. The project envisions investments of about $75,000 in equipment and teaching the technology and marketing techniques to the Soviets, who are to provide the raw materials and labor. That the chips should not only be sold in hard-currency, upscale stores, but in ordinary Soviet markets for rubles, is a gamble that Vice President Fritzi Cohen and her husband, Edward S. Cohen, owner and president of the company, expect will pay off in the long run. An appropriate product for countertrade and the opportunities of the potential export market in West Germany and Finland, where organically grown products are popular, are also being considered. While it may take a while for the venture to make a profit, Fritzi Cohen is willing to be patient. "So far, 'nosh' is not a Russian word," she says. "I think the Potato Trust [the entity set up under the agreement with the Soviet cooperative] will change that."[23]

Soviet Products in America

The Soviet magazine *Deloviye Lyudi* relates an experience in selling exotic Soviet commodities in the United States. Fresh loaves of Moskovski and Borodinski bread appeared in New York's Bloomingdale's and sold out very quickly at $6 for a one-kilo loaf (the usual price for a small loaf of wheat bread is $1.50). The bread was baked in Moscow and exported through the joint venture Interferma, comprised of an American firm, FNK Promotions, Aeroflot, and the cooperative Express Service, operating out of Moscow's international airport, Sheremetyevo-II.

How did they do this? The Express Service truck received 6,000 loaves of fresh bread at the Moscow baking factory, N-6, and moved the fresh bread to the airport where it was loaded, and went straight to the supermarket from the airplane. Mirei Smith, a representative of the supermarket executives, said in an interview given to the Associated Press, that the Russian bread was sold not only to Russians, though there were a lot of them among the customers. The competition started in New York when the president of a New York City bakery chain, Stuart Zaro, also bought Moscow bread in order to keep his customers happy, selling the bread at a cheaper price of $5 a loaf. The president of FNK Promotions, who was in Moscow not long ago, brought back muffins and biscuits as well as small amounts of cucumbers, onions, Georgian peaches, and Azerbaijan melons.[24]

Soviet-American cooperation in the food industry is developing in the following areas:

- processing and production of agricultural products; production of dairy and meat products
- production of pasta, cookies, cakes, drinks, and baby formula
- production of ice cream and setting up ice cream cafes; production of beer and setting up bars.
- fishing, raising and processing fish, processing wild fruits and berries.

Construction

According to Gary Gizbrekht, president of the Canadian firm Central Canadian Structures, Ltd., who built a thirteen-story hotel for the Central City Tourist Committee, one has to have enormous patience to build something in the Soviet Union.[25] One of the businesses with promising potential is the construction of hotels. In 1991 the magazine *Deloviye Lyudi* gave the following overview of the current state of the hotel construction business in the former republics of Soviet Union. The former Soviet Union is one of the greatest tourist attractions in the world, but it is lagging behind for many reasons and one of them is the undeveloped hotel business. Almost half of all currently operating hotels belong either to city authorities or to branch ministries, industrial conglomerates, and other specific organizations which provide hotel services primarily to business people who operate under their umbrella or from related businesses. The possibility of fast currency earnings in the tourist business which pay off the investments, generates interest in joint projects on the part of foreign construction companies, banks, and firms.

Sheraton Corporation has started to build two hotels in the center of Moscow. Hilton is renovating an apartment building and hotel in Moscow. The British group, Trust House Forte, is planning to build two hotels, while Holiday Inn is planning to build one hotel. The Austrian company, Varimpex, signed contracts for the construction of five hotels in Moscow, St. Petersburg, Novgorod, and Tbilisi. The French association, Pulman, is building six hotels in Moscow, Kiev, Tashkent, Samarkand, and Bukhara. Two floating hotels will be built in Singapore and then shipped to Moscow. Every hotel will be outfitted with modern copying facilities, personal computers, telecommunications equipment, faxes, and telexes.[26]

Perestroika was one of the very first successful Soviet-American joint ventures. It was created in Moscow by the Warsham Group, in the middle of 1988. Soviet partners included Construction Conglomerate Mosinzhstroi, created by the Moscow City Council (initial capital 40 percent), the Major Administration for Architecture and City Building of Moscow (5 percent), and the joint venture Dialog (7 percent). The joint venture Perestroika is involved in real estate development, such as construction, renovation of existing buildings, and leasing of office buildings and living accommodations. Jobs are done on the basis of contracts with the developers and by their own efforts. Perestroika is the first joint venture in the former Soviet Union which announced a profit. During 1989, the first year of the joint venture operation, its profits totaled $1.6 million, with a yearly turnover of $13 million. During the time of its operation a number of facilities have been developed, including a seven-story office building, Pushkin Plaza, in the center of Moscow, with a total floor space of 2,700 square meters, renovation of a building for an Estée Lauder store, and the Hotel Savoy.

An analysis of the history and operation of Perestroika indicate three factors which helped make it successful:

1. Warsham made the right choice of Soviet partner for this joint venture. Mosinzhstroi is one of the biggest construction companies in Moscow and has very large production and supply capacities. This enabled Perestroika to settle the supply problems and, as has been discussed here, the difficulties with resources and material supplies due to constant shortages under the conditions of central allocation meant they didn't supply businesses operating outside the system, causing many joint ventures to fail. Soviet joint venture partners participate in joint venture operations not only through financing, but also through resources and contacts, which enable efficient performances of the enterprise. Mosinzhstroi is the biggest organization in infrastructure construction in Moscow. Dialog outfitted the joint venture with computer

equipment. Glavmosarkhitektura contributed the architectural design for the buildings.

2. There was a serious approach to paperwork and working out legal documents from the very beginning. In the former Soviet Union it is said that first one must break apart and then unite. While forming the joint venture, the partners should first reveal their disagreements and different perspectives about goals and objectives of their cooperation, operating techniques, mutual expectations, and possible discord. A common mistake made by joint venture founders is to ignore these difficulties which result in conflicts at later phases of their work. The founders of the joint venture Perestroika spent four months working out initial legal documents; over this period they discovered and reconciled disagreements on major issues concerning their alliance. For instance, the American partners' intention to have an exclusive right on joint venture contacts outside the Soviet Union contradicted the Soviet partners' intentions to establish international contacts. In the course of negotiations, a compromise which complied with the interests of both sides was worked out, allowing for joint participation in international contacts. The success of this stage was facilitated by the participation of outside experts, in particular specialists from the Chamber of Commerce and Industry of the former USSR.

3. Finally, Warsham was conscientious about taking into consideration the specifics of working in both the Soviet and international markets. Perestroika did not resort to the typical Soviet method, where the seller dictates to the buyer. The directors of the joint venture realized that work methods that had been used under conditions of total deficit were inadequate for meeting the needs of the joint venture performance. On the other hand, the leaders of the joint venture took into account the necessity of being particularly aware of the specific business setting of the former Soviet Union and that Western business experience only was not enough. Therefore, while choosing a Western developer to fulfill the construction works the joint venture advocated using a Western developer experienced in the Soviet business setting. This same orientation can also be seen in the approach of the joint venture to training personnel. The first hard-currency profits generated by the joint venture were allocated for training forty-five joint venture executives in U.S. construction companies. Training plans also envisioned training managers and workers at all levels in construction companies of the United States, Canada, and Western Europe. If it was mainly foreign workers who participated in the first Perestroika project, in the fourth one it is mainly Soviet employees who have participated.[27]

Sometimes even a joint venture in a potentially promising business can develop serious disagreements between the Soviet and American partners, over determining priorities, goals, and the means of achieving them. An example is the Soviet-American joint venture, Intourist-Radamer (IRA). *Commersant* weekly has commented on the IRA's activities and disagreements between the Soviet and the American partners. The founders of the joint venture were V/O Intourist and the American firm Radisson Hotel International. The initial capital was 3 million rubles from the Soviet side and $3 million from the American side. According to the representatives of Intourist, construction of the hotel was financed by the Soviet side, including 50 million rubles invested into clearing dollars, partly by Soviet rubles, and by a Yugoslavian construction company, Industrogradnya. It was planned to lease the hotel to the joint venture after construction work was completed. A hotel and a business center within the hotel had to be maintained by the Americans, who were supposed to invest about $32 million into it, including equipment. The hotel and the equipment were to remain respectively Soviet and American, and were not to become the property of the joint venture. Main investments were made by the partners outside of the total stated capital of the joint venture. Such schemes seem promising, and have at least three major advantages. First, the partners' risk is minimized; in case the joint venture is liquidated, the major part of their investments will not be affected. Second, this pattern allows partners to avoid painful issues of stating initial capital under the conditions of converting rubles into hard currency according to the official ratio. In such a situation, the partners have the authority to decide the initial capital and the sharing of its profits. Everything depends on what part of their investments they think it is necessary to include in the initial capital. And, third, an arrangement such as that allows both Soviet and American sides to receive rent for leasing the hotel's building and equipment, as well as the profit due to them from the joint venture income. Thus, the founders' profit does not depend only on the amount of the expenses of the joint venture.

According to *Commersant*, by the end of 1990, when construction had been completed, a conflict arose between the American and Soviet founders. According to the director of the hotel, Alexander Kolesnikov, the Slavyanskaya was ready to begin operations; however, the Americans insisted that it should not be opened for six months because the commercial center in the hotel was not ready. The American partners did not think it was possible to open the hotel without the commercial center. The Soviets insisted on the immediate opening of the hotel.[28] In our interview with the high-level official from Goskominturist (the State

Committee for Tourism), we tried to understand why the disagreements had occurred. One reason may be the difference in ideas about the point at which one can state that the project has been implemented. Americans are motivated by long-term success in operating the hotel, by its prestigious amenities and large profits. They did not want to open it without the commercial center. The Soviets have quite a different orientation. One of the possible motivations might be their willingness merely to report the fact that the hotel was open on time and that they were able to accommodate customers. They also wanted to earn currency immediately.

An effective strategy on the part of foreign partners here might be to help Soviets understand that their concern with cost-efficiency is indispensable in considering any project and that it is in their own best interest to think realistically.

The Soviet partners of American companies doing joint construction are not necessarily big, state construction companies. They could be new business entities and independent economic structures, such as those created by regional authorities which manage the land designated for development. Some sizable joint projects have begun for building and renovating apartment buildings. Hotels and office facilities are contemplated by the joint ventures Illinois-Presnya and Ameros, created by independent economic structures.

A serious problem for the developing construction industry in the former Soviet Union, and particularly in Moscow with its acute demand for office buildings and hotels, is the limited construction personnel. According to Yuri Titov, deputy chairman of Glavmosstroi (Chief Moscow Construction Administration), the country is confronted with the painful problem that the profession of construction worker is dying out. It has zero prestige among the population. A vivid illustration to this is the fact that out of 3,230 children of Moscovites engaged in the construction industry, only twenty-seven wanted to be trained in the same field as their parents. The sociological survey showed that not a single Moscovite involved with construction would like his child to work on a construction site.[29] Successful joint ventures in the construction sector attempt to find more incentives for recruiting personnel through providing them with food products and consumer goods.

Business Services

Creating data bases is a fast-developing area of the business services sector. Analysis of the factors which determine a company's success showed that access to the necessary commercial information is of primary importance. Relevant information is primarily obtained through personal contacts, not official sources. The possibility of obtaining information through unofficial channels plays the decisive role for successful business in the former Soviet Union.

The following example illustrates this point: One American company learned that oil products had been bought at the Raw Materials Exchange in the Soviet Union by another company at certain prices which were spelled out in the contract. Therefore, a conclusion was made about the current market price of these products. The American company was interested in this business and relied solely on this official source of information and sent its representative to Moscow to explore the opportunities.

A Soviet exchange broker told us how the American representative offered a better price than was in the contract and was extremely surprised when his offer was rejected. In fact, the price that was in the contract was not the actual purchase price of the oil. It was intentionally reduced just for the contract. Through personal contacts, the Soviet and American partners had worked out an arrangement which allowed them to retain part of the monies received in a foreign bank. Such kinds of transactions are important to the Soviets for three reasons:

1. While dealing with a Soviet bank they must wait for several months for a payment order to be fulfilled, thus being unable to use hard currency from their account at the time when they need it. The money in their account in the Western bank is available at any time. Moreover, at the end of 1991, Vnesheconombank has practically ceased all money transfers.
2. The Soviets can use money on their account in a Western bank as security for a letter of credit from a Soviet bank.
3. There are huge tariffs on exports. Lack of awareness of these circumstances may cause a lot of confusion, because American companies might make their decisions on the basis of official information from the contract.

One of the promising business opportunities for Western companies in the former Soviet Union is providing middleman services. From an analysis of the research findings, it is possible to identify five factors which provide special opportunities for American middleman companies:

1. The complexity of work in the Soviet market, the business environment, and constantly changing regulations mean that the role

of a middleman takes on a decisive and added importance in establishing contacts and services.

2. The lack of initiative, disinterested attitude, and inertia of the state foreign trade organizations.

3. The entire perestroika period has seen many restrictions imposed on the middleman activities of independent entities. These restrictions were due to the desire of the former foreign trade monopolies to maintain control over the foreign economic activities of those who by reforms were given the right to engage directly in foreign contacts.

4. The overwhelming majority of Soviet organizations and enterprises that have entered the external market do not have the necessary information, experience, or stable contacts, and therefore, cannot operate without middleman services.

5. Joint ventures created for middleman services are not confronted with the complex difficulties of industrial, construction, and other types of joint ventures, such as shortages of resources and materials in the former Soviet Union, leasing of industrial facilities, and putting production facilities into operation. In addition, joint ventures specializing in middleman services do not require big investments. The words of the chairman of the Chamber of Commerce and Industry of the former Soviet Union, Mr. Malkevich, explain why the middleman business has been undeveloped in the country.

> Our restrictions policy seems to be very strange. The right to sell only one's own products, which represents a notorious protest against the activities of any middleman dealers and trade is, by the way, one of the major reasons a number of deals go awry. These are the deals of new businessmen. Having forced out professional middlemen, we pushed forward a lot of unprofessional dealers, the consequence of the policy of each businessman trading himself. And now we are in a hurry to compound these errors by enacting new restrictions. All this damages the interests of exporters and deters the initiative of entrepreneurs.[30]

The following publication about the activities of the World Trade Center in Moscow tells about the state of affairs in the Soviet middleman business caused by the ungrounded prohibitions.

> A curious thing is happening. The number of Soviet middlemen hardly constitutes 1 percent of the representative services market in the country. And we have been trying hard to force our own cooperatives out of this market, just to clear the road for foreign agents. And, of course, they are

not passive. No less than 200 companies and banks have been officially accredited in our country, and are moonlighting with representative services. Besides, 100 non-accredited Western middlemen rented apartments and offices in Sovincenter. The number of small and middle-sized companies of the developed capitalist countries to whom they render their services is huge.[31] (Sociocultural reasons for the restrictions on middleman services will be considered in Chapter 5.)

The consulting business in the former Soviet republics is a new, but quickly growing field, where a large, unsatisfied demand exists. It is by nature a low-investment field and provides quick returns on investments, including investments in hard currency. An ever-increasing involvement in this activity by well-known and powerful Western consulting companies is obvious. They either act independently in opening their offices, or through cooperation with Soviet organizations in creating joint ventures.

The American firm Ernst & Young has been active in assisting foreign companies in setting up their operations in the former Soviet Union. They offer their consulting services in a number of areas, including counseling on the specifics of the Soviet market, legal frameworks for doing business, areas of potential interest for foreign investors, and evaluation of the reliability of the partners, etc. The firm Ernst & Young became one of the founders of the joint venture Ernst & Young-Vneshaudit, whose objective is to offer tax, audit, accounting, and consulting services to Soviet joint ventures.

Ernst & Young became one of the first foreign firms to provide services in the former Soviet Union according to Western standards. "There is no public accounting profession in the Soviet Union because, until recently, there hasn't been any need for one," says James A. Searing, an Ernst & Young partner and the firm's director of international business services; "Concepts such as profit measurement and the differences between external and internal auditing are new for them; setting up businesses there requires far more than just adapting one country's accounting standards to another's."[32]

Joint venture attorneys in general offer a valuable edge over in-house law staffs. They are usually international trade specialists who bring not only hands-on experience in shaping joint venture deals, but also extensive contacts in both Washington and Moscow. One attorney observes, however, that maintaining a good rapport with ministries in the former Soviet Union is becoming increasingly difficult. "With decentralization, you have to know many people," says Eugene Theroux, a partner at Baker & McKenzie in Washington, D.C. "It's a bit confusing on the Soviet side now; the 'Ministries' are not sure about the extent of their authority."[33]

An acute need for timely commercial information, and an overloading of the traditional information systems, generate an information hunger for those who work in the Soviet market, and make it profitable to create computer information communication networks. Some joint ventures, including Sprint-Network USSR and Information Computer Enterprises, made an attempt to capitalize on these new opportunities of providing computer information services in the former Soviet Union.

Furthermore, issuing various reference materials containing necessary information about potential business partners in the former Soviet Union has become a promising venture, due to decentralization of foreign trade and inefficient information about new participants. The thousands of new Soviet foreign trade participants also lack practical specific information about American markets and export opportunities. Business directories such as *The 1991 USSR Business Guide and Directory*, for example, published by the publishing firm Market Molage jointly with VNIKI (a Moscow-based institute engaged in market research), and *The Directory of American Exporters* by Thomas International Publishing are designed to make a lot of important specific information available to American businesses and Soviet entrepreneurs.

Interesting observations about the advertising market in the Soviet Union are published in a new monthly magazine called *Moscow*. According to Gerry Roberts, European general manager of Ogilvy & Mather,

> Eastern Europe is the last frontier for us hotshot advertising agencies, like Latin America was twenty years ago and Europe fifty years ago. . . . In the Soviet Union, McDonald's, Pizza Hut, Kodak, Adidas, Ford, Johnson & Johnson, Colgate, Pepsi, Rank Xerox, British Airways, ICI, Visa, Amex, and Mastercard are all touting their wares now, right under Lenin's nose. . . . A blank slate on which the West can write its name. . . . Who would have thought that after all the talk of nuclear weapons and wars, the battle of world ideologies would take place over the shop counter with stakes no bigger than a Big Mac? Even Khrushchev saw it coming when back in 1950 he complained that, "Private cows multiply while Socialist cows do not."

"We got all excited about Pan-European advertising," says Gary Burandt, who heads Young & Rubicam's operations, "but Pan-Soviet advertising is a much bigger challenge."

In many ways, the former Soviet Union could well be a dream market, a virgin territory waiting to be delivered to the West. "Why go through the whole '40s, '60s, '70s, and '80s again when you can apply the lessons you've learned to this uncharted territory?" asks Burandt. Although salaries are low, many Soviets save because there is nothing to spend income on. "If you want to get your name in the market in order to spearhead a campaign two or three years down the road, that's where the real market lies," argues another executive. "Establish the brand so that when the goods come along everyone will know who you are."[34]

Management Review published a story about an arduous undertaking by Young & Rubicam in the former Soviet Union. Company representatives met with the Soviet Chamber of Commerce Presidium in 1988, when the Chamber's members wanted to learn firsthand about Western-style marketing. After the American company had formalized a partnership with Vneshtorgreklama (one of the leading Soviet advertising organizations), and negotiations had covered how to value each partner's assets and contributions, how profits would be split, and how they would be taxed, there was still plenty of red tape to unravel.

The first obstacle was lack of office space. Due to its partner's influence, accreditation for the space was received in eight months, which was unusually swift. Until then, Young & Rubicam had been barred from renting offices and apartments. The managing director and his employees, most of them Soviet citizens, had to improvise, "We set up offices in hotel rooms, paying hotels rates," the managing director recalls. Next came a budgetary oversight, where Young & Rubicam was told that the minister of finance required them to designate funds, such as wages, for three years. Belatedly, they discovered that freelancers' pay is supposed to come out of that wage fund. Ignorance of customs regulations was the biggest problem, "In the USSR assume nothing and choose a partner with clout and understanding." Y&R's Burandt relates the traumatic story of just getting a copier, "The machine arrived at the airport and we sent someone over to pick it up. He came back saying, 'I need twenty signatures on a form signed by the militia,' which is a process requiring two months. We managed to get around that, but the point is that it may not occur to the Soviets that there is a problem until it happens.[35]

Out-of-home advertising is currently the major means of acquiring brand exposure in the Soviet Union, as the three television stations are government owned and run very limited advertising. Thanks to the Transportation Displays, Inc. (TDI) deal concluded with the Soviet government, U.S. tobacco companies, which in the fall of 1990 received the right to sell Marlboros and Winstons in the Soviet Union, have now advertised those brands on busses and bus shelters.[36]

While there are several avenues open to American businesses for marketing their products in the former Soviet Union, trade exhibitions in various parts of the country are heavily relied upon. The magazine *Vneshnyaya Torgovlya* published a report about one such exhibition which illustrates their huge potential value. In October 1989, in Moscow, at the Krasnaya Presnya Exhibition, "USA-89: Opportunities for Business Cooperation," 150 American firms took part. The corporate giants attending the trade show included Philip Morris, General Electric, American Express, Johnson & Johnson, Procter & Gamble, Estée Lauder, Eastman Kodak, Federal Express, E. I. Du Pont, Caterpillar, and Ralston-Purina. Though direct trade was not the main objective of this exhibition, a number of deals were made:

- American General Resources signed a contract with Vtorchermet Enterprises worth $3 million, for scrap metal supplies.
- The firm Chilewich signed contracts with Soviet organizations for supplying footwear, for a total of $15 million.
- The firm Chick Master is planning to supply a chicken processing plant to Ukraine, with equipment worth $100,000.
- Combustion Engineering conducted negotiations on cooperation at the Tobolsk and Surgut enterprises. In November, these negotiations were completed and an agreement to create the joint venture was signed.
- A protocol of intent to create a joint venture for international parcel mailing was signed with Federal Express, including use of Soviet aviation technology.[37]

The Service Industry

New opportunities in the service industry are illustrated by the delivery of services in the former Soviet Union today. The findings of the survey conducted by Sociological Surveys at a number of enterprises and organizations in Moscow show that many people do not even attempt to use what services might exist for the following reasons:

- Lack of necessary services
- Services too far away logistically
- Poor quality of services
- Lengthy time requirement for fulfillment or delivery of services.

Most respondents in the survey indicated they would agree to a 20–30 percent price increase for quality services delivered in a timely fashion.[38] The poor state of the Soviet service industry is explained in great measure by the attitude of the Soviets to service-delivering professions. Their feeling about these professions, fostered by Soviet society, is that they are unworthy and people who deliver services can't be respected. It is interesting to note that the old Russian word "lakei" (which meant a service person) gradually acquired new connotations, moving from a neutral term to an abusive one. To engage in heavy industry or defense industry occupations deserves respect. Working in a service industry is a kind of shame. The people employed in the service sector learned to make up for the damage to their self-esteem by humiliating and abusing people they served. The attitude of the Soviets towards service, and how they deliver it can be illustrated by the following examples.

While on tour in one foreign country, a Soviet economist was accommodated by the firm for which he was working in a first-class hotel. Inadvertently, he damaged a beautiful sink in the bathroom. The Soviet man was in a desperate state. He had little foreign currency and was very concerned that the hotel administrators will tell him to buy a new sink and he would not have money to pay. He called the manager of the hotel and showed him the damage, and was shocked when the manager said: "Sir, do you insist that we should fix everything today or could you wait till tomorrow?" Happy and relieved, the Soviet reassured him that he could wait till the next day. The next day everything was fixed absolutely free of any charge.

The Soviet writer Alexander Ivanov, who described this incident, writes that he was trying to imagine what would happen in the same situation in his own country. He shuddered as he imagined representatives of the hotel administration coming into the hotel room. He imagined how the written claim would be put together about the damage to state property and the second one—about recovery. Ivanov also recalls the dramatic difference between service delivery in the Soviet Union and in foreign countries when Air-India served the passengers an additional meal when the flight was several hours delayed. Even if the flight is delayed for several days, the Soviet Aeroflot would do nothing of the kind.[39]

The following story of an American representative in the Soviet Union unveils the psychological mechanisms that underlie the attitude of the Soviets towards service and how they deliver it. The permanent American representative in Moscow met the president of his firm at Sheremetyevo Airport, together with the Soviet driver who was a new employee. This representative expected the driver to help with the luggage, but the driver was not willing to do this and even murmured something like "I am not a carrier." The American was both surprised and angry. And this episode was the cause of subsequent conflicts and tension. What was exhibited here is the entirely different perception of the idea of service by the Soviets and foreigners. For a Soviet man, personal and professional roles merge. Lack of these boundaries, along with the fact that service positions in the Soviet Union have not been traditionally perceived as respectable jobs, lead to a situation where providing a service is damaging to a person's self-respect. The driver was working for the foreign firms accredited in Moscow and was driving a Mercedes, so it was an insult for him to be asked to carry somebody's luggage. It indicated that he felt degraded, because to perform the functions of a porter was beneath his dignity. The kind of service on his part that was taken for granted by the American and in the American view should be delivered automatically, with Soviets can only be willingly given on the basis of informal contacts.

One of the sectors of the service industry with promising business opportunities is the restaurant business. The initial success of the McDonald's and Pizza Hut invasion in the Soviet Union has spurred other companies, such as Nathan's, to start joint venture restaurant projects. Soviet citizens are luring these businesses because of their dense population, high proportion of disposable income, and immense vacuum of quality food services throughout the country.

The well-publicized McDonald's and Pizza Hut successes were due to the expertise, contacts, special relationships, and long-standing friendships generated over years of determined effort. Endless tenacity and tact are required in dealing with Soviet bureaucracy, with its maze of various organizations. Establishing an adequate distribution system and finding sources of quality food are also challenges in the shortage-plagued society. Though there are plenty of workers in the former Soviet Union, Russian tradition does not foster the smiles and courtesy required of a customer-service mentality. By tradition, the main task of Soviet food-service employees has been to keep customers out of the restaurant or discourage them from returning. Massive efforts are required to overcome this mentality, by persistent training. Despite the complexities of operating in the Soviet Union, U.S. chains and independents can succeed there if they are willing to give the necessary monumental commitments in time, energy, and resources.[40] Moreover, the potential of the service industry is very large because of the size of the untapped market, including those services which are sold for hard currency to foreigners and Soviet citizens, and because of the possibility of starting a service business without large hard-currency investments.

Publishing and Film Production

There are examples of both successful and unsuccessful commercial publishing activities. One unsuccessful pattern is to have hard-currency investment in publishing in a foreign country and selling in the former Soviet Union for rubles. An analysis of experiences so far shows the importance of locating the right partner with good contacts and the ability to buy equipment, raw materials, and services in the domestic market for rubles.

The weekly publication *Commersant* reported information about publishing ventures in the USSR. *BusinessWeek* began publishing in Russian at the end of 1990. According to the vice president and publisher of BusinessWeek International, Herd Hinske, a completely new business arrangement has evolved, that fully orients the journal to the Soviet market. The journal will be put out monthly: the volume is 72 pages long. A yearly subscription is 60 rubles. Advertising space in the journal costs from $6,000 to $9,000. Every issue presents a digest of four weekly American issues and four weekly European issues of *BusinessWeek*. The good relations of the publisher Kniga with the former Goskompechat SSR helped to solve printing problems. According to Mr. Hinske, just locating the right partner enabled the joint edition of BW/USSR to outpace smaller publications that were under way, of business journal competitors such as *Forbes* and *Fortune*, which are just preparing to enter the Soviet market. According to editor in chief of the BW/USSR, Vladimir Shvedov, the success of the journal is due to its ability to pay for printing in rubles. According to *Commersant*, the ruble profit from the sale of the journal (50 percent of whose the hard-currency earnings come from advertising), will be received by Kniga publishers. Hard-currency profit will be reinvested into purchasing Finnish paper and typographic paint. According to Mr. Shvedov, almost the entire hard-currency profits from the first tentative issue have been used in this way. Printing services are paid for in rubles, according to contract prices and not exceeding 30 to 40 percent of ruble profit. The profit from circulation is assumed to be about 225 thousand rubles.[41]

In the cases where paper, typographic paint, and preliminary typesetting are supplied by Americans, currency cost accounting problems arise. Publishers are trying to solve these problems through offering advertising space to foreign companies. However, this market is rather limited at present and in general is tapped.

The following illustrates cross-cultural differences and the way they were overcome in an American-Soviet publishing business as reported by Vladimir Nadein, a Soviet journalist. Americans had a different vision from the Soviets of the way to achieve their mutual goals, including inappropriate stereotypes and unrealistic expectations which played out while developing joint strategies for publishing their Soviet-American magazine WE. The Soviets thought that their own minds would be restrained by propaganda and that American thinking was free from propaganda stereotypes. As it turned out, the Americans sometimes worked from stereotypes as well. For example, both sides were discussing the terms of publishing the initial issue. The Americans asked the Soviets for their suggestions. And the Soviets, laboring under their proverbial stereotypes, answered, "We'd rather have it published at the end of May, on the eve of the summit meeting." The Americans laughed and explained, "Nobody will care about our magazine then! We should publish it after Gorbachev's visit, somewhere closer to the 4th of July, We'll celebrate Independence Day."

The Americans set up the following criteria to test the reality of glasnost: If the article by the president's former national security adviser, Zbigniew Brzezinski, who was famous as a "'die-hard anti-Soviet," was accepted without editing or reduction, it meant that glasnost was working. It was impossible to convince the American partners that Brzezinski's straight-forwardness was not a surprise for anybody anymore, and that interviews with him had already been published in *Pravda* and other Soviet newspapers. It was not only initial mutual distrust that inhibited the cooperation at first. There are great stylistic differences in Soviet and American journalism. Soviets value a lot of analysis along with a light style, whereas Americans value facts. Soviets assume that the reader will read between the lines. Americans like precision: "Who said what?" "When was it said?" "What might be inferred from this to other expressed opinions?" etc. Soviets consider this style dry.

American journalists tend to reiterate information throughout an article. Soviets assume that the reader retains everything from the first reference and that there is no need for repetition of information. Americans are more precise regarding context; for instance, when introducing politicians into an article, information is repeated regarding their state of origin, party affiliation, age, and recent statements of note. From the Soviet perspective, the president of the United States seems to be the only politician who is not introduced in context every time.

It was difficult for the Soviets who worked with the Americans on this venture to understand that the magazine was supposed to raise money.

The Soviets discussed all kinds of issues, such as when it would be published, who was it published for, why are we publishing this particular magazine, but they never got down to the issue about how much to sell it for.[42]

With the ongoing changes in the Soviet Union, opportunities for new business arrangements have appeared in the film industry. Just a few years ago, access to filming in the Soviet Union was through co-production with Mosfilm, the state-run film agency. *Management Review* told how Australian producer–director Fred Schepisi worked out a deal to independently film the movie *The Russia House* in the former Soviet Union. He managed to get into the Soviet Union through his old business acquaintance, Jerry Rappaport, who had had business dealings with the Soviet film industry for twenty-five years. Jerry Rappaport helped Schepisi make the right connection by arranging his meeting with Elam Klimov, the head of the Soviet filmmakers' union. It turned out that Klimov needed some help on his own project. He wanted to film *The Master and Margarita* in Israel. But both Klimov and Schepisi were faced with the problem of the inconvertibility of the ruble. Paying for a movie filmed outside of the USSR when he couldn't convert the ruble into Western currency was a problem for Klimov. To solve the problem, a reciprocal agreement was worked out. Corona Films, an independent production company, which Klimov had formed with other Soviet directors and German backers, agreed to pay *The Russia House* expenses in the USSR in rubles. Pathé Entertainment, the company backing Schepisi, in turn agreed to pay Klimov's hard-currency expenses. One of the problems that emerged as Schepisi started shooting was that the crew—consisting of Soviets, Americans, British, and Finns—went into culture shock. "I thought I might have World War III at the end of the first week," says Schepisi. "I had to make everybody understand that we all work differently and that everybody has something to contribute."[43]

Business Contacts with Regional Organizations

The newspaper *Moscow News* published sociological surveys for 1989–1991 aimed at determining the development of entrepreneurship in various regions of the country. In order to ascertain where the best climate for entrepreneurship had been created, sociologists studied the occurrence of advertisements about commodities and services. The following chart specifies the percentage that various cities had in the total flow of advertising material.

Proportion in the Total Volume of Advertising Material

1989–1990		1991	
%		%	
Moscow	16.0	Moscow	28.7
St. Petersburg	6.0	St. Petersburg	4.5
Kiev	3.3	Yekaterinoburg	2.4
Minsk	3.0	Kharkov	1.6
Donetsk	2.3	Novosibirsk	1.6
Volgograd	2.0	Saratov	1.6
Stavropol	2.0	Kiev	1.4
Baku	1.5	Kazan	1.4
Krasnodar	1.3	Riga	1.0

Two tendencies can be identified here: the dynamics of entrepreneurial endeavors is higher in Moscow (the proportion of Moscow and Moscow region in the total volume of the advertising material is even higher—36.5 percent). The proportion of advertising material accounted for by the cities on places 2–9 of this list fell from 21.4 percent to 15.5 percent.

Studies of the flow of advertising material show that that the role of Moscow in the establishment of interregional economic ties is less than it was supposed to be. The bigger proportion of Moscow advertisements against the advertisements from the periphery of the country testifies to the fact that the entrepreneurs from the provinces are not so much interested in Moscow as the unique coordination center. The increasing independence of the regions and their willingness to establish horizontal economic links outside the capital of the country can be seen.

Besides the sixteen cities listed in the table, the most entrepreneurial-spirited in 1989–1990 were such cities as Brest, Gomel, Lugansk, Dnepropetrovsk, Astrakhan, Voronezh, Samara, Nizhni Novgorod, Odessa, Yaroslavl, Tver, Ribinsk, and Chelyabinsk. In 1991, Krasnoyarsk, Perm, Zaporozhye, Penza, Volgograd, Mariupol, Vinnitsa, Vladimir, Tver, Ufa, Ylyanovsk, Orsk, Aktyubinsk, and Chelyabinsk were added to this list.

The following table shows the dynamics of business activity in the regions, as reflected by their proportion in the total volume of advertising material:

Regions	Proportion in the total volume of advertising material	
	1989–1990	1991
	%	%
1. Severni (Northern)	2.3	1.0
2. Severo-Zapadni (North-Western)	4.0	5.3
3. Pribaltiiski (Baltic)	4.3	2.2
4. Belorusski (Belorussian)	6.5	2.0
5. Tsentralni (Central)	23.8	43.0
6. Tsentralnochernozemni (Central Black Soil)	3.3	0.6
7. Yugo-Zapadni (South-Western)	6.5	4.1
8. Yuzhni (Southern)	3.8	1.2
9. Donetsko-Pridneprovski (Donetsk-Dnieper)	8.0	7.1
10. Uralski (The Urals)	6.3	7.1
11. Volgo-Vyatski (The Volga-Vyatka)	3.5	1.4
12. Povolzhski (The Volga)	6.3	7.5
13. Severo-Kavkazski (North-Caucasus)	6.0	4.7
14. Zakavkazski (Transcaucasian)	2.5	2.0
15. Credeneaziatski (Central Asian)	2.3	0.8
16. Kazakhstanski (Kazakhstan)	2.8	2.6
17. Zapadno-Sibirski (Western-Siberian)	4.0	3.5
18. Vostochno-Sibirski (Eastern-Siberian)	1.5	1.8
19. Dalnevostochni (Far Eastern)	2.8	2.0
20. Moldova	0.8	0.4

SOURCE: Sergei Modestov, "The Map of Business Activity," *Moskovkie Novosti Surveys*, October 1991, p. 15.[44]

We conclude this chapter by presenting findings from studies on opportunities for independent economic development in the republics cited from the Russian translation of information compiled by the Deutsche Bank, which was published in the business supplement to the newspaper *Moskovskie Novosti*. Each republic was assessed on a ten-point scale according to twelve economic, social, and geopolitical indices.[45]

	High Level of Economic Development			Modice Level of Economic Development					Zero Level of Economic Development				
	Ukraine	Baltic Republics	RSFSR	Georgia	Belo-russia	Kazakh-stan	Moldova	Armenia	Azerbai-jan	Uzbeki-stan	Turkme-nistan	Kirgiz-stan	Tadji-kistan
1. The level of industrial development	9	10	8	6	8	5	2	3	3	3	2	2	2
2. Proportion of the production which can be exported	6	5	6	3	4	4	2	1	2	2	1	1	1
3. Agricultural production	10	8	6	7	5	5	9	3	3	3	3	2	1
4. Proportion of agricultural production which can be exported	6	3	3	6	3	4	7	1	2	3	3	3	1
5. The extent to which the republic can be economically self-sufficient	7	6	8	3	5	3	2	1	2	1	1	1	1
6. Mineral resources	8	0	10	4	1	9	0	4	7	6	5	4	3
7. Proportion of the production from all raw materials segments which can be exported	8	0	10	4	0	9	0	4	8	6	5	4	3
8. Welcoming to market reforms	3	10	2	9	3	1	5	8	2	2	1	1	1
9. Distance from Europe	6	10	4	6	7	5	7	6	4	1	1	1	1
10. Level of education	6	9	5	5	7	3	5	4	4	2	2	2	2
11. Homogeneity of population	6	6	5	2	6	2	2	6	6	1	1	1	1
12. Development of infrastructure	8	10	5	6	6	5	8	6	4	2	2	1	1
Total	83	77	72	61	55	55	49	47	47	32	27	24	18

Important Sociocultural Dynamics of Doing Business

Major Results of the Experiment

W hy is the country that occupies one-sixth of the earth's territory, has rich natural resources, scientific breakthroughs of world importance, world-famous art and literature, and a highly educated population, in such a tragic condition? The answer is multi-faceted. Democracy, freedom and openness have been introduced. Free market transformations have started and alternative economic structures have been allowed. State enterprises are establishing direct business contacts, forging relationships, trading at the commodities exchanges, engaging independently in foreign economic relations, conducting negotiations, and so on. On the surface, everything seems to be the same as in the rest of the civilized world. But actually, innovations which seem progressive have acquired distorted forms, have an adverse effect, do not result in the expected, positive changes. Instead, they aggravate and compound the disastrous economic situation, leading to social disasters. It is becoming more and more obvious that something in the people themselves is hampering the implementation of the reforms. This something is not confined to such well-known traits of the Russian mind-set as a parasitic existence, lack of initiative, the "Avos" orientation, servility, and leveling down.[1] We became convinced that there are also some other basic, specific peculiarities of the Soviets when they act as business people that do not facilitate the implementation of the reforms. They surfaced with the appearance of independent economies, when millions of people quite unexpectedly, even for themselves, became businessmen and started conducting international business.

Soviet and American CEOs on the Moon and an Uninhabited Island

Before perestroika, when the entire Soviet economy was one huge factory ruled by Gosplan, Gossnab, and other state organizations, there could be no business except on the black market and the shadow economy inside it. Outside the country, in foreign trade, the Soviet Union was represented by a select few—the elite—handpicked and raised in incubators. What exactly is the new phenomenon of millions of Soviets acting in the capacity of business people?

Our research was devoted to finding an answer to this question. In the course of conducting simulations of various business and non-business situations, we managed to reveal decisive sociocultural differences in ways of doing business through analysis of videotapes of Soviet and American business people in specific situations. These exercises included "Shipwrecked on the Moon" and "Uninhabited Island." These experiments visually illustrated typical qualities of Soviet participants, who could not:

- Enter into business relationships
- Build business relationships on the basis of certain laws, rules, and standards and not just on personal preferences
- Proceed democratically in decision making, which would conform with the complicated, ever-changing reality with which they are confronted.

What are typical Soviet people doing when they appear to be on an "uninhabited island"? We will try to summarize the findings of several experiments by making up a somewhat simplified picture out of an otherwise complicated and multi-faceted reality, in order to illustrate the typical behavior patterns of the Soviets that give a clue to understanding their business conduct.

· First of all, they complain to each other that everything is bad. They discuss for a long time whether they will be rescued or not and who might rescue them. Different opinions are expressed and disagreements become emotional. The participants' behavior and interactions become very personal according to the model: "You are a bad person, and I don't like you because your point of view is different from mine." Then they come to the conclusion: "If we do not quarrel, if we get along, if we trust each other, everything will be okay. If we had something to drink (vodka), we would drink to 'friendship.' "

· As soon as their relationships are based on friendly terms, and they become more intimate, like a family, they start "family quarrels." They begin to lie to each other in a petty, personal way.

· If a group is rather large and is broken down into small groups, the same kind of relationships develop inside these small groups.

· All the participants are divided into "us" (members of the small group), and "them." Those who are "them" are guilty of everything and just identifying the guilty ones is tantamount to solving all the problems. The major focus of attention is figuring out if somebody else (the members of one's own group included) is in possession of something better and trying to prevent this. The major orientation is that everyone should be doing equally poorly. They rely on miracles, on "Avos." (Avos is the name for the string shopping bags that Russians carry with them everywhere in the hopes that they will unexpectedly come upon a line for something they need or desire.)

In the Moon Crash Exercise a group of American, West European, and Soviet business people participated in working out a group solution to a survival problem. They were given a list of things which they could take with them to the moon. They had to take everything which they considered necessary and then prioritize them. We deliberately chose a situation that was outside their political or socioeconomic context because Soviets tend to put forth differences in the sociopolitical systems as the reasons for their inability to cooperate, to reach an agreement, or reach mutual understanding. Such a situation allowed them to trace sociocultural differences without arguments over the political and economic specifics. The result of the experiment was that they were unable to work out a mutual solution, or even engage in a productive discussion.

First of all, no one took on the role of discussion leader to help facilitate the discussion of views. One Soviet took the initiative and immediately imposed his opinion, never offering the opportunity to start a discussion. He interrupted, did not listen to others, was obviously listening only to himself, and was not motivated by solving the problem but by getting his opinions heard. Because the members of the group did not clarify everyone's understanding of the objective of the discussion, they got stuck constantly when different ideas were generated. Many times, in the course of the conversation, participants had to stop and figure out what the task was and how everybody understood it. When it became obvious that the group was unable to find a solution, one of the Soviets suggested that the participants should be divided into two groups, American and Soviet, each one coming to its own agreement. Then the two groups should get together and arrive at a final solution. It is interesting to note that just before this suggestion, the Soviets had accused the organizers of the seminar of separating the Soviets from the foreigners. For example, they indicated that Soviets and foreigners were taken around the cities in separate busses, although this was related to the necessity to have separate guides, one speaking Russian, and one speaking English. They also complained about being seated at different tables for meals. But now that everything was up to them, they decided to isolate themselves into separate groups. When the groups broke down into two subgroups, they were able to work out certain decisions. But when they tried to come to a mutual solution with the second group, they failed.

Soviet People Are Totally Unused to Entering into Business Relationships

The important thing is not that there are no adequate laws or specific conditions for doing business, but that there is little readiness for entering into business relationships interpersonally. A typical characteristic of the Soviets is lack of awareness of opportunities for agreement with other people, arising out of mutual benefit, exchange, and trade. Typically the Soviet does not want to be used for someone's benefit, even if it is mutually beneficial to him also. From this, one can understand the reasons for the behavior of Soviet directors of enterprises in the following experiment.

In this exercise, participants were divided into two teams with instructions to accomplish a specific task. In the room there was a blackboard. A 6 × 6 matrix was drawn on it, and the teams were instructed to place either a plus or a minus sign in the squares. When five similar marks were formed in a row, the team would receive one point. The exercise was not designed as a contest between two teams, playing against each other. The teams were instructed to generate a maximum number of points, but the exercise did not include the task of trying to take the lead. The teams were instructed before the exercise to work out a joint strategy for generating a maximum number of points. Though they were not supposed to play against each other, the Soviets' perception of the exercise was that they were opponents with each other and that their goal was to impede the opposite team's ability to generate points, not to cooperate in such a way that each team could win. Throughout the entire game, each team placed a symbol opposite to that written in the preceding move by the "adversary." After the game was over, they were asked: "Why did you do it this way? What kind of strategy were you working out for twenty minutes?" They were reminded that there was no assignment to hinder each other, but to think about how the most people would gain.

The blackboard was designed in such a way that it was possible to make seven crossings. That means that each team could receive three scores. As to the seventh one, it was even possible to flip a coin in order to reach a fair solution, but it didn't occur to anybody.

The Soviet participants in the experiment exhibited a lack of cooperation skills, mutual trust, or mutual gain. The ideas of collectivism have been instilled for over seventy years, resulting in people who have no concept of cooperation, common effort, or mutual benefit. The directors and managers participating in the exercise were told "this is what the concept of communism has resulted in." And the Soviets were extremely surprised. "Why, what has this got to do with communism?" To which they were told, "How else can you account for all of this? You are not less intelligent than the representatives of the capitalist system, but your behavior is absurd." Instead of giving each other an opportunity to generate a maximum number of points, the participants posed obstacles to impede each other's ability to gain points.

Six people participated in the next exercise. Each participant was assigned a role as director of an enterprise located near a lake used for dumping water from the enterprise. There were no fish in it. In conformity with the environmental protection regulations, a certain level of water purity had to be maintained. The "directors" were given the following instructions: Once a month, they were entitled to take one of five actions in regard to dumping the water. Colored cards were used in the exercise, each color designating one of these five actions or options, which the players would throw into the center when they were making their choice. A certain number of points representing profit was designated for each action:

- The first action, designated by a red card, indicated that the purified water was dumped. A score of 30 points was given for this action, and was not the highest possible. But under the terms of the exercise, the figure could increase for each participant later if certain agreements on coordinating the activities of other players were made and the game shifted into different matrices.
- The second action represented the "director" dumping contaminated water into the river. It was designated with a green card and the number of points for this move was 50. However, now the lake is contaminated, and in the next round the figure would decrease for each participant.
- The third option was to throw the yellow card to reward the one who dumped the purified water. The one who threw the yellow card received some points and the one whom he rewarded received some points too.
- The fourth option was the black card, and included a fine. The person who made this choice received no points, but the player who dumped the contaminated water lost 20 points.
- The fifth option, the white card, guaranteed a fixed, small gain which did not depend on anything else.

After each move, a participant was told the score he had received. The actual accounting of the game is in the first two options, dumping purified or contaminated water, and the exercise was designed in such a way that in every round no more than one dumping of contaminated water was allowed without increasing the admissible level of contamination. The terms of the exercise suggested a sophisticated interdependence among the players based on the idea of mutual gain. The participants were told that their objective was to raise as much money as possible and that they could work out a joint strategy which would lead to their mutual benefit. The paradox of the game was that if the participants agreed among themselves and if they worked cooperatively, each could win the maximum score, which is approximately 3,000. Each participant just needed to realize that in order to do this, he should in turn be either the source of profit for others, or they should be a source of profit for him.

While engaged in the exercise, the participants sat in such a way that nobody saw what card the other players chose, although they were never given instructions to hide their cards. After a discussion the group arrived at a strategy. At first, they seemed to follow this strategy, but suddenly they became aware that someone was violating their agreement and was dumping dirty water when he was not supposed to. They determined this by the difference in the money which they each received. Immediately they began to act according to the principle of "every man for himself." The masks of friendliness were cast off. Somebody tried to determine the wrongdoer. Everything was falling apart. In spite of the fact that the initial strategy was correct, nobody reconsidered the situation to try to return to the profit path. Everyone reacted to the situation without thinking either of his own profit or gain. Their arguments were unrelated to business or to the ideas of personal and mutual benefit. They were not discussing their failure to reach the objective of the exercise in terms of "You want to raise money. I'm offering you the way to do this." Everything was confined to ethical and moral categories, to what kind of people they were, and not how they could make money. They offered arguments such as "it is bad to deceive," describing the behavior of the players as immoral, etc. All this stemmed from basic Soviet ethics which condemned actions directed toward receiving benefit as a disgrace, and which were rooted in the moral imperatives of the Russian orthodoxy as opposed to the Protestant religion, and, carried to their extreme, ugly forms by the communist regime.

People's Mind-set under Non-existent Private Property

The following analysis of the concept of private property and the consequences of having rejected it for many years in Soviet society is given by the Soviet author Sergei Panasenko.

From childhood, Soviets were accustomed to declaring private property and other such awful things anathema, because they denote exploitation of one person by another. But getting rid of private property does not mean getting rid of exploitation, for now exploitation comes from the State. Everything that makes private property the foundation of a viable social order was rejected by the Soviet power. It was not in its interests to recognize that private property gives freedom to a man. Nobody has the right to dictate how he could manage his property.

The concern of an owner is the profitability of his business, and whether, after paying taxes, it provides him enough reward to make a living and act at his own discretion in everything. His sense of confidence in being able to provide the necessities of life is supported by other people, like himself property owners, who are also concerned about the profitability of their businesses. Unlike the position of an individual under the conditions of private ownership, the position of a Soviet man in terms of obtaining the necessities of life hinges in many ways on what he is given by the powers and, therefore, depends on his standing with them.

Under a system of private ownership, even those who do not own any property and are employed by others feel more independent than employees under a system where no private property exists. Of course they are not totally independent because they must meet the requirements of those providing the jobs. But there are also many employers because the property is scattered among many owners and is decentralized. Therefore, political freedom is the other side of economic freedom. Economic freedom always has the potential of sending forth the shoots of democracy and political freedom. Soviet power shuns private property, which enables individual existence and, regardless of the attitude of an individual towards power, turns out to be that inner force which strengthens the glue of society.

When the merciless war against private property as the biggest evil had been declared, giving birth to poverty and luxury, injustice and humiliation, the revolutionaries were pursuing two goals. One of the goals was the creation of a new, ideal economic order, the first phase of which was a society where "all citizens turn into employees . . . hired by the state." All citizens, as it was written by Lenin, become employees and workers of one All-Union state "syndicate." The first reaction of the rulers to somebody expressing his own opinion was to fire him and, in a number of cases, deprive him of the right to live in his place of residence. This indicated the state's awareness of the powerful tools at its disposal. Nothing actually changed because of the need to change one's occupation or to move from a plant to an institute, or vice versa. All the institutes and all the plants were elements of the all-powerful State and the rules of order were practically the same everywhere. Figuratively speaking, everybody was sailing in one ship, and though each was free to walk on the deck in any direction, he was always moving in the general direction of the ship's route. Nobody could choose a different ship.[2] We will look at how the sociocultural consequences of forbidding private property for seventy years and the peculiarities of the Russian mind-set reveal themselves in the present conduct of Soviet people.

No Idea of Mutual Benefit

That the Soviets are hostile to the idea of mutual benefit can be illustrated by the following typical reaction of Soviet officials to one of the Americans' undertakings.

Businessman Dennis Sokol is excited about his creation, the American Medical Konsortium (AMK), that plans to create Soviet-American joint ventures producing baby formula, drugs, medical equipment, hygienic supplies, deodorants, and soap. Twenty to twenty-five joint ventures are being planned with AMK, which could radically change the quality of health care in the former USSR. Dennis Sokol is optimistic and is fully aware of the importance of the challenge. He says success in any business depends on determining three elements: personnel, commodities, and profit. Of course, American companies are not in the business just to help the Soviets. They also want profits. The major part of the profit will be reinvested in product development.

Sokol, being a patient and tactful person, is not complaining about the fact that in over two years, the Soviets have not formed the equivalent of AMK. Now they might be approaching the signing of a corresponding document, which is assumed to occur at the yearly meeting of ASTEC (Trade and Economic Council) in May in Moscow. Over 500 businessmen from the United States will be going there. But how much time has been lost? How many projects have not been accomplished? One of the deputy ministers of the USSR Ministry of Health answers the question about the medical consortium by stating: "These Americans want to benefit from us!" But the Soviets must learn how to be motivated by profit, must base their behavior on the principles of mutual benefit in the best commercial sense of the word, to enable their earnings to benefit from joint ventures with the United States.[3] He is not thinking about the benefit he or his organization will derive from the prospective venture, but he is concerned about somebody else's benefit from doing business with him. And this is something he can't live with.

This peculiarity of the Soviet mind-set is one of the major reasons for the negative attitude of both officials and the general public towards middleman activities in the alternative market economy. This accounts for the difficulties of starting and operating a middleman business. The motivation of state structures in restricting middleman activities was retaining their control over the economy. Their leveling mentality could not accept the very idea of a middleman business, i.e., generating profit from something that was not regarded as a job or as labor by those functionaries and bureaucrats. This mentality resulted in the decree of the Presidium of the Supreme Soviet of the former Soviet Union from October 17, 1989, "Regulations for the Activities of Trading Cooperatives and for Pricing the Commodities and Services from Cooperatives." According to estimates by *Commersant*'s experts, this decree caused revenue losses of 340 million rubles for the State. It cost the buyers approximately 1.5 billion rubles quarterly because of the difference between black market and cooperative prices. In other words, the commodities that consumers could have bought from cooperatives were bought from the black market.

Every TZK (trading cooperative) purchased agricultural, industrial, and consumer products in the market for 1 billion rubles. (Trading cooperatives are not involved in production and are engaged in selling the commodities produced by others.) After closing most of them, the majority of these products were channeled for sale through the black market. The price increase as a result of this meant an additional cost for buyers (taking into consideration the difference between the black market and TZK prices of approximately 1.5 billion rubles quarterly, or about 75 rubles per person. The 1989 earnings of TZK, which employed 69,000 people with salaries of 160 million rubles, totaled 1.5 billion rubles for the nine months before this decision was passed, according to Goskomstat USSR (the State Statistics Committee). As a result of the local "measures," estimates are that in six months, the State will lose about 300 million rubles from TZK profits, and about 40 million rubles in taxes from the salaries of TZK employees. The major motivation while discussing the question of TZK was a battle with those who "are not doing anything and are only engaged in middlemen activity"). Market lows of the consumer deficit occur at different times in various regions of the country. Only mobile trade capital is able to balance regional deficit peaks. It is much easier for trade capital than the state structures to arrange purchases of products by small lots in the remote regions and deliver them to the consumer. In Georgia, for example, the purchasing price for oranges in trading cooperatives was 20 kopeks per kg. The cooperatives purchased everything on site and on more favorable terms. Those who restrict middleman business ignore the fact that a producer need not necessarily be involved in selling his production. In order to deliver it to the consumer, trade capital exists. Its appearance within the framework of the Soviet economy is a phenomenon caused by the actual demands of the producers. That is why all the attempts to fight with trade capital can have only one result at present. The capital forced out of the legal sphere passes inevitably into the black market economy. Correspondingly, commodities sold on the black market are not only considerably more expensive for the customer, but do not provide a profit to the State budget.[4]

Profit Motivation and Satisfying Personal Interests Are Not Related to Professional Duties and Responsibilities

Among the reasons for chronic inefficiencies in the Soviet economy over decades is the lack of private property and the specific way people think because of this. State-owned property has no master, and is managed by people whose interests are unrelated to the condition of that property, and therefore people do not care or take pride in it. For example, in spite of an acute need for hard currency in the former Soviet Union, equipment worth 8 billion converted rubles has been bought which is lying all over the country and is eaten by rust. What does it mean? It was bought by officials of state foreign trade organizations, the former monopolists. Naturally, they paid with money which did not come out of their own pockets and bought it not for themselves, but for enterprises which they often might not have ever seen. They had only a vague idea of whether the equipment they were buying would fit or whether it would function under the conditions of those enterprises. The representatives of the enterprises for which this equipment was bought had no access to the negotiations. What could have motivated the purchase? The Soviet delegation purchasing the equipment might have been welcomed in a foreign country and wanted to repay the invitation and hospitality. Or, they might have wanted to play up to the authorities, or accomplish some other political objective. Equipment and supplies were purchased by individuals who had no stake in the negotiated deal, no investment in the outcome, or pride and interest born out of ownership.

Two examples illustrate this. In February of 1975, the Council of Ministers passed a ruling allowing Novomoskovskbitkhim to produce synthetic detergents. The firm Minvneshtorg-USSR purchased the technology from Sumitomo Corporation of Japan for more than $40 million, including technical documentation, equipment, and the components for an extended warranty period. Documentation was completed in June 1980, and the equipment was supplied in August 1981. The terms of the contract included thirty months' warranty period starting from the date of the last supply of equipment. The warranty expired in February 1984, but it wasn't until March 1989 that the first production line was put into operation.

The following is a typical example of Soviet lack of interest and indifference. The Belgian firm Aveve, involved in the production of frozen strawberries, signed a contract with the Soviet Union to supply equipment for the year-round growing and freezing of strawberries, at the rate of five tons per hour. The State allocated hard currency to buy the equipment and insisted that the enterprise had to be in Estonia. In spite of bureaucratic procrastination and the inconvertibility of the ruble, the Belgians decided to proceed with the project because they believed in perestroika.

The Belgians delivered a turnkey production line, and the president of Aveve was ready to clip the logo of his firm to the location of the firm's new facility on the map when an electrician, whom nobody knew, generated a short circuit, and the entire industrial strawberry center, stuffed with expensive Belgian equipment, burned to ashes. According to the president of Aveve, Van Rompui, the worst part was that the construction was not insured. The Soviets had to pretend that the event was really something extraordinary for a Soviet enterprise, although it is actually very typical.[6] Such a disinterested attitude had been overwhelming before, but now that the market economy has emerged, it is changing in some measure. The following example, cited by the newspaper *Izvestiya,* can be interpreted as an illustration of not only lack of business motivation, but the replacement of business interests by personal interests, in this case, by trips abroad. Business discussions are typically aimed at concealing their personal interests and justifying their actions through lying and subterfuge.

A Spanish company producing franks sold in half of Europe offered free products for tasting in St. Petersburg. According to the president of the company, they saw the franks only once in St. Petersburg, not in a store, but at the Kirov Meat Processing Plant. The director of this plant went to Spain several times to meet with his prospective partners who were willing to conclude an agreement on supplying the equipment, revealing their know-how, and training groups of Soviet specialists and workers in the country. He was accommodated in luxury hotels, taken on tours around the country, and shown everything. Spanish media reported about the big deal being contemplated. The protocol of intent to form the joint venture was ready, the only thing left to do was signing the agreement. The Spanish partners were willing to start production immediately, that is, to supply the equipment, reveal all their production know-how, and train a group of specialists and workers in their country. But after the Soviets saw a highly automated plant in Burgos, which had been built the previous year, they rejected the first modest version of the deal in favor of the same kind of plant. The Spanish agreed, warning that it would cost more and require currency investments from the Soviet side. St. Petersburg representatives promised to think it over and left without signing the agreement. After waiting for an answer, the president of the franks company left for St. Petersburg. The Soviet plant director insisted that the Spanish partners should invest in the joint venture and the Soviets would pay them back later. The idea that capitalists were expected to invest their own capital in the project without unequivocal agreement about the profit they would receive was astonishingly naive. The director formally stated that instead of being eager to help, the Spanish wanted to benefit from the Soviet troubles. The Soviets went to Madrid again and signed a nonbinding protocol of intent. But when the time came to give their final answer, they balked. One of the Soviet director's statements was that, purportedly, Soviet people would not eat Spanish franks because they had a low meat content. He also demagogically justified the lack of results of his trip by pretending he was developing a strategy for indigenous meat processing. He also stated that in other countries he was given technology, while in Spain, company officials were only interested in setting forth their terms and conditions.

One of the Soviet officials told us, "A result does not mean anything; it is the process that matters." What he meant was that before signing a contract with a Soviet partner, Western companies interested in moving a project ahead normally invite the Soviets to visit their company, give them souvenirs, and so on.

It should be noted that from January to October the director of the Kirov Meat Processing Plant made seventeen foreign business trips, each one lasting an average of one week, totaling 119 days. It means that for almost four months out of ten, the director was absent from the plant. Over all this time, an agreement about the formation of a joint venture with a foreign firm had not been signed. The trips abroad gave this director an opportunity to bring souvenirs and to enjoy the hospitality of his foreign partners. He was also pursuing his personal interests, such as his desire to be perceived as a progressive boss active in establishing business relationships with the West and able to boost production at his enterprise at the cost of Western investors.

This story gives rise to many questions, the first of which is: What impression is being formed abroad about the Soviet entrepreneur?[7] There are some other questions too. Does the would-be buyer really intend to make a purchase or is he just pretending he is going to make a deal in order to be able to go on trips abroad? How should foreign partners regard the requirements for negotiated products and technology: perceive them seriously and consider this useful information, or try to understand that the Soviet counterpart is not serious and is discussing the matter for his own personal ends?

Successful companies overcome difficulties like this through their personal contacts in the former Soviet Union. Through these contacts foreign companies can receive leads regarding the best way of dealing with their Soviet counterparts. In order to motivate people who can assist them in overcoming a lot of difficulties, it is necessary for a Soviet to be involved in the arrangement as a partner and not as an employee. According to the opinion of the French businessman Viktor Loshak cited by the newspaper *Moskovskie Novosti,* if a Soviet is an employee, you may pay him as much as 100 rubles, 200 rubles, or even 2,000 rubles (and after liberalization of prices and with increasing inflation, 20,000 rubles), and his performance will still be poor, because any money for him is unearned money. The amount of a salary is not perceived as the result of his own efforts. Employees perceive any payment as something taken for granted. The sum of the payment might also cause feelings of envy or resentment between the employee and his neighbor.

A representative of a big state foreign trade organization, trading natural gas, told us that big American companies often underscored the significance of good personal relationships with Soviet officials who make decisions about accepting a project from this or that company. Americans commonly make the mistake of believing that because a company has a good reputation, high visibility, and substantial financial resources, its project will be preferable to the Soviets than projects offered by small and mid-sized companies. To support his statement, he told about a time when he was invited to the United States by one of the biggest oil companies. He received a daily allowance of twenty-five dollars per day, but on another business trip, while dealing with a far less-known, mid-sized company, he received seventy dollars per day. His opinion about an oil giant was that by dealing with them he got no benefit but only headaches.

Lack of Initiative

Soviet officials of state foreign trade organizations try to avoid responsibility in decision making. Soviet bureaucrats believe that: "A decision which has not been made is not dangerous," or, "To make a decision means to decrease by 50 percent the probability that you are right." Bureaucrats also say: "The safest answer is no answer at all." The slogan of the bureaucrats is:

- Don't think
- If you think, don't say it
- If you say it, don't write it
- If you write it, don't sign it
- If you sign it, reject it.

Soviet officials are not fully confident of their own power. They are afraid of making mistakes and engendering a negative reaction from their superiors. Americans often complain about the fact that they can't find out who decision makers are—where can they find a precise answer? Many deals are discussed, and when they sign a protocol of intention, everything seems in order; then, everything gradually unravels. What is behind these scenarios?

*   *   *

Initiating a possible agreement on a joint venture means that you are a progressive boss, a progressive director, and that you understand the goals of new policy. During a recent business trip to the former Soviet Union, one of the authors met with the representative of an All-Union scientific organization whom she had met previously while he was on a trip to the United States. The purpose of the meeting was to follow up on an initial discussion regarding a possible joint project. Upon entering his office, her attention was directed to a large board upon which hundreds of names and organizations were noted, all purported to be "joint ventures" which were under way, and prominently displayed so his superiors would know exactly how many contacts had been made. Whether the "joint ventures" ever materialized was clearly secondary to the recognition he received for establishing contacts. But actually fulfilling an agreement involves the risk of failing, losing your job, or your trips abroad.

An interesting example comes from the story told by Richard Parker, an economist and journalist specializing in Eastern Europe and the Soviet Union, about a retired Los Angeles businessman, Harold Willens, who had an ongoing interest in East-West affairs. This is how he went about learning more about the work of his Soviet counterparts and overcame the lack of initiative on their part:

> With glasnost and joint ventures all the rage in Moscow, Willens wrote a letter to a Soviet newspaper which said simply: "American business-man available to consult to Soviet enterprise without charge." The letter brought 4,000 replies. Sifting through the responses, Willens settled on a brassiere manufacturer in Moscow (he had once been a clothing manufacturer in California). Arriving at the Cheryomushki Sewing Factory late one summer afternoon two years ago, he was shocked at what he found. The plant itself was huge, employing more than 2,000 workers. It had been built a half-century ago and showed little sign of maintenance or repair in the intervening years. But inside the plant the equipment was relatively new, two to ten years old, and for the most part in good condition. Over the next two weeks, as Willens and several associates he had brought along spent time with managers, book-keepers, shop foremen and workers, talking through interpreters, the scope of the plant's troubles became clearer. As with almost all Soviet enterprises, the appropriate Ministry determined labor and material inputs and set production goals. The factory obediently churned out 22 million bras each year and turned a profit on the books by selling this product back to the Ministry. The problem, though, as Cheryomushki's veteran manager, Lyudmila Plachunova, explained it was that Soviet women wouldn't buy the bras. Production was, in the Russian phrase,

"For the warehouse." The Soviets were being forced to import bras from the West. Willens decided that a little market research was in order. He conducted an American-style focus group. Among the seventeen women who gathered at the first meeting, there was initially a lot of nervous laughter at the sheer novelty of being asked what a consumer might want. After an hour or so, though, reticence gave way to candor. None of the women was wearing a Soviet-made bra. Fewer than half believed that the Soviets could make a bra women would want to wear. Back at the plant, senior staff told Willens they thought they could solve the problem if only they could import some foreign-made lace that would soften the feel of their product. But their Ministry, short on hard currency, prohibited it. It was much more important, the bureaucrats insisted, to focus on output. Seven minutes per bra was the new work norm decree.

Willens met with officials in the Ministry and realized that skepticism was the kindest word to describe their feelings toward Westerners. So the American decided he needed to demonstrate the solution on his own. Willens decided on a blind test, a Soviet lingerie version of the Pepsi challenge. Through a friend who owned a successful brassiere company in the United States, he arranged for the manufacture of one-hundred bras using precisely the same specifications and the same materials that the Soviets used, down to the thread, but including the imported lace the Soviet factory manager wanted. He also had the Soviet factory make a hundred bras with the imported lace. Willens then deliberately mislabeled fifty of the American made bras as Soviet and fifty of the Soviet bras as American, and distributed all of the bras among a new group of Soviet women, who agreed to return three weeks later to discuss their opinions of the "American" and "Soviet" bras they had been wearing.

Packaging beat product: Bras labeled American were the women's favorite; bras labeled Soviet were the subject of general derision, whether in fact they were Soviet or American made. The results made clear to Willens and his associates just how deep a prejudice Soviet citizens hold against the products of their own country. . . . He feels that the Soviet people he worked with have learned something important, while he himself has a new understanding of the difficulties Soviet industry works under and a newfound respect for its capacity.[8]

Form over Substance

The attitude of "form over substance" is illustrated by the following exercise conducted during a training program. A drawing of a fish was shown to the participants under which was written a "bird." We asked the participants of the experiment to correct the mistake. Instead of crossing out the word "bird" and writing "fish" they tried to modify the drawing, adding elements that would make it similar to the "bird." This is one of the basic characteristics of bureaucratic conduct to attach more significance to the words than to reality when words conflict with reality. The behavior of the three categories of participants differed in the degree of formal approach. Among the functionaries from the state ministries, the most form-oriented responses were observed. Among the directors and managers of enterprises the tendency was noticeable. The least form-oriented responses came from the representatives of the alternative economic structures.

Americans generally have no idea what motivates a purchase by the Soviets. Decisions that appear to make no sense and are, in fact, completely absurd by Western standards, do have a rationale from the perspective of the Soviets. The following is a case in point:

After the warranties had expired on some Western equipment parts, some of the parts needed replacing. The Western company proposed to sell these parts to the Soviets, for a total cost of several thousand dollars. Instead, the Soviet foreign trade firms bought eight new machines, spending hundreds of thousands of dollars in order to break them down into the separate parts which they needed. For Western businessmen this seems like a ridiculous decision. Why weren't the separate parts bought for $3,000 instead of new machines costing several hundred thousand dollars used for the parts? The reason is that the state foreign trade organization has a plan which envisions a specific amount of trade for a year. Three thousand dollars is a small sum, which does not make a substantial contribution to fulfilling this plan (besides, concluding a contract worth several thousand dollars, with all the many related issues, can be as time-consuming as making a deal worth hundreds of thousands of dollars). In order to purchase separate parts, the foreign trade executives would have to find out whether they fit the machines which broke, and most importantly take responsibility for deciding on their appropriateness. The Soviet obsession with following orders, which has been shaped over many years, is directly related to their fear of making the wrong decision. Just to buy the very same machines in which the parts had to be replaced could avoid making a decision about the fitness of the separate parts and therefore avoid taking responsibility. Moreover, they make their contribution to fulfilling the trade plan on the trade scale. So while the decision seems irrational to Westerners, it allows the Soviets to simultaneously avoid the risk of making a bad decision as well as contribute towards the fulfillment of the trade plan. While nonsensical to the Western mind, it provides a rational option for the Soviets which is totally unfathomable to others.

The typical tendency of the Soviets to be obsessed with following orders is directly related to their fear of making the wrong decision. If they are only doing what their superiors have ordered them to do, they cannot be blamed when things go wrong.

The following example about an extreme case of formal mechanisms operating in all spheres of life, even in matters of life and death, comes from a story by Eduard Polyanovski: In the village of Stolpische, in the Mogilyov region, some women discovered a live military shell in a beet field. A tractor driver put it in his truck and took it to the village. At the village store he met the safety engineer. The safety engineer said when he was giving his account of the events: "I went by bicycle to the collective farm's office and called the Kirovsk Regional Division of Internal Affairs, who said they would come immediately. I returned to the shell and waited." The sergeant of the militia related in his testimony what had happened: "I called the Military Office and spoke to an officer. He told me to go to the village and settle everything myself. I answered that I was not a field engineer."

It takes fifteen minutes to get from the regional center to the village. An engineer was waiting for one hour and then two hours. Collective farmers who were passing by again called the militia. The sergeant of the militia in turn called the Military Office and field engineers. When it became dark and it was understood that nobody would be coming, the sergeant of the militia took the shell into his car, went to the collective farm administration's office and threw it near the border of the flower bed. In the morning he asked the administration workers to take it with them in case they were going to be going to the regional center. It was a Friday and in the Military Office no instructions had been written to the field engineers. Saturday and Sunday passed. Only on Monday did the Military Office put together the papers for the Military Division to attend to the shell. But on that day, there was no typist to type them. On Tuesday, the papers were typed but there was nobody to sign them because all of the officers were at training. On Wednesday, the Chief Commander of the Military Office signed the papers and they were sent to the Military Division. At the same time a letter to the militia was written to authorize a cordon around the shell. It takes about five minutes to walk from the Military Office to the militia office, but the Military Office mailed the letter, taking five days to get to the militia. The commander of the militia endorsed the letter for the militia men to follow the order. The secretary put the order into a folder, where it remained because the precinct militia man was on vacation. The message from the Military Office came to the Military Division earlier than to the militia, but again it was Friday and the weekend was beginning. The paper was not registered. It was not shown to the commander and then it was misplaced. The paper did not reach the field engineers.

The shell was originally found on October 12; a frost set in on the twentieth, and the flower bed became bare, allowing the shell to be easily seen. At lunchtime on the twenty-sixth, again a Friday and the end of the week, three children, aged seven, eight, and nine, were coming home from school. There was no one in the administration office. The children saw the shell, picked it up, and threw it on the concrete porch. Immediately after the explosion, militia men, field engineers, and regional authorities came. The next day a fire engine came to hose everything down. In the morning the mothers of the three dead children put flowers on the asphalt. Several years later there was a TV announcement regarding another bomb that had been discovered in the Gatchinsk region. The Military Division had been notified twelve days before, but nobody came. The next morning, the anchorman said that during the night some calls came in indicating that there were about ten bombs in the same region, at three dacha lots. The military men were advised about this two months ago, but they are still lying there. These explosions may or may not happen; such is our life.[9]

Another example highlighting these issues comes from E. Velichko, chief bookkeeper of the Trams Administration:

> I (the chief bookkeeper) was assigned to account for the year's activity. . . . But the problem was, what should I go with. No record has ever been mailed to us. I did everything in the way I got used to doing it for twenty years' work in the system. When I found the room I needed I saw five people and each one was accepting only one form. I had thirty forms and all of them were for different divisions! In despair, I asked one of the employees to help me figure out what to do. Looking at my forms he told me: "This is not the form you need. This form is not completed correctly. This form must be completed now. This form is not completed correctly. This form must be completed now. This form must be submitted, but we have no blank forms and we have no directions." And then luckily I met a colleague from a neighboring city. He gave me the form which he completed with his own hand; stamped it and got the signatures of the officials. I took this form to an office where I could get on my knees, put the abacus on the floor, and completed the form, having first erased the figures of the neighbor's enterprises. Greatly relieved, I took this account to the head of the division where I was held up by the crowd, which wanted to do the same. The head of the division was not in a hurry to look at the results of our work and asked me to come back tomorrow. The second, third, and fourth division head also put off our meeting until tomorrow. In the morning it all started again. Some officials accepted me right away. But with others I had to force my way

through a living wall of colleagues four times, and then the chief book-keeper wouldn't look at me, though I was looking into his eyes like a loyal dog. When the time came to go home I left without having ob-tained his signature.[10]

The popular catch phrases, "I need verification that you need verifica-tion," "You are worth something only with the proper paper in your hands," are a good satire on this kind of bureaucratic conduct.

Many years of totally regimenting production in agriculture have created an almost insurmountable obstacle for doing real work. It has been estimated that in agricultural management there are twenty-three steps in an administration ladder—from the highest managerial posi-tions to farmers. Huge amounts of paperwork serve the purpose of hiding lack of professionalism. The State Control Committee checked on how enterprises under Ministry of Tractor and Agricultural Ma-chine Building have to complete 159 forms with a total number of 117,000 indices in order to put together their reports. In general, 1,200 people from this industrial sector with wages totaling 2 million rubles were engaged in collecting and processing additional data. The worst thing is not even the waste of money but the impediment which those piles of paper create for doing actual job.[11]

In a country where there are formal but unrealistic requirements for output, production is not consumer-oriented, i.e., in conformity with customers' needs and market shortages of products of certain type and quality. It is instead oriented towards all kinds of formal quantity in-dices. This orientation can be illustrated by the following three exam-ples of the consequences of this type of production evaluation for an economy. They are cited by the economist Otto Latsis:

- Only 40 percent of the energy potential of the 300-hp giant tractor, Kirovets, is utilized in the collective farm system. Simply speaking, these tons of iron damage the fields and are not needed by collec-tive farmers. On the other hand, small one-ton tractors are badly needed. But the industry is not in a hurry to reorient itself and make customers pay for more expensive and less-needed technol-ogy. Machine builders agreed to develop a new tractor, yet they did not want to meet this goal through retrofitting existing plants, but demanded an investment of about four billion rubles for the new production.
- The United States produces ten times fewer grain harvesting com-bines, but considerably more grain is harvested in the United States than in the former Soviet Union. American agriculture also has

enough machines for timely harvesting, up to ten days. In the
former Soviet Union they are always short of combines. The major
reason is well known: Soviet combines are worse than American
combines in every major way; however, the low technical level and
low quality are made up for by quantity, resulting in useless machinery requiring a lot of fuel.

- Transportation of one million tons of merchandise in containers
  and not in railway cars saves about 3,000 tons of metal, 200 cubic
  meters of timber, and provides 20 million rubles profit due to the
  increase in labor productivity while loading and unloading. Under
  present conditions, the life of some enterprises, industrial segments,
  and entire regions hinges on this. Merchandise also arrives more
  safely in containers. Plans for converting from railway cars to containers fall through every year. Thousands of empty containers lie
  for months in the ports. Twenty percent of them need fixing and
  nobody is going to fix them. Sometimes a damaged container is
  loaded and sent on another road. With such maintenance, there are
  not enough containers and more and more are produced, using a
  lot of metal.[12]

Research conducted by the sociologist Dr. L. Khotin gives one more
example of absurdities associated with devising production plans. In an
interview he asked the former chief engineer of the Construction Administration if he had personally participated in putting together the
plan for his organization. The respondent answered that even though
his organization had a Planning Division he had to do this. He just
couldn't stay out of it because the Planning Division dealt with con-
forming to approved standards but he, as chief engineer, dealt with
reality. In a second interview, Dr. Khotin asked the manager of another
plant whether he believed the Soviet statistical figures on profits from
inventions. "I would never believe them," he said. "They are nonsense!
Ninety percent of the proposals for inventions are thrown away. I used
to be Chief Engineer. I was only interested in fulfilling the given plan on
inventions . . . couldn't care less that they were thrown out (after being
accounted for)."[13]

Leveling Down of Wages, Parasitic Existence, and the Attitude toward Business and Business People

The following metaphor by the Soviet economist V. Kulikov gives an
illustration of state paternalism, which destroyed the natural links between labor and profits and has reflected upon people's way of think-

ing. The existing economic system is only familiar with two arithmetic operations, subtraction and division, resulting in the principle "At first we 'undress' an enterprise and then we think how to 'dress' it." This principle is not metaphorical, but quite realistic. To work efficiently becomes unprofitable. If you give more to society, you will have more taken from you, so the result will be the same. Because the consideration of production efficiency has been ignored for many years, it was felt that to suffer losses was not so bad. The State was not supposed to leave you in trouble and you were supposed to receive the same amount as everybody else. But the natural results of labor and profits are destroyed. Practicing this kind of philosophy for many years distorted people's ideas about social justice. In Soviet society there are many people in whom the leveling mentality is deeply ingrained and it can be observed by:

- the negative attitude towards high income regardless of its source
- the wish to receive a guaranteed income
- the importance of reallocating existing resources, but not increasing them.

Requirements of this kind were included in the pre-voting programs of a number of candidates for the people's deputies of the USSR, who reflected the sentiments of certain groups in the society.

An understanding of social justice has been distorted along other lines, too. In the public's mind social injustice is related to what is known as the "parasite inclinations." Under the conditions of central management, the "top" must financially support its decisions. People have gotten used to relying on the State for fulfilling their needs. The popular saying, "Everyone loves the tree that shelters him," highlights this attitude. If expectations are not met, it is perceived as a violation of the idea of social justice. Parasitic tendencies are pervasive in all spheres of society, from the individual to enterprises, segments of the economy, and entire regions. People quickly get used to receiving income without earning it, and this applies to both individuals and entire collectives at all levels.[14] The leader is always concerned with the well-being of his people. And people think: "If the leader is thinking about me, I do not need to think about myself, and I won't need to feel guilty if incorrect decisions are made." Therefore, the thinking goes, it is good for a man to have somebody who will advise him on how he should act, who will take the responsibility off of him. One must pay for freedom with anxiety and fear. Soviets are not used to paying and are used to everything being given free. And that is why many people, however paradoxical it might seem, are against freedom.

In our studies we attempted to find out what qualities in people have been either encouraged or suppressed over more than seventy years of Soviet domination. Though officially just the opposite may have been declared, the actual qualities fostered in Soviet employees were the following:

Encouraged	Suppressed
1. obedience. 2. submissiveness 3. servility 4. following directions from "above" 5. compliance with commonly accepted standards, modesty 6. fulfillment of the "letter of provisions" without penetrating into the substance. 7. putting ideological dogmas above economic reasonableness 8. results justifying the means (such as coercion, limited freedom) 9. sense of social dependence, parasitic existence, inertia.	1. expressing one's own point of view (particularly when it differs from the opinion of superiors, officially accepted point of view), new, non-traditional ideas 2. ability to think along legal lines (following legal norms, notwithstanding directions from "above" which violate them) 3. independence which might go against directions from authorities 4. creative, enterprising spirit, aggressiveness, initiative, risk taking

As the new economic structures emerge they stimulate such new qualities as initiative, risk taking, having one's own point of view, etc.

We conducted a survey among the directors and managers about their opinion of ways to encourage employees to work better. They pointed out that in order to create such incentives it is necessary:

1. To provide better living standards (food products, consumer goods which might be available at the plants, assistance in providing housing, recreation facilities)
2. To eliminate leveling down of wages (the system of wages dependent on the end results of the labor), to hold employees accountable for defective products, and to establish no limits on salaries

3. To provide good working conditions, up-to-date equipment, timely delivery of materials, and instruments of high quality
4. To ensure compatibility of the job to be fulfilled with employees' qualifications, to provide a system of professional training and retraining
5. To provide maximum involvement of the workers in the management process, to grant them more independence and allow more initiative
6. To be more concerned with employees' needs, to encourage them to work better
7. To ensure protection of employees' rights and to make information about them available.

We also conducted a survey among the managers of enterprises to find out how these incentives are actually used by managerial personnel. It turned out that within the limited scope available to them, directors and managers are trying to use an incentive, such as providing better living standards. It was done by the majority of the directors and mangers. Only one out of ten used a stimulus such as allowing more initiative.

It can be seen from the following example that there used to be no system motivating employees. Although the authorities give bonuses for each new model of the well-known "Kalashnikov" rifle, discoveries in the military area are not patented, and no fee tied to production volume is paid to the inventor. Kalashnikov just receives small sums for authors' certificates. The bonuses are shared among the employees of his design bureau. He himself has little part of it. He has a small fixed salary, just like everyone else.[15]

Who is impacted by these dynamics of the parasitic mentality and leveling down? First of all, those employees and collectives who are able to give more to society. Parasitic psychology undermines people's labor and social motivation and is an anti-incentive for efficient labor. The paradox is that the system established for imposing strict discipline has led to almost total irresponsibility and enormous losses of working time.[16] An excellent example of the popular philosophy is exemplified in the common saying, "Perfect order creates great disorder."

Ordinary consumers have gotten used to the "ironclad law" of wages and are hostile to something different. When they don't see cheap goods and can't afford to buy expensive commodities, it is only natural that their anger is turned against new businessmen. They feel resentment when looking at the prices, and the smallest pretext is enough to vandalize cooperatives. The high wages of the employees of independent entities, which are higher than those in the state sector, arouse resentment from top to bottom. The new businessmen are working hard to earn their high incomes, but they do not subsidize the ministry, GLAVK, nor anyone else with their incomes either. Compare state and cooperative construction companies: In the state construction company Karelstroi, there are 226 managers for 1139 workers. In the Karelia cooperative Stroitel which generates the same volume, there are fifteen managers for 442 workers. The share of managers' wages in the total salaries fund of the construction company Karelstroi is 27 percent, in the cooperative Stroitel, 4.4 percent.[17]

The very complex process of transition to a law-governed state and a society where commonly accepted ethical values prevail has revealed that people do not respond easily to these changes. The following analysis of this process was published in the journal *Sotsiologicheskie issledovania* by sociologists Vladimir Bakshtanovski and Yuri Sogomonov.

This process has been complicated by a heritage of concepts fostered by years of totalitarian government and a specific ethical background which was behind the administrative-command management system.

These ethics suggested the incompatibility of the market economy with morality, and the spirit of entrepreneurship and initiative with decency. These ethics were based on blindly following instructions from above, servility, unconditional compliance with all orders in an entirely vertical hierarchy that excluded one's creativity, aggressiveness, and ambition and fostered misperceptions about what genuine human values are.

Bureaucratic management ethics instilled a perverted moral logic that facilitated social and economic backwardness. Now bureaucratic management ethics are being forced out by the first shoots of entrepreneurial ethics that suggest quite opposite human values: entrepreneurial spirit, independence of opinion, flexibility and creativity, ability to make decisions, to take risk, initiative, and responsibility. But these new norms of entrepreneurial ethics are confronted with a lot of old moral prejudices.

This encounter shows up in two extreme ethical positions which can be called "market welcoming" (marketphilia) and market hostility (marketphobia).

The ethical principle which is at the basis of the second position suggests that usefulness, the idea of benefit, contradicts morality, and kills the positive feelings of an individual. Those who are hostile to the market state that its adherents have only profit aspirations, that the only value is the size of the profit, that private property alienates individuals and separates them from each other. Among the postulates of this position is also the idea that a market that touts economic freedom is incompatible with true equality. That is why from the point of view of anti-market loyalists the market society is anti-democratic.

For the representatives of "marketphilia," the arguments against the market held truth only in regard to the period of "wild" incipient capitalism, the period of accumulating capital and early industrial civilization.

They contend that modern history shows the hypocrisy of the concept of "labor without reward" fostered by socialist ideology, that this "labor without reward" kills initiative, distorts moral and ethical orientations, and gives birth to a lot of falsifications. They report that under civilized market relationships the seeming incompatibility of spiritual values and material wealth is successfully overcome.

Ethical norms, laws, and rules of the market economy set forth the demands for honesty, decency, and mutual trust as essential conditions for effective business relationships. And this has a favorable impact on the moral health of society as a whole. Competition is tough, of course. But this is play in accordance with certain rules, and public opinion carefully guards how the rules are followed.

In the opinion of market adherents, it is being equally poor that leads to the crisis and perversion of public moral values.

The process of transition to relationships determined by market forces and the formation of new ethics essential for the new economic structure and overcoming this split in the public consciousness are intrinsically connected.[18]

The consequences of fostering poverty and sacrifice in the country are shown in an analysis by the historian A. Kiva. A willingness to rise above poverty has always been criminal and resentment has been fostered not only towards the rich, but also towards those who are doing well. The philosophy of "purifying poverty" has become an important element of public consciousness. Add to this a careless attitude toward labor and the result is the prevailing crisis in the economy. However, this is also a consequence of despair, when citizens have no opportunity to contribute something reasonable and rational to the process. Receiving unearned money, on the one hand, and mismanagement on the other, generates a desire for leveling, for a parasitic existence and social envy. It has also generated a willingness to distribute the material wealth created by somebody else. These deeply engrained traits cultivated by the socialist order are reflected in several popular Russian sayings, such as "The smallest thing of your neighbor always looks big," and "The eyes of an envious person see too far." It is fertile soil for seeding a military communism mentality. Stalinists managed to cultivate "a new man" with a dependent way of thinking, without a distinct civil position, who does not fit into a highly efficient system of production. This is one of the most serious crimes against the people of which the ideologists of military communism can be accused. The people, however, turned out to be exceptionally stable and capable of self-renewal. Many people have managed to save their own personalities.[19] According to one of the leading Soviet economists, P. Bunich, "If an American makes little money, he is not satisfied with himself and does his best to make more." The American expression "keeping up with the Joneses" (or the attempt to live at least as well as one's neighbors) is in contrast with the Soviet mentality which spies on one another to make sure somebody doesn't have an extra chicken to eat.[21]

In summer and autumn of 1990 in six agricultural regions of Bashkiria, the Center of Sociological Research under the Soviet Sociological Association conducted a poll aimed at determining the attitude of farmers to the alternative economy and the new problems associated with it.

When farmers were asked about their attitude to alternative economic structures if they existed along with State and collective farms, 87 percent of the respondents were in favor. Four percent were unsure, and 9 percent were against. The last group believed that the collective farm was the only acceptable form of agricultural production. About 40 percent of those who were polled admitted that it was possible to start farming on their own but only 10 percent were ready to do this immediately. On average they would like to take 20–30 hectares of the land and 20–25 head of cattle.

The rest of the would-be farmers (about 30 percent) were more cautious about the possibility of starting to farm on their own. They believed that it was too risky then when many problems existed concerning technology, transportation, and fuel. An impediment to introducing the new economic structures into agriculture was also a subjective factor, i.e., a very negative reaction by some parts of the rural population to the possibility that some of their neighbors might have a sharp increase of their income. This negative attitude is a result of many years of indoctrination by a leveling ideology. In the opinion of 39 percent of respondents, this might seriously deter the development of an alternative economy in agriculture.[21]

Recently, an American consultant visited a Soviet paper plant and said he had an idea which would enable the plant to produce twice as much paper in the same amount of time. As compensation, he wanted 10 percent of the surplus product. The reaction to his proposal was interesting. Nobody was interested in his proposal which could lead to increased production. Instead, everybody began to count up how much the American could make as a result. A Soviet man's attitude, which has been instilled over more than seventy years of Soviet power, is not to let your neighbor do better than you. The slogan of the October Revolution was not "There Shouldn't be Poor People," but rather "There Shouldn't be Rich People." There is also a Russian fable about a man who caught a goldfish. The goldfish asked what wish the man would like granted, and the man began to think. But the fish said, "Remember, whatever you want, your neighbor will get twice as much." And then the man said, "Stick out one of my eyes."

> As the well-known Soviet political scientist, A. Izyumov, writes in the magazine *Moscow*, Soviet people just don't like the rich. In fact, there are few places in the world where the wealthy are hated as intensely and by so many people. Not long ago, the Soviet pop star Alla Pugachova was involved in a minor incident with the administrator of a St. Petersburg hotel. Both ladies let off a considerable amount of steam but it was no real hassle. Yet when the press got hold of the story, newspapers were inundated with letters, all supporting the hotel administrator, even though no one actually knew any details. Interestingly, what readers suggested as punishments "to teach the singer to behave well," included rehousing her from her large apartment to a small one and making her live on an average Soviet salary for a couple of years.

The rich and famous in the Soviet Union don't need news articles to find out how people feel about them. In a recent interview, a newly elected beauty queen confessed she was receiving a stream of hate mail. The most widespread example of how Soviets feel about their luckier compatriots is the hostile attitude towards cooperatives. Resentment at the higher incomes of cooperative employees and complaints about high price and poor service, which are often valid, promptly led to calls for a total ban on cooperative activities. All too often this call is translated into action, and cooperative premises are vandalized. In some extreme cases, employees have been beaten up and even killed by angry mobs.

According to A. Izyumov, envy of wealth among ordinary Soviets has a solid economic background. Historically, Russia was always a widely polarized society consisting almost entirely of the extremely rich and the extremely poor, with very little in between. The middle class, which makes up a stabilizing majority in Western societies, hardly exists in the Soviet Union. According to demographic experts, the Soviet middle class makes up about 15 percent of the population, while the figure is around 60 to 70 percent in the West. About 80 percent of Soviets are poor and around 5 percent are wealthy. The Soviet dislike of the rich is also rooted in history. Russians just don't like the rich, but they never did, and for very good reasons. The Russian rich long ruled the poor with a ruthlessness that could hardly have endeared them to people who were, in every sense, oppressed. Serfdom was only abolished in Russia in 1861. The poor's response was frequent revolts, killing their landlords, and hatred of the rich. Orthodox religion did not do much to promote wealth as a positive aim either. In contrast to the West, where the Christian ethic endorses hard work and does not condemn the resulting accumulation of wealth, Russian religion glorifies poverty, urging charity along with abstinence and asceticism. The traditions are packed with fairy tales and stories portraying the poor as positive heroes and therefore role models, and the rich as cruel, stupid, and otherwise negative characters. From Stalin's time onward, Soviet citizens were imbued with the ethic that getting rich was morally unacceptable and, in practical terms, almost impossible.[22]

Business Conduct Distorted by Totalitarian Mentality

Attitude to Power: The Feeling of Anxiety and Uncertainty While Interacting with Various Types of Power Structures

When we asked representatives of the alternative economy about their relationships with the authorities, we thought of the following analogy which illustrates their attitude to power. They were like teenagers who are eager to be emancipated from their parents. If the lack of adulthood, their position of being like a child in their relationships with authorities (parents) had caused passivity and fear of power before, now a lack of adulthood reveals itself in juvenile rejection of parents' authority, subconscious rebellion, and aggressiveness towards power. We saw that this position had serious negative consequences for doing business. Instead of admitting that there is power on one side and individuals on the other, each with rights and responsibilities, Soviet business people often do not try to establish productive interaction and avoid cooperating with authorities.

We conducted several interviews with very experienced directors of large industrial enterprises, who have worked for many years in various segments of the economy and regions of the country. Our aim was to understand the sources of anxiety towards authority, and its impact on how they conduct business. In particular, we asked them to recall situations in which they felt threatened or which threatened their business. There appear to be two reasons for deeply rooted anxiety in Soviet managers. We became convinced that the most important characteristic of operating Soviet organizations is the non-continuity of authority.

Newly appointed managers are not responsible for fulfilling obligations generated from the decisions of their predecessors. There are also no distinct boundaries between personal and business spheres. Soviets tend to establish personal relationships and then build business contacts on that basis. The major impact on decision making by state bureaucrats is through personal contacts, not regulations, provisions, and business considerations. This attitude is illustrated by popular Russian sayings, such as "It's better to have a hundred friends than a hundred rubles," and "Do this because of our friendship, not because of your duty." Therefore, on any given day, an enterprise may be deprived at any moment of financial resources, new equipment, or supplies, just because the specific Ministry official who promised it all has been replaced. A situation which threatens a director of an enterprise even more is the ministry official who, due to good personal relationships, shuts his eyes to the director's violations of regulations, and the director doesn't know how the new official will respond to those same violations. One of the directors of a food industry enterprise in Moscow complained to us: "I just established contacts in the ministry and with suppliers. Someone has been replaced and everything fell through. Before I establish new contacts, the enterprise will be in a furor, won't be able to operate normally, and we won't know where we are."

This feeling of constant anxiety is the reason why Soviets who come to the United States can be identified in a crowd on the street. It applies even to those who are adequately dressed and have been abroad many times. This anxiety causes serious difficulties for American businessmen entering into contacts with Soviet representatives.

During videotaped simulated negotiations with subsequent tape analysis, we saw that there are two types of reactions of Soviet representatives to their inner anxiety:

- They "show off" before the representatives of American companies, demonstrating to everyone that they have many possibilities, broad contacts, and no difficulties.
- They keep the actual state of their affairs in the dark, and don't give away any information.

Both types of behavior interfere with the ability of foreign partners to evaluate the commercial risks of embarking on a joint business venture. We attempted to explain to our Soviet clients who try to show off for Americans that they are mistaken if they think they can resort to the same techniques when dealing with Western businessmen that they would with the commission coming to control their enterprise. We attempted to make it clear that by not informing their partners about potential difficulties they increased the uncertainty of the existing situation, hampered their planning, and risked negative evaluation. Our advice to those who are trying to keep everything in the dark is that during the course of negotiations they must articulate what information they are *not* able to provide and what issues will take time to explore.

The roots of totalitarian thinking have been analyzed in the well-known book *The Way to Understand Stalin* (H. Kobo, ed.). Under a totalitarian regime, power turns out to be a super value. A person in possession of power has everything: luxury, servility of those who surround him, the opportunity to express his opinion on every occasion, to have his whims catered to, and protection from suspicious enemies, whereas if one doesn't have power, there is nothing: neither money, nor security, nor respect, nor the right for one's own opinions, tastes, and feelings. Everything that a person can attain, he attains from power. The talented scientist can do scientific work only if he becomes the head of the laboratory or director of the institute. A good worker, doctor, or scientist can make a little more money only by special permission from his authorities and much more only if he becomes a boss himself. The apparat bureaucrat understands pretty well that in order to live better he needs to occupy his boss's position. Any other transfer will mean a decline in his well-being and lower self-respect. One of the many paradoxes of totalitarianism is that being in possession of everything, the owner of the power has nothing of his own. The luxury, house, car, dacha, and food allotments don't belong to him but to power, and if he loses power, he loses all the things of value that are significant to him. He has no friends or relatives.

There is a story about Stalin's secretary, Poskryobishev, who, himself, filed an arrest warrant for his wife. When he came home, he found an unknown woman with whom he then lived for the rest of his life. Everything a man treasures is exchanged for power.

An important attribute of the totalitarian society is control over all spheres of life without exception. Not a single sphere remains untouched by the pursuit of power. Everything is X-rayed by it and is embraced by its tentacles. There is no opportunity to evade the state's control, neither over friendly intimate relationships, nor over personal tastes, opinions, and habits.

Many potential projects have died just because the corresponding agencies could not guarantee 100 percent control. The existence of something beyond control or under partial control is, in itself, an insult to power. Totalitarian power exaggerates the significance of all of its functions and mystifies the means through which power is exercised.

The party functionary has gotten used to attributing the agrarian achievements of his region to his skillful leadership, though this might be the region where the climate is better or available land is more accessible. From his standpoint, there is nothing that occurs by itself without the intervention of power and its all-encompassing control.

The continual reorganizations of agriculture are based on the steadfast faith that power is able to directly influence the objective processes of interactions between humans and nature. Where reorganization did not provide improvements, failures could be explained by subjective factors, such as lack of organization, lack of enthusiasm, or sabotage. The failure of an experiment designed to deny the fundamentals of genetics was even explained by a lack of belief in its success.[23] When asked in an interview with the newspaper *Argumenti i Fakti* about what factors contribute to shaping totalitarian political orientations, the first, according to the psychologist Gozman, is "the peculiarities of our history. There are no examples of its development without authoritarian rule."[24]

When transformations in the society had led to looser control of power and less regimentation in all spheres of life, the power structures, which had gotten used to authoritarian means of ruling the country and had no skills in exercising control through democratic institutions, felt frustrated.

Analyzing the position of an individual under a centrally managed system, the well-known economist P. Bunich comments that workers under such a system were pawns, with no economic independence. Therefore political freedom is non-existent. That social order was sustained by people, who longed to obtain wealth, not to create it. They identified and associated with those who have blindly adjusted to hierarchical subordination. Under this system, everyone was transformed into an impersonal entity. Catch phrases originated which reflect this position, such as, "Let our superiors think. They are the ones with the big salaries," and "Their business is to think, our business to live and wait." Soviet employees actually could not change their activities. They had only a nominal right to choose their jobs. In reality, it was not so. Until recently, millions of people have worked like prisoners. Collective farmers were deprived of their passports, without which they couldn't go anywhere. The forced labor of students, scientists, and engineers engaged in harvesting and working in vegetable warehouses and repairing railways is still being used.[25]

Of course, the fact that there is no more Politburo in the country inspires optimism. But decision-making procedures have to a large extent retained their old stereotypes and routines. The authoritarian style of working out the decisions on various levels has sociocultural roots which are not easy to eradicate. The reflections of Boris Yeltsin about the meetings of the Politburo of the Central Committee of the CPSU, where the major decisions in the life of the country were made, show very well the conditions under which the Soviet style of running the government and economic management was developed.

When Politburo sittings were conducted by Brezhnev, decrees were normally drafted in advance and everything was settled within fifteen to twenty minutes. Objections were asked for. There were none. Then the Politburo was dismissed. Under Gorbachev the proceedings were quite different. Politburo members gathered in one room. Candidates for membership to the Politburo, followed by secretaries of the Central Party Committee, waited in line in another room, i.e., the conference hall, for the appearance of the general secretary. The others followed by rank: Gromyko, Ligachev, Ryzhkov, and so on, in alphabetical order. Everybody sat down at the table at an appointed seat. Then the issues on the agenda were discussed, for example, appointing a new minister. The candidate would come up to the rostrum and would sometimes be asked a few questions. The questions were insignificant, as a rule, only asked to hear the sound of the candidate's voice, rather than to figure out his standpoint in relation to an issue or problem. Sometimes Gorbachev talked with the would-be minister before the meeting, but sometimes there was no preliminary discussion and the candidate was just called to the meeting. Normally, appointing a new minister took five to seven minutes.

The sittings were held each Tuesday. The distinction between these two party bodies, the Politburo and the Council of Secretaries, was quite conventional. When the issues discussed were important, joint meetings were held of the Politburo and Council of Secretaries. On the surface, they appeared to be held in a democratic manner. But actually, the drafts were worked out by the party apparatus and they passed in a vacuum divorced from real life and lacking awareness of the actual state of affairs.

The ritualistic methods of these meetings were in direct contrast to the conflict that Boris Yeltsin began to raise. Yeltsin remembers how the reprisals were aimed at him. He was called directly from the hospital to the plenary meetings of the Moscow City Committee of the Communist party where he was dismissed. By itself, it was an extraordinary action to call a person from a hospital sickbed to the meeting. Chief party bosses were sitting in the presidium, he recalls, and the rest of the participants of the plenum were looking at them obediently, obviously scared. The plenum proceeded to commit murder with words, although it was incomprehensible why it was necessary to arrange all that when it was possible to just dismiss him by the plenum. As soon as they were given an order they were ready to betray their colleague Yeltsin, just because they were scared not to obey. Because they couldn't reason and had no arguments, they resorted to conjecture, demagogical statements, and outrageous lies.

Analyzing the behavior of the people surrounding him after his dismissal, Boris Yeltsin came to the sad conclusion that the souls of the people became irreversibly distorted over those "black decades." It seemed to him a circle had been painted around him and nobody dared to cross over it or to approach him. The worst part was that it had happened not only to the people who turned into obedient servants, but also to "normal people," who always seemed scared of something. Many turned their backs on him. Among them were those who once pretended to be his friends, but who only needed him when he was a big boss. In Yeltsin's opinion, the rank-and-file party functionaries would hardly ever act with an independent mind. Subservient and compliant behaviors were rewarded with special privileges: By health care not accessible to ordinary people, by exclusive restaurants and opportunities to buy good food, and by transportation. The higher one was in the hierarchy, the more privileges were available and the more painful it would be to lose them. It was not uncommon, for example, for a secretary of the Central Committee of the CPSU, or a member of the Politburo, or a candidate for membership, to be alone on an airplane, apart from an escort of security men and a service staff, whose only job was to make sure their boss's wishes were met. What was incredible was that these privileges did not belong to anybody personally. All amenities, dachas, good food, comfortable hospitals, even the part of the beach to which ordinary people had no access, belonged to the system. The system granted privileges and could take them away.

A man who moved up the hierarchical ladder of the system was granted his first level of special privileges. With one more step up, the level of privileges was higher, and so on. Then this man began to think of himself as an important person, eating food that other people could only dream about, vacationing where other people were not even allowed to come and touch the fence. But he did not understand that the privileges belonged to the position that he occupied and not to him, personally. If he was not loyal to the system, somebody else would occupy his position. Nothing belonged to an individual under the system. Stalin perfected this mechanism to such an extent that even his colleagues' wives did not belong to them, they belonged to the system. And the system took away the wives of Kalinin and Molotov, who didn't dare speak a word about it.

Times have changed, of course, but the bottom line is the same. A certain number of privileges are given to the position. But, in every privilege there is a seal of the system, so that a man will not forget that he is a pawn and all of this does not belong to him.[26] On the one hand, many privileges have been eliminated. But the old mentality continues to reveal itself under new conditions. It can be seen, for example, in the process of dispensing new privileges. The suggestion of one health-care official to grant special privileges to doctors who participated in the defense of the "White House" is a case in point.

Simplification of Reality—Making Simple Decisions

We were amazed at the naive ideas many Soviet business people had about business mechanisms and production management. They do not begin to understand the actual level of complexity of those processes with which they are dealing, resulting in disastrous economical, environmental, and social decisions. In the course of our research study, we became convinced that this decision-making style had been shaped over many years of total control in the political and economic organization of Soviet society.

In order to study the degree of simplicity and complexity of the Soviet's vision of the world, we conducted a series of three experiments:

We asked participants to think about the foreign partners with whom they have met and to divide the total number of partners, for example, 15, into groups of three people each. We asked them to compare the three people in each group and single out the criteria which distinguishes two partners from the third one. In the second series of experiments we asked them to divide their fifteen subordinates at work into groups of three and make the same comparison. In the third series we asked the directors and managers to recall the elements of their business communication in the course of the day, i.e., what they do in terms of interaction with other people, such as conducting meetings, participating in meetings, accounting for their work, going to workshops to talk with lower-level managers, and talking with senior authorities or others about personal matters. These elements were also grouped into threes. In each series, the participants' simplified vision of the world was common.

Actually, Soviets most often see their foreign business partners in terms of their usefulness to themselves individually (whether or not they are comfortable in business dealings with them, whether these contacts improve their standing with authorities, or provide an opportunity of going abroad), and not in terms of their usefulness to the organization or company. This usefulness was treated within the general context of the inextricable link between their personal and business life. The concept of the reciprocal usefulness of mutual benefit was most often missing. They differentiated among the partners, indicating they were preoccupied with insignificant, irrelevant, superficial indicators, such as whether the partner invited him to his home country or the partner came to the Soviet Union to negotiate. One comparison was "This partner made concessions and these other two were difficult to deal with."

The same simplified approach could be observed in the way many directors and managers related to their subordinates. With the beginning of perestroika in the Soviet Union there has been much talk about the importance of the human factor, about attention to the individual, to his personality and his needs. In reality, however, all of this is still ignored. It is ridiculous to talk about an individual approach when directors and managers, as a rule, differentiate among their subordinates on a limited number of characteristics. For example, one director talked a lot about human issues, but when his assessment of the characteristics was analyzed it appeared that all the subordinates were divided into two groups: "ours—not ours," "reliable—unreliable," "obedient—not obedient." Some directors might say that employees must be creative, must take initiatives, and be aggressive, but when asked about the differences among the employees, they could not identify these characteristics as important in assessing personality strengths. The following matrix analysis was conducted on characteristics assigned to the subordinates. The participants were asked to compare three people in each group and single out the characteristic which distinguishes two of them from the third one.

The analysis showed that very often many personality traits ascribed to them correlated with only one trait. For example, if a person was marked in the matrix as "efficient," it turned out that he also received the marks for being "cunning," "obedient to the superiors," "stupid," and "undependable." The director might use various appropriate words while describing the efficient employee, but actually subconsciously "efficient" meant for him subservient, cunning, lacking initiative, and not very smart.

The same kind of simplified, undifferentiated attitude can be seen in breaking down the elements of business communication. One director of a State foreign trade organization described in detail his daily communication, but in actuality, all that he was doing was listening to his superiors and giving orders to his subordinates. In the matrix analysis the elements of communication were matched against the characteristics of these elements. In principle everything in his interaction with his authorities correlated with the element "listening" and with the category "speaking." He would talk about the democratization processes in management, about waking up the initiative of employees, about suggesting innovations to higher-level management, but the actual activities he engaged in were listening but not talking. An amazing contradiction can be witnessed here: a person might set forth some suggestion and at the same time psychologically the bottom line of what he is actually doing is listening and being sensitive to the reaction of the authorities. One example of the simplified picture of the world is the centrally planned economy and the unprecedented level of concentration in the production of certain commodities at a few enterprises by monopolists. The statistics that illustrate this point were published by the magazine *Deloviye Lyudi/Business in the USSR.*

The average number of industrial personnel employed by a Soviet enterprise totaled 800 people in 1989. Meanwhile, in the Western European countries, Japan, and South Korea, this index did not exceed 80–90 people. Such a high level of concentration of the labor force and industrial capacity primarily within big enterprises has resulted in narrow technological specialization and led to a monopoly of production and management. As was shown by a number of industry surveys, almost 2,000 kinds of 11 billion rubles' worth of commodities are produced at one enterprise.

According to these sources, in the case of 219 large categories of commodities one huge enterprise provided more than 50 percent of the total production volume. And as for 215 products, the single, big enterprises monopolized 100 percent of the total volume of production. Therefore, more than one-third of the most important machine-building products are produced at one enterprise and the same part is produced at two. For example, almost every one of 11,000 varieties of bearings is produced by the single, absolute monopolist. Now 96 percent of diesel production is concentrated at the industrial conglomerate "Voroshilovogradteplovoz," 100 percent of sewing machines at the Podolsk plant, 100 percent of film projectors at the industrial conglomerate "Lomo," and so on. The dependence of the economy and individual customers in their operations on one enterprise can be easily traced.[27]

The Proportion of Industrial Enterprises with the Number of Personnel
Exceeding 1,000 People
(the numbers are given in percent)

USA	USSR
Industrial enterprises	
0.5	17.3
Industrial personnel	
25.2	74.6
Relative net production	
31.6	74.5

Absolute Monopolists

Enterprises which are the only producers of the given type of commodities in the USSR	Level of supplying the demands of the market (in percent) (a rough guide)
1. Kirovogradsk seeding machines industrial conglomerate (Ukraine, Kirovograd). The seeding machines are for beets, vegetables, corn, hayrick	Beets—80 Vegetables—80–90 Corn—90 Hayrick—15
2. Kharkov bicycle plant (Ukraine, Kharov). Bicycles for sports and tourism	20
3. Research and Manufacturing Conglomerate "Svema" (Ukraine, Sumsk region, Shostka). Color high-sensitive film	50
4. Volzhsk Industrial Conglomerate "Khimvolokno" (Russia, Volgograd region, Volzhski). Textile synthetic fiber	90
5. Petrozavodsk machine-tool construction plant (Russia, Karelia, Petrozavodsk). Wood processing machinery for production of parquet	20–40

Absolute Monopolists (*continued*)

6. Industrial Conglomerate "Donetskgormash" (Ukraine, Donetsk region). Lifting machines for mines	90
7. Kambarsk machine-building plant (Russia, Udmurtia, Kambarka). Narrow-gauge diesel locomotives with a capacity of over 150 horsepower	100
8. Machine-building plants named after Dzerzhinski (Azerbaijan, Baku). Deep capacity pumps	100
9. Nesvizhsk biochemical plant (Belarus, Minsk region, Nesvizh). Bacterial fertilizers	100
10. Yasnogorsk machine-building plant. (Russia, Tulsk region, Yasnogorsk). High-pressure pumps for pumping water out of mines[28]	90

It is easier to perceive the mind-set of managers and officials if we consider the specific conditions under which it has been shaped over many years of Soviet power. According to the mayor of Moscow, Gavriil Popov, who reveals the essence of monopolism, the logic of administration requires not only central control but also absolute concentration of responsibility. Elimination of duplication is one of the administration's major concerns. In this administrative system, specialization of production results in economic monopolies: in ministries and committees, in the system of enterprises, and in the regions. As a result, it is decided that the country should have one airline—Aeroflot, and in the Ministry one administration body, with one research institute under it. Every problem must be concentrated in one hand. In each neighborhood there should be only one school, one drug store, one bakery.

In practice, in every segment of the Soviet economy, Popov continued, one monopolist or another is operating. The monopolist is protected on all sides by the state order, all kinds of norms, and so on. Administrative monopolism results in deficit and bad quality. But if this monopolist becomes economically independent, his entry into the market without permitting competition and lifting price controls will result not in market prices but in monopolist pricing. In practice, the conditions for price inflation will be created. It can easily be foreseen that this absence of control will have no less negative consequences in the sphere of scientific-technical progress and consumption than the present administrative-bureaucratic monopoly. Therefore, in Popov's view, transfer to a truly free-market economy would be impossible without a consistent policy of demonopolizing the economy. Demonopolization must create the situation of competition and the market.[29]

By developing a system of total control in all areas of life, and the economy in particular, central management provided a simplified framework of reality, and, as a consequence, simplified solutions. If the center makes decisions on all problems in the life of a society, no intellectual resources will be enough to take into account the entire complexity of all the facets of real life. An example of the way decisions were made is seen in the anti-alcoholism campaign. A very complicated problem, having deep roots in Soviet society, was "cured" by restricting the sale of alcoholic drinks. Naturally, the campaign was unsuccessful and had very negative consequences. While the Soviet economy was relatively simple, such an approach worked to some extent. This was during the time when it was necessary to concentrate all resources and labor on the construction of the three "most important" plants, or the atomic bomb, or bringing hundreds of thousands of people together and giving them spades to dig a canal. Though economic life is much more complicated now, the typical problem-solving style of the Soviet leader remains the same.

As soon as the political situation is aggravated and society is confronted with the necessity of bringing about economic transformations, the minds of many functionaries, bureaucrats, ideologists, and analysts turn towards the customary clichés of the enemy image. Political labels like "sabotage" and "conspirators" become common again. Allusions to the scheming of external and internal enemies, who through their intrigues help the country choke in the daily morass of political and economic troubles, again lead to the simplification of reality. The old rage against and the threats towards those who "are not with us" are heard instead of innovative ways of addressing complicated historical problems.[30]

According to the psychologists L. Gozman and E. Etkind, the basic characteristic of a totalitarian mind-set is a belief in the simplicity of the world and the possibility of confining any phenomena to the visual and easily described combination of several elementary phenomena. This belief in the simplicity of the world is responsible for the consequences of disastrous administrative decisions. People who believe in this simplicity tend to evaluate issues in black-and-white terms and neglect the subtleties arising out of complexity. If something is bad, it is completely bad. If good, it is completely good. Therefore, any social event or phenomenon of nature should be either fully supported or uncompromisingly attacked. If the world is simple, it means that the actions aimed at its improvement must also be simple in idea, if not logistics. The problem of lack of water is solved by redirecting the rivers; of the shortage of money, by printing new money; of underpopulation problems by forbidding abortion; of spreading unauthorized ways of thinking by placing those culprits in asylums. The illusion of simplicity creates the illusion of omnipotence. Any problem can be cured. It is just a matter of dictating the right orders. The result is usually the opposite of what was aimed for and the cost of the measures many times higher than the possible benefits. But there is an explanation here: enemies scheming. The simple picture of the world dictates a special way of curing social problems which is consistent with the struggle between "them and us. The one who is not with us, is against us."[31]

We live in a diversified world, but the representatives of conservative ideologies tend either to complicate it or simplify it. If the world is simple, it does not need a sophisticated ruling system. It is only necessary for everybody to work honestly and to have one leader who rules everything. When the world is simplified, the majority of people tend to be conservative in their thinking. For example, it is well known that people who criticized Stalin before the war treated him far better during the war with Germany. Why? Because at that time the world was divided into "our people" and "aliens," and he was one of "our people."

Another extreme perception is that the world is overcomplicated. "The world and its problems are so sophisticated that ordinary people are just unable to solve them." That is why they need a "special person," a leader who always knows what should be done.

Third is a psychological rejection of diversity and the tendency towards unification. Centralization turns out to be the most reasonable system because one center provides maximum unification and all ideals are personified in one person. Thinking along these lines, one proletarian poet is needed, such as Mayakovsky, one proletarian writer, Maxim Gorky, and so on. In other words, it is necessary to have one dominant figure in all spheres and areas. This logic inevitably leads to conservative thinking in most people. A man who accepts such unification of thought becomes conservative in practically all spheres of life. At the level of political conduct, the result is extremism—whether political, cultural, or religious.[32]

One example of simple decisions was the law about mandatory and fairly complex comprehensive secondary education in the former Soviet Union. In one of our interviews, a representative of public education told us that this law completely ignored enormous differences in children's potential to study, their capabilities, and the education children receive in their families before they start their studies at school. The necessity to comply with the law about general education compelled teachers to fake the results of studies, falsify students' test scores, and falsify the average at the end of the terms. For example, during Russian exams almost all the teachers corrected the students' mistakes in the tests, to be able to give them better scores. Furthermore, all the children received high school diplomas even when some high school graduates were diagnosed as mentally retarded when they underwent medical checkups before the draft.

Another negative impact of this process of falsely indicating consistent excellent school results was the distorted performance criteria of teachers, which were institutionalized and existed for many years. The teacher who had more students with high scores in his class and no children doing poorly was regarded as performing well. A very easy way to meet this requirement was to fake students' scores and submit corresponding records to the authorities. A hard-working teacher who really cared about education and the development of his students, and who approached the value of their knowledge and skills realistically, received reprisals from his superiors. On the contrary, a dishonest and irresponsible one was praised. This situation was destroying the motivation of honest and decent teachers.

One of the examples of simple decisions was the anti-alcohol campaign. Boris Yeltsin remembers the anti-alcohol campaign and, in his opinion, it was terribly senseless and pointless. Neither the economics of the campaign nor the social consequences had been taken into consideration. And though the situation was aggravated with every passing day, the campaign continued. It was obvious that deeply rooted habits could not be eradicated just by a policy of restriction. When the sale of alcoholic drinks was reduced, people started to drink all kinds of surrogates. The profit from the sale of alcoholic drinks just passed to the black market manufacturers. The poisoning and mortality rate from surrogates increased dramatically. At the same time, Ligachev was optimistically reporting the success achieved in the battle against alcoholism and drinking.[33]

Ignoring the Changes

In one of the experiments we singled out a number of tasks which directors and managers fulfill in their work in five major areas:

- Their foreign economic relations involvement
- The work in joint ventures and participation in the joint production
- The decentralization processes in the economy
- Democratization and the new role assigned to workers in managing their own affairs, strikes, etc.
- The emerging alternative economic structures and the necessity to consider them in terms of competition, the possible migration of the labor force to the new economic sector, etc.

The people participating in the experiment had to identify fifteen tasks which were supposed to include the ones from these new areas of challenge. If they failed to single out the tasks from these new areas, we added them ourselves. Then we combined the tasks into groups of three in such a way that two of them referred to their former activities and one was from the new area. We asked participants to name the characteristic which distinguished two of them from the third one. Most of the participants did not distinguish the sign of innovation. New tasks were often combined with old ones. For example, negotiations with Western representatives were coupled with the meeting at the enterprise; they together were designated as different from talking with the visitors only by such superficial and irrelevant signs as dealing with the group or with a single individual, although negotiations with Westerners represented a new task and the other two old ones. The typically closed Soviet vision of the world was demonstrated here in the inability to see new developments and in placing them into their usual frame of reference. The simplified picture of the world entails an unwillingness to see and to seek changes. Applying standard answers to non-standard problems arising in new realities inevitably suggests searching for enemies who can be blamed for the social disasters, economic collapse and political impasse.

We participated as consultants in negotiations with leaders of a Soviet industrial conglomerate. At the beginning of negotiations, the Soviets were ready to buy. The price and main feature of the technology appeared suitable, but, as we later became convinced, American representatives might have been the victims of their own sales job. They tried to emphasize how the equipment would revolutionize Soviet production and make it profitable. At that, we noticed an expression of tension on the faces of the Soviets and they expressed frustration to the Americans because their expectations were not being met. For Soviet managers, in dealing with big, successful enterprises like the one they were dealing with, there is nothing more terrible than major changes, because the Soviet, as a rule, is not motivated by increased future potential profit which hinges on these innovations or changes.

We recommended that representatives of the American company change their strategy by making it more in keeping with the expectations of the Soviet side. The Americans then tried to show their Soviet partners that they could incorporate the new equipment with a minimum of major changes and offered their practical assistance in doing this. They also shifted the focus of their proposal by emphasizing a lower price than that of their competitors, as well as dependability, installation, and maintenance service. Here, an important trait of Soviet managers generated by the totalitarian society emerged. Many of them exhibited a typical inability to make decisions which are adequate to a complicated and constantly changing reality. Even the need for minor improvements is ignored.

In 1983, a St. Petersburg social scientist was excluded from the party because he conducted a poll among the workers on the topic "Are You Waiting for Changes?" The question about change was a violation itself of a silent agreement between the holders of power and society which had gotten used to each other. Everything in the status quo is reasonable. The best news is no news at all. All the elements of social life, leaders, institutes, structures, norms, and styles are cast in concrete. Discoveries are not introduced. Inventions are secret. The system of passports ties people to their place of residence and the law regulating labor favors those who have been in the same working place for a lifetime. The stability of prices and profits is promoted as the highest achievement of leaders.[34] Belief in an unalterable world generates distrust of change. According to Boris Yeltsin's evaluation of how decisions were made, not a single, critical situation had been anticipated and prevented. Every dramatic situation (the new laws, Nagorno-Karabakh [a regional republic area involved in ethnic unrest], the independence of the Baltic Republics, and others) first came to a dead end, then reached several poorly derived decisions, and, only after many losses was there an attempt to cure the problem.[35]

The Hope of Wonders, Relying on "Avos"

To a great extent, the isolation of the totalitarian mind-set reveals itself in a belief in the miracle properties of the world. A. Platonov, in *The Juvenile Sea,* painted a comprehensive picture of the world where miracles come true, something emerges out of a void, and the relationships between cause and effect are destroyed by submitting to the will of enthusiasts. Shepherds, who do not even have nails, build a wind-generated electrical power station in the desert. It is built through a miracle and designed to work wonders. Only in this way is it possible to fulfill the meat and milk production plans which are so out of touch with the real world that the plant itself is a wonder. "Wonderplanning" was a typical practice in Stalin's five-year plans. Russian fairy tales are full of stories in which magic and "magical thinking" result in good fortune for the protagonist.

Unrealistic plans were amended by decreasing the numbers, so that after failure the achievement of success could be declared. It was in the vital interest of power to create a cult of technology while being engaged in industrialization. Magical properties were assigned to the wonders of progress. These magical properties were designed to justify all at once the investments which were exceeding all reasonable boundaries. Ordinary technical developments of the twentieth century became sacred objects, having direct links with the greatest sanctuaries of the cult of power.[36]

The belief in "The Wonderworld" has subtle aspects which have not yet been realized. In many ancient cultures great significance was attached to the name of an idol. Some people believed that uttering the name of the devil gives power over it. Other people, on the contrary, believe that security is guaranteed by silence; the non-uttering of certain names and words. The idea is that a word can change reality. Surprising enough, we come across similar things in everyday life. Keeping silent about some plots and the obtrusive repetition of others reflected a primitive belief on the part of those who were in charge of propaganda, that frequent use of certain words influences citizens more than everything that they observe.

The Soviet people are waiting for quick, magical decisions which will solve all their problems at once. Practically everybody is ready to believe any magician, any wizard. This readiness to believe has its historical roots in three old superstitions to find: (1) one medicine that can cure for all diseases, (2) one man who knows the answer to every question (either a czar or a ruler for "all times and peoples"), and (3) one or several guilty ones. How wonderful life could be! One could just take a drug, follow orders and directions, and eliminate the guilty ones. It is hard to understand that people do not believe that decent and honest cooperators exist who produce commodities and services which are worth billions of rubles. At the same time, they believe television healers. According to the press, one famous television healer earned 300,000 rubles in Volgograd for one performance. However, this is considered to be honest money, not like the earnings of cooperators or leaseholders.[37]

According to Yeltsin, it was a tragic and comical situation when Gorbachev visited the VAZ automobile plant in Toliatti, declaring that the Soviet Union would become the trendsetter in the automobile industry in the near future. Newspapers and television were ready as usual to pick up this new slogan calling for new achievements. At the same time, the experts were ashamed and horrified. To make such a statement meant he was absolutely unaware of the situation. This is totally characteristic in a country where any nonsense originating from leaders is passed along as the height of wisdom and insight through the excellent propaganda machine.[38]

The Old Mind-set under the Changed Political System

Many changes have occurred in the Soviet Union, particularly since the attempted coup of August 1991 failed. Many new radicals have come to power both before and after the coup. But the sociocultural specifics of Soviet society and the Soviet people have persisted so that even with the new progressive tendencies in the society those deeply rooted traits continue to manifest themselves in the very people who are supposed to introduce the innovations.

Trips abroad have always been the most powerful driving force for people who have some access to this privilege. According to the newspaper *Chas Pik*, there was tension among the members of the various Deputy Commissions of the Leningrad City Council at that time concerning specific opportunities to go abroad and arising out of their positions and the obsession with this desire. There were those who felt hurt and offended that their intellect and energy had not been fully used in the commission's foreign trade activity. These personal grudges were vented against the chairman of the commission in their intention to re-elect him. The eagerness to make a trip overseas by any possible means is exhibited in the "sample of diplomacy" below, a letter from one of the people's deputies of the City Council:

Dear Mr. Mike Purey:

I recalled with pleasure our meeting on the 14th of November 1990 in the Red Room of the Leningrad City Council when I received your fax message from 26.03.91. The political and economic situation in our beautiful Leningrad is very complicated but the Leningrad City Council has full control over the situation . . .

The complex process of privatization of trade enterprises and restaurants is now under way in Leningrad. This is the economic and political backdrop for development of foreign economic ties between Leningrad and the countries of Western Europe, England included. Your fax message of 26.03.91 made me think again about the best ways for developing cooperation with the counties of Northern Yorkshire and Cornwall in Great Britain. The best and the quickest way of promoting mutually beneficial ties is, in my opinion, personal contacts. If there is an official invitation in my name for the Leningrad City Council from officials and authorities of Cornwall county to visit Cornwall and Great Britain for the purpose of establishing business, cultural and tourist ties between Leningrad and the county of Cornwall, Northern Yorkshire and so on, I'll be glad to accept this invitation for this spring or for the beginning of summer.

Many proposals from Leningrad enterprises and organizations regarding setting up mutually beneficial cooperation in the areas of tourism, joint ventures, and hotel construction were addressed to the Permanent Deputy Commission on Foreign Economic Relations and to me personally. We would not like this significant economic potential for foreign economic ties and goodwill of the prospective partners to remain unused.

In case I make this visit I am willing to meet with municipal councils of the countries, to participate in business contacts and seminars, and to make presentations about the situation in Leningrad and Russia as a whole. If there is a Rotary Club in Cornwall, I would be glad to visit them too.

Yours sincerely,

People's deputy of the Leningrad City Council
member of the Commission on
International and Foreign Economic Affairs[39]

V. V. Chervyakov

The failed coup in August 1991 and the victory of democratic forces gave a powerful impulse to the transition to a market economy and the general democratization of the society. The very behavior of the citizens who courageously rallied support of the "White House" during the coup and the morale of the Soviet army testified to a certain shift in the mentality of the people.

But on the other hand, in interviews taken after the coup, many Soviet and American business people admitted that despite changed conditions familiar behavioral stereotypes are being reproduced. It is characteristic, for example, of bureaucratic conduct which exhibits the same old traits in spite of the changing business setting and obvious shaping of a "free market" mentality. These old traits reveal themselves in the bureaucratic desire for concentration of power, for keeping people dependent on them, for being surrounded by staff selected not on the basis of merit but for being loyal. The old tendency of closing access to necessary business information has also remained.

Such manifestations of the old mentality as idealization of a leader, spreading a lot of myths and legends about past success, the desire to obtain positions and privileges, servility, and search for enemies are also present. In our interview the director of an enterprise complained that he is now afraid to reprimand his employees because they might square accounts with him by denouncing his sympathy with the putschists. An old anecdote has become popular in the former Soviet Union. "At the meeting of the collective farmers people expressed their willingness to re-elect their chairman on the grounds of his unscrupulous behavior; at the expense of the collective farm he built houses for himself, his son, his son-in-law, bought cars for him and members of his family, expensive clothes and jewelry for his wife. Then one wise old man takes the floor and says: Why should we do this? The old chairman has already obtained everything at our expense and the new one has nothing as yet and we will be ripped off again."

A director of a joint venture told us about his acquaintance who was one of the first to get out of the Communist party and one of those who rallied support for the "White House." He was an advocate of enterprises' independence from central control. But after he had been appointed to one of the key positions in the Russian Federation's Parliament, his behavior changed abruptly. He made up a coterie of his deputies and unapproachable secretaries and deliberately created lines in the reception hall to his office. His major objective became obtaining his portion of amenities belonging to nomenklatura, such as office space, furniture, and cars. He became self-righteous and rude in his attitude to visitors. He got out of the habit of listening to other people's opinions and became intolerant of their views and ideas. It became typical for him to hide information in order to have control over people to whom such information might be relevant. The most extreme and ridiculous example of this attitude was his behavior as a head of the delegation on a business tour in the United States. He hid information from the members of his group, such as the meal schedule or possible free time allotted for shopping. By using these tactics, he increased the anxiety and frustration that people typically feel in a foreign country.

CHAPTER 6

Discrepancies between Law and Reality

There are businessmen in civilized countries who, because of their eagerness to make big money, violate laws and seek loopholes in them. In the old Soviet Union, the environment was very different. Managers and directors polled in our surveys often mentioned that they had to violate laws every day merely for the sake of more or less normal operations. "You can't drive straight on a twisting lane." There is a popular Russian fairytale which vividly illustrates the predicament of honest people having to operate under laws which change very rapidly and are not enacted in the same way as in a law-governed society: "If you turn right you'll lose your horse. If you turn left, you'll lose your kingdom. If you go straight ahead you'll meet your death." People's daily routines sometimes lead them into predicaments where they have to do things for which they can literally go to jail or their enterprise won't operate. It is in bypassing the laws that the creativity of responsible and decent Soviet managers often reveals itself.

We believe it is no exaggeration to state that in those fortunate cases where an American businessman has found a really motivated partner who is concerned with the interests of his enterprise and the state, this businessman might be dealing with a gangster, though a noble one. An American businessman is dealing with a very specific type of person, one who is operating under such conditions that he is able to make a socially useful contribution basically only through daily violation of the law.

As one of the Soviet representatives of joint ventures said with frank self-criticism: "One of the typical prevailing traits of all Soviet people, not just managers and executives, is that they do not have a sense of legitimacy deep in their soul. The circumstances under which those people operate daily invoke the situations where their creative energy is aimed at law violation. Under this distorted structure the borderline between legitimate and illegitimate, between good and evil, tends to be obliterated." An American partner encounters this typical feature of Soviet business people, both in minor things, such as being late to meetings or not answering letters, and in more serious ones, such as non-fulfillment of contract terms. Analysis of our survey findings showed that successful companies can achieve positive results in dealing with the Soviets and have them fulfill their long-term contract obligations only by taking into account this sociocultural context of their business performance and the restrictions which the Soviet reality and the Soviet bureaucratic structures impose on them. Of primary significance is understanding that personal preferences outside the business and professional realms, not laws, rules, and provisions, determine in large measure the way people conduct their professional lives.

One of the objectives of our research was to confirm our hunch about one possible reason American businessmen fail to start businesses in the former USSR: The underestimation of the considerable discrepancies in business law regulations between the two countries.

How are laws, resolutions, and departmental instructions on the one hand, and real business practices on the other, related? Why do they differ? How must these differences be taken into consideration by American companies when doing business in the former USSR? When these issues were discussed in the interviews, interviewees reported various reasons for discrepancies between the laws and reality most often related to the following points:

- the actual contents and wording of the laws
- bureaucratic concerns about violations of laws and instructions
- multiple departmental instructions and barriers to implementing laws
- transformations at the local authority level
- arbitrary resorting to punitive measures
- legal nihilism and ignorance of laws
- laws, rules, informal contacts, bribes, and the black market.

We shall consider each of these points in detail.

1. The Actual Contents and Wording of the Laws

Most of those interviewed admitted the progressiveness of the laws and resolutions which granted enterprises the right to engage in free international trade, legitimized privatization, permitted the creation of independent economic structures and the establishment of joint ventures. At the same time, those participants polled pointed out that the laws themselves contain euphemisms, and even have apparent contradictions in the way they are formulated. (For instance, at the time when private property was still not allowed, in the Law on Ownership adopted at the beginning of March 1990, the term "the property of the citizens" was used as a euphemism instead of the term "private property.") These contradictions reflected the struggle between progressive and conservative forces and were the result of compromise between them. This example is also interesting from the perspective of the history of allowing private property, of the gradual transformation of the legal basis for its introduction, and of the compromise achieved at one of the phases in the process.

Enterprises and cooperative heads thought the laws ought to guarantee that rights granted today would not be revoked tomorrow. The December 1989 amendments to the law on cooperatives, which gave local officials the authority to limit cooperative activity substantially, served as an alarming example. The amendment's sponsors justified these restrictions by pointing to the public outcry against cooperatives. Directors of joint ventures, and not only those which were established by cooperatives, find this ability of the bureaucracy to base its actions on public dissatisfaction disturbing. An example of vague and contradictory drafting in the past was the well-known USSR Law on Ownership, authorizing citizens to own capital goods and hire employees, but declaring impermissible the "alienation from the workers of the means of production," and the "exploitation of man by man."

Summarizing the interviews on the contents of the laws and the ways the texts are worded enabled us to identify five reasons for discrepancies between the laws and reality:

1. Vague, contradictory, inconsistent formulations
2. Dependence on the laws on ideological trends and tendencies
3. Isolated lawmaking, divorced from international legislation
4. The conflict between laws which had been centralized and the republics, between the republics themselves, or between the republics and their autonomous territories. According to the prognosis expressed in the interview, this tendency will be increasing.

5. The instability of laws which are unclear and change from day to day.

Many years of existence under the "iron curtain," and seclusion from the rest of the world, generated disagreement between some areas of Soviet jurisdiction and international laws and norms. For example, the generally accepted legal framework for international business and property is missing in the Soviet legal system. Furthermore, some provisions in Soviet law contradict GATT rules and the accepted norms of the European Economic Community. There is also a difference in the generally accepted treatment regarding certain concepts such as "leaseholding property" and "commercial bank." For example, according to Soviet jurisdiction a "commercial bank" is a "non-state bank." Also, as "stockholding" is universally accepted as the way of managing and disposing of property, under Soviet jurisdiction "stockholding" is a variety of property.

According to the opinion of the deputy chairman of the Legislature Committee of the Supreme Soviet of the former Soviet Union, K. Lubenchenko, the lawmaking activity of the deputies in the Supreme Soviet of the country may be compared with attempts to grow a garden in the desert. Sometimes, it seems that the laws worked out by Soviets are pushed out in the same way as seedlings not accepted by soil. We are confronted with a contradictory situation. New laws are required from the deputies and, at the same time, the legislative acts adopted at three sessions of the Supreme Soviet of the former USSR are either not enacted at all, or are not fully enacted. The fundamental, systemic laws about land, property, leasing, or strikes, are not becoming norms of life in any sphere, whether economic, political, or social. One of the reasons for this is that when laws used to be ideologically steadfast, the main criterion was whether they corresponded or didn't correspond to Marxist-Leninist dogma. One could hardly say that the laws were worked out through deputies' creative work. The legislative acts were developed by the apparatus. The representatives of the people are only there to approve the legislative acts unanimously. The discussion was a parody of democratic procedure. The desire to regulate social relations from the standpoint of the ideological lawmaker generates totally paradoxical situations where the lawmaker is creating laws behind which there are no realistic conflicts and contradictions. The laws in this case are an attempt to legally formulate the ideological perception of reality. Nobody is able to enact or enforce them because they are dead from the start. There can be no law where the guideline is an ideology, rather than reason, common sense, or society's expectations.

The absence of more or less clear and reasonable guidelines in law-making and distinct boundaries between the legitimate and illegitimate is found in many Russian proverbs, such as, "The icon and the shovel come from the same tree." Lawmaking activity is also hampered because it is carried out hurriedly, which results in strange situations. An example of discord in lawmaking may be found in passing the law about secession of the republics from the Soviet Union by the Supreme Soviet. A referendum was set forth as the main provision for this. But the law about referendums had not been worked out and was not even on a future agenda. At the same time, the issue of secession was in the forefront of events in the country.[1]

The American lawyer Alexander Papkakhristu discusses the major shortcomings of the Soviet legal system in the context of the existing discrepancy between laws that are being adopted and those which have existed before. He comments that every new law has little connection with the preceding decrees. Almost nothing is said about how the new law would be adjusted in the existing system or alter it. There is an impression that every new law is adopted in a legal virgin land, and that its articles and paragraphs have no precedent. Thus, the law about taxes on the income of enterprises adopted in the summer ignores the law about stockholding companies which had been approved in spring. Normally, only the decree about enforcement of this or that law points to the necessity for coordination between the old and the new norms, but in reality, this coordination is not provided. In the current process of lawmaking, no attention is paid to the laws which existed before perestroika, though the latter are formally valid, and often include provisions that contradict the "new laws." For example, the law about joint ventures says that the wages and labor terms are determined as a result of negotiations. But the labor law code guarantees various rights to the employees. The new legislation needs codification, or at least a system of indices. At present, every law appears and operates on its own.[2]

How vague and inconsistent formulations appear in the text of laws can be illustrated by a typical discussion in the Soviet Parliament. The following statement was proposed to the Parliament for discussion and adoption: "To consider the accelerated transition to a market economy the major objective of economic reform."

First, the word "objective" was replaced by the word "contents." Then the suggestion was made to remove the word "accelerated," leaving just "transition." Then, a timid female voice suggested "best of all, 'gradual transition.' " In the draft decree, the suggestion was to reduce the budget deficit through the cost of allocations on capital construction, defense, maintenance of State agencies, and other means. The Parliament members ended up having to do it by capital construction. There were doubts and objections. It is impossible to reduce capital construction in rural areas, though nobody mentioned this. It is impossible to reduce construction at the cost of enterprises, although nobody mentioned this either. In general, one cannot reduce construction. Wording was sought that would satisfy everybody: To reduce the volume of construction from the central resources, to leave everything as it was, but to add "taking into consideration the Central Asia conditions," excluding any capital construction at all. The majority voted to economize in order to reduce uncompleted construction, even though everybody knew it was impossible. Such votes have been taken many times and the amount of uncompleted construction is still growing. If it were possible to reduce the amount of incomplete construction by just wishing, the country would have no problems.

In the streets, on the subway, or in large stores, there are many people who are walking with the general flow of traffic, but are looking in a different direction. Or vice versa, they go their own way, but are looking in the direction in which everybody is looking. They can't understand that one either should look in the direction that they are walking or walk in the direction they are looking. This seems to be happening along the road to the market economy.[3]

In our interviews, we often heard complaints from American business people about being prevented from evaluating risks because of frequent changes in laws. At the same time, Soviets are often well informed about future changes. For example, when the ruble rate against Western currency changed, it turned out to be unexpected for Western businessmen who were engaged in the currency trading business and suffered losses because of these transformations. But Soviet black market dealers involved in currency transactions were well prepared for the reform and generated profits from it. The same can be said about the reform of the 50- and 100-ruble notes. That they would come out of circulation was unexpected by the general public, but the business people were quite well aware of the fact in advance.

A year ago, at an international conference in Washington, Artyom Tarasov, the first Soviet millionaire, jokingly asked serious economists: "Do you know what the difference is between a Soviet and an American businessman? Let's say that they are playing Black Jack (or "21"). The Westerner opens his card. 'I won, I have 21!' The Soviet also opens his card, 'I have a new government decree. The game is continuing now until 23!' " The participants of the conference burst out laughing, but Artyom Tarasov remained grim. He knew very well what was behind the joke. In the opinion of people from the government law enforcing agencies to the public, the image of a businessman as a questionable figure has been shaped by many years of propaganda.[4] Because business and businessmen have been forbidden for many years, they have been under the arbitrary control of the authorities.

Many of our respondents complained about the difficulties confronting them due to the battle of laws between the center and the republics. An example cited in the interviews told about uncertainty regarding authority to allocate resources, about lack of coordination and contradictions in operating the central and republican banking systems, about discord in the activities of the republican foreign trade organizations, and the customs which operated under the authority of the central government. Now that the center does not exist any more, there is no agreement and accord between the liberated republics concerning their authorities and powers.

Here are two examples typical of the confusion of jurisdictions which had existed before the dissolution of the Soviet state. A Leningrad company obtained permission from the government of the Russian Federation to export scrap metal. But customs did not authorize the shipment. The reason for their refusal was that customs, though located on Russian Federation territory, operated under the authority of the central government. One more example. A stockholding company excluded one of its members by a majority vote, a proceeding which was in compliance with the Russian Federation's jurisdiction. But later it appeared that according to central jurisdiction, such a decision required a unanimous vote by partners.

After the failed coup and victory over putschists, the current process of lawmaking is more strongly oriented towards market transformations. And in this regard, certain positive changes have taken place. But the impediments to implementing these laws are still alive because in great measure they are determined by general disrespectful attitudes toward law and lawmaking, which includes inconsistency and paradox, lack of motivation by certain parts of the bureaucracy to decentralize the economy and to actually democratize the political and economic life of the country, and develop private entrepreneurship. Despite new demands to institute new legal policies, the old forms of thinking and behavior are still being reproduced.

One Soviet lawyer compared the legal situation with the big construction sites. Construction materials (laws) are delivered in large amounts in varying degrees of quality from good to poor. But no design or working drawings are provided, and the "foremen" fight among themselves. The highest authorities cannot agree on what they are going to build. The ordinary workers are doing everything but working. The construction site is gradually scrapped.[5]

Analysis of the experience of successful American companies showed that while working out their business strategies in the Soviet Union, they were seeking answers to issues relating to legal spheres, not only in the text of actual laws, but in life, itself. As their practices demonstrated, one of the most important factors in being able to navigate the non-sensical legal waters in business was a close informal relationship developed with Soviet partners. Soviet partners with whom informal relationships had been established and who were able to get around the Soviet business environment and legal system offered significant help by providing information on such critical points as:

- anticipated changes in the law
- realistic new business opportunities which emerge, due to the adoption of new laws
- ways to operate efficiently within existing legal frameworks, in spite of new restrictions which might be imposed
- niches for doing business which have not yet been "found" or touched by the law
- preferred orientations in cases of contradictions between jurisdictions of the countries that made up the Soviet Union and autonomous areas on their territory, as well as in cases of their disagreement with the provisions passed by regional authorities

2. Bureaucratic Concern about Violations of Laws and Instructions

Regarding the adoption of a Law on Ownership, academician A. Abalkin said: "The law is a piece of paper. It is very important to break up the stereotypes of behavior and thinking. Traditions are pulling us back."

Over the years of perestroika, the same problem arose in connection with putting into practice those laws which expand the rights of enterprises in foreign economic activity. Bureaucracy has succeeded in blocking the implementation of progressive laws. Deliberately capitalizing on the law's vague and inconsistent language, the ministerial bureaucracy even after the victory of democracy tries to continue tripping up enterprises with a multitude of instructions (such as provisions for operating inside individual entities, e.g., inside the state committee, ministry, and organizations operating under the state committee or the ministry), catching directors between contradictory obligations. As a factory director from Ukraine described it, "the powers that be will purposefully create a situation whereby any director, in order to keep an enterprise going, has to violate the law." "Where there is a person, there is a law to punish him," has become something of a catch phrase.

While summarizing the findings of the interviews, we became convinced that bureaucracy accomplishes its objective of making everybody feel guilty because of the inevitable violations of the law, and by doing this, seeks to retain its total control in three ways:

1. It sets tasks which cannot be accomplished even if one follows all the laws.
2. It issues contradictory provisions.
3. It restricts information about what laws and regulations operate at any given moment.

We shall now consider examples of specific cases, situations, and episodes treated by the Soviet press.

The former leader of the Soviet State, Leonid Brezhnev, who had been in power many years, said in one confidential conversation in reply to a question about the poor living standard of some groups who received low salaries: "You don't know the life. Nobody is living on their salary. I remember as a young college student we made a little money unloading trains. And what were we doing? Three bags and one box there, one you take for yourself. This is the way everybody lives in the country."[6] In the Brezhnev era the phrase was coined "Everything that is not hidden properly belongs to us." The idea is expressed well in the old Russian proverbs "with loose firewood around even the priest will steal," and "the hand that takes never tires of its work." When the Law on Ownership was adopted, it allowed private entrepreneurship in a certain sense, but on the other hand, it was worded in such a way that according to the well-known Soviet economist Nuikin, "Any leaseholder or farmer who hired his neighbor to milk the cow while his wife is ill could be declared a state criminal if the authorities wanted to press the issue."[7]

In one of the interviews conducted by the sociologist L. Khotin, a former Soviet manager cited an example of the conditions under which Soviet managers operate, saying that they are in a very special position. Normally, they know very well how to bypass the rigid system which is cast in concrete and which can lead to the failure of the enterprise if all the laws are followed. If the manager sticks to the rules, there will be no money to pay the workers and they will quit their jobs. Only the ingenuity of the managers ensures the successful performance of the enterprises.

What Soviet managers are doing has an impact on them. Almost every manager has received reprimands for violating certain rules. For example, the construction company Mostopoyezd was created to build bridges. Many employees in this organization work there all their lives. After retirement they used to have no living accommodations. One senior manager of Mostopoyezd decided in the early fifties to spend resources that had been allocated for the construction of temporary housing on permanent units. Since the end of the fifties he has built eight family brick houses for his workers, which was actually prohibited by law. However, he didn't spend any more money than the others who built temporary housing.

The managers interviewed calculated that over the course of their working lives they violated laws on enough counts to put every one of them in jail for 200 years, even without violations for mercenary purposes.

According to L. Khotin, a Greek communist wanting to participate in the development of communism came to Kiev to live. He was trying to work in compliance with all the technical norms and rules. He didn't know how to work in any other way. While working harder than others, he earned only twenty rubles a month, while the rest earned no less than 200 rubles.[8]

Managers who resort to various tricks and violate the laws, making false reports on the fulfillment of their plan, and providing salaries and bonuses for their employees, may hope that the functionaries of the ministry under which they operate will come to their rescue in case they are inspected or checked up on. In one of the industrial conglomerates engaged in coal mining, the manager discovered that at enterprises which were not fulfilling the plan, phony duplicates of the ore output had been written down in the book. These phony entries were duplicates of the ore that had actually been mined, entered into the books, and was kept in the warehouses. The organization was just faking the entries on ore output. This enabled them to hand out more salaries and bonuses to workers, engineers, and managers. All of this was discovered by the legal agencies engaged in such investigations. But corporate mutual assistance worked this time. The ministry prepared a revision and a control group which consisted of only ministry functionaries who rejected the idea of wrongdoing several times on the part of the organization under their umbrella. The real state of affairs was revealed only when officials from the procurator's office started investigations and put together the relevant documents.[9]

An example from the newspaper *Izvestiya* reports how officials from the City Council used the opportunity to take revenge on officers from OBKHSS (the Division for Protecting Socialist Property). The chief official of the City Division of Internal Affairs (GOVD) applied to the City Council for a footwear order which he told them was needed for uniforms. The City Council granted permission to do this. The boots were received personally by the chief official of OBKHSS GOVD, Farkhutdinov. For some unknown reason, Farkhutdinov did not receive the expected uniform boots from the warehouse, but high-quality imported boots. Having delivered them to the store, Farkhutdinov did not wait for the salesman but started selling the boots himself, thus personally participating in exactly what he was supposed to be enforcing, demonstrating the Russian proverb, "The law is straight but the judges are crooked." At the order of the deputy chairman of the City Council, an immediate on-site investigation was conducted. Some sources said it was initiated to square accounts with Farkhutdinov who was poking his nose into City Council affairs. For example, he had been inquiring why food was sold in the cafeteria of the City Council which was never found in ordinary stores. He was also interested in why high-level officials were buying deficit goods in the stores which maintained services for disabled veterans of World War II and the war in Afghanistan. The chairman of the City Council personally warned OBKHSS not to poke their noses into City Council affairs. Attacks and counterattacks began with both sides harboring grievances about each others' violations.[10]

Engaging in middleman activities in the former Soviet Union, especially export transactions, is a perilous business. Many contradictions and inconsistencies exist in this sphere of the law, and the ideological and political situation is changing constantly. This can be illustrated by Eduard Dolot's story about the perils to which the joint venture Burda Moden was subjected. The German firms, E. Burda and Ferrostal, together with the Soviet association Vneshtorgizdat, founded the joint venture Burda Moden, in order to publish a modern fashion magazine under the same name. The magazine is published in Germany, with expenses paid in marks, and is sold in the former Soviet Union for "wooden" rubles. The plan was to build a printing plant in Moscow over a period of two to three years which would save part of the currency expenses in the future. Under the Decree of the Council of Ministers of the USSR dated August 25, 1987, Goskomizdat (the State Publishing Committee) was permitted to borrow 10 million converted rubles from the bank for eight and a half years, and finance the construction of the printing facilities for Burda Moden. It was a strange decree. Who would pay the loan? If it was paid by Goskomizdat, it would mean that the future printing facility would not be the joint venture's, but the government's property. If the joint venture paid the creditor, it didn't need a middleman such as Goskomizdat. How can a joint venture repay a currency debt if it trades for rubles?

The general manager of Burda Moden, Vladimir Melentyev, says that the government's order was bound not to be fulfilled. No money was allocated for the construction. Meanwhile, the popularity of the magazine required an increase in circulation, increasing the hard-currency expenses. The joint venture had millions of rubles in its account, but all the currency expenses had to be covered by the German partners. A possible way out of this situation would have been for the government to grant permission for the joint venture itself to earn marks. In December 1989, the government granted the joint venture permission to engage in import-export transactions worth 10 million converted rubles. However, in March, several months before, the government prohibited representatives of alternative commercial structures "torgovo-posrednicheskuyu," or middleman activity (this term means that the alternative commercial entities were prohibited from selling commodities which were not produced by them and purchasing commodities and supplies which were not needed for their production). If the joint venture conducted these transactions, it would be under constant threat, or the deal could be annulled. And that was exactly what happened when the newspaper of the Central Committee of the CPSU, *Rabochaya Tribuna* (which called itself "the Newspaper for the social protection of the working people") published an article entitled "A Shady Deal under the Name of Burda." The joint venture was charged with violations, connections with the criminal world, selling foreigners strategic resources, and the country's wealth, in general. Judging by what was written in the article, a lawsuit could be filed against the authorities of Burda Moden. In order to be on the safe side, the joint venture applied to Inaudit, a stockholding company which renders auditing and advisory services to oversee all their economic and financial operations in case they inadvertently violate the laws.[11]

The bureaucracy deliberately obscures certain provisions, will not provide even elementary information, and complicates even the simplest issues by all possible means so that an entrepreneur feels dependent on officials. One of the ways to enforce the dependence of business people and make trouble for them is through the existence of a number of laws and regulations which are designed only for internal application. They are called DSP (which stands for "internal use"). The authorities themselves understand these laws and their operations, but ordinary people aren't aware of them. One example of information in the area of joint entrepreneurship that was not available to the general public, was the minimal amount of Western investment in the initial capital. In order to figure it out, one needed to have the documents which were not available in the regular, formal, registering procedure. According to an American lawyer, it has never been easy in the Soviet Union to learn about its laws, even to see what they look like on paper. Not a single periodical runs full information about current lawmaking and some decrees are not published at all. The major mass media have recently begun publishing laws, decrees, and provisions passed by new independent states. Also, new journals issued by private firms and joint ventures contribute to the flow of information. However, rumors coming from personal and business contacts retain their significance. The lawyer concluded that through rumors, it was possible to learn about the latest measures and about draft laws to be considered. However, because there is no normal procedure for the preliminary discussion of the draft laws, there are often several versions of the same laws which increases anxiety. A year ago, in order to obtain the text of a draft law, it was necessary to show resourcefulness and guarantee anonymity. The major problem now is getting around a lot of information and singling out the authentic elements, if possible. Thus, the number of versions of the law about foreign investments was no less than the total amount of such investments. A more reliable method of collecting legal information has originated lately as lawmakers are more and more interested in advice from representatives of foreign companies.[12]

3. Multiple Departmental Instructions and Barriers to Implementing Laws

The majority of our polled participants didn't speak out against departmental instructions as they agreed they are necessary as additional explanatory documents and that all details can't be specified in the laws or in the resolutions. For example, the necessity to specify statements protecting the government against unfair competition or unjustifiably low prices is obvious. How does abnormal competition differ from normal competition and who will determine whether the prices are high or low? It is not the departmental instructions themselves but their confining nature and ungrounded prohibitions which cause such negative reactions from the majority of the directors of enterprises, cooperatives, and joint ventures.

At the same time, many ministry and State foreign trade organization workers suggested that there had to be even more limitations. Since they are indispensable for preventing errors and abuse by "new participants of foreign trade activity." According to professional foreign traders, many "new businessmen" do not have the necessary experience or special knowledge to conduct business and violate laws, damaging the interest of the country in their quest to possess foreign currency. On the other hand, the heads of the enterprises and cooperatives said "Every day new instructions and resolutions appear and one cannot keep track of them. Many instructions are deliberately hidden so that nobody can know their requirements." This gives bureaucrats the pretext to punish and show "who the boss is" to those who violate the instructions.

The most frequently cited example of bureaucratic interference arises in the context of export licensing. New restrictions are often enacted unexpectedly. Many difficulties exist for enterprises and foreign trade organizations, trying to obtain export licenses, caused, among other things, by bureaucratic procrastination. Often applications for export licenses are denied. It is especially difficult to obtain a general export license designed not for licensing a separate or one-time deal, but for exporting certain commodities for certain periods of time, for example, one year. The logic of those who initiate restrictions on exports may be illustrated by their statements with regard to shortages of certain raw materials and production supplies, as well as the State's consequent inability to fulfill its international obligations in supplying these goods. For instance, while the Soviet government faced the possibility of forfeiting payments on a 2 million ton shortfall in deliveries of coal exports, individual Soviet enterprises managed to export 600,000 tons of coal. According to the opinions of the advocates of strict regulations for export licensing, the lack of control over waste paper and scrap metal exports caused a 20 percent shortfall in the capacities of enterprises for recycling old paper and processing scrap metal. For the sake of getting hard currency by any means, rolled metal is cut into pieces, simply because it is easier to sell rolled metal that has been transformed into scrap metal by cutting it into pieces rather than rolled metal itself.

At the same time, state foreign trade organizations created by the ministries used to enjoy substantial advantages in obtaining export licenses and, in particular, general export licenses. A plant director from Donetsk expressed his opinion about this: "We are compelled to decline exercising the right granted us to engage independently in foreign trade and must conduct business using the foreign trade organizations of the competent ministry." At the same time and particularly due to the restructuring of the economy, enterprises are becoming more independent and acquiring more autonomy from the state. The powerful levers of restricting the independence of enterprises have weakened both in terms of their strength and amount.

From our interviews, we discovered three common obstacles that impede the enactment of progressive laws:

1. Necessary details are not spelled out in the provisions about law enactment.
2. Entrepreneurs are entangled in all kinds of prohibitive provisions and restrictions.
3. Laws and restrictions can be interpreted by the whim of the bureaucrats, and while some laws are enacted, others are ignored.

In some of our interviews, senior managers of enterprises told us that over the entire perestroika period ministry foreign trade organizations that wished to retain their monopoly interfered with the enterprises' foreign trade activity. They picked on the texts of the contracts, pointed to the errors, and by doing this, implied that all the enterprises' foreign economic activity had to be under their control.

Another example of what impedes the enactment of the laws is provided by the chairman of one collective farm who told us in the interview that when the collective and state farms were allowed to sell part of their products to the State for hard currency, the bureaucracy set up three obstacles in order to defer, by any possible means, the establishment of the contacts of the collective and state farms with foreign firms and created difficulties for registering as a foreign economic participant. These obstacles were:

1. Very high, fixed prices for commodities which should be bought through State foreign trade organizations.
2. Prices on grain which were set twice as low as world prices.
3. A severalfold increase in state orders.

The combined effect of all this discouraged the collective and state farms until they were not interested in trying out the new system. The way the enactment of the new laws is impeded may be illustrated by an American lawyer's comments cited in the magazine *Deloviye Lyudi*. He remembers the period in perestroika when new laws were being adopted. As they were being passed, a comprehensive, though not entirely coherent, legal framework for business activity was being created. However, the state structures who were to enforce these laws were reinforcing their own bureaucratic practices, and using every opportunity to attach strings to these laws.

From the beginning of 1987, when the creation of joint ventures was allowed, the provisions, which were more like general normative decrees, had to be included in any agreement about establishing joint ventures. When such decrees appeared, the Ministry of Finance, which registers and oversees joint venture activities, insisted on comparing the joint venture agreements to the acts of the legislature. A joint venture was not approved if it did not include various decrees, especially those dealing with insurance policies, bookkeeping, and the activities of the Soviet auditing and controlling agencies. In certain cases, ministry functionaries insisted on including references to such laws as taxes on the enterprise's income. If it was impossible to overcome bureaucratic resistance, the agreement was considered temporary and had to be amended with all the changes in the corresponding laws.

Adding to the confusion in the country at this time, a number of guidebooks appeared which advised on contracts and deals with foreign companies. In principle, the sample standard documents they recommended were quite professional and useful for drafting contracts. But there was a hidden threat in these publications. First of all, many Soviet organizations with whom foreign companies wanted to set up joint ventures, were treating those samples as ironclad rules. Often, these organizations submitted the draft documents to their foreign partners before starting detailed negotiations. Very often, these documents did not reflect the specific economic activity they were going to talk about. Therefore, one had to adjust these drafts in the course of negotiations to the specific reality instead of dealing with documents worked out properly from the outset.

The officials who were to consider and approve the joint venture documents were also relying on the standard samples. These bureaucrats often demanded that, along with including this or that decree into the agreement, the agreement itself had to correspond exactly to the sample taken from the guidebook (though these books did not have the impact or effect of the law).[13]

In our later interviews, people noted that positive changes had been made in registering joint ventures and processing paperwork, due to the new powers of the republics. Though in some respects the procedures for forming and operating joint ventures have been simplified, there are complications too. Some people we polled noted that because the rights and powers of liberated republics are still being determined, it sometimes takes time and effort to achieve all the necessary coordinations. According to the opinion of the former deputy chairman of the Legislature Committee of the Supreme Soviet of the USSR, K. Lubenchenko, in many cases, the laws are not enacted because there is no mechanism for making them function. Instead, there are general "formulations and wishes" which result in the executive bodies interpreting the laws very broadly. Certain moves to solve the problems referred to by A. Sobchak have been made recently in liberated republics, for example, in Russia.

What has been said regarding the law about land can also be applied to laws about property. Many other things, such as laws about individual labor, cooperation, and leasing, remain uncertain. To what extent is the executive body able to enact or enforce laws? Are they ready and willing to do this? Are they aware of the fact that the basic foundations of life are being changed? Often the answers are discouraging. It is not ready, does not want to understand, and is not able to do anything. It is no easy task to understand the law, but without this, there is no hope that it will be enacted.[14]

4. Transformations at the Local Authority Level

As they are enforced at the local level, laws undergo significant transformations. The director of one joint venture, formed by a large-scale cooperative, related that his joint venture is under the complete control of local officials because they can, at any time, suspend the joint venture's lease on its building, alleging that it is needed for some other purpose. Local officials do not even acknowledge clear violations of the law. Here is an example of the behavior of the former high official of the Krasnodar Region which was typical of the "I-have-everything-under-my-thumb" mentality and which caused general feelings of instability in independent enterprises. This official ordered hundreds of cooperatives closed without any warning or proof of wrongdoing required by law. He also fired a procurator who protested the "violations of the law," and demanded the recall of judges who intended to insist on the letter of law. As a result, 332 cooperatives were closed down. When one of the leaders of a cooperative movement from Moscow complained to the regional authorities, he received an answer: "What has the law got to do with it?" That such problems and difficulties continue to exist after almost a year since the attempted August coup is explained by the fact that former Communist party officials retain half of the ruling positions in the regions. The more conservative minded local officials are, the more hostile they are to a market economy, and the more distorted the progressive laws appeared to be on the territories under their control, and vice versa. The more progressive the representatives of the local authorities are, the more efficiently the market reforms are being enacted. One Soviet entrepreneur explained how he was registering his company in the October district of Moscow. Before the coup, there were jokes about this region, where Deputy Zaslavski had set a goal of institutionalizing capitalism in one separate region. When he was registering his company, the All-Union bureaucracy delayed the paperwork on the registration procedure. But the regional authorities, not waiting for the documents, took the responsibility of registering the company. Their conduct was guided by the principle "Everything which is not prohibited is permitted."

But this rule has its exceptions. Progressive representatives of the Moscow City authorities made the joint venture pay for its utilities in hard currency. This is an infringement of the law because the joint venture may act as a person on the territory of the Soviet Union, and therefore, pay in Soviet rubles.

5. Arbitrary Resorting to Punitive Measures

The unstable political situation in the country, the unstable economic status of joint ventures, and lack of awareness of regulatory frameworks for joint venture operations on the part of agencies which oversee their activities, allow them to act on unchecked assumptions and general suspicion which the alternative economic structures often provoke. Thus, the fourth department of the St. Petersburg OBKHSS (the administration for dealing with pilfering socialist property) constantly disrupted the work of the concern Lenvest, by continually checking on its activities and financial records. For example, in the middle of the day, armed officers of OBKHSS rushed into the Lenvest store and started searching without providing a warrant. When the employees protested against the unsanctioned actions, the officers tied the hands of the supervisor and made her stand with her face to the wall. In one of the warehouse rooms they discovered some boxes of shoes with names written on them. They seized the footwear, sure that it was designated for unauthorized sale, but the next day they discovered it was intended for disabled veterans of World War II, whose names were written on the boxes. (Disabled veterans are a category of Soviet citizens who enjoy privileges in obtaining commodities which are in short supply.)

In addition, the officers tore open everything, from drawers to wardrobes, searching the employees' personal belongings. The manager of the department was even accompanied to the rest room by one of the officers. According to the deputy president of Lenvest, Nikolai Nazarov, who is in charge of commercial secrecy and confidential information protection, the actions of OBKHSS disrupt the work of the concern and destabilize its economic and financial position. During six investigations no illegal actions of Lenvest have been discovered. One has to conclude that this attention isn't caused by some authentic information received by the alert officers of OBKHSS, but by a general suspicion and preconception with which authorities and officers of OBKHSS are treating the company. Lt. Colonel A. Bukayev and his officers are sure that they are dealing with dishonest people. Bukayev, himself, counted the toilets, checked the furniture, warehouse, and number of automobiles. At the same time, they are not doing their own jobs, footwear is reported to have been stolen from the factory Proletarskaya Pobeda, and is supposedly used in underground footwear workshops, but no measures have been taken by OBKHSS.[15]

The overwhelming manipulation of statistics benefits both authorities (on the surface, everything seems to be okay) and subordinates (they have less work to do). Only the people do not benefit from it. Seventy years of pressure to account for fulfilling the plan by generating illegal reports and not through concrete accomplishments may also explain the evasion of professional duties. Striking examples of manipulating the statistics of law enforcement agencies were cited by the newspaper *Kriminalnaya Khronika*. Summing up the results of the work of the Moscow militia for the last year, its head, Gen. P. Bogdanov, said proudly that there were only 671 crimes per 100,000 people in the capital. According to the chairman of one of the departments of the Academy of the former Ministry of Domestic Affairs, Prof. A. Alexeyev, such figures can be explained only by the desire to replace wishful thinking for reality, or by coloring the truth and excluding the crimes from the records.

Several years ago, there was a scandal in one of the Moscow Divisions of Domestic Affairs. In certain militia precincts, the crime rate increased two to three times. It appeared that more crimes were being committed in that precinct than in the entire region. But the explanation proved to be very simple. The officers from these precincts decided not to fool themselves or the people and were recording 100 percent of all crimes committed. This resulted in a scandal and the employees were reprimanded because the annual criminal growth rate in the country was never more than 35 percent, and here it had jumped up to 140 percent.

According to the head of the division of the Omsk Regional Procurator's Office, V. Grin, over ten months last year, 847 committed crimes were concealed. The normal practices by officers of the Domestic Affairs division are to refuse to file a lawsuit, hide the crime, or punish the criminal. The Scientific Center for the Management and Sociology of the Academy of the former Ministry of Domestic Affairs of the USSR gave questionnaires to the employees of Domestic Affairs divisions in Moscow, Tuvinskaya Autonomous Republic and the Gorkovsk Region. The question was, "What illegal actions on the part of the legal bodies are most common?" The choices were as follows: Failure to report the crimes committed; hiding the crimes from being recorded; and, falsification of pertinent documents in order to refuse a case. One officer explained how these things were concealed, "Let's consider a typical situation. A handbag was taken from an old woman, resulting in an Article 145 Robbery. We are trying to persuade the plaintiff not to write the application. Then we take the application and say, 'You had three rubles in your bag and your pension is seventy rubles. Is this a big deal for you?' Then we begin to tell the old woman about horrible crimes. The woman is scared and says that she won't die from hunger if she doesn't get her three rubles returned. The word 'insignificant' appears on the application and we don't file a lawsuit. Even if someone had 300 rubles in the bag, after the psychological attack, everybody will agree that the money was not so important ('thank goodness the life was saved')."

Every lawsuit filed requires a lot of work, and when there are many of these cases there is no time to do anything else. In addition, there is sometimes little chance of finding the criminal. How could they find him, if the merchandise was stolen from a train traveling through the country? Militia officers turn a blind eye.[16]

6. Legal Nihilism and Ignorance of the Law

During our interviews we observed that many difficulties were caused by lack of awareness of the laws. It is typical for the Soviets to have simplified ideas about what is required in many joint venture contracts. They might understand the documents differently and have different expectations which can result in conflict and the threat of serious financial loss.

One Hollywood businessman told us about a famous Soviet film director who was concluding a contract with Hollywood. The Americans, as usual, were drafting the contracts very seriously, with great attention to all major and minor details. Everyone was surprised when the Soviet film maker alone, without a lawyer's assistance, browsed casually through the contract, not even reading the whole thing. It took him very little time to familiarize himself with the contract and sign it. Such a casual attitude to a document where serious business terms were spelled out was a shock for everyone.

A Soviet author of a book, which had been published in America, told the story of how his author's rights were infringed upon. He was a well-known man in the Soviet Union and applied for Gorbachev's assistance to get VAAP (the All-Union Agency for Author's Rights Protection) to settle the matter. This organization concludes deals on behalf of authors. But this powerful organization did not protect his rights because the organization had no knowledge or expertise in doing what they were supposed to do. They also explained to him that they had no hard currency to hire a lawyer in America who would uphold the author's rights.

Twenty percent of attempts by Soviets to establish an economic business alliance with Westerners turn out to be a failure because of the Soviets' ignorance of the law. The head audit and finances-bookkeeping offices of the Ministry of Foreign Economic Relations of the USSR and the Commission for Considering the Violations of the Soviet Law on Foreign Economic Activity carried out a survey in 20 percent of the enterprises and organizations which were granted the right to enter the foreign market independently. These offices calculated that over the first year of their independent activities in the foreign market, the total damage from deliberate and non-deliberate violators was 2 billion rubles. Of the total number of violations, 40 percent were in joint ventures, 39 percent in State industrial enterprises, 7 percent in cooperatives, and 14 percent in other organizations. The most typical offenses included exporting quality goods and materials under the cover name of by-products, smuggling, attempts to import commodities without tariffs, and non-conformity of the exported and imported goods to the given licenses. As to unintentional violations, the most common was a Soviet organization unregistered as a foreign trade participant striking a deal with the foreign partner.[17]

According to the story told by the Soviet analyst Yuri Alexeyev, lack of legal knowledge and experience in concluding contracts caused losses for the big Soviet space firm NPO Energia. Energia has suffered losses because its Japanese partner, Pax Corporation, went into bankruptcy. Soviet compensation was hampered by the lack of clear provisions in the contract. Under the contract, Pax Corporation leased for $2 million some samples of Soviet space technology and equipment, Soyuz apparatus, the rocket carrier Vostok, and technology for assembly and launching of spacecraft for exhibition, for a one-year period. On May 5, the contract expired. But because Pax Corporation went bankrupt and there was no clause about bank guarantees from the Japanese side, Energia not only lost its profit, but also suffered losses totaling about $350,000. According to the deputy director of the foreign trade firm

Energia, Vladimir Nikitski, the contract was signed by the president of the company, Heromika Saeki, during his visit to Moscow in the spring of 1991. Vladimir Nikitski said that because it was urgently necessary to deliver spacecraft and equipment to Japan for the opening of an exhibition arranged by Pax Corporation, Energia incurred all the delivery expenses both ways on the terms of their full future repayment, and these expenses totaled $350,000. At present, the amount of losses suffered by Energia is limited to the transportation expenses on the delivery of the exhibits to Japan, totaling 100,000 rubles and $95,000. But, according to Nikitski, Energia needs the equipment which is in Japan now to continue its work on launching rockets, and the NPO is ready to pay for its return delivery out of its own pocket, thereby increasing the amount of loss. The prospects for loss compensation do not appear good because the provisions about bank guarantees from the Japanese are not spelled out in the contract. This was a very bad mistake. However, the Soviet trade representation in Japan had recommended Pax Corporation as a reliable company and helped to establish contacts with it.[18]

The following example is about a quite common practice of drafting initial legal documents of a joint venture in an offhand manner that may later lead to attempts by the Soviet side to reconsider the terms of a business partnership. *Commersant* reported how lack of experience of the Soviet founders in the joint venture Shanghai-Leningrad caused conflict between the partners and postponed the opening of the Soviet-Chinese restaurant. The task of drafting the contract was assigned to the Chinese, and after a year and a half, the Soviet partner came to the conclusion that the terms of the contract were not beneficial to him. The initial agreement about creating the joint venture Shanghai-Leningrad was signed in the summer of 1989. The initial capital of 2 million rubles was stated, with equal participation from both sides. In the autumn of 1989, the investment of each partner increased to 1.5 million rubles. Under the agreement, the Chinese personnel in the joint venture could not exceed 30 percent. But the Chinese partner, the Shanghai company Khua Tin, obtained control over key positions in the administration. Chinese employees were to receive 80 percent of the salary in hard currency and 20 percent in rubles. Hard-currency earnings were to cover the expenses of the Chinese for the delivery of food products from China. According to the founders of the joint venture, the agreement with Khua Tin was signed by an official who thought it necessary to give the Chinese a number of advantages. After the official quit his job in 1991, the provisions of the contract were reviewed.

The Soviet founder of the joint venture demanded a record of expenses from the Chinese and insisted on revisions in the contract regarding the distribution of profits and losses.[19]

The Soviet analyst Anastasiya Solodikhina cited the example of violation of trademark laws by the firm Prodtovari. After the firm Prodtovari, part of Vneshposiltorg, a State foreign trade organization, tried to sell 10,000 deciliters of Stolichnaya vodka in Greece through the Greek firm Cosmos, the Greek firm Apka, which is the trade agent of Soyuzplodimport in Greece, filed a lawsuit against Cosmos charging it with violating the Greek trademark law. The Stolichnaya vodka trademark belonged to the Soyuzplodimport (the State foreign trade organization for fruit, vegetables and their products), which registered the trademark of Stolichnaya in Greece in 1975. Actually, Soyuzplodimport monopolized the trade in Soviet vodka. Of the total 3.4 million deciliters of vodka exported per year, Soyuzplodimport trades 3.1 million.

According to the Law on Trademarks, before starting to trade vodka in the foreign market, Vneshposiltorg had to obtain a license for using the trademark from Soyuzplodimport. However, violation of the Soviet and Greek laws on trademarks won't cause serious trouble to Prodtovari, since under Soviet law the firm is threatened with a fine of only 300 rubles, and under Greek law the trade partner of Prodtovari in Greece, Cosmos, will be liable. In the event of an unfavorable outcome for Cosmos, Prodtovari may not suffer considerable losses because vodka delivered in Greece has already been paid for in full by the Greek partner.[20]

Because of looser power control, legal nihilism has surfaced even more lately. However, the typical inability of the Soviets to think along legal lines has deep roots. One of the reasons for legal nihilism is the feeling of disappointment in the existing social order that people have experienced for many years. It seems to be neither fair nor humane, and there are serious and deep reasons for this. If the legal and ethical consciousness of people is being destroyed, and if the legal and moral principles are vague, it would be naive to hope that people would respect the State and therefore, the laws which it produces. This was shown in Rome thousands of years ago. In Rome, all aspects of lawmaking were perfect, including law drafting, lawmaking, and interpretation. That era gave the world outstanding philosophy and legal literature. Roman law was perfect and sophisticated, and even today, it is cited. But even the most perfect law loses its value if the social order is losing its attraction in the eyes of society. Citizens cannot respect a State-based coercion in everything, from labor, ideology, and place of residence, to the educational system. As a result, inner ethics disappeared from the society. Rejection of humane values relegated the country to the sidelines of the process of world development. One of the testimonies to this is an almost entire absence of legal consciousness, without which the most perfect laws cannot function. The result of this impasse is distrust of the State order, its fundamental principles, and therefore, the fairness of the laws which the State passes and enforces.[21] There is a phrase in the Soviet Union which goes, "Illegitimacy is adopted and enforced as law so that it doesn't seem so awful."

7. Laws, Rules, Informal Contacts, Bribes, and the Black Market

According to the Soviet economist Tatyana Koryagina, the Soviet economy differs from a Western economy in terms of the types of economic activities which are outside general accounting systems. In the West, these activities are either purely criminal or tax evasive. In the Soviet shadow economy, many kinds of socially useful activities refer to it. Entrepreneurs have to produce commodities which are in extremely short supply and services which are in great demand. This state of affairs is related to the many years of rejection of private property. Many entrepreneurs do not operate openly, not because they try to evade taxes, but because public opinion is not in their favor. Tatyana Koryagina thinks that this is how inherently honest people are becoming criminals. According to her estimates, shadow capital totals approximately 100 billion rubles, and the majority of it is not criminal in the Western sense of the word. A big share of the shadow economy is becoming legitimate. Koryagina believes that joint entrepreneurship will be infected with this black economy. Joint ventures will need enormous bribes to cover themselves, affecting their income. It means that, on the one hand, it will cause prices to increase in order to raise the amount of profit which will actually go to the owners of the capital. On the other hand, Western firms, who often might not know about the source of their partner's income, could get into a scandal. Western businessmen must be aware of the difficulties of the Soviet market, difficulties which emerged because of the amount of corruption, and must be very cautious while evaluating their Soviet partners. If Soviet partners have no problems with obtaining space, supplies, and equipment, or with entering external markets, suspect the red light of danger.[22]

In our interviews, we heard many times that all the prohibitions and restrictions in the laws of natural entrepreneurial practices caused individuals to search for ways to bypass them, generating the black market. For example, even after the law restricting middleman activities in foreign trade was enacted, these services were still being offered in

disguised form. Agreements about locating partners, and putting together contracts and other documents were being concluded. But actually, they were engaging in the same middleman activities. Only the
clients whom they help bring together put their signature on the contracts. While a lot of legal restrictions on middleman activity have been
lifted, it is still discouraged.

Americans tend to underestimate the typical inability of the Soviets to
think along legal lines, the extent of their mistrust of laws and rules, and
their reliance on personal relationships. In the Soviet way of doing
things, hardly any business can be developed without personal ties. We
witnessed this conflict between American and Soviet partners caused by
the Soviet mentality and the lack of awareness about it on the part of
the Americans. When a famous and influential person in the Soviet
Union was flying from one city to another in the United States, his
luggage got lost along the way. For the Soviets, a typical response in
such a situation would be to call somebody he knows at the Ministry of
Aviation, which is in charge of all airports, or somebody who is on a
first-name basis with the minister and ask him to intervene. The Soviet
guest later told us that he was hurt when his American partner, instead
of getting in touch with the number one person in the airport or finding
somebody who is acquainted with him, just acted in compliance with
the regular standards for such an occurrence, i.e., calling the ordinary
clerk in charge of the luggage and asking him to settle the matter. The
Soviet could not believe that merely acting according to the rules could
lead to any positive results, because for him, it is personal contacts that
matter most of all. It took effort to negotiate this conflict by explaining
to the Soviet that the ways he was used to in the Soviet Union are not
necessarily appropriate in America. The attitude toward rules and regulations is quite different in this country. On the other hand, we tried
to explain to the American clients that for a Soviet man, the loss of his
suitcase creates more difficulties in his daily routine than it would create
for a foreigner who has hard currency, because what little hard currency he has is designed to buy commodities to take back to the Soviet
Union, and not the basic necessities to replace what was lost in the
luggage. We also explained he needed support from his American partner to get out of this difficult situation.

The following stories told by the *Commersant* weekly show how the
regular business practices of many joint ventures can be regarded as
illegal and acquire criminal significance. In spite of the fact that the
same grounds for illegality can be found in many deals, official claims
were submitted to the joint venture Ferster, and the joint venture InNis.
The joint venture Ferster bought fifteen "music centers" for hard cur-

rency in the West, each set consisting of tape recorder, equalizer, speakers, record player, and radio. The joint venture sold ten sets to senior executives of the enterprise on which Ferster depends for supplies of raw materials. Allegedly, the price at which they sold the sets was far lower than the market one.[23]

The next case also lends itself to different interpretations in terms of being legal or illegal and whether it is justifiable to ascribe criminal significance to it. In the summer of 1990, the State Education Committee of the USSR invited a Japanese group for a week's tour of Moscow. There are several competing rent-a-car firms in Moscow who would like to receive an order to take the guests of the city around Moscow. In order to bypass the competitors, the Soviet-Japanese joint venture InNis worked out the following arrangement with the State Committee. The State Committee asked InNis to take the Japanese guests around Moscow. InNis, on its part, agreed to buy tele-video appliances for hard currency and sell them to the Committee for rubles as if it were "for the admissions office for foreign students and specialists." All sides fulfilled their obligations. Forty-two Japanese paid for the services with $16,000. The joint venture paid $10,500 for the appliances which it sold to the State Committee for 64,000 rubles. When the appliances were delivered, the manager of the admissions office of the State Education Committee and three of his subordinates kept the appliances for themselves, having paid the joint venture with their own money. The regional procurator called this a bribe. But the general director of the joint venture and the Japanese, who discussed the problem at a meeting of the board, regarded the fact that the appliances were sold at discount prices as a regular business transaction.[24]

According to a survey conducted by the Center for Sociological Surveys, the scale of the black market, its viability and influence, are determined not so much by the amount of capital accumulated by it, but by the common routine of a great number of people who use its services and who have no other alternative. As they say in Russia, "If you live with wolves you begin to howl like them." One of the most typical indicators of the shadow economy is the small bribery which remains on the periphery of big scandals connected with the corruption of high-level authorities. Many people condemn the bribery, but this phenomenon exists because people are totally dependent on the corrupt system of distribution for satisfying their needs. When asked whether they had expressed their "gratitude for favors through gifts or money," 62 percent of the respondents answered that they gave gifts, and 42 percent that they gave money. There are indications that such practices are increasing. While answering the questionnaire, the respondents and the analysts noted that within the range of black market redistribution, there are minor services and important social wealth. What are the most frequent commodities obtained in the black market? Here are the answers given in percent according to the number of respondents:

	%
Clothing and footwear	70
Food products	57
Consumer durables	37
Drugs	35
Books	30
Transportation services	28
Construction materials	23
Custom design clothing	21
Doctor & dentist services	19
Domestic appliance repair services	17

To this list, add construction services, instructor's fees, apartment rentals, dachas, and so on. The black market penetrates all segments. This is confirmed by the findings of the polls of experts and from ordinary employees who testified that they often observe cases of nepotism, pilfering, and cheating, etc. The findings of these polls are as follows (in percent according to the number of respondents):

Personal Encounter With	Experts %	Ordinary Employees %
Nepotism	71	51
Pilfering	77	50
Doing another job during working hours	76	38
Faking the amount of work and production output	67	38

The social and political damage from the black market is exhibited in the disintegration of power. By virtue of the existing economic conditions and the legal framework for economic conditions, the black market is the reason for many crimes among workers and managers.[25]

An experiment was conducted where a researcher worked incognito as a member of a group of construction workers who were building a dacha under private agreement at a lot located not far from the construction sites of the State construction companies. One of the aims of the experiment was to study the structure and operating mechanisms of the shadow economy, in this case plundering and selling construction materials from neighboring state construction companies. The conclusions reached by the researcher who participated under a false identity in all illegal shadow deals were that it was possible to steal and sell everything without exception. All employees, notwithstanding their age and profession, were doing this. One could just contact them to see if the material in short supply was available, and they would not hesitate to steal and sell it.

During the forty days of the experiment the researcher dealt many times with plunderers but he had never met anybody who would be on guard (or the watchman) to protect the company's property. It appeared that the watchman's functions had to be fulfilled by the militia. But what was the militia actually doing? The officers from the local Division of Protection of Socialist Property visited the construction site many times. But everybody had been advised of their visit ahead of time. By the time the inspector was arriving, all the necessary papers, documents, and records were available. To check their authenticity was impossible, because the inspector would need a week to do this. He did not have sufficient time at his disposal because he was responsible for a third of the region, with many trading outlets, construction sites, warehouses, and other organizations.

Theoretically, before the experiment began it had been supposed that the plunderers are normally people (1) with a criminal record; (2) people who had been on trial before for similar misdemeanors; or (3) "bums." But the research findings expanded the contingent. The conclusion was: everybody who can steal something is capable of doing this. It seems that to make plundering easier, the most favorable conditions are being created: there are practically no responsibility mechanisms, a total lack of control, and orders are issued by authorities to "ship" merchandise to destinations which nobody knows about. Once the observer was watching a scene that made a deep impression on him. Two foremen were fighting over who should be the first to sell the contraband. The absurd logic of the shadow economy prompted them to threaten each other with reporting to the militia, though in the long run they understood that both of them would be discovered in such a case. Nobody knows what the end of the dispute might have been if they had not been convinced that the stolen goods would be bought from both of them in turn.

The "shadow" structure of the construction company might be described as a cake with many layers. Plundering occurs at each level: rank-and-file workers and foremen commit crimes undiscovered by supervisors. Supervisors do not steal what they need by themselves, but with the help of "trusted" subordinates. In their turn, higher-ranking executives do the same but through "trusted" supervisors. This is trust of a special kind: it is based on conspiracy. Once the researcher asked the supervisor if he wasn't scared about being confronted by the law. He answered calmly that for him personally there was no threat or danger. Everything was being done by the workers. He saw his function as to provide a timely shield. It is quite natural that under such circumstances the supervisor depends on his subordinates. He is not able to fulfill his controlling functions. Control is exercised by the person who is involved in crime.

Acting in such a way in relations with his subordinates he suggests the same mode of behavior to higher-ranking people in the company. During the period of the experiment the researcher contacted suppliers of the stolen goods sixty times and only twice was there no deal. Once the person was afraid of his boss (he did not know that the boss himself was selling stolen construction materials). The second time the reason for refusal was lack of availability of the needed material. According to the researcher's observations, in approximately 50 percent of all cases, the executive knew about the deal and had his "commission" from it. That is why he pretended not to know about it. In every third case, the authorities arranged thefts through their subordinates and at the right time left the construction site.[26]

The question might arise whether the construction materials are in such excess supply that it is possible to sell them through "shadow" channels and whether it is possible to account for those materials. In one of our interviews, a former supply manager explained this situation by saying that first, the supplies system under centralized mismanagement allows for loopholes to place bigger orders than are actually needed for each specific construction site. Second, transportation and storage conditions are so poor that up to 30 percent of construction materials might turn out to be unfit for use in the long term and everybody knows that it is possible to write them off the books for these reasons.

CHAPTER 7

Categories of Soviet Organizations and Business People as Partners of American Companies

A Western businessman must be prepared for getting around the labyrinth of Soviet organizations and entities in choosing potential partners. In this chapter, a general overview is provided of the types of Soviet organizations as potential partners of American companies: former foreign trade monopolists, i.e., organizations of the Ministry of Foreign Economic Relations, foreign trade organizations that have been moved from the former Ministry of Foreign Trade under umbrellas of branch ministries and other foreign trade organizations under the ministries, their divisions, and under state committees, and categories of new foreign trade participants. Among new foreign trade participants there are both traditional entities such as state enterprises and organizations which had had no right to engage independently in foreign trade activity before and also new types of organizations, such as cooperatives, private enterprises, commodities, raw materials and stock exchanges. There is also an intermediate type of organization, such as some traditional foreign economic structures which start operating as shareholding companies. Finally, we will provide an analysis of the sociopsychological background and motivation of Soviet employees at different levels under the conditions of the ongoing economic and social transformations.

Over 400,000 new commercial structures have emerged lately, in addition to hundreds of thousands of traditional state structures. The correct identification and choice of a partner are becoming major difficulties in solving a whole range of problems in the business foray into the former Soviet Union.

The examples of deals and joint ventures illustrate the special significance of choosing the right partner for a successful business venture. At the same time, failures have also occurred due to specific characteristics of the Soviet partners chosen. After April 1, 1989, when Soviet organizations were allowed to engage directly in foreign trade and tens of thousands of prospective partners appeared, it became more difficult to locate the right partner. According to one Italian businessman, the situation in the country changed considerably and quickly and now it is necessary to ensure that partners are involved in realistic, reasonable projects. In this respect, it was easier to find partners before perestroika began. All the projects came from the State. They were based on a thorough choice and a technical-economic analysis of the options. The only thing left to do was to negotiate the price.

Now everything is different, and Western businessmen have to look for partners themselves, study their proposals, and verify their technical and economic reliability because financing is not always straightforward. The process of concluding contracts has also become more complicated, for they must be endorsed by many agencies.[1]

According to businessmen Paul Richardson and David Kelly, a businessman who arrives in Moscow is immediately plunged into an atmosphere of unpredictability, absurdity, and the absence of usual amenities. They warn about Soviet lack of awareness of basic business concepts which serve as guidelines for the rest of the civilized world. In their opinion, there can be no illusions about the Soviet bureaucrats, who are both inefficient and corrupt. The businessmen recommend bringing gifts, which are absolutely necessary for establishing contacts and striking deals in the former Soviet Union. They recommend seeking people for joint venture work who are not only honest but also know how to find their way around many difficulties. Otherwise one would just go crazy.[2]

According to the French businessman Viktor Loshak, the same Soviets keep going abroad. They just change their titles as they move from the ministry to the association, from foreign trade association to the kontsern, and in the process of moving they become far less reliable. Many potential Soviet partners engender obligations, accept gifts, and sometimes extort them, but do not fulfill their commitments. Frequently, a Soviet "businessman" will have an office and a car, and nothing else. He will have no actual authority, but that doesn't hinder his efforts. He will make any promise and sign all papers, and by doing so, discredits all Soviet foreign economic activity. Perhaps not all Soviets engaging in foreign trade are like this, but many are. Cooperatives are generating many varied proposals for business, from venom extraction to the hides of unknown animals. The offer is: We have something and we want to sell it. All of them claim to have licenses. But what is behind these proposals?

According to Charles E. Hugel, chairman and CEO of ASEA Brown Bover, Inc., and chairman of the National Foreign Trade Council:

> As government officials negotiate specifics of a trade agreement, it is important that they address another impediment to furthering economic relations—the difficulties for Americans in understanding how to deal with the multiple layers and labyrinths of Soviet agencies. As part of the Soviet's ongoing process of streamlining their bureaucracy, officials may want to consider the benefits of establishing one central office, focused solely on expediting decisions with foreign companies.[3]

An interview with the former Soviet ambassador to Tanzania given to a Soviet newspaper is a good illustration of the difficulties of identifying the right partners in the former Soviet Union. Even a knowledgeable diplomat who attempted to assist a foreign firm experienced difficulties.

The Soviet ambassador reported his attempts to create a joint venture for growing tea together with Tanzanian partners. Everything seemed very simple. Problems started when the ambassador started seeking prospective founders for the joint venture. At first he applied to the cooperative which offered services in locating business partners, but the cooperative did not deal with commodities such as tea or coffee. In addition, cooperatives were forbidden to engage in middleman or brokering activities. Next, the ambassador applied for assistance to the Ministry of Foreign Economic Relations. The ambassador doubted that the person from the ministry who is involved with Tanzanian affairs would look for a tea partner all over the country, but the ambassador applied there anyway. The ministry has been looking for a partner for two years but has not found one. Then the ambassador started to look for partners on his own and he seemed to have found one—*Georgian Agroprom* (Agr.-Industrial Committee). A Georgian team went to Tanzania to develop the project and worked out many details, but when the time came to work out the technical-economic analysis and estimates and conclude the joint venture agreement, it turned out they could not finance even the analysis and estimates. The ambassador couldn't understand why so many people were generating expenses, when they did not have the capability to follow through. Finally, the ambassador contacted Gosagroprom (State Agri-Industrial Committee). They seemed to appreciate the idea but they didn't make a decision because there were different points of view on the issues. The ambassador agreed with the journalist who was interviewing him that the bureaucratic system would not like any venture being out of its control, as is the case with joint ventures and cooperatives.[4]

The various types of foreign trade participants should be approached differently. Often, American and other Western businessmen don't take into consideration the differences among their potential partners. There are State foreign trade organizations and foreign trade firms of enterprises, State enterprises, and cooperatives, as well as cooperatives and shareholding companies. The Westerners also tend to perceive familiar words, such as "stock exchange" or "commercial bank" in their own frame of reference and ascribe to them the same meaning that these words have in Western societies. But in the Soviet business setting, "stock exchange" might appear to be an auction, and "commercial bank" might be just a non-state bank and not the concept familiar to them from the Western business environment.

An Overview of Soviet Organizations

Industrial Enterprises (Promishlennie Predpriyatia)

Industrial enterprises consist of workshops, specific production sectors, or production lines. At some industrial enterprises there are only production sectors or production lines. Some entities of an industrial enterprise might fulfill primary functions (such as assembly), or secondary functions (like repairs), maintenance functions (such as transportation workshops), or subsidiary functions (such as processing the by-products of the main production). A typical industrial enterprise is a mill, for example, metallurgical and textile mills. Mills are involved in processing raw materials and by-products.

Industrial Conglomerate (Proizvodstvennie Obyedinenia—PO)

Production associations are created to coordinate the management of several industrial enterprises, with one head enterprise in the association. A production association can be comprised of several enterprises engaged in coal mining, oil extraction and processing, etc. It differs from Research Industrial Conglomerates (NPO), which also include scientific-research institutes.

Scientific-Research Institutes (Nauchno-Issledovatelskie Instituti—NII)

There are several types of scientific-research institutes:

- NII which were the Academy of Sciences of the former USSR before.
- NII under the Republican Academies of Science
- NII under Branch Academies of Sciences (e.g., of the Academy of Medical Sciences)
- NII under Branch Ministries
- Regional NII
- Independent NII

Interbranch Scientific-Technical Complexes (Mezhotraslievie Nauchno-Teknicheskie Komplexi—MNTK)

This type of complex has been created recently for large-scale production to implement large scientific projects. One of the most successful is the Institute for Electric Welding named after E. O. Paton.

Republican Foreign Trade Organizations (Respublikanskie Vneshneekonomicheskie Organizatsii—RVO)

RVOs are created by the Council of Ministers of republics according to the approved guidelines. The specific export potential and the import needs of a republic are reflected in the focus of the activity of a republican V/O. (V/Os are foreign trade organizations under ministries and committees, which are being transformed into stockholding companies.) RVOs have subdivisions with a specific specialty. For example, included among firms which belong to Rosvneshtorg are Siryoexport (exporter of various resources such as fertilizers) and Mashimpex (importer of technology and equipment).

Foreign Trade Organizations under Ministries and Committees (Vneshneekonomicheskie Organizatsii Ministerstv i Vedomstv)

These organizations act as legal entities and operate according to the code approved by those ministers and committees under whose umbrella they operate. For example:

- Soyuzvneshexport specializes in the field of oil exports;
- Soyuzkhimexport specializes in exporting chemical products;
- Exportkhleb specializes in grain imports;
- Prodintorg specializes in food products;

- Stankoimport, Elektrointorgtekhnika, Sovelektro, and Tekmashimport specialize in the import and export of machinery and equipment;
- Medexport is engaged in exporting medical equipment and supplies;
- Litsenzintorg is involved with licenses and intellectual know-how.

Specialization is not rigid, and several state foreign trade organizations can be involved with one kind of product. Every foreign trade organization, no matter what its specialty, can purchase consumer goods, food products, or medical supplies upon assignment of the ministry or enterprises under the ministry for their employees.

One of the latest developments in the system of foreign trade is some State foreign trade organizations becoming independent of the ministries and operating as shareholding companies. An example of this tendency is re-organization of Soyuznefteexport and Soyuzplodimport. The owners of Soyuzplodimport have become enterprises and organizations of the Russian Federation, Belorussia, and other republics. These organizations are collective and state farms, some food products factories, and banks. Soyuzplodimport keeps on functioning as a middleman and brokering organization but on a more independent basis. One can hope now that a commercial approach to foreign trade decisions, which had been determined in great measure by political concerns before, is becoming more of a reality, now that these organizations are becoming interested in profitable business.

Foreign Trade Firms (Vneshnetorgovie Firmi—VTF)

VTF of industrial enterprises and organizations are normally created inside them. In these cases VTF cannot act as a legal entity, but must remain under the supervision of the organization or enterprise under which it has been created.

The name VTF (no matter whether it is a legal person or not) comprises the name of an organization and/or the enterprise under which it was created. Hence, examples of VTFs are VTF "Polyot" Pervogo Moskovskogo Chasovogo Zavoda (Foreign Trade Firm of the First Moscow Watch Plant), VTF "Avto Lada" Proizvodstvennogo Obvedineniya "Avtovaz" (Foreign Trade Firm of the Industrial Conglomerate "Avotovaz"), VTF Mezhotraslevogo Territorialnogo Obyedinenia pri Yaltinskom Gorispolkome (Foreign Trade Firm of the Interbranch Territorial-Production Association under Yalta City Council), and VTF "Intersiba" Sibirskogo Otdelenia Akademii Nauk SSSR (Foreign Trade Firm of the Siberian Branch of the Academy of Sciences of the USSR).

Many new commercial entities, such as leaseholding companies, small enterprises, or cooperatives, have been created recently. American clients often ask what the differences are between various types of new commercial structures. The following provides a short description of some of these new economic structures.

Cooperatives (Kooperativi)

Since 1987, 255,000 cooperatives have been established in the Soviet Union. By the end of the first year of their existence, their production was worth 300 million rubles; in 1988, 6.3 billion rubles; in 1989, 40.1 billion rubles. Tentative estimates for 1991 are over 100 billion rubles.

According to the laws, the three types of companies—cooperatives, shareholding companies, and limited liability companies—which are jointly owned. In reality, all three types of collectives (either individuals or legal entities) form the assets of these enterprises from the property belonging to them. Collective executive bodies operate in all three types of companies. A cooperative is different from these due to the requirement for the members of the cooperative to participate with their own labor in the work of the cooperative. Hiring employees is allowed only as an exception and there are certain limitations by law. The classic example of a cooperative is a company with collective labor whose profit is generated from the labor of its members. Compared to the cooperative, the shareholding company and the company with limited liability are not obligated to participate with their own labor. They are free to hire employees and can receive dividends from their investments without participating in the production. Many of the modern cooperatives are not cooperatives by their economic characteristics, but rather, being private enterprises, they use the label "cooperative" for other forms of entrepreneurship.

Shareholding Companies (Aktsionernoye Obshchestvo)

According to the law, a shareholding company is a company with the stated capital divided into a certain number of shares which is equal to the net cost and which is liable for its obligations only with its property. Shareholders can incur losses only to the amount of the cost of their shares. The total net cost of outstanding shares constitutes the stated capital of the company which cannot be less than 500,000 rubles. In the stockholding company a shareholder making his investment receives shares or securities, a specific type of financial document which can be used in certain financial transactions. A security can be sold, used as collateral, etc. No agreement by other shareholders is needed for these transactions.

Limited Liability Companies (Obshchestvo s Ogranichennoi Otvetstvennostyu)

In certain aspects, the limited liability company is similar to the shareholding company. It can also attract investments from individuals, organizations, and enterprises for joint entrepreneurship. The partners in this company also set up executive boards and make joint decisions on the distribution of profits. The USSR Law "On Enterprises in the USSR" refers to both limited liability companies and shareholding companies because of similarities as enterprises based on joint property. But there are specific differences between these two types of companies:

1. The limited liability company does not issue securities. The partner to this company receives a written certificate about his investment which is not a security. This written certificate cannot be sold or handed over to another person. In the limited liability company what can be transferred is not the security but the rights for investment into the joint assets. This transfer requires the consent of other partners. This type of company is characterized by a greater degree of interindependence of its partners.
2. In shareholding companies, any legal person can buy shares. In comparison with this, in the limited liability company, the partners are agreed upon by all members. No changes can occur without their consent. The minimum stated capital of these two types of companies also differs. The initial capital investment for the limited liability company is 50,000 rubles.

Small Enterprises (Malie Predpriyatia)

Small enterprises are created by enterprises operating on a cost-accounting and self-financing basis. The major purposes of creating small enterprises are:

- speeding up the formation and tapping of commodities markets
- operationalizing the results of research and development
- production of export commodities on a small-scale basis
- more effective use of local raw materials and by-products
- development of service industries.

The founders of small enterprises can be enterprises, organizations, associations, or government bodies, divisions, and committees of the Council of People's Deputies. A small enterprise acts as a legal entity, has a bank account, is independent in its operations and production management and distribution, and can spend the profit left after taxes and other necessary payments.

The form of property owned by a small enterprise is not its distinctive characteristic. It can be either state, or private, or cooperative. The law about property spells out provisions which allow for small enterprises to be the property of families or other individuals acting together. This property might be a shop, a service enterprise, a restaurant, a catering enterprise, or others. Therefore, small enterprises can be private property. The major distinctive feature of small enterprises is not the form of property but the number of personnel:

- in industry and construction—up to 200 employees
- in science and related industries—up to 100 employees
- in other fields of production—up to 25 employees
- in retail trade—up to 15 employees

Small enterprises can cushion the harsh social effects of mass closing costs, inefficient enterprises, and mass unemployment. Small enterprises might be created on the basis of shops or divisions of big enterprises which have become cost-inefficient. These will be economic structures which will combine features of both state and cooperative organizations.

Many associations for fostering business cooperation with foreign countries and other associations with foreign trade and trading houses have emerged recently. Being grouped together in associations enables enterprises to unite their efforts and apply for professional services in locating business partners overseas, in operating foreign trade transactions, in obtaining export licenses, and in providing transportation and delivery services.

Types of Associations

Associations with Broad Business Representation
• Association of Exporters • Association of Foreign Economic Cooperation of Small and Middle-Sized Enterprises • Association of Joint Ventures
Branch Associations (Otrasleviye)
• Association of Business Cooperation with Foreign Countries (Agropromservis) • Foreign Economic Association for Cooperation in Metallurgy (ACMET)
Regional Associations (Regionalniye)
• Leningrad Foreign Economic Association • Western-Siberia Association for Foreign Economic Cooperation • Uzagropromservis (Uzbekistan) • Consortium Rodon (Ukraine) • Association Diyaz (Azerbaijan) • Interazia (Kazakhstan)

There are a number of organizations which facilitate American-Soviet business relationships in many ways. The Intergovernment Soviet-American Trade Commission was created in 1972 to facilitate agreements on strategic issues of American-Soviet trade, or long-term projects for economic cooperation, for example, joint development of natural resources.

The Trade and Economic Council (ASTEC) was created in 1974 and encompasses American and Soviet companies, enterprises, and banks. ASTEC is an organization involved in counseling and assisting in foreign trade transactions, as well as disseminating information about economic development and foreign economic relations between the United States and the USSR. Registered in the United States as a non-profit organization and located in New York, with offices in the Soviet Union, ASTEC includes among its members American companies, banks, Soviet foreign trade organizations, and industrial conglomerates.

Chambers of Commerce and Industry of the former Soviet Union and the former Soviet republics, as well as regional Chambers of Commerce and Industry, offer business information and assistance in entering the Soviet marketplace. Its foreign trade organizations are designed to assist foreign and Soviet business people in establishing contacts, conducting joint events, advertising their products and services, organizing exhibitions, and offering logistical support. For example:

- Sovintsentr (the International Center of Trade and Scientific and Technical Relations with Foreign Countries) assists in forging foreign trade contacts and in preparing and conducting congresses, conferences, and seminars.
- V/O Expotsentr offers a complete package of services connected with the arrangement of exhibitions.
- V/O Vneshtorgreklama is involved in advertising.
- V/O Vneshekonomservis is engaged in consulting and assists in locating foreign business partners.
- V/O Soyuzpatent carries out the functions of a patent attorney. It also registers trademarks in the former USSR and abroad, and advises foreign firms on legal and patent issues.

General Characteristics and Categories of Prospective Soviet Partners

Through our analysis of the difficulties which American companies have to overcome while locating partners, and interviews with representatives of the major types of Soviet enterprises and organizations, we put together practical guidelines for clients which have helped them to achieve success.

We have identified three advantages and three drawbacks to working with the traditional participants of foreign trade activity, State foreign trade organizations, and with new participants in foreign trade activity, State enterprises and independent entities which have been given the right to engage directly in foreign trade.

Three Advantages of State Foreign Trade Organizations

- *Experience and professionalism in the area of foreign trade.* They represent an elite group which has been trading for many years and has trained at the one academy used to train Soviets in foreign trade activity.
- *Greater opportunities in overcoming various difficulties during the course of cutting a deal.* For example, in getting licenses, permissions, or making all kinds of provisions. If they actually undertake a venture they have a greater possibility of realizing it.
- *A certain amount of reliability.* Officials of State foreign trade organizations value their work very highly because it is directly connected with trips abroad.

This type of potential partner also has three drawbacks:

- *Lack of incentive.*
- *Lack of flexibility.* They act only according to instructions and try to avoid risk.
- *Lack of familiarity with enterprises.* They often do not know the conditions under which factories for which they buy the equipment and whose products they sell really function.

Three Advantages of Working Together with New Participants in Foreign Trade Activity

- They have incentive and they are interested.
- They are very familiar with the conditions of the enterprises in which the equipment they purchase will function, and they know how the product they sell might be used.
- They can take some risk and are more flexible.

Three Drawbacks to Working with New Participants in Foreign Trade Activity

- They may not be familiar with the norms relating to foreign trade activity. They are not very aware of what is going on in the external market.
- They have fewer opportunities to obtain licenses and overcome various bureaucratic hurdles.
- Very often, they promise more than they can fulfill, substituting what is desirable or expected for what is realistic.

While trying to establish contacts with "new" businessmen, it is necessary to figure out whom one is actually dealing with. It is understood that with so much chaos in the former USSR, foreign partners are interested in details of this kind. Experienced companies ask the following questions while initiating contacts with the Soviets:

1. Was the enterprise officially registered (which would enable it to participate in foreign trade activity)? What was its registration number? What kinds of foreign trade activity were on its registration *card*? When organizations were allowed to engage directly in foreign trade, they were also required to have a registration card. These could take a long time to acquire. The experienced companies preferred to figure out whether or not a foreign trade organization had a registration card *before* starting negotiations, because the Soviet organization might first seek a partner and then pursue acquiring the registration once it found a partner. In this case, implementing the deal might have to wait until this procedure was over. In addition, the exports and imports the Westerner was interested in might not have been included on the registration card which the partner already had.

2. Was it necessary that the product they proposed for exchange or sale should acquire licensing? And, if so, how realistic was it that they could get a license? Had they tried before? Often, the Soviet partner did not even know if the product was subject to licensing because the list of products to be licensed was constantly changing and increasing. Often, he might have not considered it necessary to find out until he had a buyer.

3. What experience had the potential partner had, if any, in actually selling the product abroad? What experience did he have in overcoming bureaucratic obstacles? If a Soviet firm hadn't sold a product before, that could be a plus, on the one hand, because it meant that he had no other stable business partners. But, on the other hand, it also meant that the Soviet partner had no experience and probably couldn't overcome the many bureaucratic obstacles, transportation problems,

customs problems, etc. It did not necessarily mean that it made no sense to work with the potential partner because one could actually establish contacts and work with him for many years. But, in this case, short-term profits were not contemplated, even if the Soviet partner promised them. The director of the enterprise just might not be aware of the difficulties that might stand in the way. He usually spends a lot of time working on internal affairs and probably doesn't have expertise in foreign trade. He might not know himself about difficulties that crop up.

4. What was the availability of hard currency and what were its sources? Perhaps an enterprise had produced something and sold it in the West for hard currency or had received hard currency from the ministry and was just waiting to get it.

The opposing points of view to advantages and disadvantages of dealing with various types of partners can be illustrated by the opinions of foreign businessmen and Soviet experts. Here are some examples illustrating the advantages of developing business contacts with former foreign trade monopolists. J. Yuryeff, from Allen-Bradley, believes that American firms have more difficulties now, because they don't really understand cooperatives, joint ventures, or other new organizations. They prefer to deal with partners whom they have known for a long time. But firms which have been doing business in the Soviet Union for a long time and have had stable contacts, might want to reconsider those contacts in light of the appearance of many newcomers. The newcomers are unknowns. No one can provide any substantial information about them. Often, they are non-professionals whom directors of the enterprise assign to do marketing. They might be highly competent in their professional area, but are very inexperienced in foreign trade.[5]

The following examples illustrate lack of awareness on the part of some new Soviet businessmen of the rules, procedures, necessary formalities, and specific steps in working out a deal. The director of a Moscow plant applied to Korean trade representatives and asked for their assistance in locating a partner who would be interested in buying wire cable. He submitted the samples which were sent to Seoul. After some time the Soviet was informed that there was a prospective partner. The Soviet director received a call from the Korean representative who asked him to quote the price. The Soviet director got indignant: "Do you consider me a fool," he bellowed. "Let the firm representative come here and we shall talk, or we shall go to Seoul ourselves."

Here is one more example. One businessman from Indonesia, who came to the conclusion that doing business with the Soviet Union is an uneasy route to take, complained that the Soviet partners seem to drag on the negotiating process deliberately. "The deal could be finalized in one day in my country and here it takes a year." After some time the same businessman complained again: "We had already signed the contract and I was about to fulfill our contractual obligations when I suddenly figured out that our counterpart intends to conclude the same deal with another firm and is going to void our agreement." A businessman from overseas cannot understand the motivation of his Soviet partner. In "normal" business practice, the faster a deal is moved ahead, the more profitable it appears. For the Soviets, the deal as such is not so important. The process of negotiations themselves is the direct profit because it involves the trips abroad, gifts, and the opportunity to purchase clothing which can be sold in their country for profit.[6]

An Austrian businessman, Mr. Guss, states that previously, the Soviets [they dealt with] were considered conservative, but when they entered into business relations with their firm, and were satisfied with them as partners, they still intended to change partners. More and more frequently, non-professional people are becoming involved in foreign trade. Representatives of various cooperatives, industrial conglomerates, and joint ventures, who are engaged in foreign trade, are presenting business proposals. What's their orientation when they approach the firm? They don't want to pay for working out the proposal. They are coming and asking for $20–30 million worth of business. For instance, one proposal was to sell production-line technology. To put together this proposal would cost $600,000. Why should the firm take the risk? There have been significant changes in the economy. Sometimes they occur so quickly that people are not able to adjust to them. Many big enterprises which have been granted the right to enter the external market do not make use of the opportunity. According to Mr. Guss, this is because they are currently working together with a foreign trade partner and are gaining experience from them.[7]

Here is the opinion of a typical former Soviet foreign trade monopolist, the Soviet trade representative in Finland, about the advantages of developing business contacts with traditional foreign trade structures— the former monopolists. He believes that the existing foreign trade mechanism with well-qualified, competent officers does not hamper foreign trade, acting as Cerberus [the terrifying, three-headed dog in Greek mythology], protecting the government's interest, but rather, this mechanism provides counseling, assistance, and coordination.

According to the opinion of the Soviet trade representative in Finland, Soviet enterprises were sometimes selling their products at lower prices than state foreign trade structures which had adequate knowledge about prices and were not so ready to make concessions. Often the deal that the new foreign trade participants were concluding might remain a secret. It was extremely difficult to catch such "exporters" red-handed. The association Interlatvia (one of the new participants in foreign trade activity) supplied window glass to Finland for a price 34 percent lower than Stroimaterialintorg (the traditional foreign trade participant—state foreign trade organization).

According to estimates, about 900 organizations, including cooperatives, were engaged in the Finnish market. Most Soviet exporters did not inform the trade representatives about negotiations, business trips, or contacts. As a result, the influx of incompetent people who were not aware of marketing, competition, or prospective partners and who were attempting to negotiate foreign business has increased. The trade representative said that instead of going to existing foreign trade structures (state foreign trade organizations), such as Raznoexport, and buying consumer goods or food products at reasonable prices, the delegations ignored these structures and went on business trips abroad, eventually purchasing goods for higher prices.

Because of lack of awareness of local conditions and jurisdictions and basic information about the partners, the association Ukrimpex (one of the new republican foreign trade participants), concluded a contract for exporting vodka and women's clothing with the Finnish firm Terro Koski which soon went bankrupt. Only then did the Ukrainian organization apply to the foreign trade representation for help and though it might be possible to get back some of the merchandise and payments Ukrimpex might still suffer big losses. Later it turned out that the exclusive right to import alcohol in Finland belongs to the State company, Alco, and only upon its approval could vodka and wine be imported by other firms.[8]

The same point of view can be illustrated in a case related by a consultant of the School of the Ministry of Foreign Economic Relations. He happened to be a participant in a ridiculous conversation with Soviet "merchants" who came overseas to trade with foreign firms. The consultant was sure that in compliance with world standards, Soviet business people had already contemplated from whom and for what price they were going to buy. In answer to his questions about who was the partner and what was the price they were considering, he heard the answer, "the partner has not been located yet and the prices are unknown." Soviet business people often have only a vague idea about competition and about the prices in the world markets.

There are two reasons why many Soviet enterprises who independently conclude export and import contracts do not care about going after the best prices. First of all, their objective is to generate hard currency by any means as soon as possible. Second, they have no idea what the criteria are for success in foreign trade transactions. Often, enterprises attempt to unload resources or prefabricated goods from the plants' inventory on foreign customers at any price, and for the currency they have received buy personal computers for the plant or consumer goods for their employees. Such deals seem to be good for enterprises on the surface, exporting resources which have been bought for low domestic prices and importing commodities which are very expensive on the black market in the country. But often, the actual cost of exported goods exceeds the cost of imported goods, an unequal exchange which is detrimental to the country. In the foreign trade organizations of the former Minvneshtorg (Foreign Trade Ministry), a rule existed forbidding the purchase of goods without a proposal package from three foreign suppliers. For big transactions, the minimum number of proposals increased to five or more.

According to the consultant, one experienced Soviet foreign trade organization invited several competing foreign firms to Moscow for negotiations and accommodated several of them on the same floor of the Ukraine Hotel. Negotiating simultaneously with representatives of several foreign firms, the Soviet importer managed to strike a good bargain, getting a better discount than the initial price suggested by competitors. Purchasing from one supplier, without comparing proposals of other competitors, the importer has no chance to determine the best price. Newcomers in foreign trade often ask whether it is acceptable business conduct to ask other firms for commercial information. They are afraid that the foreign competitor whom they have already contacted will learn about it. Experiences teaches the contrary. Your partner must know about his competitors.[9]

Here is an example that serves to illustrate the logic in favor of strict state control over foreign trade. After the decree of 1986 reorganized the management of foreign economic relations in the Kazakhstan, Kalmikskaya Autonomous Republic, and some other regions, a number of organizations, including the Kzil-Ardinsk City Hospital, began developing Tibet Medicines (made from herbs and other natural materials), a commodity in great demand in the world market. The reason was high profits with practically no investment. Competitors began inflating the purchase price of supplies which were bought from hunters and from those who picked the plants. At the same time, they reduced export prices for each other, leading to a reduction in total hard-currency earnings generated in the country, and threatening some species of wild animals and plants with extinction. The government decided to take measures to restrict the exploitation of these rare resources, and to stiffen the control over them.[10]

With the influx of new Soviet organizations onto the market, questions of non-compliance and ethical norms often arise. The co-owner of a New York foreign trade firm, Arthur Goldstein, agreed with a Soviet manufacturer to distribute his product in the United States. Goldstein conducted an expensive advertising campaign and then learned that the Soviet partner had given the right for distribution in the American market to another firm. The competitor did not spend a penny on advertising, took advantage of the demand which had been generated through the efforts and money of the first company, and began to force Goldstein's firm out of the market. Goldstein was also surprised by the avoidance of long-term contracts by Soviet organizations, and said that he couldn't start a marketing campaign if he couldn't count on a long-term supply from the country, because one-time deals did not pay off the sales expenses.[11]

Another aspect of the problem is illustrated in the example cited by the Soviet economist Vladimir Tikhonov. According to him, everything which is reasonable and efficient in other countries is unreasonable and inefficient in the former Soviet Union. To the contrary, everything which is unreasonable and contradicts common sense appears to be the only way for Soviets to survive. It seems as if they are living in an anti-world. Tikhonov gives an example which illustrates the essence of the economic system.

The technique of floating timber downriver leaves at least one-third of this timber in the water. Billions of cubic meters cover the beds of Siberian, Far Eastern, and European Siberian rivers. Nobody in the State cares about this. Only cooperatives were ready to lift it, process it, and sell it in the external market. Operations like this were started only because the Law on Cooperation in the USSR did not forbid them. Within six months, the State shut them down to the detriment of the country. The grounds for this were that the timber was being sold overseas at a time when the Soviets were short of forest products. The result of such measures is that the timber just disintegrates on the riverbeds. But government officials are satisfied. Nobody will reproach the official for not doing his job. He is a monopolist, once again, with nobody competing against him. And, once again, he deceives Gosplan officials and the government by saying that they are running out of timber, so it is necessary to increase prices for the timber which he is producing. This is what the economic system does: It is based on shortages, and in maintaining them. Monopolism cannot live without shortages and that is why it is reproducing them.[12]

While counseling American companies, we became convinced that distinguishing between potential Soviet partners as "former monopolists" and "new businessmen" does not provide all the necessary information. It is necessary to break them down into more detailed categories and it is obvious that a different approach should be taken to the new types of foreign trade participants as alternative economic structures and State enterprises.

Independent Economic Structures

In interviews with representatives of the independent economic structures, a number of projects were considered, including the objectives and goals of their organizations, their idea of commercial activity, and their methods of achieving business goals, enabling a breakdown of respondents into three categories, which we have characterized as romantics, swindlers, and realists.

Romantics

Romantics are Soviet individuals or organizations who are enthralled with the mere idea of entering the foreign market. This is attractive in itself for them, totally aside from the profit concern. It is implied that the profit will somehow come by itself, somewhere in the future. What lures them is the well-known name of the company with which they might be working. A potentially large project may be a remote but exciting prospect. They are sometimes called "the traders of air." The aim in itself, which is by no means related to increasing their profits, is expanding their organization, increasing the number of personnel, renting bigger offices, acquiring modern equipment, and so on. There is often the unconscious desire to feel like a "rider on the horse at the head of the parade." Romantics might be unreliable, but rather because of their unrealistic evaluation or assessment of abilities than because of the conscious intent to cheat. As a rule, they are well educated and often worked previously in the scientific sector of the economy, but did not occupy positions of authority and have no experience working in that capacity in traditional State structures.

Swindlers

Swindlers comprise a large category. Their idea of doing business corresponds to a primitive type of capitalism, that is, they are sure that the main principle of doing business is to cheat and run, and that the norms of business ethics are outdated prejudices. Before the co-operatives were legally allowed, many of these people operated within the framework of the black market. They possess foreign resources which are legal now with the help of the alternative commercial structures that they created. They have, as a rule, stable contacts with the corrupted elements of state apparatus, law enforcement agencies, and criminal groups. The most successful of them were the first to start setting up companies overseas and open accounts in foreign banks. In doing this, they have generated their own vehicle for retreat, if and when required.

Realists

Realists create their alternative economic structures in lines of business close to those in which they worked in the state economic sector. Often, they occupied positions of authority there and retained viable, normal (not criminal, like swindlers) contacts in their ministry, state enterprises, or other organizations. They do not keep themselves isolated from those structures because they understand the advantages of these contacts. They replicate many of the methods they got used to while working in state organizations. They seem to do the same things, but better, and more reasonably, because the alternative economy provides relative freedom and independence and minimizes intervention by state bureaucrats. They differ, as a rule, from their colleagues who remained in the State sector in a number of ways, which have facilitated their migration to the alternative economy. These traits are: more creativity, an informal approach to what they are doing, enthusiasm, initiative, and willingness to take risk. The strategies used by them are a major vehicle for the free-market transformation of the country. Realists are different from Romantics in that they are motivated, as a rule, by reasonable organization and expansion of their production, reasonable commercial activity, and reasonable means of generating profits. They differ from Swindlers in that they are not "profit-by-any-means" oriented. If they violate the rules and regulations, they do it reasonably, when their enterprises cannot operate otherwise, and not because they are after super-profits.

We analyzed several cases of cooperation of American companies with each of these three types of representatives from the alternative economy. Realists are naturally the most serious partners. Romantics are unreliable, however some small American companies are able to benefit from Romantics, striking one-sided, beneficial, and lucrative deals. It was quite enough to show respect for their romanticism and to let them feel like "international class businessmen."

Some companies entered business relationships with Swindlers and have managed to take advantage of an immediate, favorable situation. For example, a small lot of cheap, outdated computers was exchanged for raw materials, bypassing legal restrictions with the help of the Soviet partners who monitor the ways this can be done.

There is a certain benefit in assisting Romantics. This assistance is not designed to facilitate contacts in the international market, however, but to expose them to business culture and principles of management and marketing. Though their business is, as a rule, more like a children's game, while "playing" they do acquire business skills. Under the conditions of the market economy, they will be able to find a niche for themselves in the near future.

Let us consider some aspects of the difference between alternative commercial structures and state structures by examining cooperatives, which are the most typical form of alternative structure in the analysis of the leading Soviet economist Vladimir Tikhonov. This difference reflects among other things a certain business style and performance typical of directors and managers of State enterprises, which has been shaped over the years of central management and which is, though with great difficulty, undergoing changes now.

First, every worker in a cooperative knows that he raises money through his own labor, not the accumulated, impersonal labor of many people which minimizes personal responsibility, but his own labor which produces a product and then a profit. The profit enables him to support his family and himself and safeguards his ability to work. The worker in a cooperative is well aware whether or not his product has sold, and, if sold, whether the consumer was satisfied or unhappy. His income and life-style depend on the salability of his product, initiating the desire and necessity to study consumer demand. Cooperatives try to produce only those goods which are needed by consumers.

Second, the structure of the cooperative is completely determined by the demand for certain products, with each cooperative having to adjust to this demand. A State enterprise does not care whether the consumer wishes to buy his products. His consumer and supervisor is The Plan. Those who work out this Plan decide how to pay for the production and from what source. It is both easier and more difficult for a cooperative to operate now than under a normally functioning economy; easier because of the shortages and excess rubles that the Soviet people have; more difficult because the supplies are not easy to obtain and cooperators have to think about how to bypass the law on occasion.

Third, production in a cooperative is shaped only by the influence of demand that can be backed by payment for products and services. So the flexibility of the structure and the production technology can operate at an optimum size.

The major difference between cooperatives and the State enterprises, trade, and service organizations today is having more freedom of action. A cooperative may engage in any line of business if it is not prohibited by law. A state enterprise has no such power. Its production structure is determined by the Plan. The Plan is the law.

The following situation illustrates the typical business style of directors and managers under a centrally managed economy. The legacy of such a style is still present in the transforming society. If an enterprise is mining copper ore, the activities of the director and managers responsible for the Plan are oriented only towards copper ore, although many other valuable substances are being wasted. Managers do not care about the other substances that are not in their line of business, and nobody will provide supplies, personnel, or salaries to extract the valuable material. Even though it might be profitable, the Plan does not include this particular product which is meant for somebody else.

Fourth, there is a direct link between the personal income of workers in a cooperative and the economic activity of a cooperative. Such a worker knows that his personal income hinges not only on how well he is working and what he is producing, but also on whether he will make a good sale. Market prices are related to many things, primarily to the product's quality. A cooperative worker's income depends fully on the total business performance of the cooperative, including supplies, production, operations, choice of buyer, and finally, the sale.

The fifth source of strength in cooperative production is economic responsibility for the results of the economic operations. Here, everything is very clear.[13]

Foreign business people have a different attitude to alternative commercial structures. When Japanese firms were asked whether they could work with cooperatives, some of the firms replied:

1. *Toyota:* "Our firm has no experience in working together with cooperatives. I'm not very familiar with this form of entrepreneurship in the USSR, but it seems to me that the development of cooperation in working with cooperatives in this country does not have big potential."
2. *Mitsu:* "Cooperatives are not popular in the Soviet Union. That is why they cannot stand competition."
3. *Progress Training:* "Cooperatives have not interested our firm so far. Maybe we will need this in the future."

The president and chairman of the board of directors of Dresser Industries, Jim Murphy, noted that the future scenario for American entrepreneurs is most promising for small and middle-sized business. The U.S. deputy trading minister, Thomas J. Deusterberg, touching upon the problems of the developing cooperative movement, small businesses, and joint ventures in the former USSR, and noted that the economic reform of the country should be oriented to cooperatives as a form of entrepreneurship, in that this form lends itself more easily to a transfer to a market economy.

Attitudes towards cooperatives on the part of certain categories of Soviet people differ too. Typically, the negative attitude to alternative commercial structures encompasses all such structures, including joint ventures. The especially negative attitude towards joint ventures may be combined as well with certain anti-Western sentiments, i.e., being oriented to the isolated development of the Soviet economy, aside from international contacts.[14]

Economic structures that operate outside central planning (state order) and are not part of the command system are considered to be alternatives and include:

- Cooperatives in the service industry (must not be confused with consumers cooperative societies)
- Leaseholding companies (including the agricultural segment)
- Stockholding companies
- Private enterprises
- Independent foreign economic organizations
- Commercial banks
- Commodities, raw materials, and stock exchanges
- Joint ventures.

Let's look closely at the work of one of the first successful cooperatives as it is described in the magazine *Moscow*.

Konstantin Buravlyov (director of the Gonchars Ceramics Company) heard about the problems confronting Gonchars in March 1988. The factory dates from long before the 1917 Revolution and formed a part of the production department of a large umbrella State construction company. But the plant was antiquated and operating at a loss for years. Buravlyov was working elsewhere in the company as an engineer when he heard the government, in this case the local authority, say they were determined to get rid of the factory and would be open to ideas for turning the business into a private cooperative. Buravlyov discussed the matter with his friend, Evgeni Zalyoshin, an economist at one of Moscow's numerous ministries. The friends approached others, primarily technical engineers, and a small group of partners was soon formed who were willing to take on a new challenge. More than a year later, the former lumber room was transformed into a director's office with an enormous desk, a red telephone, a flipchart with felt marker notes, a conference table, and a cabinet displaying Gonchars products: square bathroom tiles in various soft pastels or with flower motifs, some rather exuberant molded bowls, and a small collection of fragile-looking vases.

To eliminate any doubt about the extent of their achievement, the two young directors first sketched a lengthy description of the deplorable state the factory was in, including understaffing, low morale, lack of management, and low wages. Not surprisingly, only half of the plant's annual production actually came off the line, and with that, only 5 percent was of A-standard, or in other words, undamaged. Losses in 1987 had risen to 700,000 rubles, and no one was responsible. "In our system, making losses is like an act of God. It just happens," quipped Buravlyov. When the company became independent from the umbrella State concern on September 1, 1988, and had to stand on its own two feet, the task ahead seemed almost insurmountable. The most difficult part was to keep up the workers' morale and convince them the whole exercise had a point.

But enthusiasm grew visibly when the directors raised wages to an average of 300 rubles a month after only a few months' trading. "Production soared immediately, and the quality improved," grinned Zalyoshin, who had put together a wage system based on performance and productivity which he considers both ingenious and fair. With wages around 500 rubles a month, technicians at Gonchars earned twice the salaries made by colleagues employed by state companies. This appeared to be a winning combination for a young enterprise, as quality had improved enormously in the first year of operation. Turnover in rubles increased from 180,000 to 460,000 a month in 1989. The annual 1989 turnover reached almost 6 million rubles, of which 1.3 million, or about 20 percent, was profit.[15]

Our poll among the major representatives of the alternative economy revealed the following major difficulties with which they are confronted in their foreign economic activity:

1. Absence of a distinct and consistent government policy towards the alternative sector of the economy.
2. Contradictory and vague laws regulating the activities of alternative economic structures.
3. Frequent changes in the legal framework for these activities.

4. Lack of professionalism, business culture, and experience in doing international business.
5. Short-term, immediate results orientation, disregarding prospects for the future.
6. Resistance to market-economy transformations with which they are met sometimes by State foreign economic structures, the ministries, legal bodies, and the directors of state enterprises.
7. Lack of accessibility to many resources, materials, and equipment because of shortages in the country.

State Enterprises and Collective Farms

In the interviews with representatives of state enterprises, we analyzed their possibilities as potential partners of American companies, using classifications based on three variables or parameters: (1) Influence (influence and role in the Soviet economy), (2) Independence (the degree of independence from higher authorities), and (3) Potential (their responsiveness to free-market transformations by having the potential to work under market conditions). Let's look at each of these more closely.

1. *Influential* enterprises possess resources which:

- under Soviet shortages can be exchanged for needed supplies, such as resources, materials, or equipment. One example is enterprises producing oil products.
- are able to exert pressure on the bureaucratic and economic structures, for example, enterprises which have a monopoly on manufacturing chemicals due to using world-class technology. If they stop supplying them, operations of entire industries might be threatened. If they demand something, they are listened to as opposed to enterprises manufacturing outdated production needed only by a few customers. Thus, we are talking about influence based on scarcity or superior technology, not on the volume of production or the financial situation.

2. *Independence.* We isolated three types of enterprises:

- *Enterprises which are practically independent,* and therefore, similar to alternative economic structures. One of the directors of such an enterprise said in the interview: "They have a long umbilical cord linking them to the ministry or other State structures which in principle remained the same whatever other name the ministries might assume."

- *Enterprises restricted in their authority to make decisions.* In particular, those which practically have no right to negotiate with foreign partners without the participant being controlled from the ministry (a short umbilical cord).
- *Enterprises which seem to be a separate economic entity only on the surface,* but actually, according to one of the directors of such an enterprise polled by us, is "a small part of the big, monolithic rock."

3. *Potential* (responsiveness). Five types of enterprises were identified, which we gave the following names— *The Bankrupt, Monsters, Corpses, Fat Cats, and Optimists:*

- *The Bankrupt.* This type of enterprise has a desired commodity, but due to a substantial reduction in state support, has no resources now to generate production. A typical example of this type of enterprise is a wood processing mill. In spite of the fact that part of its lumber production is sold overseas for hard currency, which is profitable for the Soviet State, the enterprises are in chronic financial crisis, resulting in delayed employee wages because the bank will not loan them money. Before the beginning of the economic reform, money for salaries was given automatically by the state bank, without considering the financial performance of the enterprise. The wood processing enterprise performs poorly because of the low purchasing price of lumber by the State. When they acquired relative independence as a result of economic reforms, the bank stopped automatically giving money for salaries, and now the enterprise is falling apart.
- *Monsters.* The Monster is an enormous industrial conglomerate such as one that produces tractors, which is stable, and not subject to any market transformations. The monster has no technological and personnel prerequisites for changing outdated equipment or personnel practices.
- *Corpses.* Corpses are enterprises which should be eliminated because the state of their production, operations, and management, and the complete disinterest in the results of labor, make revitalization impossible. These include most collective farms.
- *Fat Cats.* These enterprises happen to generate a product which has a market in the West, resulting in the exportation of most of the production of the enterprise, but which exhibit a laissez-faire attitude towards market transformation. An example of a Fat Cat is the first watch plant in Moscow. One of the reasons for the disin-

terested attitude toward market innovation, according to our survey, is their satisfaction with their current position. Most of the hard currency in these enterprises remains in the possession of the enterprise and is allocated for purchasing consumer goods for the employees.

- *Optimists.* Companies in this category have business potential and are ready to make the market-oriented transformations necessary to maximize their potential. In comparison with the Bankrupts, they are in a favorable financial position. In comparison with Monsters, they have modern technology and highly qualified, motivated, and disciplined employees. In comparison with Fat Cats, they are in acute need of innovations. An example of an industry in this category would be the aerospace industry.

State enterprises acting as foreign business partners generally reveal two types of personality traits among their managers:

1. One group is results-oriented, knowledgeable about production, identifies with the enterprise, is interested in its development, and, as a result, increases its efficiency through establishing reasonable contacts with foreign firms.
2. The second category uses the traditional, formal approach: Good reports, fulfillment of orders, following directions, and approval by the authorities. As a rule, these managers have moved to their position from a bureaucratic job and are really pseudo-directors, since the major operations are managed by a chief engineer, or operations and production manager. The directors' function is mostly a representative one.

Often, the examples of the Uralmash plant, on the one hand, and of Turbo Engine, on the other, are cited. Both are located in the Yekaterinoburg District. Uralmash has been trying for more than a year to win the right to do its own planning. In a risky battle, it won the right of independent management, free from central control. After it had started operating independently, the ministry, which previously shared responsibility for the poor plan, turned into a severe critic. Looking at it from the outside, it laughed at the hardships of the plant and sometimes compounded its difficulties. Turbo Engine Plant, on the other hand, agreed with each plan that it was given, just as before, whether timely or not timely. It had its supplies delivered. If the plant didn't fulfill the plan, it was adjusted and bonuses were not affected. As usual, the higher officials were not satisfied with the director's performance, but his life remained more or less peaceful.[16]

One of the typical management styles is cited in the example by Boris Yeltsin, who remembers how in his work as a chief engineer he encountered petty tyranny from the general manager of his organization. The general manager couldn't tolerate his subordinate's claim to a right to have his own opinion. Sometimes ridiculous situations occurred. Yeltsin remembers that they would fight while riding in the car, and if he would not give in, his boss would stop the car and yell "get out." Or sometimes in the office, the boss, angry over a subordinate's words, would grab a chair as a weapon, the subordinate would do the same thing, and they would both approach each other. Such were the relationships. The general manager once issued a record number of seventeen written reprimands to Yeltsin in one year. Yeltsin collected all the reprimands, walked up to him, threw them on the table, and said that with the first reprimand next year, he would start a scandal. On the second of January, there was a reprimand for not working on the first of January, which is an All-Union holiday in the Soviet Union. Yeltsin complained to the higher authorities and the reprimand was revoked. For a while, the boss was more cautious, but later, he filed a lawsuit against Yeltsin over non-compliance with some accounting regulations. The plaintiff on behalf of the company was the accountant, and Yeltsin was the defendant. Fortunately, the judge was a smart man and did not find a cause of action in this lawsuit. At the end of the trial, the judge said, "In the performance of every manager, a certain amount of risk is justified. This was exactly so in Yeltsin's case. That is why Yeltsin is found not guilty and all the court expenses must be covered by his company." This was a severe blow, both for the general manager and the accountant. The accountant tried to seek revenge during the process of admitting Yeltsin into the Communist party membership. The accountant asked on what page and in what volume of Marx's *Kapital* the issues of commodities-financial connections were considered. Yeltsin was sure that he hadn't read Marx and had no idea about either the volume or the page. Without thinking, he answered that it was the second volume, page 387. The answer was accepted as if it were true and as if the accountant knew it. The petty tyranny with which the general manager treated Yeltsin lasted until Yeltsin was appointed chief engineer of the plant, which was a bigger company than his former place of work.[17]

One of the points of view about high-ranking personnel of state enterprises can be illustrated by the opinion of a leading Soviet economist, Pavel Bunich. Many directors of big enterprises fall into the following category: They are treated very kindly by the highest authorities, as laureates, as heroes who are able to rob the State, to threaten and demand with their fist beating on the table. They can't and don't want to use their brains to work. They, of course, don't want to change anything.[18]

A source of confusion is that many new enterprises have no infrastructure and no personnel, especially in the outer regions of the country. According to the estimates cited by the economist I. Ivanov, in order to satisfy the demands of doing business with foreign companies, Soviets need to begin training, or retrain, about 50,000 people. Under present conditions, this process will take five to seven years. This training has to be done at every level, including former teaching personnel who have a vague understanding of the new economic mechanisms. A lot of specialists are transferring from the state sector to the cooperative and joint venture sectors.

Many of the dysfunctional habits which developed in the domestic market have been transferred to foreign economic relations. Despite the introduction of contractual relationships, export shipment plans are not being fulfilled. Over the last five years, the number of complaints about Soviet machines overseas reached 1 million. Unreliable business correspondence, "business tourism," or the signing of non-binding "protocols of intention" instead of contracts, have become widespread. Only a few enterprises are using commercial risk guarantee systems and act overseas not only as traders but as industrial production manufacturers and investors.[19]

There are many obstacles in the way of collective and state farms that wish to enter the foreign market. They have to overcome the bureaucratic resistance of the agro-industrial and foreign economic complex.

The following example illustrates how even under the old conditions, with all the hurdles to entrepreneurial endeavors, some individuals with clout and initiative realized the opportunities that entering the foreign market offers. Those bold individuals were capable of finding creative, non-standard solutions and managed to chart their way through multiple obstacles using all kinds of economic and human resources.

Alexander Dubkov, the chairman of the collective farm, "Progress" of the Grodnensk Region, has toured around almost all of Europe trying to research the market thoroughly and figure out opportunities for commercial deals. He was not embarrassed to learn the basics about this new area in the West, but in his own country he got no support. Only through the assistance of the prime minister of the USSR was the collective farm granted the status of a collective farm which has the right to enter the foreign market. The collective farm began by supplying mushrooms to a Dutch firm. The first deal was successful and satisfied both sides. The Dutch company asked for more mushroom supplies and the collective farm bought the unique agricultural technology from the Dutch. In order to avoid losing a good partner, the Dutch company offered to supply refrigerator and wood processing technology.

The first order was from a Finnish firm for wooden items for bathrooms. The order was filled to the client's satisfaction, who could hardly believe the Soviet collective farm could produce items of such quality. A Swedish company also offered wood processing equipment. Now, the collective farm had an opportunity to choose their supplier and to bid on sales for higher prices and on buying for lower prices. They had made a good start. It turned out there were other sources for generating currency earnings, such as cattle feed. As soon as they started the production, they found a buyer, a West German company. Then, the Austrians heard about the Belorusian farm. They sent a request for game meat, resulting in a contract for DM 100,000. Their main source of hard currency for the future is the products of their own animal farm, furs of foxes, mink, etc. Not only sales from supplies of furs are planned, but now they are also developing a project with Italians for tanning and sewing fur coats. They are also planning to raise lobsters after learning the cost for two lobsters in European restaurants is over $12.00. The collective farm also decided to study business and a representative was sent to Moscow for training. They wanted to start their own training program after his return. They are now planning to have their own computer center, international teletype, and trade representatives in London, Paris, and other European cities.[20]

Over the last years some State enterprises have started to transform themselves into new types of entities. The journal *Sotsiologicheskie Issledovania* cited the findings of a sociological study which was conducted at Lvov Industrial Conglomerate Konveyer in 1989 to research the response and reaction of the population to the emerging capital market. Authorities of the enterprise offered their employees shares based on their performance and number of years of work at the enterprise. This approach helped people to realize their own interests, and during the first month, their investment in shares increased and sometimes totaled 1,000 rubles. In general, 83.5 percent of the personnel became shareholders.

In the poll, the question was asked, "Will shareholding exist in your organization as a new form of owning state enterprise property?" The answers were as follows: In April 1989, 22.2 percent of the managers said yes, no one said no, and 77.8 percent gave no answer. Among the workers, the answers were as follows: 41.7 percent answered yes, 4.2

percent answered no, and 41.1 percent gave no answer. In June 1989, the personnel in general gave the following answers: 62.5 percent answered yes, no one said no, and 37.5 percent gave no answer.

This research study has revealed a positive trend towards willingness to become shareholders. Because shareholding in a state industrial conglomerate is still new, there is a great deal of confusion about it. Even managers cannot answer definitely who is in charge of selling shares (38.9 percent think that it is a shareholders' meeting; 33.3 percent believe that it is the Council of the Employees Collective; 21.7 percent mention their authorities).

The general director of the association, V. M. Vologozhin, believes that in terms of both short-term and long-range goals, shareholding at state enterprises is very important for increasing employees' motivation to work better.[21]

Operations and management of a new kind of entity—kontzern— have been described in the magazine *Biznes*. Kontsern is considered an intermediary stage between state and alternative economic structures. In its form it is new, but still retains links with central control. The first kontserns, interbranch state amalgamations of enterprises, were created in 1989. The first three kontserns, Tekhnokhim, Energomash, and Kvantemp, were created on a voluntary and independent basis and managed to become independent of the control and supervision of their ministries. As a new kind of entity in the former Soviet Union, the kontsern is defined as "an amalgamation of enterprises with centralized production, research and development, investment, financing, foreign trade and other functions, and cost-accounting operations."

The kontsern Tekhnokhim is comprised of seventeen enterprises and organizations, with a total of 55,000 employees. The management is based on democratic principles: the directors of enterprises have equal rights with the workers, and the decisions made by them are implemented by the executive board. Under Tekhnokhim, certain organizations have been created such as a stockholders' bank, a foreign trade division, and other divisions responsible for certain operations of the kontsern. The enterprises included in the kontsern delegated some of their duties and functions to the executive bodies of the kontsern. The executive bodies, in their turn, represent the interests of the Tekhnokhim enterprises and act on their behalf in contacts with ministries and committees and also with other organizations and enterprises. To provide functioning of the kontsern as an independent entity, part of the profit of the enterprises and organizations included in the kontsern, previously withdrawn for the centralized ministries fund, now goes to the centralized fund of the kontsern.

The main channel of spending from this fund is financing research and development in areas of high scientific and technological priority. The financing provisions of research and development envision the results of this activity to be the joint property both of the kontsern and the scientific organization which fulfills the order from the kontsern. The profit is shared accordingly.

Such centralized financial management resulted in an improvement in a number of social programs of the kontsern. One such program, "Housing-2000," guarantees housing for the Tekhnokhim, St. Petersburg, and St. Petersburg region residents from 1993 to 1998.

The chairman of the executive board of the small kontsern is convinced that without the supervision and control of the ministry it would be impossible to survive. But as it turned out, the kontsern successfully accomplished all its functions without help from the ministries. The performance of the enterprises and organizations of Tekhnokhim in fulfilling contractual obligations turned out to be the best among the enterprises in the same industries. Enterprises which have voluntarily joined the kontsern retain their independence and the right to leave the kontsern at any time. The enterprises in the kontsern have maximum freedom and maximum responsibility. They can use any cost-accounting economic measures to improve the efficiency of their operations, including leasing.

Cooperatives are being created at some enterprises. All major decisions are made by the staff of the enterprises. The major positive result of operating the first Soviet kontsern is working without ministry control. The major reason for this is undeveloped wholesale trade. All the resources are still primarily distributed through state channels. Only with true market mechanisms can kontserns be fully independent from government bodies.[22]

State Foreign Trade Structures

In our interviews, many American business people, primarily those who had started doing business in the Soviet Union in the last few years, told that they had had their own experience of being traditional state foreign economic structures, who were not interested in new contacts and were passive and inflexible compared to new foreign trade participants. Many of these American companies, which have created joint ventures in the former Soviet republics, have been confronted with restrictions imposed by the ministries and committees which were attempting to retain their monopoly.

With decentralization and the gaining of independence by the republics all the organizations are in a state of transformation. These organizations use various types of levers to compel foreign trade participants to do business through state foreign trade structures rather than through alternative economic entities.

Western companies' experiences of being confronted with a formal approach and lack of motivation by the state foreign trade officials may be illustrated by the following examples. According to the opinion of the representative of the American-French company Chlumberzhe Nina Bylon, Soviet trade representatives overseas have neither the expertise nor the ability to seek a partner in the business world. Not long ago, she visited one such Soviet trade office. The two experts considering business proposals from the country had a list of tens of enterprises looking for prospective partners overseas. They could not provide information on the location of the enterprise, their line of business, or the scale of their production, or anything that could satisfy the minimum, preliminary interest of a businessman. In general, she finds it hard to imagine how the small staff of the Soviet trade office can give a Soviet enterprise the leads it needs into the world market, especially if we assume that the influx of requests and proposals will increase dramatically.[23]

The newspaper *Moscow News* published a story about the joint venture Mono-Al, created by the American businessman J. Ross, and illustrates the lack of motivation of Soviet ministry officials. Mono-Al manufactures condoms. A great deal has been written about the shortage of condoms in the former Soviet Union. Only three condoms per year are available for an adult, even amid the growing AIDS epidemic and the absence of other contraceptives. It seems that this joint venture would be given the green light, but this was not the case. One of the ministry officials refused to endorse the written permission of his predecessor which would allow the export of by-products necessary to produce and package condoms overseas. In reference to the agreement regarding the concern about the AIDS epidemic, the official answered: "At my age, I'm not concerned about the shortage of your products."

It seems that people with a similar "understanding" of state interests are working in St. Petersburg customs. Two containers from the firm filled with important equipment required to produce the condoms for the Soviet market were plundered and detained by customs. Customs made Mono-Al apply to the procurator's office to recover the containers. Who benefits from this kind of attitude? The country? The joint venture? The customs which began operating on a cost-accounting basis? Nobody is personally responsible, meaning that nobody will pay out of their pockets or will sacrifice their career. That is why such situations are the rule rather than the exception.[24]

The ministries and foreign trade organizations have gotten used to not knowing the specific enterprises for which the technologies and licenses are purchased. They do not want interference from managers of enterprises making independent decisions about purchasing or taking part in negotiations, thus losing their control. The periodical *Eko* published comments by a Soviet engineer on the consequences of such control. He remarked that our personnel may be given an assignment such as the one to study licenses of the German company, Bosch. It is more likely that in this automated system the components come from the United States, Japan, and South Korea. One would have to pay in hard currency for them, which we cannot afford. So, we have several questions.

1. What should we do? There are solutions here. The first one is to dig into all the specifications of the Bosch company and find comparable Soviet components. Every designer knows that this probably will not be successful. The alternative is to try to understand how these components operate and to develop them ourselves. This is acceptable, but in this case, it was not necessary to buy licenses. It was possible to develop everything ourselves.
2. How much do these licenses cost our State? This purchase cost our State 1 million dollars. To make this technology operational in the Soviet plant will cost millions more, but this time in rubles. The system will not be identical but similar to the German one, and will be produced by our enterprises. It is difficult to explain why the license from another country must be bought if your own production has been developed.
3. What is the technical level and consumer quality of the license production line? To say that the Bosch company sold the product embodying the latest breakthroughs of science and technology would be an exaggeration. Neither can they say that Soviet designers are familiar with these systems. It means that we spent time and effort to adjust somebody else's product, but will be excluded from the process of improving quality and refining our own developments. Besides these considerations, a different approach to the design of the production line is being considered in developed countries.

Given the expense of all the operations and the cost of the license itself, one cannot count on a fast payoff of this deal given the current state of the economy. The currency which has been invested will not yield benefits, either in the development of technology or in increasing labor productivity. Engineers who must make all necessary Russian adjustments and fit the technology will temporarily not be participating in the development of their own technologies. Don't such licenses hamper progress? Moreover, they increase State indebtedness and are a wasteful use of currency. Figuratively speaking, if you are poor and feed the cow of your neighbor, your cow will die.[25]

The widespread opinion of Italian businessmen is that the biggest problem in doing business in the former Soviet Union is breaking through the wall of inertia and lack of initiative of Soviet foreign trade organizations. In spite of restructuring agencies involved in foreign economic relations in the former USSR, Italian businessmen and official representatives of the government are often confronted with procrastination, and frequent incompetence on the part of their Soviet colleagues. They are surprised by the willingness of Soviets to purchase non-quality items for low prices. As a rule, it is explained by the lack of currency and the necessity to save "the State's money."[26]

The Soviet economists M. Osmova and A. Sokolov have also analyzed the inefficiency of the State foreign trade system as follows. Soviet State foreign trade organizations frequently give up unexpected orders because the existing delivery terms for industrial equipment, from six to twelve months, do not accommodate fast commercial transactions. If a customer needs the equipment immediately, he will not wait for six months but will go to a competitor. The laws of the world market are still being ignored in foreign trade practices, such as supply, demand, product quality, and position stability in the market, etc.

If a Soviet foreign trade organization is selling its products successfully in the market, it would be logical to conclude a long-term contract on these products to get a toehold in the market. But foreign trade organizations have no guarantees that these products will be allocated for export in the required amounts. There are many reasons for this: unpredictable slowdown of the production might occur, state orders might be underfulfilled, the demand of the internal market has to be tapped, or the enterprises might have managed to trade their production in the foreign market independently. Soviet organizations appear and disappear sporadically in the market depending on current needs, while the market requires a continual presence. Inside the country, a company that does not fulfill its commitments is often forgiven. But foreign partners are not tolerant of this. Shortcomings turn into currency losses.[27]

Boris Yeltsin remembers when, at the time of perestroika, the activities of the Moscow State Institute of International Relations, Ministry of Foreign Trade, and Ministry of Foreign Affairs were checked into. The results were terrifying. Cheating, nepotism, and shady dealings were uncovered. The double standards and pervasive hypocrisy of the entire society are strikingly embodied in the performance of these organizations. From the podiums there was a lot of sloganeering about the evils and vices of Western society and its collapse. At the same time, high-ranking officials finagled to get their children into educational institutions which prepare citizens for overseas trips. Alongside the thinking about "developed socialism" and collapsing capitalism, they dreamed of the trips, during which they could save their daily allowance and buy tape recorders which could be sold in the Soviet Union for good money.

It took a lot of effort to streamline these organizations which had been closed to criticism for many years. With the Ministry of Foreign Affairs it was easier. Shevarnadze quickly got rid of pseudo-specialists who were on the staff of the major foreign affairs agencies of the country. In the State Institute of International Relations and the Ministry of Foreign Trade it took longer to eliminate many of these problems, but the process started. The party leaders and administrative leaders were removed.[28] In spite of the changes going on in this area, much of its legacy still remains, as cited by the opinion of a famous Soviet businessman, Artyom Tarasov, in 1990. He states that retaining the monopoly position of foreign trade organizations provides the basis for a number of wrongdoings and leads to many billions of rubles in losses. It can't be otherwise. Because the well-being of their officials is related little to the profitability of the deals, they are not afraid to lose the trust of enterprises whose products they are trading. It is no secret to say that for many of them the most important incentives are gifts and trips abroad, arranged by foreign partners. It is quite natural that they should be paid off, but this is a special kind of payment and not from their pocket.[29]

The following opinion illustrates another aspect of the problem of choosing a partner among State officials. One experienced Soviet foreign trade official said that American companies who offered sizable projects often had wrong ideas about choosing a partner. They count, for example, on regional authorities whose power was obtained as a result of new democratic trends. They underestimate the role of traditional bureaucratic structures, which seem to have changed only on the surface, and the role of multiple functionaries who retained their control over decision making. He said that Americans listened to the opinion of people who might be not worth listening to, and might not invite the right people to make an overseas trip and visit their enterprises.

Soviet Employees under Economic and Social Transformations

Differences in the types of partners considered so far have been related to the type of entity they represent, the degree of its independence, and its place within the state or alternative economic structures. But there are other social and psychological characteristics of partners that also determine their position in the current business and social setting.

The following findings come from surveys conducted by social scientists from the Informsotsiologia Scientific Research Center and State Research Institute of Labor. One of the sociological research studies conducted by the Informsotsiologia was aimed at figuring out correlations between the destruction of economic ties and subsequent dysfunction of the USSR economy and major differences among Soviet populations in their value orientations, interests, and norms of behavior that had a direct impact on their role in accomplishing perestroika. Two thousand employees from electrotechnical enterprises participated in this survey. Among them, the author singled out five groups which differ by their involvement in social ties and connections, and in their behavior.

Fighters

Members of this group are not satisfied with the existing social order, welcome radical changes, and make their own efforts to implement those changes. They are trying to fight those who hamper progressive transformations in the society. The majority of "fighters" are highly qualified workers. They are 35–45 years of age. Half of them have college educations, a feeling of empowerment, and identify not only with their specific workplace but also with the enterprise as a whole. Many in this group are engineers, or research, and scientific personnel who, due to their education, turned out to be more responsive to economic and political innovations.

Fellow Travelers or Sympathizers

These are people who are not taking an active role in the fight for innovations, but just approve of the behavior of fighters. As a rule, they are older people (45–55 years old) with a substantially lower level of education. More than half of the women working at an enterprise belong to this group. Usually, these people are reliable and responsible employees, though passive. They never criticize higher-ranking personnel even if they do not agree with them. These employees would not attempt to increase their production even if it resulted in a salary increase. Seventy-five percent of them would not try to master a new profession and 15 percent would quit their job if offered certain changes in their working functions. In the event of possible radical economic transformations at their enterprises, a part of the "fellow travelers" or "sympathizers" might be labeled "conservative" or even "reactionary," because they would be willing to retain the status quo which does not encourage them to change their profession, increase productivity, or take responsibility for solving new problems.

Conservatives

These constitute one-third of the employees of all enterprises. This group includes representatives of all age groups and of various educational levels. Two-thirds of the employees from this group are satisfied with their life and do not want any changes. Any transformations in the economic status of their enterprise might entail changes in their life and they are concerned about this. The priority in their set of values is having a happy family, and their well-being and the well-being of their family are identified with their stable position at their enterprise. In this group, 61.3 percent of the employees are hostile to the introduction of economic reforms, do not want to learn to operate new technology, or to improve their education and qualifications. A bigger part of the "conservatives" believes that operating the enterprise on a cost-accounting basis would lead to negative practices among employees: The willingness to obtain a more profitable job to the detriment of others, inaccurate estimates of the amount of the job accomplished, and lack of fairness in the distribution of bonuses.

The greater proportion of "conservatives" is among foremen, shop managers, and division managers—48.3 percent. This testifies to the fact that a great part of the managers and executives are satisfied with their position, status, and profession. Any reforms in their enterprises and the life of society can negatively impact their status and life-style.

The Morass

The researchers singled out a large group of people in Soviet society whom they labeled "the morass" (in Russian it is *boloto,* the word which figuratively connotes lack of clear identification with any side or position, non-adherence to any distinct political and economic mottoes and tendencies). The behavior of this group is considered to be the most unpredictable during periods of radical, revolutionary changes in the society. For *bolotos,* apathy and indifference to what is going on in the society, at their enterprise, or in their region is characteristic. All their energy is directed towards satisfying their personal needs. Poorly qualified and unqualified workers and employees constitute the majority of this group. Part of this group consists of people of retirement or pre-retirement age. They are not concerned with the future of their enterprise. This group constitutes 43 percent of the *boloto* category, and in some measure they are similar to "conservatives," that is, if their personal interests are affected by new economic mechanisms they may actively fight them.

On the other hand, among this group are young people (under twenty-five). In general, they are also indifferent to the problems of society. Their personal interests are outside the sphere of material well-being. This group is not afraid to voice its opinion, or to hold non-traditional views.

Reactionaries

They, like fighters, are not satisfied with the existing order and actively move toward political and economic restructuring at the enterprises. Their activity is not directed at progressive changes, but rather changes to restore the totalitarian order. They obstruct the regular and timely fulfillment of production orders, violate technological regulations, and in their personal relationships are involved in scheming and intrigue.

To determine various aspects of motivation in the workplace of the Soviet people, a specific technique was developed by the Research Institute of Labor that has been tested at one of the Tomsk enterprises.

Types of labor motivation among Soviet employees can vary from the intense desire to work and apathy, indifference, and the willingness to satisfy unfulfilled needs through non-labor sources. Various combinations of types of motivation are given in the accompanying table.

Types of Worker Motivation

Degree of Development of Motivation	Types of Motives Combination
All types of motives are well developed.	Interest in the process and result of labor are combined with the desire for material and personal reward

Types of Worker Motivation (*continued*)

Labor is a value in itself, and not seen partially or at all as a means of achieving reward.	Desire for the process and result of labor is combined with the desire for material reward.
	Desire for the process and result of labor is combined with the desire for (personal?) moral reward.
	Desire for the process and result of labor
Labor as a value in itself is partially developed. The motives of labor as a means of achieving material and moral reward are fully developed.	Desire for the result of labor combined with the desire for material and moral reward.
	Motives of the process of labor combined with the motives of material and moral reward.
The motives of labor being a value in itself and of labor being a means of achieving reward are not fully developed.	The motive of the result-oriented labor is combined with the motive of material reward.
The motive of the result or product of labor is significant.	The motives of the result of labor combined with the motive of moral reward
The motives of labor as the value in itself and labor being the means of winning reward are not fully developed. The process of labor is significant.	The motive of the process of labor as a value is combined with the motive of material reward.
	The motives of the process of labor as a value are combined with the motives of moral reward.
The motive of labor being a value in itself is developed. The motive of labor as the means of achieving reward is not developed at all	The motives of the result (product)-oriented labor.
	The motives of the process-oriented labor
The motive of labor being the means of achieving reward is developed. The motive of labor being a value in itself is not developed	The motives of material and moral reward
	The motives of material reward.
No motives are developed	The motives of moral reward
	Intense, strong motives are non-existent

One of the sociological studies conducted at seven agricultural machine building plants in various regions of the country was aimed at analyzing the lack of motivation for efficient performance by workers, brigade leaders, and foremen. In order to avoid losing working time and resources, each of them has to perform in compliance with certain instructions and if necessary to take initiative and be resourceful. During the poll it turned out that about 8 percent of the respondents do not even fulfill their mandatory functions spelled out in the instructions; 43.4 percent perform only some necessary functions; 11.8 percent fulfill everything envisioned in the instructions; 33.2 percent take initiative, i.e., try to improve the organization of their work, to introduce technical improvements, and so on.

The disinterested attitude of the employees and lack of motivation shows up also in their indifference to what is going on at the enterprise: 63.7 percent of the respondents do not react to the drawbacks (the attitude to efficient spending of the resources was researched) in the work of the enterprise; 26.7 percent respond only to the drawbacks in the performance of the brigade; 7.1 percent respond to the drawbacks in the work of their shop; and only 2.0 percent respond to the performance of the enterprise as a whole.

This behavior was contrasted to their behavior at home, where 6.7 percent of the respondents do not react to squandering at their homes or in their household, 11.2 percent react in a passive way just making comments, 26.3 percent react actively, trying to make improvements themselves not trying to involve anybody, 33.0 percent react actively and try to involve others in this effort, and 22.8 percent of the respondents did not give any answer. The reasons for such an attitude to State property were the lack of encouragement of the efforts and the concrete input of every individual that has been characteristic of Soviet power for many years.[30]

CHAPTER 8

Negotiating with Soviet Business People

Changes in Soviet life and the Soviet economy have created a demand for people who are able to participate in negotiations. We were assigned the task of putting together a training program to teach Soviets to negotiate, so we developed a program based on American practices.

As we conducted negotiation workshops for Soviets, we began to observe a strange phenomenon. The Soviets seemed to assimilate everything they were taught. They found all the negotiation techniques interesting and useful. They understood the various strategies and tactics and understood the ways of reasoning, types of arguments, and questions and answers should be articulated. However, when it came time to practice or use what they had been taught, they did not negotiate that way. Their interest in all of the training appeared to be abstract. A similar kind of negotiation workshop for Soviets was conducted by American professors who had been successful in teaching negotiation techniques in the United States. It appeared their program did not result in the expected improvement in the outcome either, i.e., the participants did assimilate the techniques, but they did not relate anything they learned to their actual way of negotiating. They seemed to find it very interesting, but didn't seem to connect the material to their own lives and work at all. We decided to conduct a series of exercises to figure out where the problem lay.

233

The exercises showed that Soviets negotiated primarily through emotion. If we listened carefully to how the Soviets negotiate, we could understand that they are often not business-oriented, but rather relationship-oriented during negotiations. This means that while they are conducting negotiations, they are actually concerned with personal relationship problems and satisfying their needs in this sphere. What they are often concerned with is how to win recognition, how to win approval from their authorities, and how they are treated (with respect or disrespect? Are they being hurt or overlooked?). Everything that happens during negotiations is related to issues of power and influence. We observed that all the minor issues were the focus of attention, not the subject of the negotiations themselves. If they are not talking about it, they are thinking about it.

We were surprised to see that it was typical for them to perceive negotiations in the same framework as they perceive family relationships. For example, they may be hurt in the same way that a wife feels slighted by her spouse. We observed the same sensitivity to status and esteem issues, as seen in the distribution of family roles, such as the roles of grandmother, mother, and father. Acting during negotiations in the capacity of a director of an enterprise, minister, or head of a state foreign trade organization is a similar type of family role playing. The problems, we realized, are not in the sphere of business, but in the sphere of power and the distribution of influence. We often observed that when talking about business issues, they were typically not preoccupied with better ways to solve problems and issues, but rather, were absorbed with emotions associated with status, self-respect, and similar problems.

The following example illustrates how the Soviets are emotionally involved in negotiations. For Soviets, a souvenir or commemoration distributed during international negotiations is not an element of conventional ritual which has nothing to do with the course of negotiations and their role in them. Correspondingly, the absence of a souvenir in return for their giving of one might be perceived by them as a personal injury. Once during negotiations we observed that the Soviets had given souvenirs but had received nothing in return. We tried to explain to our Soviet clients that it is socially acceptable in American culture not to respond by giving souvenirs in such situations. It might be incomprehensible to the Soviets that giving or not giving a souvenir is not regarded as an expression of personal attitude and that Americans don't attach the same significance to this. The significance which Soviets attach to even the smallest items becomes more understandable in view of the fact that the value of the souvenir which the American presents him might often exceed his monthly salary, and in some cases might be more important than winning concessions that could result in better terms of a contract. In his set of values, this five-dollar souvenir might be more significant. *He is not negotiating a deal which will come out of his pocket.* The price of equipment in a deal might be of the least importance. This refers, first of all, to a category of negotiators, such as representatives of a foreign economic complex and of ministries. In practice it hardly refers at all to those directors of state enterprises who are not indifferent to the fate of their enterprises or to Soviet owners of private businesses whose number are rapidly increasing. Representatives of the State foreign economic complex used to be the only negotiators that the Westerners dealt with. Now, with the emerging independent economies, there appear to be other categories of negotiators too.

However unusual and unexpected it might seem, we realized that in order to teach Soviets negotiation techniques it would be more appropriate to turn to training programs and techniques used in family therapy. Just as members of a family are taught to handle their conflicts and disputes and reach mutual understanding, they are instructed to approach the family issues as a type of negotiation in which the sides must come to an agreement. The objective of this family training is to make a shift from the sheer emotional sphere to a rational one and to resolve conflicts on a rational basis.

All our training, especially negotiations counseling work, is analogous to family coaching and is aimed at finding ways to help people set aside personal preferences, and conquer personal relationship and self-esteem concerns in order to focus on rational negotiations. We try to help them realize that all those personal motives must not be confused with business concerns that hamper reaching reasonable agreements. Whether we work as consultants to Soviet or American teams, our strategy is to help the Soviets reach this rational level. So, however strange and paradoxical it might seem, we work with Soviets in terms of family coaching, where tremendous efforts must be taken to help them get to a level where they can think rationally. Otherwise, negotiations will continue to resemble a family quarrel.

We also observed that in the same way families differ and certain categories of families, family problems, and conflicts exist, the same categories seem to fit Soviet negotiation participants. We used those specific techniques to bring people to a rational level, teaching them phrases to say in order to start thinking rationally, especially during complicated negotiations. We encountered lack of awareness of the reality of situations and their place within them during negotiation sessions. On the one hand, Soviets often do not comprehend what it is all about. On the other hand, the Americans might be unaware what specific kind of negotiators they are dealing with. In some measure, our role is that of the family therapist, being a trusted person of both sides. We do not make decisions for them, but help them carry on a reasonable discussion. We also help the Soviets formulate their objectives and goals. If we see that there is something emotional or irrational behind what they are going to do at negotiations, we help them overcome this "off-line," or outside the negotiation sessions.

We often observed that the people who participate in negotiations know no boundaries between their professional functions and their personal lives. They might not care about losing a lucrative deal because it doesn't matter for them personally. The Soviet negotiator might not understand what his job as a negotiator is. Instead, he may be constantly thinking about all kinds of personal issues, such as whether he was hurt or whether he was being treated with respect. It is characteristic behavior of the Soviets to be influenced in large measure by all these motives while making decisions. Even a minor slight, as perceived by the Soviets, might be transformed into an obstacle to normal business dealings. It is striking what impact some insignificant occurrence sometimes can carry which is emotionally charged for the Soviets and might affect the result of the deal. Interestingly, there is also an unexpected side-benefit when a man's job functions are perceived personally. A director of an enterprise who is motivated by his job might spare neither time nor effort to achieve better results without getting paid more money. With bureaucrats and state foreign trade organization officials, it is different. They do not identify with an enterprise. When a director of an enterprise is participating in negotiations, his personal emotions are less likely to have an impact on the result of negotiations. He is concerned with the interests of his enterprise and with the millions that he spends. The bureaucrats identify with their account to their authorities. And though a director may also have difficulty maintaining a rational discussion, the absence of a souvenir is less likely to influence the course of negotiations.

The following examples illustrate the behavior of Soviets at negotiations.

At one negotiation session where Soviets were purchasing high technology from an American firm, a multimillion-dollar deal was being discussed. One of the Soviet negotiators, quite unexpectedly from both the American and the Soviet teams' perspective, took an adverse position, and it was obvious that he was torpedoing the negotiations for some irrational reason. During the break we discovered that before the negotiations, there was a meeting at a business club where all the members of the Soviet delegation were given pens and pads with the logo of the American company. By mistake, the representative of the American negotiation team missed that particular Soviet negotiator while handing out the souvenirs. He happened to be just the kind of a person who attached much significance to giving souvenirs. Moreover, he had not been abroad before, had just got access to overseas trips, and his family was expecting him to come back with souvenirs. But the most important reason for him feeling hurt was that he hated the thought of everybody else receiving something he failed to get. We advised the American negotiator to correct his mistake, which he did, and the behavior of the Soviet changed abruptly.

In another situation, a delegation from one of the Union Republics was negotiating with Americans about creating a joint venture. The Soviet delegation included three officials from the Council of Ministers. The officials were not the head of the delegation, but members of it, and though they did not answer questions concerning the joint venture, many things during negotiations depended on their position because they were in charge of transportation, supplies, and resources. During the discussions, the Americans, quite naturally, asked questions and discussed their positions with the representatives of the enterprise who controlled the major issues. At one point, the Soviets and the Americans taking part in the discussion even shifted to one side of the table so that the representatives of the Council of Ministers appeared to look like outsiders. The officials began talking with each other and were obviously bored. As they felt more and more out of the discussion, they started to generate obstacles to the productive resolution of both Soviet and American issues. When the negotiators started to talk about the clause in the contract which would spell out who would have responsibility for supplies, one of the Americans asked who would make decisions on these issues. The general manager of the enterprise answered that he would. Then, one of the officials from the Council of Ministers said to another, "Let him think so." Their authority allowed them to deny the resources which the joint venture needed in order to operate. They were ready to stiffen their opposition and not provide the technology, raw materials, or transportation. During a break in the negotiations, we advised the American negotiator to involve the people from the Council of Ministers in the discussion, to ask them questions, and ask for their advice. As soon as the bureaucrats felt that they were included in shaping things, they changed their position and contributed to making productive decisions. The recognition of their active participation in the deal was more important to them than the deal itself, since they, themselves, felt superfluous in the situation.

A delegation of one of the Union Republics was discussing opening its office in an American state. The Americans offered a choice of two large trade center cities. The prime minister of the republic, who was at the head of the delegation, did not know much about American business life or what the guidelines should be for opening such an office, and he was hurt that the prospective location offered for the office was not the state capital. He knew that the governor's office was in this small capital. The prime minister was operating from his Soviet experience, where operating in the capital is more prestigious, and without knowing the American ways, he made the same assumptions about the American business world. When the Americans did not offer the state capital for the prospective Soviet office, he felt humiliated, and though some members of the Soviet delegation were more knowledgeable about American ways of doing business, they did not dare tell the prime minister that he was wrong.

The Soviet individual's psychological characteristics affect his business conduct. This is a significant obstacle which must be dealt with during negotiations. The individual characteristics of a Soviet strongly affect his behavior at work. A Soviet at work is often less likely to act according to special rules and regulations, but he does reveal his moods, attitudes, preferences, personal interests, and peculiarities. The rules functioning at his job might be used for solving personal problems, and the opportunity to interpret them in different ways, to use one rule in one case and different rules in another case (depending on whom he is dealing with—somebody from his circle or not, or whether he is interested in solving a problem or not), provides an opportunity to use the rules for solving his own personal problems.

Personal relationships and favors are important for survival in the former Soviet Union. Because of limited food and other commodities, people must rely on favors, sometimes illegally, rather than written instructions. With personal relationships, it is possible to do even what is not written in instructions. When there are no personal relationships, even what should be done under the instructions is not being done. Such is the general tendency of a system where social functions are inferior to personal interests. What contributes to this desire to use the laws for one's personal purpose is that, as discussed in Chapter 6, the laws and rules are vaguely formulated, enabling individuals to ignore them or to use them to satisfy their personal interests.

The director of a foreign economic division of a large enterprise told us that while participating in a training program of an American firm, he was amazed at how the people who worked in different divisions of the firm and did not know each other, but occupied similar positions, still held similar attitudes to their job duties and responsibilities. He told us that it would be impossible to do that in the Soviet Union, as it is impossible to predict how a person will behave at work according to the duties and responsibilities of the position. Everything depends on his personality, his mood, interests, preferences, how he obtained the position, who he is dealing with in a specific situation, and whether the person belongs or does not belong to his circle. All of these influence his business performance.

In the Soviet mind-set, business relationships are distorted by personal relationships to such an extent that personal interests, contacts, and preferences tend to supersede such driving forces of business conduct as rules, norms, and even concern about profit. In Russia one says, "Don't have 100 rubles, have 100 friends." According to an opinion of an Austrian businessman who worked successfully in the Soviet Union, it was impossible to have a partnership without liking each other, without having good relations.[1]

Soviet representatives tend to be conservative when establishing business contacts. They prefer to deal with those with whom they have stable relationships. There is another saying which goes, "An old friend is better than two new ones." Here is an example of why personal contacts are so important.

A Soviet official from a state foreign trade organization forgot to send some papers on the chartering of his ship cargo on time. As a result, his Greek partner had enormous losses but did not claim anything and did not demand compensation. He did not want to damage the reputation of his Russian partner, who could lose his job because of the mistake he made. Established contacts with the Soviet partner were more valuable for him than getting back money which he had lost. For the Soviet official, choosing such a partner is a security against any unpredictable problems he might have in the future. We recommend to our clients to take into account all these points, the sociocultural specifics, when they are drafting the provisions of a contract.

Many years of fostering the idea of not serving each other, but some abstract goal which exists somewhere outside the people in some remote future, led to a distorted perception of the concept of mutual benefit. As a result, it became typical for the Soviets to shun the idea of service for mutual benefit. In the Soviet scheme of things, it used to be insulting to benefit someone or even do something together so that both might benefit. These traits, together with the typical inability to think along legal lines, may lead to the situations when the Soviets do not comprehend the necessity of complying with contract obligations and terms.

This point is illustrated by the experience of the administrator of an international education and exchange program in Vermont. In our interview she recalled that while addressing a group of international students about the specifics of the cross-cultural education seminar they were about to begin, a Soviet participant asked, "What is the higher scientific purpose of this program?" If we take into account these concepts, as well as the situations which allow a person to reveal these characteristics, we see that they create an impossible situation in terms of complying with contracts and obligations. On the one hand, people do not care about rules and provisions. On the other hand, they do not obey the spirit of the agreement. If a Soviet is following an agreement, it means that he is serving somebody or somebody will benefit from him. It is his nature to resist this. That is why it is very important how clauses of the contract are formulated. We recommend to our clients who want their contracts to be fulfilled to put them in the form of instructions or orders which spell out very precisely the job that should be done by the Soviets. The contract should not reflect responsibilities in terms of serving anyone, and, moreover, never in terms of achieving mutual benefit, which is sometimes sufficient in the Western world but is not a motive for the Soviets.

We met with a hotel administrator to discuss the concept of good service in order to help her and the staff treat their customers better. The administrator would treat people better if she were given a clear and unambiguous order to do this. She knows the actual rules and guidelines about how she should treat customers, but doesn't care about them. If she perceived the guidelines as an order, containing concrete instructions, non-fulfillment of which could result in punishment, she would obey them. If she believed that she was doing it for mutual benefit, such as helping somebody make money in which she would share in the profits, she would not do it.

The idea of service, which is at the root of interpersonal activities in the Western world, is the opposite of the idea which was in existence throughout all the years of the Communist experiment, that everything was being done for the sake of some ideological goal somewhere in the distant future. People might mine coal, but coal is to make trains run and trains serve people's needs. In the former Soviet Union, everything was being done for the sake of some higher ideological purpose, such as the "good of the State." It is preferable not to set forth objectives in a contract, because Soviets tend to change or ignore them, but clear definitions of a job to be done which will be perceived as an order.

As to their obligations spelled out in the contract, Soviets tend to avoid any definite commitments and terms. For example, they are often not able to set any deadlines for themselves because too many things are beyond their control. The everyday reality of a manager is in a constant state of flux. The manager seeks resources to find loopholes for explanations about why he did not fulfill this or that obligation. Once at negotiations we asked a director of an enterprise why he had signed the contract to supply chemical resources produced by his plant without figuring out for himself whether he was able to obtain a license and provide transportation. He answered that he "was concluding such contracts" with the ministry every day. What he actually meant was that he was giving promises and was successful in finding subterfuges and loopholes to avoid fulfillment of the commitments to the ministry. The Soviets are accustomed to unpredictable and constantly changing conditions. Avoiding concrete commitments and contract terms is a way of life.

In general, attitudes towards contracts are different among bureaucrats, directors of enterprises, and representatives of the alternative economic structures, in terms of how the contract is related to reality and how it affects the actual state of affairs. Bureaucrats aim for maximum definition in spelling out the obligations of the other side. They ascribe to the other side their own resourcefulness in finding loopholes in contract provisions. Bureaucrats are motivated by the attitude of their superiors and the contract, and consider the contract more binding than the director of an enterprise and representatives of the alternative economy. One of the most common complaints of Americans is that Soviet negotiators will not make decisions or take responsibility. They delegate everything to their superiors. We became convinced that often the Soviet team actually does *not* have decision- and deal-making authority. The problem regarding the actual range of power becomes critical. There are basically three categories of Soviet negotiators with whom Westerners deal in their business discussions:

- Some negotiators do have actual power to conclude deals and make decisions and travel to foreign countries to generate positive results and sign agreements.
- Some negotiators discuss contract details with their superiors every day, or, if negotiations are conducted overseas, have frequent telephone talks with their boss to discuss the next moves. They have no authority to decide anything themselves.
- Other Soviet negotiators have not come to the negotiating table for the purpose of achieving any real results or making any decisions,

but are just exploring possibilities. Sometimes a member of the Soviet negotiating team is present at negotiations just for the sake of somebody being present. The actual decision maker may be busy with something else, while the person substituting for him is just marking time.

Making the distinctions among the various negotiating categories and identifying whom you are actually dealing with is a major difficulty. It is very difficult to judge if the person in front of you has any actual power or authority. Sometimes a negotiator might be the president of a large enterprise and still not have any real power. At the same time, some assistant might be the person who actually possesses authority and clout.

The Soviets do not have any system for delegating negotiating or decision-making authority on a consistent basis. We often observed that the Soviet representatives who arrived to participate in negotiations got into the negotiating team not because of professional duties and responsibilities that require their presence and allow them to make their own judgments, but perhaps because they are in good standing with the authorities and were rewarded for this by participation in negotiations. Perhaps they were not busy at the time it was necessary to make a business trip, or, in keeping with the principle of equality, were sent simply because their other colleagues had already been abroad. In that respect, we often observed that for Soviets, negotiations could be a process unrelated to any kind of activity which might bring about positive results. Frequently, "negotiations" were for the purpose of obtaining some information, for training, or just for a report to superiors. Therefore, identification of the partner and his actual authority is of critical importance.

The bases upon which Soviets appear to make negotiating decisions are quite often perplexing or nonsensical to Westerners. The following example illustrates the typical kind of transaction which confounds and frustrates Westerners.

A Soviet trade representative was buying equipment for a chemical plant. He had proposals from two companies. Company No. 1 had previously provided equipment to the USSR. It was already fitted out for the Soviet chemical plant. Company No. 2 offered similar equipment. It had never sold to the Soviets. The Soviets had doubts about how well the equipment would function under the conditions of the Soviet chemical plant. Company No. 1 wanted $300,000 for the equipment, and, as a result of negotiations, agreed to sell it for $250,000. Company No. 2 wanted $450,000, but went down to $300,000. The

Soviet representative bought the equipment from Company No. 2. It is obvious that this decision does not make sense in the context of Western business. So what happened?

One of the chief criteria for evaluating how foreign trade officials do their job is the discount they generate during negotiations, which is supposed to show how persistent and uncompromising they are as businessmen. Western companies who know about this criterion sometimes deliberately raise prices in order to create a greater discount later. However, this strategy doesn't always work for several reasons. First of all, comparison price lists are generated in many companies for prices on necessary equipment or commodities. On the basis of this information a market price list is developed, and if the prices of one company are much higher than those of others, negotiations might not begin there. Secondly, new participants in foreign trade activity who use their own hard currency to buy for their own enterprise, are less interested in discounts than in buying the proper equipment at lower cost. We will look at five specific characteristics of Soviet negotiations.

1. Susceptibility of Soviets to Hierarchical Distinctions

There is a saying in the former Soviet Union: "If I am a boss, you are stupid. If you are a boss, I am stupid." A Western company which was working with a Soviet enterprise often traveled to the country with a translator. The translator later created his own trading company. When he came to the Soviet Union as president of his own company, he met with the same people he used to work with before. They were surprised. How can this be? Who allowed this? It was difficult for them to understand how someone who was just an employee could become president of the company.

The deal with an American company was nearly destroyed because an ordinary worker tried to call on one of the Soviet high-ranking officials of the state foreign trade organization, rather than the president of the company, to resolve some issues. The call by the worker was taken as an insult.

Richard Worthy, USSR program manager for GE Transportation Systems, described in our interview his initial difficulty with the Soviets in being taken seriously as GE's chief negotiator for locomotive products. Worthy, twenty-nine, was perceived as too young, and therefore, by Soviet definition, too junior, to be dealt with in negotiations. On one occasion, while participating in a negotiation session along with several senior GE executives, including the general manager of GE Transportation Systems, Worthy visibly played the key role, while the other executives were clearly in a secondary role. "That was important in establishing my credibility as a senior player—a decision maker," stated Worthy. "The Soviets are sensitive to hierarchy and only want to deal with decision-makers. You have to prove to them that you're the one they want to negotiate with."

How can you use hierarchical structure to your benefit? For six months an American and a Soviet company were unable to complete a deal. Within that six months, the president of the foreign company came and, correspondingly, the head of the foreign trade organization went to the negotiations. The difficulties were overcome in a week's time because many issues were resolved by the right person from the Soviet delegation unlike previous "negotiations," when even insignificant issues needed many provisions and approvals from non-participating negotiation members.

2. The Psychology of Shortages

Everything is in short supply in the Soviet Union, so there is no aim to satisfy customers or meet their requirements. Those who sell dictate their own terms. One Soviet organization wanted to sell honey to an American company, but the Americans indicated they were only interested in transparent honey. Although the Soviets were interested in selling the honey, their response to the Americans was "Do something to keep it transparent."

Soviets joked that the former Soviet Union had created the optimum distribution system: Goods and commodities produced all over the country were brought to Moscow. Everybody had to go to Moscow to buy the goods and commodities and then distribute them in their own regions, bringing them to their friends and relatives. One could see this constantly going on at Moscow train stations. Now the provinces are taking revenge, limiting food and consumer goods supplies to the capital and so generating a vital necessity for Western aid, particularly in Moscow and St. Petersburg.

A Western company opened a business center in Moscow. Soviet representatives of a machine building plant suggested that they put their products in the hall, explaining that Western business people who would visit the business center might be interested in their products and buy them. They believed this was enough to promote their products for Western companies. They could not understand that in order to enter Western markets it was necessary to launch a promotional campaign in the West. Because the Soviets are often unaware of some basic market mechanisms, American partners must take on the marketing responsibilities when undertaking a joint venture with them.

3. Negotiating from a Closed Position

Very often Soviet participants take a closed or secretive position at negotiations and the attempts to hide information can reach ridiculous levels. In a recent example, a Western company decided to buy worn-out scrap metal from submarines for £5 million. When the Westerners inquired about the chemical compound of the metal, the Soviets informed them it was secret information and that they could not reveal it. At the same time, this very scrap metal had already been sold to an American company and the information about the chemical composition of the metal had been given. The secretiveness of the Soviets is rooted in their entire history of deliberately secluding themselves from foreigners. An example of the absurdity they reached in their xenophobia dates back to tsarist Russia, when the railway tracks were narrowed so that foreigners would not be able to ride directly into Russia. Since that time, the space between the wheels of a train has to be increased before it can cross the border of the country.

One of the aspects of the Soviets' position in negotiations, which requires clarification, is the actual power of a Soviet partner. Analysis of successful deals shows that this is one of the factors critical for achieving success. In our interviews we managed to figure out what techniques are used by successful companies to identify the decision- and deal-making authority of their counterparts. Three criteria are used here as guidelines:

1. One guideline is the type of organization that the Soviets represent. The closer the status of this organization to independent economic structures, the more this representative is free to act at his own discretion within this organization. But on the other hand, it is more probable that his organization is restricted from the outside, i.e., by the state structures which have the authority to allocate all kinds of resources. For a more detailed analysis of the advantages and disadvantages of dealing with representatives of alternative economic structures, see Chapter 7.

2. Another key is the status of the members of the delegation within their organization. Because of the many specific factors that contribute to the distinction of status, there can be no steadfast guidelines here. The entire situation is contrary to the American way, where the job title of a specific position suggests what duties, responsibilities, and authority a negotiator has. On the one hand, the general sensitivity of the Soviets to hierarchical distinctions makes it more likely that if the number one person is present at negotiations, he has the authority to make decisions. On the other hand, because of the obliterated borderlines between professional responsi-

bilities imposed by a specific position and a lot of non-business, non-professional factors, one's performance may be affected by non-formal distinctions.

3. One of the important factors in purchasing arrangements is the source of hard currency at a negotiator's disposal or his prospects for obtaining it. If members of a delegation represent an organization that earns hard currency and has the power to spend it, i.e., it is not frozen in its account in a Soviet bank, the deal is more likely to be concluded. But the situation in regard to the source of hard currency might be different. Negotiators might rely on the State for hard-currency allotment. Or they might be representatives of local authorities from a city or the region where, in compliance with the new decision, enterprises generating hard currency allocate part of their earnings to the city's needs. In such cases, the power of negotiators to spend hard currency needs verification because it hinges on a lot more factors in contrast with enterprises which generate hard-currency earnings themselves.

Furthermore, when Soviets sell something, it is necessary to figure out whether a license for the product is needed and whether they have this license.

4. Negotiations as Dividing a Pie

Soviets see business deals as fixed and finite entities. Only when ensuring that they will end up with more and the negotiating partners end up with less, do they feel the negotiations are successful. To Soviets, negotiations are like cutting a pie: To receive more means to get something at the expense of your counterpart, or, vice versa, he gets it at your expense. Negotiations are regarded as bargaining and not necessarily as looking for creative solutions which would benefit both sides. There is no concept of win/win. Together with their attitude toward secretiveness, situations like the following can occur:

In order to illustrate that such behavior was nonsensical, we cited the following analogy: Three people were dividing an orange, bargaining over who got what. The first one said he should have half and the others a quarter each. The second proposed to divide it in thirds. So they took the orange and divided it and used the portions they each had for their individual purposes. One squeezed the juice. The second took off the skin. The third one took what was left after he had squeezed the juice. If they had originally indicated what they required, everybody could have had the whole orange for what they needed. But, because they hid their positions, they could not find a creative solution that would allow everybody to benefit from a deal.

5. Soviet Rigidity

There are usually two reasons for the lack of flexibility of Soviets at negotiations:

1. Very often, Soviet representatives do not have the full right to make decisions. They first have to check with their authorities on any amendments in a previously approved program, including objectives, goals, strategy, projects, or contract documents.
2. Often, compromise is seen as a sign of weakness. At the same time, taking a very hard "no compromise" position is showing their strength. Often, the tendency on the part of foreign partners to compromise is viewed by the Soviets as a sign of weakness.

The Impact of Poor Soviet Listening Skills in Negotiations

We conducted a series of exercises to study the listening skills of senior Soviet executives, including the children's game commonly called "telephone." The exercise was videotaped while the information was transmitted from one participant to another and then subsequently analyzed. Among the groups who took part in the exercise were general managers of foreign trade organizations, directors of enterprises, and directors of cooperatives and joint ventures. Besides the task of studying Soviet listening skills, we also wanted to determine the differences in these skills between Americans and Soviets. Over the course of the series of experiments, both Soviet executives and American businessmen participated.

The task of the exercise was to memorize and transmit a message to another participant. The Soviets exhibited the following typical general behaviors in this exercise:

1. In general they remembered less of the information in the message and distorted it more than Americans.
2. Unlike the Americans, the Soviets in general would not admit that they could or had made a mistake, and regarded making a mistake as damaging to their reputation. They would agree that they made a mistake only when they viewed it on the videotape. While the Soviets did not doubt their ability to remember and transmit the message adequately, the Americans often began their communication with remarks expressing their doubt as to the degree of exactness of what they were about to transmit.

Americans treated the experiment casually and with humor while the Soviets were serious and tense.

Non-Verbal Behavior during Negotiations

A paradox of Soviet behavior at negotiations is that, while they purposely conceal facts and information, they do not hide their emotions. They have little understanding of the dynamics of non-verbal behavior and even less experience in attempting to manipulate it for their benefit, frequently communicating attitudes that they would otherwise wish to conceal.

Knowledge of Soviet non-verbal conduct, however, can help Americans during business dealings by:

- Providing a steady stream of feedback on the progress of the negotiations, potential breakdowns, or the need to restore rapport
- Determining whether the Soviet negotiator rejects an offer flat out, or is merely trying to win more concessions
- Determining the balance of power within a Soviet negotiating team since there is considerable confusion about who has what power
- Potentially improving the all-important informal contacts outside of the actual negotiations

The following examples illustrate each of the above processes and were taken from actual Soviet-American negotiating sessions:

1. How did Soviets provide information feedback on the need to re-establish damaged rapport?

During negotiations involving a multimillion-dollar contract in which we facilitated the deal in terms of cross-cultural support, it was obvious through a number of non-verbal indicators that some of the Soviets were taking an adversarial position and, in addition, did not completely understand what their American counterparts were saying. One member of the Soviet delegation was jerking his shoulders and crossing his hands with the palms open on his chest. Some of them stiffened and became rigid. One negotiator bit his lips. The American partners had a feeling that something was wrong but couldn't articulate where their uneasy feelings were coming from. We suggested that one of the possible reasons for the behavior of the Soviets was their disbelief of the estimated expenses and profit calculations by their American partners. The Soviets were sure that they had a commodity which was in high demand and couldn't understand why the Americans included advertising expenses in the estimates. Because their expectations were that Americans would cheat them, they did not trust the estimates.

During the break we tried to explain to the Americans that some non-verbal indicators gave the general appearance of mistrust and lack of rapport on the part of the Soviets. When the Americans provided a detailed description of how the market in the West operates, explaining that even a quality commodity required promotional expenses, rapport was re-established and the talks went on smoothly.

2. What clues indicated the offer was rejected flat out?

During negotiations for selling video and audio equipment, a lucrative deal was offered to the Soviets. They did not give a definite answer, and though the Americans explained in detail the profitability of the deal, it soon became clear that the Soviets were stalling. There were signals, however, which indicated that the offer would not be accepted. One negotiator threw his head back and a little bit aside in a sharp movement which conveyed that he had made a decision to do or not to do something right away. Another obvious signal of discrepancy between the discussion about "considering the proposal" and "taking next steps" and the actual intentions came from the member of the team who was shifting his eyes from one object to another. Another negotiator dropped his eyes and looked aside, which indicated evasiveness and insincerity. When we talked with the Soviet negotiators during the break we found that they were not decision makers and came to negotiate because the people with authority were away on another business trip.

3. What non-verbal clues indicated who had decision-making power on a particular negotiating team?

While negotiating the contract for construction of a hotel in a large Soviet city, we noticed that the American businessman mostly addressed the Soviet who was sitting just opposite him who did not clearly articulate his position, obscuring the situation. However, he was not the person with decision- and deal-making authority and actually was not in a position to give definitive answers. An actual decision maker was sitting at the end of the table. His posture and facial expressions were indicative of his authority. He was holding his hands on his chest and his body was leaning back. During some of his associate's answers the decision maker tapped his knee or raised his chin, signaling that he had the final say in the discussion. When the American understood who person number one was, the talks went more quickly and more constructively.

4. How did non-verbal behavior improve an informal relationship?

Soviets send messages in informal settings which indicate willingness to be on friendly terms with their partners. Bodily contact, distance, and touching convey their attitudes and feelings.

For example, the Soviets extended a greeting in the form of the traditional handshake with hands open and palms up, when they wanted friendly contact with them. Using the second hand on the handshake indicated even more friendliness. They also conveyed their willingness to engage in friendly contact through "body space" a half step of distance between speakers, elbows bent, and hands almost at chest level. Through friendly gestures, such as touching the speaker, either on the hand, arm, or shoulder, or a sudden reduction of space between parties, the Soviets signaled their friendliness and also a change in communication status from official to unofficial. Adequate response by the Americans helped reinforce the rapport.

Soviet Decision-Making Practices

Over many years of consulting for Soviet organizations we became convinced that one of the major reasons for poor performance was the lack of training at all managerial levels in decision-making practices and group discussion skills. Senior-level authorities of enterprises engage in discussions in the same way as foremen who talk about their minor problems, as well as Parliament deputies and the people who have been making the country's most important decisions. In specially designed simulations, we studied how Soviets conduct their meetings, analyzing videotaped recordings of real meetings of Soviet enterprises and organizations. During the interviews we also tried to find out what Soviets were thinking about the meeting itself, about the group decision-making process, and what their idea was of a good meeting. For example, we wanted to determine what results must be accomplished in or by the meeting for it to be regarded as a good one in their perception. What kind of a meeting would bring satisfaction to them? Some answers included, "When I managed to convince everyone that I was right," or "When the majority of the participants voted for the right decisions suggested by me," "When there was not a lot of disagreement," or "We managed to find a simple solution." We became convinced that they did not have a viable model for productive meetings. It was typical for senior managers to see no relation between their behavior and the way the meetings were being conducted; between the ways they conducted meetings and the failures in performance of the enterprises. After one training program, a senior manager was stunned when he saw for himself how the Soviets were conducting meetings, and cited the following analogy:

> Imagine people who do not see any connection between sexual intercourse and the birth of the child. Can a society that does not see this connection control the birth rate? Of course not.

The same is true here. Can an enterprise improve its performance if it does not see the relationship between the initial stages of an operation such as decision making, and the end result of their activities? We observed how American students who were on a tourist trip in Moscow discussed and solved their problems and were amazed to see that they were far more efficient than the directors in charge of large enterprises with hundreds of thousands of employees.

As we observed how Soviet senior executives sometimes worked out solutions to problems, we began to see how these decisions existed separately from the life they were designed to correlate with and did not correspond to the degree of complexity or reality. The people responsible for making decisions did not regard decision making as a complex process, but rather as a single issue covered in a textbook where the answer is given at the back of the book.

The major typical characteristic of Soviets in group decision making is that they believe there *is* one, right answer and somebody knows or can guess the right answer. When they set about making a decision, they go through the motions of working it out, but in principle, they are sure that the absolute, right answer exists at the end of the book, somebody knows it, and it is possible to verify the decision. The only thing left is to guess what it is. In reality, of course, everything is different. Therefore, typically, the objective that Soviets set for themselves at meetings devoted to decision making is to discover this "right" decision and isolate it from the "wrong" one.

The concept that the correct decision may be inferred only from life is most often totally absent, and they do not tend to treat the answer to a problem as a process where reality provides constant feedback and only reality can verify whether or not the decision was reasonable. The issues which arise out of complicated industrial and social situations are treated in large measure as problems which require a onetime decision, and not as problems which constantly develop and change as life itself changes all the time. Maybe an original decision was quite appropriate, but with later developments needs to be reevaluated. No history is traced, such as how the decision affected reality, or what new dynamics are observed. The prior decisions continue to be implemented unchanged, ignoring the changed reality.

When Americans and Soviets are discussing an issue, they might subconsciously engage in different kinds of activities. Most likely they do not understand what these differences are because they are deep and subconscious.

We designed and conducted simulations of various complicated problems in the operations of enterprises caused by some external conditions. These complex problems required an elaborate series of programs and actions. Instead of taking an approach which would be compatible with the complexity of the problem, a simple decision was made, such as, for example, whether or not to replace a manager, or whether or not to give someone a bonus which was promised. The problem was pronounced solved, set aside, and then the next problem was addressed. Perhaps in a month's time they would meet to hear how the decision was implemented, and its impact. Somebody will be punished, somebody will be praised.

Measures used to solve problems frequently only compounded them. One ministry official remarked that, "Nowhere in the world are so many 'right' decisions being made as in the Soviet Union," yet at the same time, the country was on the verge of ruin and economic collapse. The percentage of intelligent people in the former Soviet Union is just as high as in other countries. But if twenty intelligent people are not educated and trained in how to make decisions, they will be less effective than twenty average people who have received training or education in decision making.

Group discussions and decisions in the Soviet system do not enhance the probability of making better decisions. We analyzed several discussions at Soviet-American joint ventures where strategic plans were developed, and saw some of the sources for the lack of understanding between the parties.

In our interview, a railway manager compared the Soviets' vision of the world and their planning practices with a railway timetable. In this analogy the planning practices would be similar to a situation in which non-fulfillment of the original schedule is not taken into consideration when the new schedule, which is not met either, is devised. A railway is an organization that must serve the needs of its customers and if it is viewed as such, failure to keep to the original schedule may lead to closing some divisions of service and creating other ones, or result in some other changes and improvements. Instead, issues are discussed about why the timetable is not kept, the reasons for failures, and who should be blamed. The focus is shifted from the goal towards the means.

Another peculiarity of Soviet conduct at meetings and discussions is the fear of saying something considered stupid. By virtue of the same Soviet trait of merging the personal and the functional, the main objective of negotiators at the meetings most often becomes an attempt to either win the approval of the authorities or to seize power if one does not have it yet. If one has power there is no longer any discussion, because it is just imposing someone's point of view in full conformity with the principle "If I am a boss, you are a fool. If you are a boss, I am a fool." Therefore, people either don't say anything, even something reasonable, because they are afraid of being disgraced, or they say something which pleases the authorities or the boss imposing his opinion. Such planning practices create an illusion of solving all problems at once, and reflect the overwhelming tendency to declare big goals without considering the means to attain them. Soviets joke at things Soviet officials might be proud of: "Soviet computers are the biggest computers in the world."

It is typical for the Soviets not to see the difference between meetings designed for various purposes, including, for example, meetings where the manager is giving directions, and meetings to discuss how the decision which he has made should be implemented. Some meetings might be devoted to solving some technological problem. But meetings which are devoted to complicated issues are often approached in the same way as those which require group input and decision-making, although they are completely different in character and objectives. Most often, the boss thinks he already has the right answer and is just getting people together in order to share responsibility or to create the illusion of democracy. Though on the surface it may look different, typically the meeting is designed only to pass on the decision of the boss.

Skills in sharing power are also undeveloped. The situation is sometimes different when participants are equal in power. In this case, because of the lack of skills in sharing power, two or three people may start fighting, trying to assert their primary authority. It is self-assertion and not the discussion and solution of the problem which are primarily the focus of the meeting. There is no concept that the correct decision is inferred only from experience. The video recordings demonstrate this quite clearly when somebody takes the initiative or begins to tell what the truth is, what the right decision is. It was even said about Lenin that he was not seeking truth but victory in disputes.

We have not conducted special studies to determine in which country the tendency for authoritarian assertiveness and suppression of others' opinions is greater. One can assume that there are people with such styles both in the former Soviet Union and in the United States. Perhaps in the former Soviet republics such traits are more common due to the totalitarian nature of the society. But what we witnessed is that Soviets exhibit those traits more frequently in group discussions. Americans also have authoritarian traits and can be assertive, but Americans are solving business problems at meetings and Soviets are often solving their personal problems and seeking self-assertion.

There are exceptions to this deeply ingrained Soviet decision-making style. One of the leading Soviet economists, the author of the 500 days program, Grigori Yavlinski, developed a program to bring about market transformation of the Soviet economy on the basis of cooperation with developed countries of the West. The program was developed jointly with specialists from Harvard, unusual for the Soviets. In an interview with the former chief editor of the newspaper *Moskovskie Novosti,* Yegor Yakovlev, Yavlinski indicated that the program was designed as work-in-progress. It was not aimed at spelling out solutions to specific problems, but rather, at developing a philosophy which would be the basis of a search for an answer to a problem that might arise. Yavlinski stated that the program was a new, and unique example of this kind of approach in Soviet history, because up to that point everything had been done according to predetermined answers or conclusions.[2]

We believe that the overwhelming inability to compromise and find common ground is one of the reasons why talks and negotiations in the parliaments of Russia and the countries that made up the Soviet Union often end in an impasse. Distorted ideas about decision-making procedures hamper productive discussions among representatives of the former Soviet republics and among various groups of democratic movements, and between democratically elected power bodies and entrepreneurs. It is their deep, subconscious feeling that the right decision is not something that is a result of a productive discussion worked out in the process of analyzing each other's positions, sifting through them, and integrating them into a compromise. Instead they see it as one's own monopoly on the truth. Readiness to compromise is viewed as a personal weakness and the aim of the discussion is perceived as imposing one's opinion and making everybody think this way.

Epilogue

Dear Mark,

I'm not really sure what motivated me to take on the difficult, labor-intensive, and time-consuming project of co-authoring this book with you, other than it seemed like a perfect opportunity to learn more about your country, the tremendous changes you are experiencing politically and culturally, and the practice of business there. As an organizational consultant, I couldn't resist studying change in the ultimate "laboratory." I also saw an opportunity to put into perspective the business experiences I had personally had with Soviets. I wanted to understand why I experienced so much frustration. I wanted to understand why it was so difficult to get anything accomplished, and why most projects never got off the ground at all.

In working with you, my eyes opened up to a deep and complex culture and history that seemed confusing and annoying at first. As we worked together, I was initially frustrated at your apparent lack of interest or commitment to deadlines. I suggested carefully thought-out time lines for the huge project ahead of us which you agreed to, but then did not comply with. I requested information that I needed for writing text, or needed for clarification for my own understanding, but never seemed to get. I was told that a certain portion of your work was finished and "sent out today by Federal Express," and then a week would go by before it materialized at my office. Meanwhile, I searched anxiously for it every day in the daily deliveries.

During the many times we worked together face to face, usually at your home, but sometimes in an office space, I was humbled and overwhelmed by your gracious hospitality, the tea and coffee, chocolates and cookies, and of course, the lavish and delicious full Russian lunches prepared by your wonderful wife, Natasha. I was also a little taken aback by them as well. I was uncomfortable that Natasha worked so hard in the kitchen to prepare these meals, because I also viewed her as a peer and colleague in this effort. I was uncomfortable that a significant portion of our short working time was spent "socializing," and the "work time" evaporated over the course of the day. At the conclusion of these long work days, I was totally exhausted. Dealing with the complex subject matter, needing to ask so many questions and listen to so much complex information to get the answers, listening so intently for hours and hours through the translator, left me completely exhausted. (I can only imagine how Eleanor, the translator, felt at the end of these days!) The volume of your voices is different from Americans' and the unflagging "energy" with which you speak tired me. I usually felt like "my agenda" for the day or meeting got usurped somehow as you plunged ahead into the conversation. The tone of voice you used to ask or answer questions frequently left me feeling scrutinized (which I realized later was just a cultural difference that did not intend scrutiny or criticism at all). All of these dynamics combined to make our face-to-face interactions stressful and exhausting for me.

As we near the completion of this long collaborative effort, what have I learned about myself and about working with Soviets?

I am in touch with my tendency, the typical American business tendency, to shortchange social amenities in working together on a project. In my mind I saw an eight- or ten-hour workday solely as eight or ten hours in which to charge through our agenda, deal with content, get the information we needed to move ahead, and move on to the next objective. My compulsivity about time and using it fully, i.e., getting as much "work" done as possible, increased my stress level when we spent two hours over lunch in your home. In working together in the future I will be more inclined to look at our "work time" together as time that honors the socializing as much as getting through the content. Now that I understand more fully how and why social relationships are so important in developing a business relationship in your culture, I will be more attentive to those opportunities.

I have a greater awareness of the personal physical toll that working through a translator brings to the collaborative effort. It's time-consuming and leaves both parties open to the vagaries of nuance which are difficult to untangle, but imperative for authentic and accurate communications to occur. I certainly understand better the Russian historical, social, and political cultures which have led to reluctance, if not outright avoidance, in making decisions, from the most minor topics to the major ones. I also appreciate the magnitude and scope of the political and cultural process ahead for your countrymen as they attempt to learn, understand, and behave according to the new principles of business behavior. I would also hope that the years ahead can be a lesson for American business people in learning the importance of developing social relationships and not just in "getting down to business." For it is a fact, after all, that most business worldwide is conducted on the foundation of personal relationships, including much of American business as well. We are just less likely to put it "out there" as a stated agenda.

I have learned what questions to ask to determine what you can and can't do, will and won't do, instead of assuming many things that later turn out to frustrate me. In working with your Soviet managers I have learned how to evaluate who has the power to do what, and to cautiously evaluate all offers of opportunities which are proffered.

I have been reminded over and over in a hundred ways that, while we are similar in some ways, our cultures are very different. I have been in touch with many of my unconscious assumptions about human behavior and human interaction and I have learned to look at specific behaviors from several perspectives, not just my white, middle-class, American WASP perspective.

And if I had been able to articulate all of these learnings at the time we began this joint project, I would have realized that they were exactly what I had wished to learn and engage in. Our collaborations, both on this book and in our management consulting work, have provided the richest, most intense, and totally authentic laboratory for that learning. Thank you for that gift. Thank you for the gifts of your thinking and experience. But most of all, thank you for the gifts of your friendship and respect. I look forward to working together in the future.

Warmly,

Eileen Morgan

Dear Eileen,

As Eleanor and I worked together with you, we have been gradually developing the idea of what a typical American business person
is, because our working arrangement permitted us long-term observations and substantiated our conclusions. Though what we have seen
corresponded with our original assumptions about a typical representative of the Western business world, still, our long interaction en-
riched the idea and added new nuances.

We had a chance to see for ourselves what a highly professional
performance in the Western scheme of things means, and became
convinced that high motivation is demonstrated in forms other than
only stretching oneself and making many spontaneous efforts. Your
planning in advance, operationalizing every stage of the work, efforts
to be on schedule, showed us a different work dynamic.

Your different working rhythm and high self-organization put
some pressure on our interaction and impeded it at first. But as time
passed, we tried to adapt to what was more rational in terms of
achieving our shared goals with less strain and with a clear perspective at every stage.

We saw during our interactions that you had always given careful
thought to and had created a careful outline of the issues for our discussion, while on our side we acted more extemporaneously, though
it might have been determined by our varying perspectives on the
points for discussion, different perception of some concepts at the
outset, and lack of clarity at the beginning on how our mutual understanding might develop.

Being confronted with an entirely different world, you trusted and
respected my judgment. You have never started the discussion with
preconceived assumptions and myths, and have always tried to approach the problem from various angles, to penetrate deeply into it,
to grasp all the nuances, and develop an understanding adequate to
the extremely complicated reality you are dealing with. We think
that our interactions transcended the goals of the project we had
been working on. We invariably felt your friendly interest in our
country, in its people, in its destiny and hardships. We were aware of
your sympathy with the hard route our country has taken and your
desire to contribute to improving it.

During your presentations in our training groups, you made successful efforts to convey the concepts of an unfamiliar business life to people
from a different culture and with different perspectives. Their lively

interest, excitement, and response during the presentation showed that you succeeded in creating a setting which facilitated the exchange of ideas and that you provided an impetus for thinking about how to improve their business performance.

I consider that the integration of ideas from people with expertise representing different cultures has proved to be extremely fruitful, that each of us has gained far richer and broader perspectives, and that the tangible results of our collaboration are obvious. The only thing that we need to improve in our future collaboration is our organizational skills and working rhythm. I am sure we will develop further ways to work together and look forward to collaborating with you in the future.

Sincerely,

Mark Tourevski

APPENDIX

Natural Resources and Industries of the Republics of the Former Soviet Union and Contact Addresses and Phone Numbers

A Short Guide

While we were collecting these data, three new developments took place in the middle of 1991 which had a dramatic impact on the Soviet marketplace and created new business opportunities for foreign companies and new ways of establishing business contacts:

1. Transformation of the former Soviet republics into the sovereign states.
2. Foreign investors now have the right to explore and develop the natural resources of the republics.
3. Now that republican leaders are seeking more business contacts with Western partners and the political status of the former Soviet republics has changed, enabling them to create a more stable and viable business environment, the republics are adopting laws which are designed to solve in some measure the problems of creating guarantees to protect foreign investments.

In this short guide, we have put together information about the foreign economic potential of the republics and above all their natural resources and major regions of exploration and processing. The appendix also includes contact addresses and phone numbers of organizations which can assist American business people in establishing business contacts in various republics and regions. We focused mainly on independent structures, such as associations for foreign economic cooperation, cooperative unions, exchanges, and banks.

It was not only because of the emerging opportunities for Western companies to participate in the development and processing of resources that we provided information on the republican (regional, cities) reserves of natural resources, and the centers of

261

the exploration and processing industries. This information might also be useful for those companies who are interested in selling industrial equipment, computer and telecommunications technology, medical equipment and supplies, agricultural and food processing equipment, food products, consumer goods, and so on to the former Soviet Union. The hard-currency owners—enterprises involved in the development of resources and also the local authorities in the regions where these enterprises are located—may be targeted by those companies because part of their hard currency is allocated for purchasing foreign technologies and various commodities for their employees. Besides, they often have something to offer to foreign companies under the terms of compensation or barter deals.

Together with the Russian names of organizations, we gave their translations into English to give a very general idea of their activities. Because of limited space we were able to give only a selection of the organizations and contact addresses and phone numbers which might be useful in making business connections. In addition, six other types of organizations may be approached for assistance in establishing business contacts:

1. The organizations located in the United States, such as the Trade and Economic Council, Amtorg Trading Corporation, Sovfracht, and others.
2. Foreign trade organizations under former central ministries and committees which are undergoing changes now in terms of their organizational authority and forms of ownership, some of them even being transformed into stockholding companies.
3. Foreign trade organizations of the republican ministries and committees and under regional and city executive bodies.
4. Scientific-research institutes in various sectors of the economy which provide information on opportunities for exploring natural resources in various regions of the country, on the specifics of certain reserves, and on existing facilities.
5. Chambers of commerce and industry, centers of world trade, exhibition facilities, customs, shipping companies, banks, exchanges, and other organizations which can assist foreign companies in doing business in the former Soviet Union.
6. State and private enterprises, stockholding companies, and joint ventures.

Special consulting companies offer their services in providing such information.

Russia

The territory of the Russian republic extends over 17 million square kilometers. Its population is about 150 million people. The percentage of the urban population in the entire Russian republic is 73.5 percent. The working population numbers 84,058,000. There are over 20 million university and college graduates.

Central Region

Moscow, Vladimir, Ivanovo, Kostroma, Yaroslavl, Smolensk, Tver, Kaluga, Bryansk, Oryol, Tula, and Ryazan Districts

The Central Region is the part of Central Russia which includes also the Central, Central-Black Soil, Volgo-Vyatski, and North-Western Regions. There are a lot of forest resources in the north of Central Russia. The regions of Central Russia are connected through its transportation routes with major foreign trade ports of the Baltic and Black Seas. Major resources of the Central Region are *brown coal* (Nelidovo, Safonovo Regions, Tula Region, Novomoskovsk Region); *phosphorites* (Bryansk Region); *peat* (Yaroslavl Region, Kalinin Region). Processing industries are *ferrous metallurgy* (Tula); *petrochemical industry* (Yaroslav region); *chemical industry* including production of *fertilizers* (Tula Region, Voskresensk), production of *synthetic rubber* (Yaroslav, Yefremov); *textile industry* (Moscow, Orekhovo-Zyevo, Noginsk); *lumber industry* (Kaluga, Yelnya, Belaya Beryoza, Rzhev); *pulp and paper industry* (Surazh, Kuvshinovo, Kondrovo). Other industries developed in the Central Region are machine and machine tools building, and instrument making.

ROSVNESHTORG (Foreign Trade Department of Russian Federation)
123242 Moscow, Barrikadnaya Ul. 8/5, Phone: 250-80-50

SOVINCENTR (The International Center for Trade and Scientific-Technical Cooperation with Foreign Countries)
123610 Moscow, Krasnopresnenskaya Nab. 12, Phone: 253-63-03, Telex: 411486

VNESHECONOMSERVIS (Information Services on Foreign Economic Issues)
123100 Moscow, 1-i Krasnogvardeiski Proyezd 12, Phone: 259-73-53, Telex: 41238A, 41238B VES SU

INFORMSERVIS (Information Services on Foreign Economic Issues)
113324 Moscow, Ovchinikovskaya Nab. 18/1, Phone: 244-12-98, Telex: 411932 IVES SU, Fax: 244-12-98

EXPOCENTR (Services on Arrangement of Exhibitions)
107113 Moscow, Sokolnichesky Val 1a, Phone: 268-70-83, Telex: 411185

VNESHTORGREKLAMA (Foreign Trade Organization for Marketing and Advertising)
113461 Moscow, Kakhovka Ul. 31, Build. 2, Phone: 331-91-00, Telex: 411265 VTR

Rossiiski Soyuz Sovmestnogo Predprinimatelstva (Russian Union of Joint Enterprises)
103031 Moscow, Moskvina Ul. 5, Korp 7, Komn. 25, Phone: 924-22-31

Liga Bankov Rossii (Russian Banks' League)
Moscow, Novoarbatskii Prospect 29, Komn. 2116, Phone: 291-75-90

Rossiiski Kupecheski Soyuz (Russian Merchants' Union)

103012 Moscow, Varvarka Ul. 8, Phone: 298-43-94

Promishlenno-kommercheskaya Kampania "Rossiiski Dom" (Industrial-Commercial Company "The Russian House")
Moscow, Lev Tolstoi Ul. 2/22, Phone: 244-48-26

Rossiiskii Brokerskii Dom (Russian Brokers' House)
107066 Moscow, N. Krasnoselskaya Ul. 35, Phone: 267-44-82, Fax: 264-55-45

Rossiiskaya Tovarno-Siryevaya Birzha (Russian Commodities and Raw Materials Exchange—RSTB)
Moscow, Politekhnicheski Muzei, Podyezd # 2, 1-i Etazh, Phone: 262-80-80, Fax: 262-57-57

Rosagrobirzha (Russian Agricultural Products Exchange)
129223 Moscow, Prospect Mira, VDNKH, Tsentr "Moskva," Pav. # 3, Phone: 209-52-25

Tovarnaya Birzha "Konversiya" (Commodities Exchange)
140056 Moscow Region, Dzerzhinsky, Sovetskaya Ul. 6, Phone: 551-01-88, Fax: 551-01-27

Mezhdunarodnaia Birzha Intellektualnoi Sobstvennosti (International Exchange of Intellectual Property)
117418 Moscow, Novocheremushkinskaia Ul. 69-b, "VNIIzarubezhgeologia"

Torgovi Dom "Agrointorg" (Trade House for Trading Agricultural Products)
Moscow, Skatertni Per. 4, Phone: 290-51-41, Telex: 411676 ROZA, Fax: 200-02-94

Assotsiatsia Krestyanskikh i Selskokhozyastvennikh Kooperativov Rossii (Association of Farmers and Agricultural Cooperatives of Russia)
107139 Moscow, Orlikov Per. 1/11, Komn. 637, Phone: 207-80-75

Assotsiatsia Delovogo Sotrudnichestva s Zarubezhnimi Stranami v Oblasti Stroitelstva, Arkhitekturi i Sotsialno-Ekonomicheskogo Razvitiya v Rossiiskoi Federatsii "Rosstroiimpex" (Association for Business Cooperation with Foreign Countries in the Area of Construction, Architecture and Social-Economic Development in the Russian Federation)
101819 Moscow, Furkassovski Per. 12/5, Phone: 923-56-56

Moskovskaya Assotsiatsia Sovmestnikh Predpriyatii (Moscow Association of Joint Ventures)
103031 Moscow, Moskvina Ul. Korp 7, Komn. 25, Phone: 924-19-14

Moskovski Soyuz Chastnikh Predprinimatelei (Moscow Union of Private Enterpreneurs)
103104 Moscow, p/o K-104, Phone: 259-67-38

Moskovski Klub Menedzherov (Moscow Managers Club)
129010 Moscow a/ya 18, Phone: 242-22-50

Moskovskaya Mezhdunarodnaya Fondovaya Birzha (Moscow International Stock Exchange)
Moscow, Neglinnaya Ul. 23, Phone: 238-36-32

Moskovskaya Tovarnaya Birzha (Moscow Commodities Exchange—MTB)
Moscow, Pr. Mira, VDNKH, Pav. # 4, Phone: 187-86-14

Moskovskaya Birzha Stroitelnikh Materialov "Alisa" (Moscow Exchange for Construction Materials)
Moscow, Pr. Lenina 15, Phone: 137-00-06, Fax: 137-67-23

Centralnaya Krestyanskaya Birzha (Central Exchange for Farmers)

103009 Moscow, Tverskaya Ul. 5/6, Phone: 924-03-01

Birzha Tovarov Narodnogo Potrebleniya (Rosiiskaya Birzha) (Consumer Goods Exchange)
123423 Moscow, Narodnogo Opolcheniya Ul. 20, B. # 1, Phone/Fax: 946-32-98

Moskovskaya Centralnaya Fondovaya Birzha (MCFB) (Moscow Central Stock Exchange)
Moscow, 1-i Volokolamskii Proezd 10, Phone: 196-68-00

A/O Birzha "Rossiiskaya Bumaga" (Exchange "Russian Paper")
123268 Moscow, Sadovo-Kudrinskaya Ul. 9, Phone: 244-84-03

Moskovskaya Birzha Tzvetnykh Metallov (Moscow Exchange of Nonferrous Metals)
121596 Moscow, Gorbunova Ul. 20, Phone: 448-63-05, Fax: 446-18-01

Moskovskaya Neftyanaya Birzha (Soviet Oil Exchange)
Moscow, Naberezhnaya Morisa Toresa 26/1, Phone: 233-89-81

Smolenskaya Vneshneekonomicheskaya Assotsiatsia (Smolensk Foreign Economic Association)
214000 Smolensk, Pr. Gagarina 6, Phone: 3-29-77, Telex: 412574 BAIT

Smolenski Oblastnoi Soyuz Kooperativov (Smolensk Regional Cooperatives Union)
214000 Smolensk, Komunisticheskaya Ul. 17a, Phone: 3-71-97

Kalininski (Tverskoi) Oblastnoi Soyuz Kooperativov (Kalinin [Tver] Regional Cooperatives Union)
170000 Tver, Krilov Ul. 20/79, Phone: 3-78-52

Ryazanski Oblastnoi Soyuz Kooperativov (Ryazan Regional Cooperatives Union)
390010 Ryazan, Pirogova Ul. 13, Apt. 48, Phone: 53-29-26

Soyuz Kooperativov Tulskoi Oblasti Pri "Tulaglavsnabe" (Cooperatives Union

of the Tula Region under the Tula Committee for Supplies)
300600 Tula, Pr. Lenina 79, Phone: 21-83-64

Vneshneekonomicheskaya Assotsiatsia "Interservis" (Foreign Economic Association "International Service")
153000 Ivanovo, Pr. Lenina 40, Phone: 2-90-91

Ivanovski Oblastnoi Soyuz Kooperativov (Ivanovski Regional Cooperatives Union)
153000 Ivanovo 10, Avgusta Ul. 37, Phone: 2-51-46

Mezhrespublicanskaya Textilnaya Tovarno-Syryevaya Birzha "Ivanovo-Voznesenk" (Interrepublican Textile Commodities-Raw Materials Exchange)
153001 Ivanovo, Aptechnyi 17, Phone: 2-64-49, Fax: 2-76-02

Vneshneekonomicheskaya Assotsiatsia "Oryolimpex" (Foreign Economic Import-Export Association in Oryol City) 302200 Oryol, Lenina Ul. 37B, Phone: 6-99-22, Telex: 412545 RUNOK

Central-Black Soil Region and Volgo-Vyatski Region

Chuvashskaya, Mariiskaya, and Mordovskaya Autonomous Republics, Voronezh, Lipetsk, Kursk, Belgorod, Tambov, Nizhni Novgorod, and Kirov Districts

Major resources of these regions are *iron ore* (Kursk magnetic anomaly); *phosphorites* (Rudnichni); *peat* (Kirov, Nizhni Novgorod Regions). Processing industries are *oil processing* (Nizhni Novgorod); *ferrous metallurgy* (Star Oskol, Novolipetsk, Nizhni Novgorod, Kulebaki, Viksa); *chemical industry* including production of *mineral fertilizers* (Lipetsk, Uvarovo), and production of *synthetic rubber* (Voronezh, Belgorod); production of *construction materials* (Semiluki); *lumber industry* (Yoshkar-Ola, Cheboksari, Kirov region); *pulp and paper industry* (Pravdinsk, Balakhna, Volzhsk). In this region handicraft items and souvenirs are made, such as khokhloma (old folkcraft of painting on woodenware).

Vneshneekonomicheskaya Assotsiatsia "Interprogress" (Foreign Trade Association)
603600 Nizhni Novgorod, Krasnoflotskaya Ul. 65, Phone: 33-14-93

Kommercheskii Tsentr Gorkovskogo (Nizhnegorodskogo) Glavnogo Territorialnogo Upravlenia Gossnaba (Commercial Center of the Gorky [Nizhni Novgorod] Head Office for Supplies)
603134 Nizhni Novgorod, Kostin Ul. 2, Phone: 33-03-94, Telex: 151119 ARFA

Gorkovski (Nizhnenovgorodski) Oblastnoi Soyuz Kooperativov (Gorky [Nizhni Novgorod] Regional Cooperatives Union)

603005 Nizhni Novgorod, Minina Ul. 15-a, Phone: 36-95-04

Voronezhski Gorodskoi Soyuz Kooperativov (Voronezh City Cooperatives Union)
394074 Voronezh, Putilin Ul. 5, Phone: 49-59-78

Soyuz Kooperatorov Mordovii (Mordovian Cooperatives Union)
430030 Saransk, Stroitelei Ul, 15, Phone: 4-88-24

Assotsiatsia Proizvodstvennikh Kooperativov Chuvashskoi Oblasti (Association of Productional Cooperatives of the Chuvashski Region)
428003 Cheboksari, Chapaeva Ul. 14, Phone: 21-10-12

North-Western Region and Kaliningrad District

St. Petersburg, Novgorod, Pskov, Kaliningrad Districts

Major resources of this area are *aluminum ore* (Boksitogorsk); *phosphorites* (Gatchina); *peat* (Pskov, Novgorod regions); *shale* (Novgorod region); *construction stone* (Viborg region). Processing industries are *ferrous metallurgy* (St. Petersburg); *nonferrous metallurgy* (St. Petersburg); production of *fertilizers* (Novgorod, Kingisep), *pulp and paper industry* (Sovetski, Svetogorsk, Priozersk).

Other industries developed in these regions are machine and shipbuilding.

LENINGRADIMPEX (Export-Import Foreign Trade Organization)
190107 St. Petersburg, Isakiievskaya Pl. 6, Phone: 310-94-41, Telex: 121575, Fax: 319-97-09

LENFINTORG (Foreign Trade Association for Exports and Imports of Products within the Framework of Border and Coastal Trade Agreements with Finland, Norway, and Sweden)
196084 St. Petersburg, Moskovski Pr. 98, Phone: 296-11-65, Telex: 121518 LFT, Teletype: 122724 LENFIN

Severo-Zapadnoye Otdelenie Torgovo-Promishlennoi Palati (Chamber of Commerce and Industry. North-Western Office)
191194 St. Petersburg, Chaikovskogo Ul. 46, Apt. 48, Phone: 273-48-95, Telex: MOMENT LTPP

Leningradskoye Glavnoye Territorialnoye Upravlenie Gossnaba (Leningrad Territorial Head Office for Supplies)
193124 St. Petersburg, Suvorovski Pr. 62, Phone: 311-73-71

Tzentr Mirovoi Torgovli "Sankt Piterburg" (Center of World Trade)
193060 St. Petersburg, Proletarskoi Diktaturi Ul. 6, Komn. 417-419, Phone: 274-19-70, Fax: 270-18-08

Rossiiskii Brokerskii Dom (Russian Brokers House)
191119 St. Petersburg, Tushina Ul. 7, Phone/Fax: 164-94-47

Assotsiatsia Nauchnikh, Nauchnotekhnicheskikh i Nuachno-proizvodstvennikh Kooperativov St. Petersburga (Association of Scientific, Scientific-Technical and Scientific-Productional Cooperatives of St. Petersburg)

190000 St. Petersburg, Naberezhnaya R. Moiki 76, Komn. 533, 534, Phone: 314-50-52

St. Petersburg Soyuz Kooperativov (St. Petersburg Cooperatives Union)
St. Petersburg, Per. Grivtsova 5, Phone: 294-03-04

Upravlenie po Obsluzhivaniyu Inostranikh Predstavitelstv (Services to Foreign Representations)
191187 St. Petersburg, Kutuzova Nab. 34, Phone: 272-15-00

Torgovi Dom "Lenvneshtorg" (Foreign Trade House)
190000 St. Petersburg, Admiralteiskaya Nab. 8, Phone: 210-77-68, Fax: 311-14-26

LENEXPO
199106 St. Petersburg, Vasilyevski Ostrov, B. Prospekt 103, Phone: 355-19-90, Fax: 255-19-85

Leningradskaya Fondovaya Birzha (Leningrad Stock Exchange)
197061 St. Petersburg, Skorokhodov Ul. 19, Phone: 232-55-00

Interlesbirzha (Exchange for Forest Industries)
195009 St. Petersburg, Mikhailova Ul. 17, Phone: 542-90-03

Assotsiatsia Vneshneekonomicheskogo Sotrudnichestva Gosudarstvennikh Predpriyatii i Kooperativnikh Organizatssi Kaliningradskoi Oblasti (Association of Foreign Economic Cooperation of the State Enterprises and Cooperative Organizations of the Kaliningrad District)
236000 Kaliningrad Obl., Kaliningrad, Komsomolskaya Ul. 41, Phone: 1-23-83, Telex: 262125 ABC CU

European North

Karelskaya and Komi Autonomous Republics, Nenetski Autonomous Okrug, Vologda, Murmansk, Arkhangelsk Districts

Natural resources of the European North are *apatites* (Khibinskaya grupa); *ores of non-ferrous metals* including *aluminum ore* (Kirovsk) and *nickel ore* (Monchegorsk); *iron ore* (Monchegorsk, Kovdor, Kostomuksha); *coal* (Vorkuta, Inta); *gas* (Voivozh); *oil* (Usinskoye, Vozeiskoye, Verkhnegrubeshorskoye, Ukhta, Pashnya); *chloride* (Emva); *construction stone* (Kildinstroi, Svetogorsk). Processing industries include *oil processing* (Ukhta region); *ferrous metallurgy* (Cherepovets); production of *aluminum* (Monchegorsk, Nadvoitsi, Kandalaksha); production of *mineral fertilizers* (Cherepovets); *lumber industry* (Arkhangelsk, Naryan-Mar, Kestenga, Yushkozero, Umba, Pudozh); *pulp and paper industry* (Suoyarvi, Pitkyaranta, Kodino). There are a lot of forest resources and water resources in this area. The seas of the European North have a lot of fish. Murmansk is an ice-free seaport.

VOLOGDAGLAVSNAB (Vologda Head Office for Supplies)
160600 Vologda, Lenin Ul. 5, Phone: 2-11-89, Telex: 146922 SATURN

Soviet Soyuza Kooperativov Vologodskoi Oblasti (Council of the Cooperatives Union of the Vologda Region)
162614 Cherepovets, Gorkogo Ul. 61, Apt. 95, Phone: 5-37-29

Karelski Respublikanski Soyuz Potrebitelskikh Obshchestv (Karelian Republican Union of Consumers Cooperatives—Trade Coordinating Organization for Rural Area)
185660 Petrozavodsk, Pervomaiski Prospekt 1-A, Phone: 7-68-59; Telex: 165336

Severo-Zapadnyi Brokerskii Kontsern (North-West Brokers Concern)
Petrozavodsk, Kooperativnaya Ul. 6, Phone: 5-10-07

Arkhangelski Oblastnoi Soyuz Kooperativov (Arkhangelsk Regional Cooperatives Union)
Arkhangelsk, Levacheva Ul. 37, Komn. 11, Phone: 2-39-46

Murmanski Oblastnoi Soyuz Kooperativov (Murmansk Regional Cooperatives Union)
183012 Murmansk, Papashina Ul. 14, Phone: 5-92-96

Soviet Soyuza Kooperativov Avtonomnoi Respubliki Komi (Council of Cooperatives Union of Komi Autonomous Republic)
167001 Siktivkar, a/ya 1113

KOMI Tovarnaya Birzha (KOMI Commodities Exchange)
167610 Siktivkar, Oktyabrskii Prospekt 16, Phone/Fax: 3-84-43

Brokerskaya Kontora RTSB (Brokers Firm of the Russian Commodities-Raw Materials Exchange)
167018 Siktivkar, Borisova Ul. 58, #45. Phone: 26-47-42

Apatitski Regionalni Soyuz Kooperativov (Apatitski Regional Cooperatives Union)
184200 Apatiti, Bredova Ul. 9, Suite 20, Phone: 3-47-38

Volga Region

Tatarskaya and Kalmitskaya Autonomous Republics, Penza, Samara, Ylyanovsk, Saratov, Volgograd, and Astrakhan Districts

Volga Region is the part of the Uralo-Povolzhye which includes also the Urals Region. Uralo-Povolzhye has a lot of water resources. The river route Volga-Kama (Volgo-Kamski put) gives access to the Caspian, Blac, Azov, Baltic and White Seas.

Major natural resources of the Volga Region are *oil* (Frolovo, Zhirnovsk, Zhigulevsk, Chapaevsk, Sizran, Bugulma, Yelabuga); *gas* (Saushkinskoye, Frolovo, Zhirnovsk, Saratov, Stepnoye, Otradni, Almetyevsk, Yelabuga, Iki-Burul, Yermolinskoye); *shale* (Sizran); *sulphur* (Samara region); *sodium chloride* (Akhtubinsk region). Major industries are *oil processing* (Volgograd, Saratov, Samara, Sizran, Yelabuga); *gas processing* (Saratov, Almetyevsk); *ferrous metallurgy* (Volgograd, Volzhski); production of *aluminum* (Volgograd); production of *mineral fertilizers* (Toliatti); production of *construction materials* (Zhigulevsk); *lumber industry* (Volgograd).

Regionalni Soyuz Kooperativov Ul-
ianovskoi Oblasti (Regional Cooperatives Union of the Ulyanvosk Region)
430021 Ulyanovsk, Mira Ul. 14, Phone:
31-96-98

Simbirskaya Tovarno-Siryevaya Birzha
(Simbirsk Commodities-Raw Materi-
als Exchange)
Ulyanovsk, Pr. 50-letia VLKSM 23-a,
Phone: 36-54-81

Assotsiatsia Kooperativov Goroda Toli-
atti, Zhigulevska i Stavropolskogo
Kraya (Cooperatives Association of
Toliaati, Zhigulevsk, and Stavropol
Region)
445009 Toliatti, Chapaeva Ul. 158,
Phone: 29-29-60

Volgogradski Oblastnoi Soyuz Kooperativov (Volgograd Regional Cooperatives Union)
400005 Volgograd, Zemlyanskogo Ul. 1,
Phone: 34-34-32

Nizhne-Volzhskaya Tovarno-Siryevaya
Birzha (Commodities-Raw Materials
Exchange of the Lower Volga Region)
400005 Volgograd, Marshala Chuikov
Ul. 65, Phone: 34-72-95, Fax: 34-
74-19

Kirovski Soyuz Kooperativov Goroda i
Oblasti (Kirov Regional and City Cooperatives Union)
Kirov, Karla Libknekhta Ul. 119, Phone:
9-32-59

Kuibishevski (Samarski) Soyuz Kooperativov (Kuibishev [Samara] Cooperatives Union)
443010 Samara, Nekrasov Ul. 38,
Phone: 32-19-78

Mezhregionalnaya Avtomobilnaya
Birzha (Interregional Automobile Exchange)
443100 Samara, Molodogvardeiskaya
Ul. 187, Phone 33-89-80

Penzenski Oblastnoi Soyuz Kooperativov
v Sferakh Proizvodstva i Uslug (Penza
Regional Cooperatives Union in the
Area of Production and Service Industry)
440600 Penza, Gorkogo Ul. 12, Phone:
66-51-25

Engelsovski Gorodskoi Soyuz Kooperativov v Sfere Proizvodstva i Uslug (Engels City Cooperatives Union in the
Area of Production and Service Industry)
413100 Engels, Bolnichni Per. 1, Phone:
6-32-59

Urals Region

Bashkirskaya and Udmurtskaya Autonomous Republics, Komi-Permytski Autonomous Okrug, Perm, Yekaterinoburg, Chelyabinsk, Orenburg, Kurgan Districts

Resources of the Urals Region are *oil* (Buzuluk, Buguruslan, Tuimazi, Checkmagush, Ishimbai Neftekamsk, Votkinsk, Krasnokamsk, Perm); *gas* (Orenburg, Kumertaur); *iron ore* (Mednogorsk, Magnitogorsk, Yekaterinoburg, Pervouralsk, Nizhni Tagil, Kachkanar, Serov); *ores of non-ferrous metals* including *aluminum ore* (Zlatoust region), *copper ore* (Orsk, Zlatoust, Yekaterinoburg, Nizhni Tagil, Krasnouralsk, Serov),*nickel ore* (Yekaterinoburg region), *chrome ore* (Sarani); *construction materials* including *asbestos* (Yekaterinoburg region) and *marble* (Yekaterinoburg region, Kamensk-Uralski region); *graphite* (Zlatoust); *potassium salt* (Solikamsk); *sodium chloride* (Solikamsk). Processing industries are *oil processing* (Orsk, Ishimbai, Ufa, Perm); *gas processing* (Orenburg); *ferrous metallurgy* (Magnitogorski, Nizhnetagilsk, Chelyabinsk, Novotroitsk, Chusovoi); *non-ferrous metallurgy* including *aluminum*

(Krasnoturinsk, Kamensk-Uralski), *copper* (Krasnouralsk, Revda, Verkhnaya Pishma, Kishtim), Mednogorsk), *other non-ferrous metals* (Orsk, Rezh, Chelyabinsk); production of *fertilizers* including *potassium fertilizers* (Solikamsk), *phosphate fertilizers* (Perm, Krasnouralsk); *lumber industry* (Yekaterinoburg, Perm, Serov, Ufa)

Uralskoye Otdelenie Torgovo-Promishlennoi Palati (Chamber of Commerce and Industry, The Urals Office)
620027 Yekaterinoburg, Vostochnaya Ul. 6. Phone: 53-04-49

Uralskaya Assotsiatsia Delovogo Sotrudnichestva s Zarubezhnimi Stranami (Urals Association for Business Cooperation with Foreign Countries)
620043 Yekaterinoburg, Kopernika Ul. 46a, Phone: 72-36-36, Fax: 72-16-62

NII Metallurgii I Materialov (Research Institute for Metallurgy and Materials)
620219 Yekaterinoburg, Studencheskaya Ul. 51, Phone: 44-49-93, Telex: 2211291 AT Tsezii.

Sverdlovskaya (Yekaterinoburg) Tovarnaya Birzha (Sverdlovsk [Yekaterinoburg] Commodities Exchange)
620012 Yekaterinoburg, Cosmonavtov Pr. 23, Phone: 39-85-94, Fax: 34-43-01

Kooperatvini Bank "Polyarexbank" (Cooperative Bank)
620151 Yekaterinoburg, Libknekhta Ul. 45, Phone: 58-90-06

Chelyabinskaya Oblastnaya Assotsiatsia Kooperativov (Chelyabinsk Regional Cooperatives Association)
454000 Chelyabinsk 91, Truda Ul. 157

Brokerskaya Firma Moskovskoi Tovarnoi Birzhi "Chemet" (Brokers Firm of the Moscow Commodities Exchange)
454084 Cheliabinsk, Pobeda Pr. 160, Phone: 35-49-84

Cheliabinskaya Investitsionno-Tovarnaya Birzha (Chelyabinsk Investment-Commodities Exchange)
454000 Chelyabinsk, Yelkina St. 5, Phone: 33-96-02

Brokerskaya Kontora RTSB (Brokers Firm of the Russian Commodities-Raw Materials Exchange)

454114 Chelyabinsk, Box 17628, Phone: 35-17-78

Brokerskaya Kontora RTSB "Parus" (Brokers Firm of the Russian Commodities—Raw Materials Exchange)
Chelyabinsk, Pobeda Pr. 306-a, #16, Phone/Fax: 41-61-93

Chelyabinski Oblastnoi Kooperativni Bank "Rotor-Bank" (Chelyabinsk Regional Cooperative Bank)
454080 Chelyabinsk, Entuziastov Ul. 26, Phone: 34-76-83

Orenburgski Soyuz Kooperativov (Orenburg Cooperatives Union)
460000 Orenburg, 8 Marta Ul. 25, Phone: 1-99-92

Kooperativni Bank "Yuzhni Ural" (Cooperative Bank)
460031 Orenburg, Altayskaya Ul. 4, Phone: 1-19-00.

Regionalnaya Ecologicheskaya Birzha (Regional Ecological Exchange)
614600 Perm, Popova Ul. 9, Phone: 33-24-91

Permskaya Tovarnaya Birzha (Perm Commodities Exchange)
614600 Perm, 25 Octobrya Ul. 1, Phone: 31-99-98, Fax: 32-83-10

Kooperativni Bank "Zarya" (Cooperative Bank)
614039 Perm, Komsomolski Pr. 69, Phone: 44-41-28

Udmurtskii Respublikanskii Soyuz Potrebitelskikh Obshchestv (Udmurtski Republican Union of Consumers Cooperatives—Trade Coordinating Organization for Rural Area)
426034 Izhevsk, Revoluytsionnaya Ul. 217, Phone: 71-88-56, Telex: 255310 KEDR

Izhevskaya Kooperativnaya Assotsiatsia (Izhevsk Cooperatives Union)
462004 Izhevsk, Pastukhov Ul. 49/49, Phone: 76-65-75, Teletype: 255090 KARAT

North-Caucasus Region

Dagestanskaya, Severo-Osetinskaya, Checheno-Ingushskaya and Kabardino-Balkarskaya Autonomous Republics, Adigeisk and Karachaevo-Cherkessk Autonomous Oblasti, Krasnodarski and Stavropolski Krai, Rostov District

Major resources of the region are *coal* (Cherkessk Region, Shakhti, Kamensk-Shakhtinski); *oil* (Novorossisiisk Region, Khadizhensk, Neftegorsk, Grozni, Makhachkala, Yuzhno-Sukhokumsk); *gas* (Maikop, Temru, Kaneevyskaya, Stavropol, Takhta, Yuzhno-Sukhokumsk); *ores of non-ferrous metals* including *molybdenum and tungsten ores* (Nalchik), *polymetal ores* (Sadon). Processing industries include *oil processing* (Krasnodar, Grozni, Tuapse, Khadizhensk); *gas processing* (Grozni); *ferrous metallurgy* (Taganrog, Krasni Sulin); *non-ferrous metallurgy* (Ordzhonikidze).

The fertile soils and favorable climates of this region create good conditions for developing agro-industrial branches, such as grape raising, gardening, cattle raising, and food production.

Proizvodstvennaya Khozraschetnaya Firma "Impexservis" Severo-Kavkazskogo Regionalnogo Otdelenia Torgovopromishlennoi Palati. (Cost-accounting Firm "Import-Export Service" of the North-Caucasus Office of the Chamber of Commerce and Industry)
354005 Sochi, Kubanskaya Ul. 15, Phone: 92-20-03

Kooperativni Bank (Cooperative Bank)
354000 Sochi, Politekhnicheskaya Ul. 32, Phone: 93-83-38

Kommercheski Tsentr "Severoosetinglavsnaba" of Ordzhonikidze (Ordzhonikidze Commercial Center of the North-Osetian Supplies Committee)
362042 Vladikavkaz, General Pliev Ul. 44A, Phone: 4-70-33

Dagestanski Respotrebsoyuz (Dagastanski Union of Consumers Societies)
367002 Makhachkala, 26 Bakinskikh Komisarov Ul. 15, Phone: 7-26-69, Telex: 175161 Raduga

Taganrogski Gorodskoi Soyuz Kooperativov (Taganrog City Cooperatives Union)
347925 Taganrog, Instrumentalnaya Ul. 48 or Lermontovski Per. 28, Phone: 6-32-12

Kooperativni Informatsionno-kommercheskii Tsentr "Inkoservis" (Cooperative Information-Commercial Center)
344012 Rostov-na-Donu, Tselinogradskaya Ul. 1

Soyuz Kooperativov "Karachaevo-Cherkesski" (Karachaevo-Cherkesskii Cooperatives Union)
357100 Cherkessk, Per. Odesski 5, Phone: 2-77-81

Brokerskaya Kontora RTSB "Kobra" (Brokers Firm of Russian Commodities-Raw Material Exchange)
Stavropol, Tolstogo Ul. 39, Phone: 2-04-35

Birzha "Alisa" (Exchange "Alisa")
Grozni, Mayakovskogo Ul. 125, Phone: 24-15-54

Western-Siberian Region

Mountain-Altaisk Autonomous Oblast, Yamal-Nenetski, Khanti-Mansiiski Autonomous Okrugs, Altaiski Krai, Tumen, Omsk, Novosibirsk, Tomsk, Kemerovo Districts

The Western-Siberian Region is the part of the Eastern Economic Zone, which includes also the Eastern-Siberian Region and Far East. The Eastern Zone has enormous forest resources. There are many valuable fur-bearing animals in taiga (the woods of Siberia): sables, squirrels, foxes. Major resources of the Western-Siberian Region are *oil*

(Nizhnevartovsk, Surgut, Samotlor, Ust-Balik, Olenye, Shaim); *gas* (Urengoi, Medvezhye, Beryozovo, Igrim, Lunginskoye); *coal* (Kuznetski coalfield—Kemerovo, Anzhero-Sudzhensk, Leninsk-Kuznetski, Novokuznetsk, Prokopyevsk); *iron ore* (Tomski Region, Biisk region); *polymetal ores* (Rubtsovsk Region, Prokopyevsk Region); *sodium chloride* (Kulunda). Processing industries are *oil processing* (Omsk); *gas processing* (Nizhnevartovsk, Surgut); *ferrous metallurgy* (Novokuznetsk, Novosibirsk); *non-ferrous metallurgy* including *zinc* (Belovo), *aluminum* (Novokuznetsk), *tin, pewter* (Novosibirsk); *chemical industry* including production of *mineral fertilizers* (Kemerovo), *acids, alkali* (Omsk); *lumber industry* (Narim, Kolpashevo, Mogochin, Baturino, Asino).

Zapadno-Sibirskaya Assotsiatsia Vneshneekonomicheskogo Sotrudnichestva (Western-Siberian Association for Foreign Economic Cooperation)
630007 Novosibirsk, Komunisticheskaya Ul. 41, Phone: 29-91-71, Telex: 133143

Zapadno-Sibirsk Filial Obyedinenia "Soyuzpromvnedrenie" (Western-Siberian Affiliate of the Association for Patents, Licenses, and Know-how in the Field of Consumer Goods Production)
630078 Novosibirsk, Vatutina Ul. 15, Phone: 46-41-27

Nauchno-Issledovatelski i Proyektno-Konstruktorski Institut "Gidrotsvetmet" (Research Institute for Non-ferrous Metals Metallurgy)
630060 Novosibirsk, Zelyonaya Gorka Ul. 1, Phone: 32-00-33

Sibirskii Investitsionni Bank (Siberian Investment Bank)
630024 Novosibirsk-24, Mira Ul. 55,

Phone: 44-37-30, Teletype 15-74
BANK

Novosibirski Innovatsionni Bank (Novosibirsk Innovation Bank)
630081 Novosibirsk, Kamenskaya Ul. 53, Phone: 24-93-59

Institute Khimii Nefti (Petrochemical Research Institute)
634055 Tomsk-55, Pr. Akademicheskii 3, Phone: 1-86-23, Telex: 128240 Park

Komerchiski Bank "Tumen" (Commercial Bank)
Tumen, Gorkogo Ul. 44-a, Phone: 25-22-94, Fax: 22-74-85

Kooperativni Bank "Sibir" (Cooperative Bank)
644099 Omsk, Krasnogvardeyskaya Ul. 49, Phone: 22-17-42

Kooperativni Bank "Alyans" (Cooperative Bank)
626440 Nizhnevartovsk, Industrialnaya Ul. 5, Phone: 7-25-40

Eastern Siberian Region

Tuvinskaya and Buryatskaya Autonomous Republics, Khakassk Autonomous Oblast, Taimirski (Dolgano-Nenetski), Evenkiiski, Ust-Ordinski Buryatski, Aginski-Buryatski Autonomous Okrugs, Krasnoyarski Krai, Chita and Irkutsk Districts

Major resources of the Eastern-Siberian Region are *gas* (Norilsk region); *coal* (Angarsk, Kizil, Chernogorsk); *brown coal* (Kansko-Achinski coalfields, Irkutsk and Minusinsk reserves, Tulun, Chita, Nazarovo, Achinsk); *iron ore* (Zheleznogorsk-Ilimski, Abaza, Abakan); *ores of non-ferrous metals* including *copper ore* (Norilsk), *nickel ore* (Norilsk), *polymetal ores* (Borzya, Khapcheranga), *molybdenum ore* (Davenda), *tin ore* (Kharanorskaya); *gold* (Tuva, Buryatia, Khakassia); *graphite* (Kureiskoye, Angarsk Region); *asbestos* (Kizil Region); *sodium chloride* (Angarsk Region). Processing industries are *oil processing* (Angarsk, Achinsk); *non-ferrous metallurgy* including *aluminum* (Shelekhov, Bratsk, Krasnoyarsk), *copper-nickel* (Norilsk); *chemical industry* including production of *mineral fertilizers* (Angarsk), production of *synthetic rubber* (Krasnoyarsk); *lumber industry* (Igarka).

Vostochno-Sibirskaya Vneshneekonomicheskaya Assotsiatsia "Baikalit"
(Eastern-Siberian Association for Foreign Economic Cooperation)
664027 Irkutsk Pl. Im. Kirova. Dom
Sovetov, Phone: 24-68-09

Kommercheskii Bank "Aziatskii" (Commercial Bank)
664047 Irkutsk, L. Komunarov Ul. 10,
Phone: 27-46-69

Tovarnaya Birzha "Angarskii Region"
(Commodities Exchange)
665813 Irkutskaya Oblast, Angarsk,
Chaikovskogo Ul. 1-a, Phone: 3-03-
44, Fax: 3-04-73

Krasnoyarskoye Glavnoye Territorialnoye Upravlenie Gossnaba (Krasnoyarsk Territorial Head Office for
Supplies)
660049 Krasnoyarsk, Prosp. Mira 84,
Phone: 27-15-49

Krasnoyarski Kraevoi Soyuz Kooperativov (Krasnoyarsk Territorial Cooperatives Union)
660200 Krasnoyarsk, Belinskogp Ul. 1,
(Temporarily), Phone: 23-36-63

Brokerskaya Kontora RTSB "Taiga"
(Brokers Firm of the Russian
Commodities-Raw Materials Ex-
change)

Krasnoyarsk, 60 Let Octyabrya Ul. 113,
Phone: 36-61-7

Rossiiskii Brokerskii Dom (Russian Brokers House)
660025 Krasnoyarsk, Prospect Mira
129, #21, Phone/Fax: 29-20-41

Buryatskoye Glavnoe Territorialnoye
Upravlenie Snabzhenia (Buryatski Territorial Head Office for Supplies)
670045 Ulan-Ude, Poligon Buryatglav-
snab, Phone: 4-27-67, Telex: 219314
Sibir

Asiatskaya Birzha (Asian Exchange)
670000 Ulan-Ude, Sovetskaya Ul. 23,
Phone: 2-28-11, Fax: 2-26-81

Torgovo-Zagotovitelnaya Baza Ministerstva Torgovli Tuvinskoi Avtonomnoi
Respubliki (Trade- and Warehouse of
the Ministry of Trade of the Tuvinsk
Autonomous Republic)
667009 Kizil, Kalinina Ul. 25, Phone:
4-17-65

Soyuz Kooperatorov Tuvinskoi Av-
tonomnoi Respubliki (Cooperatives
Union of the Tuvinskaya Autonomous
Republic)
667004 Kizil, Kochetova Ul. 104a,
Phone: 2-40-38

Far East

Yakutskaya Autonomous Republic, Jewish Autonomous Oblast, Chukotkski, Koryak-
ski Autonomous Okrugs, Primorski Krai, Habarovski Krai, Magadan, Kamchatka,
Amur and Sakhalin Districts

Major resources of the Far East are *oil* (Sakhalin); *gas* (Sakhalin, Mastakh, Ust-
Viluiskoye); *coal* (Lenski coalfield, Zirnyanski coalfield, Chulmakanskoye, Cangar-
skoye, Galimovskoye, Partizanskoye, Uglegorskoye [Sakhalin]); *brown coal* (Anadir,
Korfovskoye, Partizanskoye region, Yakutsk); *iron ore* (Tayozhnoye, Garinskoye);
ores of non-ferrous metals including *manganese ore* (Urgalskoye region), *polymetal
ores* (Berezovskoye), *tin ores* (Valkumei, Urgalskoye region, Beryozovskoye); *diamonds*
(Yakutia); *gold* (Yakutia). Major industries are *oil processing* (Khabarovsk,
Komsomolsk-na-Amure); *ferrous metallurgy* (Komsomolsk-na-Amure); *non-ferrous
metallurgy* including *lead* (Dalnegorsk); *lumber industry* (Yakutsk, Khabarovsk, Al-
dan, Lensk, Petropavlovsk-Kamchatski, Ust-Kamchatsk, Kurilsck); *pulp and paper industry* (Blagoveshchensk, Yuzhno-Sakhalinsk); *fishing industry* (Vladivostok,
Nakhodka, Magadan, Petropavlovsk-Kamchatski, Anadir, Evensk). Far East seas and
the Pacific Ocean are rich in various kinds of fish, such as salmon, crabs, and also sea
animals, such as whales, walruses, and sea bears.

DALINTORG (Foreign Trade Organization)
692900 Primorski Krai, Nakhodka, Nakhodkinski Prospekt 16-A, Phone: 5-54-49, Telex: 213853

Primorskoye Otdelenie Totgovopromishlennoi Palati (Chamber of Commerce and Industry. Primorski Office)
690600 Vladivostok, Okeanski Prosp. 13-A, Telex: 213462 PALATA

Primorski Krayevoi Soyuz Potrebitelskikh Obshchestv PRIMKRAIRIBOLOVPOTREBSOYUZ (Primorski Territorial Union of Consumers Cooperatives—Trade Coordinating Organization for Rural Area)
690600 Vladivostok, Mordovtseva Ul. 3, Phone: 5-85-95, Telefax: 21-34-55 OMR, Telex: 213122 MRX

Dalnevostochnii Tekhnicheskii Institut Rybnoi Promishlenosti i Khozyaistva (Far Eastern Technical Institute for Fishing Industry)
690600 Vladivostok, Lugovaya Ul. 52-B, Phone: 9-52-16

Brokerskaya Kontora RTSB (Brokers Firm of the Russian Commodities-Raw Materials Exchange)
Vladivostok, Prospect Krasnogo Znameni 66-a, Phone: 6-58-19

Magadanskoye Glavnoye Territorialnoye Upravlenie Gossnaba (Magadan Territorial Head Office for Supplies)
685000 Magadan, Proletarskaya Ul. 12, Phone: 2-53-02, Telex: ZNAMYA145196

Regionalni Soyuz Kooperativov "Severovostok" (Regional North-Eastern Cooperatives Union)

685000 Magadan, Proletarskaya Ul. 1, Phone: 2-61-82

Brokerskaya Kontora RTSB (Brokers Firm of the Russian Commodities-Raw Materials Exchange)
Magadan, Proletarskaya Ul., Phone: 2-27-67

Kooperativni Bank "Magadanterkoopbank" (Cooperative Bank)
685000 Magadan, Proletarskaya Ul. 14, Phone: 2-23-53

Fond Sakhalina (Sakhalin Foundation)
Yuzhno-Sakhalinsk, Komunisticheski Pr. 39, Sakhalinski City Council, Phone: 3-14-02

Upravlenie Snabzheniya i Sbita Amurskogo Oblispolkoma (Supplies and Sales Division of the Amurski Regional Council)
675011 Blagoveshchensk, Muhina Ul. 152, Phone: 5-26-39, Telex: 154145 STRO

Amurskoye TPO Mestnoi Promishlennosti (Amurski Territorial-Production Association for Local Industry)
Amurskaya obl. Blagoveshchensk. Lenina Ul. 135, Phone: 4-39-00, Telex: 154165 KOSMOS

Dalnevostochni NII Mineralnogo Sirya (Far Eastern Research Institute for Mineral Resources)
680005 Habarovsk 31, Phone: 34-06-59, Telex: 141110 TEMP

Dalnevostochni Kommercheski Bank (Far Eastern Commercial Bank)
680000, Habarovsk, K. Marksa Ul. 42, Phone: 3-04-43

Ukraine

Major Ukrainian resources are *iron ore* (Krivoi Rog, Kerch); *ores of non-ferrous metals,* including *manganese and mercury ores* (Krivoi Rog) and *nickel ore* (Pobugskoye); *coal* (Lvovsko-Volinski coalfield); *brown coal* (Pridneprovsk coalfield). Other Ukrainian resources are *sodium chloride* (Shebelinka region, Jankoi, Glebovskoye), *sulphur* (Lvov Region). There are insignificant amounts of oil and gas reserves and construction materials such as chalk, limestone, and fire clay. Processing industries include *ferrous metallurgy* (Donetsk, Makeevka, Kommunarsk, Mariupol, Krivoi Rog, Dneprodzerzhinsk, Dnepropetrovsk); *non-ferrous metallurgy* (Zaporozhye); *chemical industry* including production of *synthetic fibers* (Kiev, Zhitomir, Cherkasi), production of *fertilizers* (Odessa, Dneprodzerzhinsk, Vinnitsa); *oil processing* (Odessa, Kherson, Kremenchug, Lisichansk). Other Ukrainian industries are machine building, aviation, and shipbuilding. In the southern part of Ukraine there are seaports (Ukraine, Odessa, Sevastopol, Kerch, Mariupol).

The territory of Ukraine is over 604,000 square meters. The population of Ukraine is about 52 million people, of which the urban population forms 67 percent. The working population is 28,826,000 people. College and university graduates constitute over 6.6 million people. The capital of Ukraine is Kiev. Other big cities are Kharkov, Dnepropetrovsk, Odessa, Donetsk.

Permanent Office of Ukraine in Moscow
Moscow, Stanislavskogo Ul. 18, Phone: 229-28-04

UKRIMPEX (Ukrainian Foreign Trade Department)
252054 Kiev, Vorovskogo Ul. 22, Phone: 216-21-74, Telex: 131384 UKIE SU

KIEVVNESHSERVIS (The Firm for Foreign Trade Facilitation)
252655 Kiev, GSP, B. Zhitomirskaya Ul. 33, Phone: 212-29-58

Soyuz Obyedinennikh Kooperativov Ukraini (The Ukrainian Cooperatives Union)
252012 Kiev, Pl. Oktyabrskoi Revolyutsii 2, Phone: 444-72-08 (Temporarily)

Assotsiatsia "Kievoblagroservis" (Association for Agroindustrial Products)
Kiev-1, Kreshchatik 6, Phone: 228-29-21, Telex: 131474

Kievski Gorodskoi Soyuz Kooperativov (Kiev City Cooperatives Union)
252001 Kiev, Kreshchatik 46, Phone: 3-78-52

Ukrainski Respublikanski Aktsionerni Innovatsionni Bank. (The Ukrainian Republican Stockholding Innovation Bank)
252001 Kiev, Malopodvalnaya Ul. 8, Phone: 229-57-95.

Kommercheski Bank "Ukrzhivmash" (Commercial Bank)
252112 Kiev, Parkhomenko Ul. 62, Phone: 446-08-12

Kommercheski Bank Razvitiya Promishlennosti Stroitelknikh Materialov

Ukraini "Ukrstrombank" (Commercial Bank for the Development of the Construction Materials Industry in Ukraine)
252053 Kiev, Artyom Ul. 73, Phone: 229-11-91

Kommercheski Bank Razvitiya Lyogkoi Promishlennosti Ukraini (Commercial Bank for the Development of Light Industry of Ukraine)
252023 Kiev, Kuibisheva Ul. 8/10, Phone: 220-81-36

DONETSKVNESHSERVIS (The Firm for Foreign Trade Facilitation)
340000 Donetsk, Pr. Dzerzhinskogo 12, Phone: 92-80-60, Telex: 115417 NORD

RADON (Foreign Economic Consortium)
340017 Donetsk, B. Shevchenko Ul. 75, Phone: 94-42-58, Telex: 115299 RADN SU

Donetskii Kommercheskii Tsentr Gossnaba Ukraini (Donetsk Commercial Center of the State Supplies Committee of Ukraine)
340086 Donetsk, Pr. Pavshikh Komunarov 7, Phone: 90-39-53

Donetskoye Oblastnoye Upravlenie Statistiki (Donetsk Regional Administration for Statistics)
340048 Donetsk, Universitetskaya Ul. 89, Phone: 55-21-44, Telex: 115153 STAT

Tovarnaya Birzha "Alisa" (Commodities Exchange "Alisa")
Donetsk, Cheluskintsev Ul. 189, Phone: 99-86-08

Nauchno-Issledovatelskii i Proyektni Institut Vtorichnikh Tsvetnikh Metalov (Research and Development Institute for Secondary Non-ferrous Metals)
340103 Donetsk, Pr. Lagutenko 14, Phone: 92-54-43, Telex: 115139 OLOVO

Regionalnaya Vneshneekonomicheskaya Organizatsia "Partner" (Regional Foreign Economic Organization)
310002 Kharkov, Ivanova Ul. 35, Phone: 42-33-05, Telex: 115177 Soyuz

KHARKOVVNESHSERVIS (Firm for Foreign Trade Facilitation)
310050 Kharkov, B. Khmelnitski Ul. 12-A, Phone: 21-32-53

Kharkovski Oblastnoi Soyuz Kooperativov (Kharkov Regional Cooperatives Union)
310050 Kharkov, Pl. Rudneva 9, Phone: 20-60-94

Assotsiatsia Vneshneekonomicheskogo Sotrudnichestva "Odessaintorg" (Odessa Association for Foreign Economic Cooperation)
270023 Odessa, Pushkinskaya Ul. 83, Phone: 22-32-08

Assotsiatsia "Intertemp" (Association "Intertemp")
270028 Odessa, Lopatto Ul. 13, Phone: 22-21-82, Fax: 22-65-04

Odesskii Kommercheskii Tsentr Odessglavsnaba Ukraini (Odessa Commercial Center of the Odessa Supplies Committee)
270039 Odessa, Gamarnik Ul. 13, Phone: 25-22-20

Odeski Oblastnoi Sovet Soyuza Obyedinennikh Kooperativov (Odessa Regional Council of the Cooperatives Union)
270009 Odessa, Perekopskoi Divizii Ul. 17/19, Phone: 68-55-78

Odesskaya Tovarnaya Birzha (Odessa Commodities Exchange)
Odessa, Proyezd Leninskoi "Iskri" 43, Phone: 44-81-56

Assotsiatsia Vneshneekonomicheskogo Sotrudnichestva "Kontakt" (Associa-

tion for Foreign Economic Cooperation)
333034 Simferopol, Kievskaya Ul. 81, Phone: 27-24-20

Krimski Oblpotrebsoyuz (The Crimea Regional Union of Consumers' Cooperatives—Trade Coordinating Organization for Rural Area)
333650 Simferopol, Samokisha Ul. 30, Phone: 27-77-66

Institut Mineralnikh Resursov (Institute of Mineral Resources)
333620 Simferopol, Pr. Kirova 47/2, Phone: 27-55-70

Vneshneekonomicheskaya Assotsiatsia "Lugan" (Association for Foreign Economic Cooperation)
348022 Lugansk, Lermontova Ul. 1-B, Suite 409, Phone: 52-22-95, Telex: 115184 Lux

Dnepropetrovskvneshservis (Firm for Foreign Trade Facilitation)
320061 Dnepropetrovsk, Vakulenchuk Ul. 3, Phone: 91-20-14, Telex: 143035 BAZIS

Dnepropetrovski Oblastnoi Soyuz Kooperativov (Dnepropetrovsk Regional Cooperatives Union)
320036 Dnepropetrovsk, Paster Ul. 2, Phone: 42-37-44

KHMELNITSKVNESHSERVIS (Firm for Foreign Trade Facilitation)
280025 Khmelnitski, Vokzalnaya Ul. 59, Phone: 6-50-97, Telex: 02-291610 ZEVS

Khmelnitski Oblastnoi Soyuz Kooperativov (Khmelnitski Regional Cooperatives Union)
290000 Khmelnitski, Ivana Franko Ul. 33/4, Phone: 6-93-10

Kirovogradski Oblastnoi Soyuz Kooperativov (Kirovogradsk Regional Cooperatives Union)
360050 Kirovograd, Gogolya Ul. 44, Phone: 2-70-03

Ivano-Frankovski Gorodskoi Soyuz Kooperativov (Ivano-Frankovsk City Cooperatives Union)
284000, Ivano-Frankovsk, Gryunvald-

skaya Ul. (Former City Council Building), Phone: 2-31-69

Chernovitski Oblastnoi Soyuz Proizvodstvennikh Kooperativov (Chernovtsi Regional Union of Productional Cooperatives)
274008 Chernovtsi, Gagarina Ul. 29, Komn. 34, Phone: 20-92-21

Kooperativni Bank "Nikolaevkoopbank" (Cooperative Bank)
327015 Nikolaev, Varvarski Spusk Ul. 1, Phone: 36-73-51

Kooperativni Bank "Tavriya" (Cooperative Bank)
334800 Feodosiya, Desantnikov Ul. 7, Phone: 3-19-68

ZAKARPATVNESHSERVIS (Firm for Foreign Trade Facilitation)
294015 Uzhgorod, Engelsa Ul. 62/29, Phone: 6-22-14, Telex: 274335 ATLAS

Zakarpatski Kommercheski Bank Razvitiya Lesnogo Kompleksa "Lesbank" (Commercial Bank for the Development of Forest Resources)
294000 Uzhgorod, Oktyabrskaya Ul. 52, Phone: 3-31-01

Lvovski Kommercheski Bank "Karpati" (Lvov Commercial Bank)
290069 Lvov, Shevchenko Ul. 317, Phone: 33-93-80

Belarus

Major Belarusian resources are *peat reserves* (Novopolotsk region); *potassium salt* (Soligorsk, Starobin). Other resources are construction materials such as limestone, kaolin, quartz sand, and small oil reserves. One-third of the Belarusian territory is woods. Belarusian processing industries are production of *lumber* (Minsk, Vitebsk, Gomel, Slonim, Osipovichi, Bobruisk, Borisov); *oil processing* (Novopolotsk, Mozir); *ferrous metallurgy* (Zhlobin); production of fertilizers including *nitrogen fertilizers* (Grodno) and *potash fertilizers* (Soligorsk); production of *construction materials* (Ros, Beryoza). Other industries of Belarus are machine building, tractor building, and radio engineering. The territory of Belarus is over 207,000 square kilometers. The population of Belarus is 10,266,000 people, of whom about 70 percent represent the urban population and 5,713,000 people the working population. College and university graduates number 1,360,000. The capital of Belarus is Minsk.

Permanent Office of Belarus in Moscow
Bogdan Khmelnitski St., 17/6 Permanent Representative, Phone: 925-57-58

BELARUSINTORG (Belarusian Foreign Trade Department)
220084 Minsk, Kollektornaya Ul. 10, Phone: 29-63-08, Telex: 252292 SONAR SU

Assotsiatsia Delovogo Sotrudnichestva "Garant" (Association for Business Cooperation)
220050 Minsk, Revoluytsionnaya Ul. 15

Assotsiatsia Vneshneekonomicheskikh Svyazei po Izdeliyam Mediko-Sanitarnogo Naznacheniya (Association of Foreign Economic Relations in

the Field of Medical Equipment and Supplies)
220013 Minsk, Surganova Ul. 6, 52

Belaruski Respublikanski Kommercheski Tsentr Gossnaba Belarusi (Republican Commercial Center under the State Supplies Committee of Belarus)
220600 Minsk, Brilevski tupik 55

Assotsiatsia po Informatsii Agropromishlennogo Kompleksa Belorussii (Informational Association of Agroindustrial Complex of Belorussia)
220108 Minsk, Kazinets Ul. 86, korp. 1

Minski Gorodskoi Tsentr Naucno-Tekhnicheskogo Tvorchestva Molody-

ozhi (Minsk Youth Center for Research and Development)
220006 Minsk, Mayakovskogo Ul. 22, korp. 2

Minski Oblpotrbsoyuz (Minski Regional Union of Consumers Cooperatives—Trade Coordinating Organization for Rural Area)
220050 Minsk, Volodarski St. 9

Minski Nauchno-Issledovatelski Institut Stroitelnikh Materialov (Minsk Research Institute of Construction Materials)
220600, GSP, Minsk, Minina Ul. 2, 3

Kommercheski Bank "Mikobank" (Commercial Bank)
220121 Minsk, Prititskogo Ul. 56, Phone: 55-75-77

Belaruski Innovatsionni Bank (Belarusian Innovation Bank)

220678 Minsk, Lunacharski Blvd. 6, Phone: 33-09-84

Vitebskoye Glavnoye Territorialnoye Upravleniye Materialno-Teknicheskogo Obespechenia (Vitebsk Head Territorial Office for Supplies)
210015 Vitebsk, 2-ya Prodolnaya Ul. 3

Vitebskaya Optovaya Torgovaya Kontora Oblpotrebsoyuza (Vitebsk Office for Wholesale Trade of the Regional Union of Consumers Cooperatives—Trade Coordinating Organization for Rural Area)
210001 Vitebsk, Beloruskaya Ul. 3

Mogilyovski Oblastnoi Soyuz Potrebitelskikh Obshchestv (Mogilyov Regional Union of Consumers Cooperatives—Trade Coordinating Organization for Rural Area)
212001 Mogilyov, Pervomaiskaya Ul. 97

Moldova

Favorable soil and climate conditions determine the development of the Moldovian agroindustrial complex. Major republican industries are grape raising and winemaking, gardening, market-gardening, and tanning. The republic also produces *cement* (Kagul) and has a developing *textile industry* (Tiraspol, Benderi).

The territory of Moldova is about 34,000 square kilometers. The population of Moldova is 4,381,000 people, of whom the urban population is 47 percent and the working population 2,408,000. The number of college and university graduates in the total population is about 500,000 people. The capital of Moldova is Kishinev.

Permanent Office of Moldova in Moscow
Kuznetski Most 18, Phone: 928-54-05

MOLDEX (Moldovian Foreign Trade Department)
277018, Kishinev, Botanicheskaya Ul. 15, Phone: 55-70-36, Telex: 163125 CODRU SU

Soyuz Dizainerov Moldovi (Moldovian Designers Union)
277001 Kishinev, Pr. Lenina 73

Gosudarstvenno-Kooperativnoye Obyedinenie "Moldvtorresursi" (State-Cooperative Association for By-products)

277018 Kishinev, Lesnaya Ul. 6

Kooperativno-Proizvodstvennaya Firma "Interproduktsia" (Cooperative Production Firm)
Kishinev, Per. Studencheski 2/4

PO Moldkoopprom (Production Association)
277023 Kishinev, Zavodskaya Ul. 9a

Moldavski Soyuz Potrbitelskikh Obshchestv (Moldavian Union of Consumers Cooperatives—Trade Coordinating Organization for Rural Area)
277001 Kishinev, Pr. Lenina 67

Kishinevskaya Khozraschetnaya Proizvodstvennaya Firma "Vneshservis"

(Kishinev Cost-Accounting Foreign Economic Production Firm)
277012 Kishinev, Komsomolskaya Ul. 28

Soyuz Agropromishlennikh Predpriyatii i Organizatsii Moldovi (The Union of Agroindustrial Enterprises and Organizations of Moldova)
277016 Kishinev, Pr. Lenina 162

Moldavski Institut Vinogradorstva i Vinodeliya NPO "Vierul" (Moldovian Institute of Grape Raising and Winemaking under Scientific-Production Association)
277019 Kishinev, Grenoblya Ul. 1, 28

Brokerskaya Kontora Birzhi Tovarov Narodnogo Potreblenia "Rossiiskaya Yarmarka"—Maloye Predpriyatie

"VolKKo" (Brokers' Firm of the Consumer Goods Exchange "Russian Trade Fair"—the Small Enterprise)
Kishinev, S. Aliende Ul. 1-92, Phone: 63-56-32

Brokerskaya Kontora Birzhi Tovarov Narodnogo Potrblenia "Rossiiskaya Yarmarka"—Maloye Predpriyatie "Mondial" (Brokers' Firm of the Consumer Goods Exchange "Russian Trade Fair"—the Small Enterprise)
Kishinev, Tigini Ul. 23-6, Phone: 26-51-25

Tiraspolski Tsentr Nauchno-Tekhnicheskogo Tvorchestva Molodyozhi "Tinzher" (Tiraspolski Scientific Development Youth Center)
278 Tiraspol, 25 Oktyabrya Ul. 45

Armenia

Major Armenian resources are *copper ore* (Kafan) and *molybdenum ore*. There are also *construction materials* including *marble* (Ararat, Artashat, Razdan) and others such as limestone and granite. Major industries are *non-ferrous metallurgy*, (Alaverdi); production of *synthetic resins and fibers* (Yerevan, Kirovokan). The chemical industry produces also synthetic rubber and mineral fertilizers.

The territory of Armenia is about 30,000 square kilometers. Its population is over 3 million people, of whom the urban population makes up over 67 percent. The number of college and university graduates is about 400,000 people. The working population is 1,969,000. The capital of Armenia is Yerevan.

Permanent Office of Armenia in Moscow
Moscow, Armyanski Per. 2, Phone: 925-57-58

ARMENINTORG (Armenian Foreign Trade Department)
375051, Yerevan, Komitas Ul. 546, Phone: 23-10-42

AIKOOP—Soyuz Potrbitelskikh Obshchestv Armenii (The Armenian Union of Consumers Cooperatives—Trade Coordinating Organization for the Rural Area)
375015 Yerevan, Marxa Ul. 7, Phone: 53-13-91

Fond Tekhnologicheskogo i Intelektualnogo Razvitiya Armenii (Foundation for Technological and Intellectual Development of Armenia)

375052 Yerevan, Asratyana Ul. 9, Phone: 28-30-12, Telefax: 28-30-11, Telex: 243323

Respublikanski Soyuz Kooperativov Armenii v Sfere Proizvodstva i Uslug (Armenian Republican Cooperatives Union for Production and Service Industry)
375033 Yerevan, Kiyevyan Ul. 19, Phone: 27-48-37

Magazin "GUM" (Yerevan Central Department Store)
375018 Yerevan-18, Marksa Ul. 33, Phone: 57-00-57

Brokerskaya Kontora Birzhi Tovarov Narodnogo Potrblenia "Rossiiskaya Yarmarka"—Maloye Predpriyatie "AS" (Brokers' Firm of the Consumer

Goods Exchange "Russian Trade Fair"—the Small Enterprise)
375028 Yerevan, Kievni Ul. 8, PTU 7, Phone: 22-70-63

Brokerskaya Kontora Mezhdunarodnoi Birzhi. Maloye Predpriyatie "Servis-Turism" (Brokers' Firm of the International Exchange—the Small Enterprise "Services for Tourists")
375002 Yerevan, Paronyan Ul. 40, Gost. "Dvin", Komn. 522, 524, Phone: 65-54-12

Abovyanski Gortorg (Abovyan City Trade Administration)
378510 Abovyan, 60-Letiya SSSR Ul. 5, Phone: 28-52-52

Kirovokanski Tsentralni Universalni Magazin (Kirovokan Central Department Store)
377201 Kirovokan, Pr. Lenina 81, Phone: 3-88-92

Azerbaijan

Azerbaijan has big reserves of *oil* (Baku Region, Artyom Ostrov) and *gas* (Karadag). At present oil is drilled from a depth of 5,000 meters and also from the sea bottom. Azerbaijan oil is mostly chemically pure and has little admixtures. Other resources are *iron ore* (Dashkesan) and *aluminum ores* (Alunitdag). The Azerbaijan processing industries are *oil processing* (Baku-Sumgait); *ferrous metallurgy* (Sumgait, Baku); production of *aluminum* (Sumgait); production of *synthetic rubber, synthetic resins,* and *synthetic fibers* (Sumgait). Through the Caspian Sea, Azerbaijan is connected to Central Asia and Kazakhstan and through the Volga to the Urals Region.

The territory of Azerbaijan is about 70,000 square kilometers. The population of Azerbaijan is 7,300,000 people. The urban population is 54.2 percent and the working population 3,941,000 people. College and university graduates constitute 625,000 people from the population as a whole. The capital of Azerbaijan is Baku.

Permanent Office of Azerbaijan in Moscow
Moscow, Stanislavskogo Ul. 16, Phone: 229-16-49

AZERBINTORG (Azerbaijan Foreign Trade Department)
370004 Baku, Nekrasova Ul. 4, Phone: 92-29-40

Azerbaijanskaya Respublikanskaya Vneshneekonomicheskaya Assotsiatsia (Azerbaijan Republican Foreign Economic Association)
370025 Baku, Telnov Ul. 28

Azerbaijanskaya Respublikahskaya Assotsiatsia Vneshneekonomicheskogo Sotrudnichestva. (Azerbaijan Republican Association for Foreign Economic Cooperation)
370141 Baku, Alekperov Ul. 82/23

DIYAR—Assotsiatsia Vneshneekonomicheskogo Sotrudnichestva s Zarubezhnimi Stranami. (Association for Foreign Economic Cooperation with Foreign Countries)
370020 Baku, Moskovski Pr. 82/1

Kommercheski Tsentr Gossnaba Azerbaijana (Commercial Center of the Azerbaijan Supplies Committee)
370005 Baku, Per. Gusi Gadzhieva 7

Azerbaijanskaya Kommercheskaya Assotsiatsia (Azerbaijan Commercial Association)
370016 Baku, Dom Pravitelstva

Soyuz Proizvodstvenikh Kooperativov Azerbaijana (The Azerbaijan Industrial Cooperatives Union)
370603 Baku, Moskovski Prospekt 81/6, Phone: 67-84-95

Bakinskaya Gorodskaya Assotsiatsia Kooperativov "Midzhlis" (Baku City Cooperatives Association)
370005 Baku, Gorkogo Ul. 5, Phone: 94-94-66

Bakinski Gorodskoi Tsentr Nauchno-Tekhnichaskogo Tvorchestva Molody-ozhi "Imrad" (Baku City Youth Center for Research and Development)
370000 Baku-Tsentr, A/YA 103

Azerbaijanskoye Obyedinenie Vtorich-nikh Resursov "Azervtorresursi" (Azerbaijan Association for By-products)
370602 Baku, A. Alekperov Ul. Block 507-511, 14B

Azerbaijanskoye Respublikanskoye Kom-mercheskoye Predpriyatie Ministerstva Torgovli Azerbaidzhana (Azerbaijan Republican Commercial Enterprise under the Azerbaijan Ministry of Trade)
370004 Baku, Gertsena Ul. 24

Mezhdunarodni Nauchno-Tekhnicheski Kompleks "Intergeo-Tetis" (International Scientific-Technical Complex)
370012 Baku, Tbilisski Pr. 73

ASINAM—Assotsiatsia Eko-nomicheskogo i Kulturnogo Razvitiya Azerbaijana (Association for Economic and Cultural Development of Azerbaijan)
370148 Baku, Mekhti Gusein Ul. 1A, Hotel *Moskva*, Room #601

Bakinski Kommercheski Bank "Universal" (Baku Commercial Bank)
370001 Baku, Ostrovskogo Ul. 39/11, Phone: 92-89-80

Kooperativni Bank Bakinskogo Soyuza Kooperativov (Cooperative Bank for Baku Cooperatives Union)
370025 Baku, Barinova Ul. 12, (370000, a/ya 221), Phone: 67-45-46, Telex: 142205 BAKOB SU

Kooperativni Bank "Gyandzhbank" (Cooperative Bank)
374700 Gyandzha, Gyandzha Ul. 24, Phone: 2-60-37

Georgia

The favorable natural conditions of Georgia have determined the development of its agroindustrial business. Major branches of this sector of the economy are raising citrus fruits, grapes, and tea. Major Georgian natural resources are *manganese ore* (Chiaturi); *coal* (Tkibuli, Tkvarcheli). Georgian processing industries are *ferrous metallurgy* (Zesta-foni, Rustavi); production of *nitrogen fertilizers* (Rustavi); *oil processing* (Batumi).

The territory of Georgia is about 70,000 square kilometers. Its population is 5,500,000 people. The urban population constitutes 55 percent and the working population 3,027,000 people. The number of college and university graduates is 619,000 people. The capital of Georgia is Tbilisi.

Permanent Office of Georgia in Moscow
Moscow, Paliashvili Ul. 6, Phone: 291-21-36

GRUZIMPEX (Georgian Foreign Trade Department)
380018 Tbilisi, Rustaveli Pr. 8, Dom Pravitelstva, Phone: 93-70-90

Torgovo-Promishlennaya Palata Gruzii (Chamber of Commerce and Industry of Georgia)
380079 Tbilisi, Pr. Chavchavadze 11, Phone: 23-00-45, Telex: 212155 Pala

Kommercheski Tsentr Gosudarstvenogo Komiteta Gruzii po Materialno-technicheskomu Snabzheniiyu (Com-mercial Center of the Georgian Supplies Committee) 380094 Tbilisi, Bakhtrionskaya Ul. 8, Phone: 38-64-30

TBILPROMTORG (Tbilisi City Trade Administration for Consumer Goods)
380005 Tbilisi, Baratashvili Ul. 8, Phone: 93-45-94

Gruzinskoye Upravlenie Optovoi Tor-govli Khimicheskoi i Polimernoi Produktsii (Georgian Administration of Wholesale Trade for Chemical and Polymer Products)
380051 Tbilisi, Pos. Lilo, Phone: 41-54-59, Telex: 212140 KHLOR

Soyuz kooperatorov v sfere proizvodstva i uslug Gruzii (Cooperatives Union in the Sphere of Georgian Production and Service Industries)
380007 Tbilisi, Pavlova Ul. 42, Phone: 39-47-70

Tbiliski Glavni Univermag (Tbilisi Central Department Store)
380007 Tbilisi, Pr. Rustaveli 2/4, Phone: 93-42-32

NII Nauchno-Tekhnicheskoi Informatsii i Tekhniko-ekonomicheskikh Issledovanii (Research Institute of Scientific-Technical Information and Technical-Economic Studies)
380062 Tbilisi, Pr. Chavchavadze 35, GRUZNIINTI, Phone: 22-16-05, Telex: 212245 FOND SU

Kommercheski Bank "Avtotransdor" (Commercial Bank)
380060 Tbilisi, Pavlova Ul. 12, Phone: 38-26-31

Kooperativni Bank "Sokartvelo" (Cooperative Bank)

380007 Tbilisi, Lenina Pl. 7, Phone: 99-85-31

Brokerskaya Kontora Mezhdunarodnoi Birzhi—Korporatsia "Tao" (Brokers' Firm of the International Exchange—the Corporation "Tao")
380086 Tbilisi, Dzhinia Ul. 16, Phone: 31-91-10

Brokerskaya Kontora Mezhdunarodnoi Birzhi—Mnogootraslevoi Kooperativ "Orion-90" (Brokers' Firm of the International Exchange—the Cooperative for a Variety of Businesses)
380000 Tbilisi, Patritsi Ul. 35, Phone: 99-88-02

Territorialno-Mezhkhozyaistvennoye Obyedinenie Sukhumskogo Gorispolkoma (Territorial Interbranch Organization under the Sukhumi City Council)
384900 Sukhumi, Pr. Mira 62, Phone: 2-42-79

Kazakhstan

Kazakhstan's major reserves are *coal* (Karagandinski coal field); *brown coal* (Kurgaiski coal field); *oil* (Embinsk reserves, Mangishlak, Buzachi, Tengiz); *gas* (Karachagansk); *iron ore* (Karazhal, Dzhezkazgan, Kacharsk, Lisakovsk reserves); *ores of non-ferrous metals* including *copper ore* (Dzhezkazgan), *manganese ore* (Dzhezkazgan, Karsakpai), *bauxites* (Arkalik), *polymetal ores* (Leninogorsk, Achisai, Tekeli), *nickel ore* (Mugodzhari); *phosphorites* (Alga, Karatau). Processing industries are *ferrous metallurgy* (Temirtau, Aktyubinsk, Yermak), *non-ferrous metallurgy* including *copper* (Dzhezkazgan, Karsakpai, Balkhash), *aluminum* (Pavlodar), *zinc, titanium and magnesium* (Ust-Kamenogorsk); *oil processing* (Chimkent); *chemical industry* including production of *synthetic resins* (Guryev), *synthetic fibers* (Chimkent), *mineral fertilizers* (Dzhambul); the *textile industry* (Alma-Ata, Karaganda, Aktubinsk, Dzhezkazgan, Kustanai). Baikonur, the spaceships' launching site, is located in Kazakhstan.

The territory of Kazakhstan is over 2 million square kilometers. Its population is 16,500,000, of whom the urban population is over 57 percent and the working population 9,227,000. The number of university and college graduates is about 2 million people. The capital of Kazakhstan is Alma-Ata.

Permanent Office of Kazakhstan in Moscow
Chistoprudni Blvd, 3a, Phone: 208-26-49

Kazakhintorg (Kazakhstan Foreign Trade Association Department)
480003 Alma-Ata, Gogolya Ul. 111, Phone: 32-36-00

Torgovo-Promishlennaya Palata Kazakhskstana (Kazakhstan Chamber for Commerce and Industry)
480091 Alma-Ata, Pr. Kommunisticheski 93/95

Vneshneekonomicheskaya Assotsiatsia "Kazakhstan" (Foreign Economic Association)
Alma-Ata, Novaya Pl. 15, Phone: 63-27-90

Respublikanskaya Vneshneekonomicheskaya Assotsiatsia "Kazsvyazimpex" (Republican Foreign Economic Association)
480091 Alma-Ata, Kirova Ul. 134, Phone: 62-02-48, Telex: 251232

Vneshneeokonomicheskaya Assotsiatsia Gosudarstvennikh, Kooperativnikh i Obshchestvennikh Organizatsii (Foreign Economic Association for State, Cooperative, and Public Organizations)
Alma-Ata, Novaya Ploshchad 15

Vneshneekonomicheskaya Assotsiatsia "Interazia" (Foreign Economic Association)
Alma-Ata, Pr. Lenina, 100 A/YA 113

Respublikanski Kommerchesko-Informatsionni Tsentr Gossnaba Kazakhstana (Republican Commercial-Information Center under the Kasakhstan Supplies Committee)
480009 Alma-Ata, Furmanova Ul. 103

Kommercheskii Tsentr Alma-Ataglavsnaba (Commercial Center of the Alma-Ata Supplies Committee)
Alma-Ata, Mukanova Ul. 245, Phone: 53-64-41

Vneshneekonomicheskaya Mezhregionalnaya Selskokhozyastvennaya Assotsiatsia (Foreign Economic Agricultural Association)
480031 Alma-Ata, Iliiskoye Shosse, IKM

Kazakhskoye Kooperativnoye Respublikanskoye Obyedinenie "Soyuz" (Kazakhstan Cooperatives Association)
480012 Alma-Ata, Kirova Ul. 151, Phone: 67-68-88

Alma-Atinski Gorodskoi Fond Molodyozhnikh Obyedinenii (Alma-Ata City Foundation of Youth Centers)
480100 Alma-Ata, K. Marxa Ul. 135 SOATA, Phone: 62-84-14, Telex: 251241 FOND SU

Assotsiatsia Tsentrov Nauchno-Tekhnicheskogo Tvorchestva Molodyozhi "Kaztekhnopolis" (Association of the Youth Centers for Research and Development)
480091 Alma-Ata Komsomolskaya Ul. 67, Phone: 62-03-31

Kazakhskaya Respublikianskaya Assotsiatsia Mezhotraslevogo Delovogo Sotrudnichestva (Kazakhstan Republican Association for Business Cooperation)
480091 Alma-Ata, Mira Ul. 115

Kazakhskoye Nauchno-Proizvodstvennoye Obyedinenie "Kazrudgeologia" (Kazakhstan Scientific-Production Association for Geologic Research)
480021 Alma-Ata, Pr. Lenina 85

Khozraschetnaya Firma "Almaatekspertiza" Torgovo-Promishlennoi Palati Kazakhstana (Cost-accounting Firm under Kazakhstan Chamber for Commerce and Industry)
480091 Alma-Ata, Komsomolskaya Ul. 45

Alma-Atinski Gorodskoi Tsentr Nauchno-Tekhnicheskogo Tvorchestva Molodyozhi "Kontakt" (Alma-Ata City Youth Center for Research and Development)
480026 Alma-Ata, Pr. 50-let Oktyabrya 167

Vistavochno-Informatsionni Tsentr NTTM (Exhibition-Information Center)
480091 Alma-Ata, Komsomolskaya Ul. 67

Institut Khimicheskikh Nauk AN Kazakhstana (Research Institute for Chemical Sciences of the Academy of Sciences of Kazakhstan)
480100 Alma-Ata, Krasin Ul. 106, Phone: 61-24-80, Telex: 02251412 Tsezii

Alma-Atinski Tsentralni Kooperativni Bank "Tsentrobank" (Cooperative Central Bank)
480091 Alma-Ata, Panfilova Ul. 98, Phone: 33-69-96

Innovatsionni Kommercheski Bank "Kramds Bank" (Innovation Commercial Bank)

480046 Alma-Ata, 16-a Linia Ul. 160, Phone: 43-67-80

Investitsionni Kommercheski Bank Razvitia Optovoi Torgovli Kazakhstana (Investment Commercial Bank for the Development of Wholesale Trade in Kazakhstan)
480009 Alma-Ata, Sovetskaya Ul. 65, Phone: 62-47-36

Alma-Atinski Investitsionni Bank (Alma-Ata Investment Bank)
480004 Alma-Ata, Furmanova Ul. 65, Komn. 428, Phone: 33-51-43

Vneshneekonomicheskaya Assotsiatsia "Chimkent" (Foreign Economic Association of Chimkent City)
486050 Chimkent, Gorkogo Ul. 49, Phone: 4-65-20, Telex: 412625-SOSNA-SU

Informatsionno-Kommercheski Tsentr Chimkentglavsnaba (Information-Commercial Center of the Chimkent Supplies Committee)
486009 Chimkent, Neftebazovaya Ul. Phone: 66-33-85

Vostochno-Kazakhstanski Soyuz Potrbetelskikh Obshchestv (Eastern-Kazakh Regional Union of Consumers Cooperatives—Trade Coordinating Organization for Rural Area)
492024 Ust-Kamenogorsk, Krilova Ul. 73, Phone: 65-17-72

Kooperativni Bank "Paritet" (Cooperative Bank)
492019 Ust-Kamenogorsk, Ushakob Ul. 3, Phone: 65-46-70

Gorno-Metallurgicheski NII Tsvetnikh Metalov (Mining and Metallurgy Research Institute for Non-ferrous Metals)
492014 Vostochno-Kazakhstanskaya Obl., Ust-Kamenogorsk, Promishlennaya Ul. 1, Phone: 49-14-60

Aktyubinski Oblastnoi Soyuz Kooperativov (Aktyubinski Regional Cooperatives Union)
463000 Aktyubinsk, 101 Strelkovoi Brigadi Ul. 4, Phone: 5-07-62

Komercheski Tsentr Tselinogradglavsnaba (Commercial Center of Tselinograd Supplies Committee)
473029 Tselinograd, Pr. Pobedi 104, Phone: 2-18-97, Telex: 264144 Ozon

Kokchetavski Oblastnoi Soyuz Potrebitelskikh Obshchestv (Kokchetav Regional Union of Consumers Cooperatives—Trade Coordinating Organization for Rural Area)
475000 Kokchetav, Lenina Ul. 13, Oblpotrebsoyuz, Phone: 4-23-14, Telex: 185229 TOVAR

Jambulski Oblastnoi Soyuz Kooperativov v Sfere Proizvodstva i Uslug (Jambul Regional Union of Cooperatives for Production and Services)
484039 Jambul, Mirzoyan Ul. 3, Phone: 4-48-94

Brokerskaya Kontora "Tabrok" (Brokers' Firm of the Moscow Commodities Exchange)
484002 Dzhambul, Sovetskaya Ul. 161, Phone: 902-17-54

Uzbekistan

Major resources of Uzbekistan are *gases* (Gazli) and *copper and molybdenum ores* (Almalik, Kalmakir). There are also gold reserves in Uzbekistan. Its major industries are *gas processing* (Mubarek); *ferrous metallurgy* (Tashkent); *non-ferrous metallurgy* including *copper, zink, aluminum* (Almalik); production of *fertilizers* including *nitrogen fertilizers* (Chirchick, Fergana, Navoi); and *phosphate fertilizers* (Samarkand). In agriculture the most important branch is cotton growing that determines the development of *textile industry* (Tashkent, Bukhara). Among Uzbekistan agricultural products are also astrakhan and silk cocoons. The territory of Uzbekistan is about 450,000 square kilometers. Its populations is over 20 million, of whom the urban population is about 41 percent and the working population 10,137,000. College and university graduates constitute over 1.5 million people. The capital of Uzbekistan is Tashkent.

Permanent Office of Uzbekistan in Moscow
Pogorelski Per. 12, Phone: 230-00-78

Goskomitet Uzbekistana po Vneshnei Torgovle i Zarubezhnim Svyazyam (Uzbekistan State Committee of Foreign Trade and Relations)
700017 Tashkent, Lenina Ul. 15, Phone: 34-44-80, Telex: 116122 ATLAS, Fax: 34-60-01

Torgovo-Promishlennaya Palata Uzbekistana (Chamber of Commerce and Industry of Uzbekistan)
700000 Tashkent, Pr. Lenina 16A, Phone: 39-40-65, Telex: 116147 TUMAN SU

TASHKENTVNESHSERVIS (Firm for Foreign Trade Facilitation)
700000 Tashkent, Pr. Lenina 16-A, Phone: 39-45-24

Vneshneekonomicheskaya Assotsiatsia "Kosmos" (Foreign Trade Association)
700077 Tashkent, Lunacharskogo Ul. 1

Vneshneekonomicheskaya Assotsiatsia "Inter-Vostok" (Foreign Trade Association)
700039 Tashkent, Kirovski Region, Mariiskaya Ul. 2

Vneshneekonomicheskaya Firma "Navruz" (Foreign Trade Firm)
700115 Tashkent, Chilanzar, Block 2, Korp 53

Vneshneekonomicheskaya Assotsiatsia "Osie" (Foreign Trade Association)
700093 Tashkent, Chilanzar, Block 2, Build. 8

Tashkentskaya Assotsiatsia Vneshneekomocheskogo Sotrudnichestva (Tashkent Association for Foreign Economic Cooperation)
700000 Tashkent, GSP, Khorezmaskaya Ul. 51, Phone: 33-41-59, Telex: 116121 Pois

UZAGROPROMSERVIS (Association for Business Cooperation with Foreign Countries)
700100 Tashkent, Generala Karimova Ul. 7, Phone: 55-35-16, Fax: 55-35-17, Telex: AGROS 116148

Uzbekistan Kommerchsko-Informatsionni Tsentr Gossnaba (Uzbekistan Commercial-Information Center of the Supplies Committee)
700038 Tashkent, Navoi Ul. 7

Vneshnetorgovaya Firma "Uzdrevintorg" (Foreign Trade Firm)
700195 Tashkent, Abai Ul. 4

Soyuz Kooperativov Uzbekistana (Uzbekistan Cooperatives Union)
700000 Tashkent, Proletarskaya Ul. 4, Phone: 33-67-25

Proizvodstvennoe Obyedinenie "Uzagroinform" (Production Association)
700043 Tashkent, Pr. Druzhba Narodov 8, Phone: 45-74-63, Fax: 45-14-43

Assotsiatsia Gosudarstvennikh Predpriyatii Leninskogo Rayona (Association of State Enterprises of the Lenin District)
700015 Tashkent, Poltoratskogo Ul. 18

Khozraschetnaya Proizvodstvennaya Firma "Tashkentvneshservis" (Cost-accounting Production Firm)
700000 Tashkent, Pr. Lenina 16-A

Glavnoye Koordinatsionno-Geologicheskoye Upravleniye "Uzbekgeologiya" (Head Coordination Office for Geology)
700060 Tashkent, Shevchenko Ul. 11

Tashkentski Oblastnoi Soyuz Potrebitelskikh Obshchestv (Tashkent Regional Union of Consumer Societies)
700060 Tashkent, Tsetkin Ul. 76

Molodyozhnaya Firma "Emkho" (Youth Firm)
700113 Tashkent, Gazeti "Pravdi" Ul. 60

Uzbekski Innovatsionno-Kommercheski Bank "Ipak Yul" (Uzbek Innovative—Commercial Bank)
700000 Tashkent, Kh. Alimjan Ul. 5, Phone: 33-48-86, Fax: 55-35-17

Uzbekski Aktsionerni Innovatsionni Bank (Uzbek Stockholding Innovation Bank)
700027 Tashkent, Beshagach 7, Phone: 45-03-02

Vneshneekonomicheskaya Assotsiatsia "Bukhara" (Foreign Trade Association)
705016 Bukhara, 40 Let Oktyabrya Ul. 8

Brokerskaya Kontora "Bukhara" (Brokers' Firm "Bukhara" of the Moscow Commodities Exchange)
705000 Bukhara, Lenina 256, Phone: 5-57-93

Samarkandski Gorodskoi Soyuz Kooperativov (Samarkand City Cooperatives Union)
703003 Samarkand, Griboyedova Ul. 20, Phone: 4-02-09

Assotsiaysia Delovogo Sotrudnichestva s Zarubezhnymi Stranami (Association for Business Cooperation with Foreign Countries)
743600 Beruni, Lenina Ul. 15, Phone: 4-33-10, Telex: (64) 116148 AGROS SU, Fax: 4-86-11

Mezhotraslevaya Regionalnaya Assotsiatsia Vneshneekonomicheskogo Sotrudnichestva "Fergana" (Inter-branch Regional Association for Foreign Economic Cooperation)
712003 Fergana, Komunistov Ul. 119, Phone: 4-51-61

Khorezmskaya Assotsiatsia Vneshneekonomicheskogo Sotrudnichestva (Khorezm Association for Foreign Economic Cooperation)
740015 Khorezmskaya Obl., Urgench, Kommunisticheskaya Ul. 23, Phone, 4-13-93

Chirchikski Gorodskoi Soyuz Kooperativov (Chirchik City Cooperatives Union)
702100 Chirchik, Lomonosova Ul. 29, Phone: 5-26-31

Namanganskii Oblastnoir Soyuz Kooperativov (Namangan Regional Cooperatives Union)
716000 Namangan, Oromgokh Ul. 5, Phone: 4-26-61

Surkhandaryinski Oblastnoi Soyuz Potrbitelskikh Obshchestv (Surkhandaryinski Regional Union of Consumers Cooperatives—Trade Coordinating Organization for the Rural Area)
732000 Surkhandaryinski Region, Termez, Kirova Ul. 2

Kooperativni Bank "Dzhizabank" (Cooperative Bank)
708000 Dzhisak, Navoi Ul. 4, Phone 2-26-12

Tajikistan

Tajikistan occupies a high mountainous part of Central Asia, with the highest mountainous peak in the former Soviet Union. There are a lot of water resources in Tajikistan. Major industries of Tajikistan are raising long-fiber cotton, silk processing, and raising astrakhan sheep and camels. Other industries are *aluminum production* (Dushanbe) and the *chemical industry* (Dushanbe). The territory of Tajikistan is over 143,000 square kilometers. Its population is over 5 million people. The urban population constitutes about 33 percent and the working population 2,522,000 people. College and university graduates number about 330,000 people out of the total population. The capital of Tajikistan is Dushanbe.

Permanent Office of Tajikistan in Moscow
Moscow, Skatertni Per, 19, Phone: 290-61-02

TADJIKVNESHTORG (Tajikistan Foreign Trade Department)
734051 Dushanbe, Pr. Lenina 42, Phone: 23-29-03, Telex: 201243

Chamber of Commerce and Industry of Tajikistan
734012 Dushanbe, Mazaev Ul. 21, Phone: 27-95-19

Soyuz Kooperativov Tadjikistana
(Tajikistan Republican Cooperatives Union)

734025 Dushanbe, Ordzhonikidze Ul. 18, Phone: 22-60-46

Dushanbinski Kommercheski Bank "Ekspress-Bank" (Dushanbe Commercial Bank)

734025 Dushanbe, Pr. Lenina 48, Phone: 22-88-60

Turkmenistan

The major resource of Turkmenistan is *gas* (Shatlik, Maiskoye, Ashkhabad region, Okarem). Other resources are *sodium sulphate* (Bekdash); *sulphur* (Gaurdak); *potassium salt* (Gaurdak). There are small reserves of oil. Major industries are *gas processing* (Krasnovodsk, Chardzhou); *oil processing* (Chardzhou); production of *fertilizers* including *superphosphate* (Chardzhou) and *nitrogen fertilizers* (Mari). An important agricultural branch is raising fine-fleeced sheep, one-hump camels, and horses. The wool of the sheep is used for the famous Turkmenian rugs.

The territory of Turkmenistan is about 500,000 square kilometers. Its population is over 3.5 million people. The urban population is over 45 percent and the working population 1,842,000 people. The number of university and college graduates is about 270,000 people. The capital of Turkmenistan is Ashkhabad.

Permanent Office of Turkmenistan in Moscow
Moscow, Aksakova Ul. 22, Phone: 291-66-36

Soyuz Kooperativov Turkmenistana "Turkmenistan" (Turkmenistan Cooperatives Union)

Ashkhabad, Labukhi Ul. 20, Phone: 5-14-35

Kommercheski Bank "Senegat" (Commercial Bank)
744000 Ashkhabad, Gogoly Ul. 20, Phone: 9-74-05

Kyrgyzstan

The agricultural sector of the republic specializes in raising fine- and semi-fine fleeced sheep. Among agricultural products is medical poppy. There are small amounts of *oil* (Jalal-Abad), *gas* (Jalal-Abad), and *coal* (Jergalan) in Kyrgyzstan. There are also polymetal ores, mercury, and stibium. The republic is rich in water resources. The territory of Kyrgyzstan is about 200,000 square kilometers. Its population is about 4.5 million people. The urban population constitutes about 40 percent and the working population 2,219,000 people. These are 367,000 university and college graduates. The capital of Kyrgyzstan is Bishkek.

Permanent Office of Kyrgyzstan in Moscow
Moscow B. Ordinka Ul. 64, Phone: 237-48-82

KYRGYZVNESHTORG (Kyrgyzstan Foreign Trade Department)
720000 Bishkek, Kirova Ul. 205, Phone: 26-63-66, Telex: 245213

Torgovo-Promishlennaya Palata Kyrgyzstan (Chamber of Commerce and Industry of Kyrgyzstan)
720300 Bishkek, GSP, Kirova Ul. 205, Phone: 26-49-42

Kommercheski Tsentr Gossnaba (Commercial Center under the Kyrgyzstan Supplies Committee)
720769 Bishkek, Lev Tolstoi Ul. 210

Kooperativno-Gosudarstvennoye P/O "Kirgozagropromles" (Production Association with Mixed—State and Cooperative—Forms of Ownership)
720300 Bishkek, Kievskaya Ul. 96

Konsultativno-Issledovatelskoye i Tekhniko-Ekonomicheskoye Byuro (The Technical-Economic Bureau for Counseling and Research)
720017 Bishkek, A / YA 688

Mezhotraslevoi Coordinatsionni Tsentr Vipuska Tovarov Narodnogo Potreblenia (Interregional Coordination Center for Consumer Goods)
720082 Bishkek, M-ON "Kok-Zhar," 1 A / YA 1392

Sredneaziatski Tsentr "Sredazzolotoavtomatika" (Central Asian Center for Gold Mining)
722153 Novo-Pokrovka, Gorkogo Ul. 139A

Kyrgyzstanski Filial NII po Izucheniyu Sprosa Naselenia (Kyrgyzstan Affiliate of the Research Institute for Consumer Demand)
720571 Bishkek, Mendeleyeva Ul. 153B

Kommercheski Bank "Kirgiztransdorbank" (Commercial Bank)
720079 Bishkek, 40 Let Oktyabrya Ul. 42, Phone: 26-50-78

Latvia

The greatest Latvian natural resource is *peat* (Riga region, Yurmala). It is also rich in forest and water resources. There are ice-free seaports in Latvia: Liepaya and Ventspils. Processing industries include the production of *lumber* (Kuldiga); the *chemical industry* (Riga, Dobele, Olaine); *ferrous metallurgy* (Liepaia); the *pulp and paper industry* (Yurmala); the *textile industry* (Riga). The machine-building industry produces railcars, buses, machinery, electrical equipment, radioengineering appliances, instruments, and ships. Latvia produces fish preserves, meat, and dairy products.

The territory of Latvia is about 64,000 square kilometers. The population of Latvia is about 2.7 million people. The urban population constitutes over 70 percent and the working population 1,506,000 people. The number of college and university graduates is about 400,000. The capital of Latvia is Riga.

Permanent Office of Latvia in Moscow Soyuz, Chapligin Ul. 3, Permanent Representative, Phone: 925-27-07

INTER-LATVIA (Latvian Foreign Trade Association Department)
226001 Riga, Lenina Ul. 85, Phone: 27-16-62, Telex: 61149 INLA SU

Torgovo-Promishlennaya Palata Latvii (Chamber of Commerce and Industry of Latvia)
226189 Riga, Lenina Ul. 21, Phone: 33-22-05, Telex: 161111, 161145 VISIT

Assotsiatsia Kooperativov Latvii (Latvian Association of Cooperatives)
226001 Riga, Komyaunatnef 24, Phone: 32-29-48

Upravlenie "Latvkhimopttorg" (Latvian Head Office for Wholesale Trade of Chemical Products)

226073 Riga, Katlakaln Ul. 10, Phone 24-39-05, Telex: PRIBOR 1338

Latvnii Nauchno-tekhnicheskoi Informatsii i Tekhniko-ekonomicheskiskikh Issledovanii (Latvian Research Institute for Scientific-technical Information and Economic Studies)
226930 Riga, GSP, Pl. Doma 6, Phone: 22-94-49

Latviiski NII Agropromishlennogo Kompleksa (Latvian Scientific-Research Institute of the Agroindustrial Complex)
226039 Riga, Peivis Ul. 14, Phone: 55-29-09, Telex: 162933 KOLOS

Brokerskaya Firma Moskovskoi Tovarnoi Birzhi "Sigma" (Brokers' Firm of the Moscow Commodities Exchange)

226080 Riga, Dzelzavas Ul. 74-342, Phone: 57-86-13

Brokerskaya Firma Moskovskoi Tovarnoi Birzhi "Agroresurs" (Brokers' Firm of the Moscow Commodities Exchange)
226168 Riga, Respublikankaya Pl. 2, Phone 32-54-49

Brokerskaya Kontora RTSB (Brokers' Firm of the Russian Commodities and Raw Materials Exchange)
226047 Riga, Box 691, Phone 58-81-33

Latviiskaya Universalnaya Birzha "Unibal" (Latvian Exchange for Various Commodities)
Riga, Dzirnavu Ul. 33, Phone: 32-17-76

Kommercheski Innovatsionni Bank (Commercial Innovation Bank)

Riga, Berzin Ul. 1/8, Phone: 3-37-31

Mezhregionalni Kommercheski Bank "Simkas" (Interregional Commercial Bank)
226168 Riga, Respubliki Pl. 2, Phone: 32-77-40

Mezhregionalni Kommercheski Bank "Baltiya" (Interregional Commercial Bank)
226050 Riga, Padamui Blvd. 34, Phone: 22-58-06

Kommercheski Bank "Riga-Bank" (Commercial Bank)
Riga, Komunarov Blvd. 6, Phone: 32-05-70

Lithuania

Republican natural resources are *peat* (Vilnus Region, Kaunas) and *limestone* (Mazheikyai). Lithuania also has amber in the coastal area. Processing industries include the production of *synthetic resins* (Kaunas) and the *lumber industry* (Vilnus, Kelme, Shilute, Panevezhis). Other industries are shipbuilding, instrument and tool making, electrical and electronic engineering, production of construction materials, the chemical industry, production of food products, fishing, and the fish processing industry.

The territory of Lithuania is over 65,000-square kilometers. It has a population of over 3.7 million. The urban population constitutes about 70 percent and the working population 2,122,000 people. There are 555,000 college and university graduates. The capital of Lithuania is Vilnus.

Permanent Office of Lithuania in Moscow
Moscow, Pisemskogo Ul. 10, Permanent Representative, Phone: 291-16-98

LITIMPEX (Lithuanian Foreign Trade Department)
232600 Vilnus, Pr. Lenina 37, Phone: 62-14-53, Telex: 278128 LIE SU

Torgovo-Promishlennaya Palata Litvi (Chamber of Commerce and Industry of Lithuania)
232600 Vilnus, Algirdo Ul. 31, Phone: 66-15-50, Telex: 261114 LCO SU

IMPEXSERVISAS Torgovo-Promishlennoi Palati Litvi (The Firm IMPEXSERVISAS under the Chamber of Commerce and Industry of Lithua-

nia for Commercial Shows, Seminars)
232600 Vilnus, Algirdo Ul. 31, Phone: 66-15-42, Telefax: 66-15-20, Telex: 261114

Informatsionno-kommercheskii Tsentr "Litinkom" (Information-Commercial Center for Market and Commercial Information)
232600 Vilnus, B. Radvilaites Ul. 1, Phone: 69-09-35

Respublikanski Agrovichislitelni Tsentr (Republican Agricultural Computing Center)
232600 Vilnus, V. Kudirkos Ul. 18, Phone: 61-01-29, Telex: 261558 DISPUT 261113

Litovski Aktsionerni Innovatsionni Bank (Lithuania Stockholding Innovation Bank)
232006 Vilnus, K. Bugos Ul. 27, Phone: 26-08-83

Kommercheski Bank "Ekonomika" (Commercial Bank)
233000 Kaunas, Mairone Ul. 25, Phone: 22-30-19

Kaunaski Kommercheski Bank Promishlennosti "Ukiobankas" (Kaunas Commercial Industrial Bank)
233000 Kaunas, Gruodzhino Ul. 9, Phone: 20-36-51

Upravlenie Torgovli Klaipedi (Klaipeda City Trade Administration)
235800 Klaipeda, Manto Ul. 26, Phone: 1-36-18, Telex: 278138 TOMAT

Estonia

Estonia is rich in *fuel shales* (reserves along the Gulf of Finland, in the Kokhtla-Yarve Region) which are used as a source of power and also as a raw material for the chemical industry. The republic has also *phosphorites* (Tallin region) and *peat* (Puarnu, Valmiera, Valga). Estonian processing industries are the production of *fertilizers* (Kokhtla-Yarve); the production of *construction materials* (Kokhtla-Yarve); the *textile industry* (Puarnu, Sindi, Valga). Among Estonian major industries are fishing and fish processing. Estonia also is developing its radioengineering industry and produces equipment for the shale industry and agricultural machinery.

Other industries are ship repairing and textiles. There are many rivers and lakes in Estonia. The capital of Estonia is a seaport located on the shore of the Finnish Gulf. The territory of Estonia covers over 45,000 square kilometers. The population of Estonia is about 1.6 million people. The urban population constitutes about 72 percent and the working population 888,000 people. College and university graduates number 232,000 people. The capital of Estonia is Tallin.

Permanent Office of Estonia in Moscow
Moscow, Sobinovski Per. 5, Permanent Representative, Phone: 290-50-13

ESTIMPEX (Estonian Foreign Trade Department)
200101 Tallin, Tolli Ul. 3, Phone: 60-14-62, Telex: 173288 ANTIK SU

Fond Estonskogo Mezhdunarodnogo Torgovogo Tsentra (Estonian International Trade Center Foundation)
200104 Tallin, Kukhlbars Ul. 1, Suite 120, Phone: 43-17-26, Fax: 43-71-73, Telex: 173225 ESTEX

Assotsiatsia Vneshneekonomicheskoi Deyatelnosti "Estwood" (Association for Foreign Economic Activity)
200107 Tallin, Pyauzukese Ul. 1, Phone: 42-71-89, Telefax: 42-71-69, Telex: 173411 KALKA

Vneshneekonomicheskaya Assotsiatsia Molodezhnogo Sotrudnichestva "Spektrum" (Youth Foreign Economic Association)

200004 Tallin, Kyaspert Ul. 24, Phone: 49-49-51, Telex: 173273 INF SU

Estonskoye Respublikanskoye Upravlenie "Estraznoopttorg" (Estonian Republican Head Office for Wholesale Trade)
200001 Tallin Suur-Karya Ul. 14, Phone: 44-09-50, Telex: 173150 LAMPA

Tallinski Dom Torgovli (Tallin Trade House)
200001 Tallin, Lomonosov Ul. 2, Phone: 42-43-90, Telefax: 42-43-90, Telex: 173517 KULON

Vyistavka Dostizhenii Narodnogo Khozyaistva Estonii (Exhibition of Economic Achievements of Estonia)
200103 Tallin, Pirit Ul. 28, Phone: 23-86-97

Aktsionernoye Obshchestvo "Kharyuski Fond Razvitiya" (Stockholding Company "Kharyuski Development Foundation")

200013 Tallin, Lauristini Ul. 19, Phone:
44-39-07

Kommercheski Bank "Esteksbank"
(Commercial Bank)
200104 Tallin, Kaukhlbarsi Ul. 1,
Phone: 43-07-81

Kommercheski Bank "Evea-Bank"
(Commercial Bank)
202104 Tallin, Kuekhl Bersi Ul. 1,
Phone: 43-30-71

Estonski Innovatsionni Bank "In-
nobank" (Estonian Innovation Bank)
200005 Tallin, Kingissep Ul. 40, Phone:
42-22-24

Pyarnusskii Gorodskoi Soyuz Kooperativov (Pyarnu City Cooperatives
Union)
203600 Pyarnu, Rozi Ul. 14, Phone:
4-37-02

Pyarnusski Kommercheski Bank (Pyarnu
Commercial Bank)
203600 Pyarnu, Ruyudli 47, Phone:
4-01-90

Tartusski Kommercheski Bank (Tartu
Commercial Bank)
202400 Tartu, Munk (Abovyan) Ul. 18,
Phone: 3-31-97

Associations and Unions

One of the ways of making business connections in various republics and regions is approaching associations and unions of the former Soviet Union that used to encompass enterprises and organizations from various sectors of the economy and with various forms of ownership. At present these associations and unions are in the process of changing their status. Some of them envision a broad scope for their activities, admitting as their members enterprises and organizations from various independent republics or acquiring international status.

Assotsiatsia Exporterov (Exporters Association)
103009 Moscow, Gertsena Ul. 22, Kab.
3, Phone: 202-70-89, Fax: 202-70-89

Assotsiatsia Sovmestnikh Predpriyatii,
Mezhdunarodnikh Organizatsii i
Obyedinenii (Association of Joint
Ventures, International Organizations
and Amalgamations)
125190 Moscow, 157, Phone: 943-94-
81, Fax: 943-00-20

Soyuz Obyedinenikh Kooperativov (The
Cooperatives Union)
107066 Moscow, Tokmakov Per. 14,
Phone: 261-33-76, Fax: 288-95-79

Soyuz Arendatorov i Predprinimatelei
(The Union of Leaseholders and Entrepreneurs)
103012 Moscow 25 Octyabrya Ul. 5/7,
Phone: 928-23-29, Fax: 975-21-85

Soyuz Aktsionernikh Obshchestv i Obshchestv s Ogranichennoi Otvetstven-
nostyu (The Union of Stockholding
and Limited Liability Companies)

107082 Moscow, Balakirevski Per. 23,
Phone: 261-82-93, Fax: 295-65-11

Economicheskoe Obshestvo (Economic
Society) 117259 Moscow, B. Cherio-
mushkinskaya 34, Phone: 120-13-21,
Telex: 411055 SNIO SU, Fax: 120-
13-20

Nauchno-Promishlenni Soyuz (Scientific-
Industrial Union)
101000 Moscow, Staraya Pl. 10/4,
Phone: 206-70-36, Fax: 975-23-26

Assotsiatsia Rukovoditelei Predpriyatii
(Association of the Plant Directors
and Managers)
101000 Moscow, Chistoprudni Blvd.
12-a, Phone: 227-31-58, Fax: 200-
32-03

Soyuz Menedzherov (Union of Managers)
113054 Moscow, Zatsepa Ul. 41,
Phone: 237-87-83, Fax: 237-87-88

Mezhregionalni Birzhevoi Soyuz (Union
of Interregional Stock Commodities
Exchanges)

Phone: 187-88-27 (temporarily)

Assotsiatsia Vneshneekonomicheskogo Sotrudnichestva Malikh i Srednikh Predpriyatii (Association of Economic Cooperation of Small and Middle-Size Enterprises)
101000 Moscow, Tsentr, Chistoprudni Blvd. 12A, Phone: 227-90-25, Fax: 925-58-28

Soyuz Obyedinennikh Kooperativov (Cooperatives Union)
107066 Moscow, Tokmakov Per. 14, Phone: 261-19-11

Assotsiatsia Marketinga (Marketing Association)
123557 Moscow, Bolshaya Gruzinskaya Ul. 13, Phone: 254-12-47, Telex: 411127, Fax: 230-28-19

Assotsiatsia Nauchno-Tekhnicheskikh Kooperativov i Khozraschetnikh Orga-

nizatsii i Predpriyatii "VANTKHOP" (Association of Scientific-Technical Cooperatives and Cost-accounting Organizations)
119034 Moscow, Kursovoi Per. 17, Phone: 927-33-33

Assotsiatsia Vneshneekonomicheskogo Sotrudnichestva s Arabskimi Stranami (Association for Foreign Economic Cooperation with Arab Countries)
109004 Moscow, Taganskaya Ul. 5/9, Phone: 271-05-61, Telex: 411069 SUPER SU

Vneshneekonomicheskaya Assotsiatsia po Sotrudnichestvu Molodezhi "Interkontakt" (Youth Foreign Economic Association) 121200 Moscow, Smolenskaya-Sennaya Pl. 32/34, Phone: 244-36-45, Telex: 411268

Notes

Preface

1. Patricia A. Dreyfus, "Negotiating the Kremlin Maze," *Business Month*, November 1988, p. 55.

Introduction

1. For review of studies of the American perception of Soviet management, see: Paul R. Lawrence and Charalambos A. Vlachoutsicos, *Behind the Factory Walls*, Cambridge, Mass., Harvard Business School Press, 1990, p. 69: Charalambos A. Vlachoutsicos and Paul Lawrence, "What We Don't Know about Soviet Management," *Harvard Business Review*, November–December 1990, pp. 51–56; Edward Beliaev, Thomas Mullen, and Betty Jane Prunnett, "Understanding the Cultural Environment: U.S.–U.S.S.R. Trade Negotiations," *California Management Review*, Vol. XXVII, No. 2, Winter 1985, p. 111.
2. Raymond F. Smith, *Negotiating with the Soviets*, Bloomington, Indiana University Press, 1989, p. 5.
3. *Doing Business with the Soviet Union*, New York, AMA Membership Publication Division, American Management Association, 1988, p. 58.
4. Stephen J. Simurda, "An American Trade Show in Moscow," *Management Review*, March 1990, p. 60.

Chapter 1. The Human Dimension of Doing Business: A Key to Success in the Former Soviet Union

1. Edward Beliaev, Thomas Muller, and Betty Jane Punnett, "Understanding the Cultural Environment: U.S.–U.S.S.R. Trade Negotiations," *California Management Review*, Vol. XXVII, No. 2, Winter 1985, p. 103.
2. Pierre-Louis Roederer, "Licensing Technology to the East," *Bloc*, August/September 1990, p. 34.
3. F. Wilhelm Christians, *Paths to Russia*, New York, Macmillan, 1990, p. 62.
4. Ronald Hingley, *The Russian Mind*, New York, Charles Scribner's, 1977, p. 253; Raymond F. Smith, *Negotiations with the Soviets*, Bloomington, Indiana University Press, 1989, p. 92.

Chapter 2. Ten Advantages of Doing Business in the Russian Federation and Other Former Soviet Republics

1. Interview with Leonid Sinelnikov, "The Price for Being Greedy," *Moskovskie Novosti*, September 2, 1990, p. 11.
2. Alexander Dotskevich, "Only Professionals Can Work under the Conditions of the Market Economy," *Deloviye Lyudi/Business in the USSR*, No. 2, June 1990, p. 28.
3. Yelena Mashovets, "Will the Novgorod Project Become a Reality?" *Moskovski Biznes*, No. 2, 1990, p. 29.
4. M. Berger, "There Is No Alternative to the Market Economy," *Izvestiya*, December 31, 1989, p. 3.
5. "The Sales Volume of Commercial Structure Is Little But They Perform Very Well," *Commersant*, February 25–March 4, 1991, p. 28.
6. Y. Znamenski, "The Author's Responsibility," *Izvestiya*, May 15, 1990, p. 2.
7. "The Professional Viewpoint," *Ekonomika i Zhizn*, No. 14, July 1990, p. 20.
8. Vladimir Tsvetov, "The Motivation Might Extinguish . . . ," *Ogonyok*, July 1989, p. 6.
9. Yuri Baranov, "America . . . America," *Karyera* July 1990, p. 6.
10. *Izvestiya*, April 14, 1989, p. 4.
11. Interview with J. Fuqua, *Ekonomika i Zhizn*, April 17, 1990, p. 20.
12. Denis Kiselev, "Four-Story Business of Americans," *Moskovski Biznes*, No. 2, 1990, p. 18.
13. Igor Kozhin, "As It Turned Out There Is Ample Hard Currency in the Soviet Union," *Commersant*, August 27–September 3, 1990, p. 21.
14. V. D. Popov, *Psychology and Economy*, Moscow, Sovetskaya Rossiya, 1989, p. 177.
15. Yuri Nechaev, "Is Foreign Trade Monopoly a Necessity?" *Vneshnyaya Torgovlya*, No. 12, 1989, p. 36.
16. Otto Latsis, "What Acceleration Means," in L. I. Abalkin and P. G. Bunich (eds.), *The Tough Route to Take*, Moscow, Misl, 1989, p. 45.
17. "Soviet Delegation Visits US," *Journal of the US–USSR Trade and Economic Council*, No. 1, 1990, p. 22.
18. Oleg Utitsin, "As It Turned Out the Soviet Union Is Able to Sell Technologies," *Commersant*, May 20–28, 1990, p. 5.
19. "New Contacts," *Moscow*, August 1990, p. 19.
20. Jay Mailin, "U.S. Firms, Soviets Join in Satellite Photo Deal," *Washington Times*, September 17, 1990.
21. Vadim Kunin, "Coffeepot Made from Tank," *Megapolis-Express*, June 21, 1990, p. 11, and Vadim Kunin, "Conversion: Social Aspects of the Problem," *Sotsiologicheskie Issledovania*, No. 5, 1990, pp. 112–116.

Chapter 3. Ten Obstacles to Developing Business in the Former Soviet Union

1. R. G. H. Siu, "Management and the Art of Chinese Baseball," in H. J. Leavitt and L. Pondy, eds., *Readings in Managerial Psychology*, Chicago, University of Chicago Press, 1980.
2. E. Bazhanov, "Adventures in the Enigmatic Country," *Izvestiya*, August 9, 1991, p. 5.
3. V. N. Shalenko, "Strikes as an Object of Sociological Studies," *Sotsiologicheski Issledovaniya*, No. 7, 1990, pp. 107–111.
4. Leon Anderson, "Barter: The Key to Eastern Europe," *Bloc*, June/July 1990, p. 33.
5. Leslie Jay, "Madison Avenue Lands in Moscow," *Management Review*, March 1990, p. 55.
6. Sergei Sedakov, "What Mineral Waters Can Do for the Finances of the USSR," *Commersant*, July 16–23, 1990, p. 7.
7. For information about Artyom Tarasov's life, see *Megapoli-Express*, No. 44, 1991, p. 13, and *Izvestiya*, November 11, 1991, p. 8.
8. I. Zhagel, "There Is No Market without a Middleman," *Izvestiya*, May 12, 1990, p. 2.
9. *Problems of Peace and Socialism*, No. 1, 1989, p. 11.

10. For more information about SPARK's quandary, see Igor Svinarenko, "The Lawsuit about Industrial Smuggling—II: Publicity Created by KGB," *Commersant*, November 26–December 3, 1990, p. 14. Igor Svinarenko, "KGB Screwed Up with One More Lawsuit about Industrial Smuggling," *Commersant*, February 11–18, 1991, p. 14.

11. Zbigniew Brzezinski, "If You Cease Pressing the Pedals, You Might Become Rocky and Fall Down," *Deloviye Lyudi/Business in the USSR*, No. 2, June 1990, pp. 54–56.

12. M. Novikov, "Doing Business in Compliance with the Rules," in *Delovoi Mir: Finance and Statistics,* Moscow, Finance and Statistics, 1990, p. 60.

13. Nina Sandin, "How Medical Firms Do Business in USSR," *American Medical News,* July 20, 1990, p. 20.

14. Kate Bertrand, "U.S. Companies Turn to Countertrade in Soviet Union," *Business Marketing,* May 1990, p. 22.

15. Laura B. Forker, "Accepting Soviet Goals in Countertrade," *Journal of Purchasing and Material Management,* Spring 1990, p. 18.

16. Anderson, "Barter: The Key to Eastern Europe," p. 33.

17. E. Bazhanov, "The Adventures in the Enigmatic Country," *Izvestiya,* August 9, 1991, p. 5.

18. For more detailed information about the projects of services to Western businesses, see "Business-Service Reuters in Moscow Obtained New Owner," *Commersant,* December 3–10, 1990, p. 9; "Business-Service Reuters in Moscow Obtained New Owner," *Commersant,* October 29–November 5, 1990; and "New Types of Postal Services," *Moscow,* July 1990, p. 7.

19. Alexei Kondratyev, "Joint Venture 'Molkom': The Gold-Mine Has Been Discovered," *Commersant,* August 27–September 3, 1990, p. 26.

20. Patricia A. Dreyfus, "Negotiating the Kremlin Maze," *Business Month,* November 1988, p. 56.

21. *Izvestiya,* January 27, 1990, p. 4.

22. Zbigniew Brzezinski, "If You Cease Pressing the Pedals, You Might Become Rocky and Fall Down," *Deloviye Lyudi/Business in the USSR*, No. 2, June 1990, p. 56.

23. Interview with P. Bunich, "To Read Tea-Leaves," *The Alternative Economy,* Part I, 1990, p. 107.

24. *Nash Sovremennik,* No. 1, 1987, p. 157.

25. "Special Credit . . . for Production of Crackers?" *Commersant,* March 18–25, 1990.

Chapter 4. Potential Opportunities in Trade and Investment Activities for American Companies in the Former Soviet Republics

1. "Soviet Foreign Trade Five Year Plan: Reduction of the Government's Role in General Slowdown. Foreign Trade Turnover of the USSR in 1986–1990," *Moskovski Biznes,* No. 4, 1991, pp. 39–40.

2. Vitali Zvolinski, "From Cold War to 'Hot' Trade," *Deloviye Lyudi/Business in the USSR,* February 1991, pp. 60–61.

3. "Statistics of Joint Ventures," *Deloviye Lyudi/Business in the USSR,* June 1991, pp. 19–21; *Delovoi Mir,* August 1991, p. 6; Alexei Smachi, "The End of the First Round," "The Volume of Production by Joint Ventures Is Increasing," *Izvestiya,* March 6, 1992, p. 4.

4. Allana Sullivan, "Texaco Sets Pact with the Soviet Union on Oil Reserves," *Wall Street Journal,* August 15, 1990, p. B8.

5. Neil Behrmann, "Soviets Negotiate Uranium Contracts with U.S. Utilities," *Wall Street Journal,* October 8, 1990.

6. *Doing Business with the Soviet Union,* New York, AMA Membership Publication Division, American Management Association, 1988, pp. 59–62; Patricia A. Dreyfus, "Negotiating the Kremlin Maze," *Business Month,* November 1988, p. 57; Alla Lipatova, "ABB—'Pris': The Quarrel" *Commersant,* October 22–29, 1990, p. 11.

7. Kate Bertrand, "U.S. Companies Turn to Countertrade in Soviet Union," *Business Marketing,* May 1990, pp. 22–24.

8. For more information about the development of the computer industry in the Soviet Union, see Vladimir Shvedov, "Computer Market in the USSR," *Commersant*, July 16–23, 1990, p. 7; Leonid Malkov, "Computers: From 'Rush' to Big Business," *Deloviye Lyudi/Business in the USSR*, July/August, 1991, pp. 30–31; "Compatible Computers for an Incompatible Economy," *Deloviye Lyudi/Business in the USSR*, July/August, 1991, pp. 36–37; "Production of Computers: The Priorities," in *The Alternative Economy*, Part I, Moscow, Mir, 1990, pp. 89–90.

9. More detailed information about IBM projects in the Soviet Union is published in the following sources: Stuart Anderson, "Bloc's Ten Leading Innovators," *Bloc*, January/February 1991, p. 18; Dmitri Bogdanovich, "IBM and Its Dealers Started Their Operations of Winning the Soviet Market," *Commersant*, November 19–26, 1990, p. 8; Dmitri Bogdanovich, "The Decision about Creating IBM USSR," *Commersant*, January 28–February 4, 1991, p. 5.

10. About Microsoft strategies in the Soviet market, see: Anton Lyubomudrov, "JV Dialog-Microsoft: The Conflict Is Over," *Commersant*, September 17–24, 1990, p. 5; Vladimir Yakobson, "Dialog Lost the Exclusive Rights," *Commersant*, August 13–20, 1990, p. 10; Dmitri Bogdanovich, "Microsoft Does Not Need Dollars, But Market in the USSR," *Commersant*, December 17–24, 1990, p. 7.

11. For information about the activities of Control Data, see: Stuart Anderson, "Bloc's Ten Leading Innovators," *Bloc*, January/February, 1991, p. 19; "Safety First," *Moskow*, August 1990, p. 29; Dmitri Bogdanovich, "Control Data: You Need Supercomputers, We Need Dealers' Network," *Commersant*, March 11–18, 1990, p. 11.

12. "US West Group Sets Pact for Moscow Cellular Service," *Wall Street Journal*, December 28, 1990, p. 2.

13. T. P. Rukavishnikova, A. M. Safo, and L. M. Khazova, "Moskovite Shopper," *Sotsiologicheskie Issledovania*, No. 7, 1990, pp. 97–101.

14. Julie A. Cohen, "Footwear And the Jet Set: Soviets do the Shuffle—American Style, *Management Review*, March 1990, p. 42.

15. Matt Richtel, "U.S.–Soviet Entrepreneurship," *Nation's Business*, April 1990, p. 46.

16. Anderson, "Bloc's Ten Leading Innovators," p. 17; Leon Anderson, "Barter: The Key to Eastern Europe," *Bloc*, June/July, 1990, p. 33.

17. Easy Klein, "Doing Deals with the Soviets," *D&B Reports*, March/April 1990, pp. 18–21.

18. Antony Ramirez, "Two U.S. Companies Plan to Sell Soviets 34 Billion Cigarettes," *New York Times*, September 14, 1990, p. A1.

19. Irina Kolkunova, "Brown Bread for America and 'Soviet Shik,' " *Deloviye Lyudi/Business in the USSR*, May 1990, pp. 36–37.

20. Nina Sandin, "How Medical Firms Do Business in the USSR," *American Medical News*, July 1990, pp. 17–20.

21. For more information about the Pepsico story, see Stephen J. Simurda, "Pepsico's Donald Kendall: Thirty Years' Patience Pays Off," *Management Review*, March 1990, p. 17, and *Doing Business with the Soviet Union*, New York, AMA Membership Publication Division, American Management Association, 1988, pp. 63–70.

22. Stephen J. Simurda, "An American Trade Show in Moscow," *Management Review*, March 1990, p. 60.

23. Klein, "Doing Deals with the Soviets," pp. 18–21.

24. Kolkunova, "Brown Bread for America and 'Soviet Shik,' " pp. 36–37.

25. Alla Romanova, "One Must Have Christian Patience in Order to Be in Construction Business in the USSR," *Deloviye Lyudi/Business in the USSR*, June 1991, p. 70.

26. Leonid Khodorkov, "The Price for the Comfort," *Deloviye Lyudi/Business in the USSR*, June 1991, pp. 36–37.

27. Perestroika's experiences have been described in a number of publications, including: Elena Mashovets, "Wall-Street Businessman Is Happy: 'Perestroika' Is Doing Fine," *Moskovski Biznes*, No. 2, 1990, pp. 14–15; Alexei Kondratyev, " 'Perestroika' in America," *Commersant*, July 23–30, 1990, p. 27.

28. For more information on the "Slavyanskaya" project, see Semyon Kuznetsov, "Hotel 'Slavyanskaya': Since November the Most American Hotel in Moscow," *Commersant*, June 11–18,

1990, p. 8; Anton Lyubomudrov, "The Soviets Believe That the Construction of 'Slavyan-skaya' Has Been Completed. But the Americans Do Not Think So," *Commersant*, October 29–November 5, 1990, p. 8.

29. Yuri Titov, "Quitting the Jobs on Construction Sites," *Moskovskie Novosti*, May 12, 1991, p. 10.

30. M. Berger, "Asking for a Helping Hand Is Not the Way to Achieve Success in the World Market," *Izvestiya*, June 24, 1990, p. 3.

31. *Literaturnaya Gazeta*, No. 49, 1989.

32. "Big Six Accounting Firm Opens in Moscow," *Management Review*, March 1990, p. 20.

33. Patricia A. Dreyfus, "Negotiating the Kremlin Maze," *Business Month*, November 1988, p. 68.

34. Tom Shone, "Adding Up the USSR," *Moskow*, June 1990, pp. 36–48.

35. Leslie Jay, "Madison Avenue Lands in Moscow," *Management Review*, March 1990, p. 56.

36. Robin Griggs, "To Russia with Tar. The Marlboro Man Rides East as USSR Lifts Ban on Cigarette Ads," *Mediaweek*, January 28, 1991, p. 7.

37. A. Kazakov, "USA—89: Opportunities for Business Cooperation," *Vneshnyaya Torgovlya*, No. 2, 1990, pp. 16–20.

38. V. I. Anikin, "The Opinion Polls Regarding the Service Industry, *Sotsiologicheskie Issledovania*, No. 7, 1991, pp. 102–105.

39. Alexander Ivanov, "The Firm 'Sir' and the Firm 'Listen!' " *Literaturnaya Gazeta*, October 17, 1990, p. 16.

40. Charles Bernstein, "The Moscow Gold Rush: Not As Easy As It Seems," *Nation's Restaurant News*, April 9, 1990, p. 27.

41. Dmitri Bogdanovich, "Business Week / USSR. The News about World Economy Will Appear in the USSR Every Month," *Commersant*, November 26–December 3, 1990, p. 5.

42. Vladimir Nadein, "The Story of How We Were Making 'We,' " *Izvestiya*, July 5, 1990, p. 6.

43. Donna Brown, "Anatomy of a Deal: *The Russia House*," *Management Review*, March 1990, pp. 50–53.

44. Sergei Modestov, "The Map of Business Activity," *Moskovskie Novosti*, Surveys, October 1991, p. 15.

45. Sergei Panasenko, "Chances of the Sovereign States." *Moskovskie Novosti*, Economic Overview, October 1991, p. 15.

Chapter 5. Important Sociocultural Dynamics of Doing Business

1. "Avos" means relying on or waiting for something that occurs by itself, without planning or an individual's own efforts.

2. Sergei Panasenko, "Our Choice Is Freedom," *Ogonyok* No. 5, January 1988, pp. 9–10.

3. M. Berger, "I Do a Favour for You—You Do a Favour for Me," *Izvestiya*, May 11, 1990, p. 5.

4. " . . . In Russia There Is Only One Remedy against Improper Measures Taken by the Government—Improper Implementation," *Commersant*, February 1990, pp. 8–9.

5. "The Plants Should Be Made Operational," An Interview with the Minister of Foreign Economic Relations G. F. Rakhembaev, *Vneshnyaya Torgovlya*, No. 11, 1989, p. 27.

6. Yuri Makarov, "Disposable Strawberries," *Izvestiya*, April 15, 1990, p. 3.

7. V. Vernikov, "Do We Need Spanish Franks?" *Izvestiya*, January 13, 1990, p. 3.

8. Sergei Kivrin, "The Myth of Economic Collapse," *Moscow*, August 1990, pp. 33–34.

9. Eduard Polyanovski, "Words and Power," *Izvestiya*, August 1, 1990, p. 3.

10. E. Velichko, "The Story about the Bookkeeper Who Put Together the Report," *Eko*, No. 7, 1989, pp. 35–36.

11. P. Oldak, "The Modern Stage of the Socialist Society," in *Economic Sociology and Perestroika*, Moscow, Progress, 1989, p. 34.

12. Otto Latsis, "What Acceleration Means," in L. I. Abalkin and P. G. Bunich (eds.), *The Tough Route to Take*, Moscow, Misl, 1989, pp. 44–49.

13. L. Khotin, "Looking from Outside," *Znanie—Sila*, No. 10, 1990, p. 31.
14. V. Kulikov, "Parasitism Is Incompatible with the Market Economy," *Ekonomika i Zhizn*, No. 23, July 1990, p. 6.
15. Grigori Viktorov, "The Sad Kalashnikov," *Za Rodinu*, August 31, 1990, p. 3.
16. Kulikov, "Parasitism Is Incompatible," p. 6.
17. Vladimir Tikhonov, "State Monopoly or Cooperatives?" in *The Tough Route to Take*, p. 76.
18. V. I. Bakshtanovski and Y. V. Sogomonov, "Social-Political Process and Ethical Values of the Society: Co-Evolution Phenomenon," *Sotsiologicheskie Issledovania*, No. 7, 1991, pp. 38–47.
19. A. Kiva, "To Be Rich Is Not Evil," *Izvestiya*, June 2, 1990, p. 4.
20. "One of the Perspectives in Which the Reform Could Be Seen," *Argumenti i Fakti*, No. 26, 1989, p. 5.
21. A. A. Akhmadeyev, "Farmers' Hopes and Hesitations," *Sotsiologicheskie Issledovania*, No. 7, 1991, pp. 102–103.
22. Alexei Izyumov, "Long Live the Millionaires!" *Moscow*, August 1990, pp. 19–21.
23. L. Gozman, and E. Etkind, "The Cult of Power. The Structure of the Totalitarian Mindset," in H. Kobo (ed.), *The Way to Understand Stalin*, Moscow, Progress, 1989, pp. 339, 340, 339, 337–372.
24. L. Gozman, "Psychology of Power," *Argumenti i Fakti,"* No. 24, 1989, p. 6.
25. Pavel Bunich, "Only Revolutionary Changes Will Work," in *The Tough Route to Take*, pp. 25–27.
26. Yeltsin, *The Confession on the Given Topic*, Moscow, Pik, 1990, pp. 139–140, 141.
27. Stanislav Skopovski, "Monopolies and the Market. Goliath against David," *Deloviye Lyudi/Business in the USSR*, January 1991, pp. 64–65.
28. Ibid., p. 65.
29. Gavriil Popov, "What Lies at the Basis of Economic Reform," in *The Tough Route to Take*, pp. 182–183.
30. Albert Plutnik, "Is the Old Mindset Still Alive?," *Izvestiya*, September 3, 1990.
31. L. Gozman, "The Cult of Power. The Structure of the Totalitarian Mindset," pp. 344, 346.
32. Gozman, "Psychology of Power," p. 5.
33. Yeltsin, *The Confession on the Given Topic*, p. 96.
34. L. Gozman, "The Cult of Power. The Structure of the Totalitarian Mindset," p. 348.
35. Yeltsin, *The Confession on the Given Topic*, p. 114.
36. L. Gozman, "The Cult of Power. The Structure of the Totalitarian Mindset," pp. 363, 354.
37. M. Berger, "There Is No Alternative to the Market Economy," *Izvestiya*, December 31, 1989.
38. Yeltsin, *The Confession on the Given Topic*, p. 114.
39. Tatyana Chesnokova, "The Unforgettable Fax. . . ," *Chas Pik*, April 15, 1991, p. 3.

Chapter 6. Discrepancies Between Law and Reality

1. K. Lubenchenko, "The Laws That Do Not Work," *Izvestiya*, July 8, 1990, p. 3.
2. Alexander Papakhristu, "Fuss about Search for the Ways of Civilized Lawmaking," *Deloviye Lyudi/Business in the USSR*, January 1991, p. 58.
3. Eduard Gonzales, "Comrades, Go Ahead Towards Market!" *Izvestiya*, June 16, 1990, p. 3.
4. Alexander Levikov, "Lawsuit against Tarasov's Children's Pictures for Adults," *Deloviye Lyudi/Business in the USSR*, March 1991, p. 21.
5. Yuri Volokhov, "What Is the Way to the Law-Governed Society?" *Delovoi Mir*, April 4, 1991, p. 4.
6. V. E. Rogovin, "The Way from Stalin's Equality to Open Income of the Brezhnev's Era," *Eko*, No. 9, 1989, p. 142.
7. Andrei Nuikin, "Are We in the Right Place to Erect Barricades?" *Izvestiya*, March 13, 1990, p. 3.
8. L. Khotin, "Can You Rely on Directors of Enterprises?" *Ekonomika i Zhizn*, February 1991, pp. 29–30.

9. V. Semyonov, "Quixote from OTK (Quality Assurance Division)," *Ekonomika i Zhizn,* February 1990, p. 11.

10. G. Shcherbina, "Imported Boots vs. Deficit Food in the Special Diner," *Izvestiya,* March 1, 1990, p. 2.

11. Eduard Dolot, " 'Burda Moden': The Test for Survivorship," *Deloviye Lyudi/Business in the USSR,* February 1991, p. 104.

12. Papakhristu, "Fuss about Search for Ways of Civilized Lawmaking," p. 59.

13. Ibid.

14. Lubenchenko, "The Laws That Do Not Work," p. 3.

15. Lev Korsunski, "OBKHSS Is Fabricating a Lawsuit against 'Lensovet.' The Fabrication Is Far Too Obvious," *Chas Pik,* May 6, 1991, p. 9.

16. T. Nurullin, "Manipulating with Figures," *Kriminalnaya Khronika,* Issue 3(8), 1991, p. 6.

17. Kirill Alexeyev, "Ministry of Foreign Economic Relations Caught Criminals Violating Foreign Trade Laws of the USSR," *Commersant,* October 22–29, 1990, p. 5.

18. Yuri Alexeyev, " 'Energia' 's Financial Troubles: To Send Spaceships into Space Turned out to Be Safer than in Japan," *Commersant,* May 6–13, 1991, p. 7.

19. Andrei Koptyaev, "Scandal in Shanghai Kitchen: Khua Tin versus Obshchepit," *Commersant,* April 29–May 6, 1991, p. 7.

20. Anastasiya Solodikhina, "Greeks Will Have to Pay for Their Unawareness of Whose Vodka They Have Bought," *Commersant,* October 22–29, 1990, p. 11.

21. Lubenchenko, "The Laws That Do Not Work," p. 3.

22. Marina Kiseleva, "In the Shadow of the Shadow Business," *Moskovski Biznes,* No. 2, 1990, pp. 38–39.

23. Igor Svinarenko, "Komi Autonomous Republic: Arrests under Decree," *Commersant,* February 25–March 4, 1991, p. 14; Igor Svinarenko, "Joint Venture 'Ferster': Division of Property," *Commersant,* March 4–11, 1991, p. 7.

24. Gleb Pyanikh, "Director of the Joint Venture Has Been Charged with Bribery," *Commersant,* April 8–15, 1991, p. 14.

25. Zh. Toshchenko and V. Voikov, "Shadow Economy," *Glasnost,* August 1990, p. 6.

26. A. Goryanovski, "It Is Possible to Steal Anything. The Findings of the Research with the Experimentator's Participation," *Sotsiologicheskie Issledovania,* No. 2, 1990, pp. 57–64.

Chapter 7. Categories of Soviet Organizations and Business People as Partners of American Companies

1. Roberta Bonometti, "An Italian in Moscow," *Moscow,* August 1990, p. 10.

2. "The Way to Survive in the Jungles of Soviet Business," *Moskovski Biznes,* Nos. 5–6, 1990, p. 38.

3. Charles E. Hugel, "US–USSR Trade: Building the Future," *Journal of the US–USSR Trade and Economic Council,* Vol. 15, No. 1, 1990, pp. 10–11.

4. I. Kruglyanskaya, "Striking a Pineapple Deal in Arbat," *Izvestiya,* March 11, 1990, p. 7.

5. A. Kazakov, "USA–89: Opportunities for Business Cooperation," *Vneshnyaya Torgovlya,* No. 2, 1990, pp. 19–20.

6. E. Bazhanov, "Adventures in the Enigmatic Country," *Izvestiya,* August 9, 1991, p. 4.

7. Alexander Datskevich, "Partnerships Cannot Be Established without Personal Likings," *Deloviye Lyudi/Business in the USSR,* May 1990, pp. 34–35.

8. V. Shmiganovsky, "The Real and Imaginary Problems," *Izvestiya,* January 14, 1990, p. 7.

9. "The Professional Viewpoint," *Ekonomika i Zhizn,* No. 14, July 1990, No. 31, p. 20.

10. Yuri Nechaev, "Is the Monopoly of Foreign Trade a Necessity?" *Vneshnyaya Torgovlya,* No. 12, 1989, p. 35.

11. Andrei Kutennikov, "How We Trade with America," *Moskovski Novosti,* November 5, 1989, p. 13.

12. Vladimir Tikhonov, "The State Monopoly or Cooperatives?" in L. I. Abalkin and P. G. Bunich (eds.), *The Tough Route to Take,* Moscow, Misl, 1989, pp. 55–60.

13. Ibid.
14. "Japanese Partners Are Willing to Trade . . . ," *Commersant*, April 23, 1990, p. 5; Mikhail Shvedov, "Businesspeople from America Recommend Doing Business with Small Companies," *Commersant*, May 20–27, 1990, p. 7.
15. Peter Van Der Klugt, "Out of the Red," *Moscow*, February 1990, pp. 26–31.
16. Tikhonov, "The State Monopoly or Cooperatives?" p. 75.
17. Boris Yeltsin, *The Confession on the Given Topic*, Moscow, Pik, 1990, pp. 39–42.
18. Interview with Pavel Bunich, "One Shouldn't Act on Guesses," *The Alternative Economy*, Part I, Moscow, Mir, 1990, pp. 105, 107.
19. I. Ivanov, "To Get Rid of Inappropriate Orientations on the Way to the External Market," *Eko*, No. 9, 1989, p. 93.
20. N. Matukovski, "There Are Many Ways to Generate Hard Currency," *Izvestiya*, December 12, 1989, p. 2.
21. A. V. Vasilyev, "The Prospects of Shareholding at State Enterprises," *Sotsiologicheskie Issledovania*, No. 5, 1990, pp. 16–21.
22. E. Skvortsov, "Kontzern," *Biznes*, No. 2, 1991, p. 16.
23. Nina Bulon, "Is It Possible to Sell Sawdust?" in *Business World*, Moscow, Finances and Statistics, 1990, p. 51.
24. Kutennikov, "How We Trade with America," p. 13.
25. *Eko*, No. 9, 1989, p. 175.
26. Yuri Sigov, "Italian Businessmen: To Break through the Wall of Inertia," *Moskovski Biznes*, No. 1, 1990, p. 35.
27. M. Osmova and A. Sokolov, *Adversity or Cooperation*, Moscow, Misl, 1989, pp. 136–137.
28. Yeltsin, *The Confession on the Given Topic*, pp. 39–42.
29. I. Zhagel, "There Can Be No Market without Middlemen," *Izvestiya*, May 12, 1990, p. 2.
30. For more details on the surveys about different orientations, values, and motivation of employees under new economic conditions, see: Y. L. Neimer and T. A. Slyusareva, "The Heroes of the 'Perestroika'," *Sotsiologicheskie Issledovania*, No. 3, 1991, pp. 45–49; S. A. Naumova, "Types of Employees: Problems of Management," *Sotsiologicheskie Issledovania*, No. 2, 1991, pp. 60–65; S. G. Safro, "The Plant Needs Responsible People," *Sotsiologicheskie Issledovania*, No. 2, 1990, pp. 103–106.

Chapter 8. Negotiating with Soviet Business People

1. Alexander Datskevich, "Partnerships Cannot Be Established without Personal Likings," *Deloviye Lyudi/Business in the USSR*, May 1990, pp. 34–35.
2. Interview of Grigori Yavlinski with Yegor Yakovlev, "Sensation for Tomorrow," *Moskovski Novosti*, May 19, 1991, pp. 5–6.

Index